S0-CMT-840

393-1
13

PRE-SCHOOL EDUCATION FOR THE HANDICAPPED

Robert Piazza

Assistant Professor Deartment of Special Education Southern Connecticut State College, New Haven, Connecticut.

Roz Rothman

College of New Rochelle

Special Learning Corporation
42 Boston Post Rd. Guilford, Connecticut 06437

LC
4019.2
.P747
c.2

Special Learning Corporation

Publisher's Message:

The Special Education Series is the first comprehensive series designed for special education courses of study. It is also the first series to offer such a wide variety of high quality books. In addition, the series will be expanded and up-dated each year. No other publications in the area of special education can equal this. We stress high quality content, a superb advisory and consulting group, and special features that help in understanding the course of study. In addition we believe we must also publish in very small enrollment areas in order to establish the credibility and strength of our series. We realize the enrollments in courses of study such as Autism, Visually Handicapped Education, or Diagnosis and Placement are not large. Nevertheless, we believe there is a need for course books in these areas and books that are kept up-to-date on an annual basis! Special Learning Corporation's goal is to publish the highest quality materials for the college and university courses of study. With your comments and support we will continue to do this.

John P. Quirk

©1979 by Special Learning Corporation, Guilford, Connecticut 06437

All rights reserved. No part of this book may be reproduced, stored, or communicated by any means--without written permission from Special Learning Corporation.

First Edition

1 2 3 4 5

ISBN No. 0-89568-082-3

90736

BELMONT COLLEGE LIBRARY

SPECIAL EDUCATION SERIES

- ● Autism
- * ● Behavior Modification
- Biological Bases of Learning Disabilities
- Brain Impairments
- ● Career and Vocational Education for the Handicapped
- Child Abuse
- Child Development
- Child Psychology
- Cognitive and Communication Skills
- * ● Counseling Parents of Exceptional Children
- Creative Arts
- Curriculum and Materials
- * ● Deaf Education
- Developmental Disabilities
- * ● Diagnosis and Placement
- Down's Syndrome
- ● Dyslexia
- Early Learning
- Educational Technology
- * ● Emotional and Behavioral Disorders
- Exceptional Parents
- * ● Gifted and Talented Education
- * ● Human Growth and Development of the Exceptional Individual
- Hyperactivity
- * ● Individualized Educational Programs
- ● Language & Writing Disorders
- * ● Learning Disabilities
- Learning Theory
- * ● Mainstreaming
- * ● Mental Retardation
- ● Motor Disorders
- Multiple Handicapped Education
- Occupational Therapy
- ● Perception and Memory Disorders
- * ● Physically Handicapped Education
- * ● Pre-School Education for the Handicapped
- * ● Psychology of Exceptional Children
- ● Reading Disorders
- Reading Skill Development
- Research and Development
- * ● Severely and Profoundly Handicapped
- Slow Learner Education
- Social Learning
- * ● Special Education
- * ● Speech and Hearing
- Testing and Diagnosis
- ● Three Models of Learning Disabilities
- * ● Visually Handicapped Education
- * ● Vocational Training for the Mentally Retarded

● Published Titles * Major Course Areas

Exceptional Children: A Reference Book

An updated and welcome resource for educators and librarians.

CONTENTS

3. Programs

4. Parents

5. Future Trends

GLOSSARY OF TERMS

Assessment Considered to be a battery of tests (formal and informal) to evaluate a person's performance.

Auditory Perception The ability to interpret what one hears.

Behavior Modification A technique which involves the theory of operant behavior and conditioning in order to change the way a person performs or acts.

Child-Find An organized attempt by public and educational agencies to seek-out young handicapped children.

Chronological Age The actual age of a person.

Cognition The process or act of knowing. Thinking skills and processes are often considered cognitive skills.

Delivery Systems The various ways educational services are offered to children and their families.

Early Identification The attempts by professionals and educators to recognize young children who may encounter difficulty in school in academic learning, the subsequent provision of appropriate prevention services.

Educational Team The group of professional individuals, classroom teachers, supportive service teachers (resource room, speech therapist etc.), psychologist, school nurse, principals who are involved in diagnosing and supervising a child's educational program.

Etiology The origin or cause of a condition.

Expressive Language The ability to produce language (verbal, written, gestural) for communication with other individuals.

Feedback The process of recognizing or receiving notice for a behavior or performance.

Fine Motor Most frequently relates to use of the hands to perform manipulative and writing tasks.

Frequency The number of occurrences of a behavior.

Function level Ability level at which a person can perform for a given task.

Gross Motor Most frequently relates to use of the large muscles of the body to perform acts of motion such as turning, jumping, running. Gross Motor also involves the ability to coordinate large muscle movements.

Handicap A disadvantage that makes success more difficult.

Head-Start A federally funded program for pre-school disadvantaged children.

High Risk Children with suspected potential learning problems.

Home Start Programs designed to bring comprehensive child development services to children and their families in their own home.

Infant Stimulation Programs which provide auditory, visual or physical stimuli to foster the development of more obvious weaker, under-developed or undeveloped abilities.

Inner Language The process by which a human being organizes and internalizes experiences without the use of language.

In-Service Education Professional oriented programs given to personnel while they are teaching or involved in public or private practice.

Intervention The prevention of a future difficulty by providing immediate methods or materials to facilitate development of a child.

Language The ability to understand, assimilate and utilize the words one hears.

Least Restrictive Environment The "most normal educational program possible" that a child can receive instructional services.

Mean Score The average score achieved on a test.

Mental Age The mental age at which a child functions based upon a specific diagnostic or achievement test.

NonVerbal The inability to talk, the cause of which may be physical, psychological, or intellectual.

Normalization Keeping the handicapped integrated within the family or community or in as near a "normal" environment as possible.

Para-Professional A person trained in a metholology to assist and help a teacher or professionally certified individual.

Perception The attachment of meaning to the reception of a stimulus. Understanding that which is received by the sense organs.

Perceptual Motor The interaction of the various aspects of perception with a motor activity, i.e. visual, auditory, tactile, kinesthetic.

Post-Test A test or examination administered after a treatment to measure the effects of the treatment.

Prescription The specific education program designed by the professional and parent to meet the individual needs of a child.

Pre-Service Professional oriented courses given to personnel before they begin to work.

Pre-Test A test or examination administered before a treatment is initiated to ascertain a baseline of performance.

Receptive Language The ability of an individual to understand that which is spoken or read by another person.

Rubella German measles.

Screening Global testing or evaluation on a large scale to detect children who may have possible areas of deficit. If a child scores poorly on a screening, then further in-depth testing is recommended.

Self-Help Skills The ability of an individual to feed clothe and attend to his/her personal needs without assistance.

Sensori-Motor A term which relates to the combination of the input of sensations and the output of a motor activity. The motor activity indicates what is happening to the sensory organs such as sight, hearing, tactual and kinesthetic sensations.

Teacher-Mom Parents or volunteers who usually work in a school in a one-to-one situation with a child who is having difficulty. Most of the time the person is trained by the teacher or supervisor for this role.

Token Reward In a behavior modification program a reward is usually given for correct response or appropriate behavior. A reward is usually withheld if the person fails to respond or perform within previously established guidelines.

Toxic Caused by a poison or toxin.

Visual Perception Interpreting that stimuli which is received through the eye. Among the subskills are visual discrimination, constancy, memory and memory sequencing.

PREFACE

Over the past 12 years, concern with, and the development of, infant and early childhood programs for handicapped youngsters has grown. The years from infancy to entry into school are now considered crucial to overall development, especially for children with special needs and whose deficits must be identified and treated during this period.

The stimulation and education of young handicapped children involves not only general theories of development, methodology and techniques of evaluation, but also procedures for the indentification of such children. The following are considered to be crucial aspects related to the purpose and importance of early identification: (1) to help ameliorate or prevent potential problems with learning in an academic environment; (2) to plan education programs; (3) to undertake the initial steps necessary to assist children to fulfill their potential; and (4) to involve parents, family and community to recognize, support, train and teach the handicapped child.

The passage and implementation of PL 94-142 will raise new issues concerning the early education of handicapped. Some professionals urge that we do not hurry to fulfill mandates. It is better to wait until more adequate services and trained personnel are available. It is paramount for teachers, physicians, and other involved professionals to be educated/re-educated to work with young special children to better understand the needs of these children and their families. Administrators and curriculum experts will need to investigate individualized programs which are vital to successful planning for handicapped children in the mainstream, both at home and in a school environment. Efforts need to be directed toward programs for all the above adults geared toward self-understanding of attitudes, feelings and awareness of young handicapped children. Most successful programs include re-evaluation of the physical, intellectual and emotional development of today's children in current cultural environments. "Disadvantaged" cannot be interpreted to apply only to low socioeconomic strata, but needs to include youngsters from wider ranges of class, race and culture.

Psychological and educational studies give credence to the value of early identification and early education for all young handicapped children. Based upon this knowledge, parents of handicapped children have urged legislators to effect laws that protect the rights of and grant education for all handicapped children from infancy. Theoretically, what has been accomplished is monumental; empirically, to be successful, enormous amounts of time, energy and money must still be expended so that educators and parents may continue to help these young special children.

EARLY INTERVENTION - A RATIONALE

While the history of preschool children with handicapping conditions receiving an early education extends back over one hundred years, it was primarily restricted to a few non-public residential facilities. Over the past two decades there has been an escalating concern for these children. Many programs have been initiated in both the public and private sectors during this time period.

In the late 1960's and early 1970's recognition of the positive effects of preschool programs was demonstrated in many state laws, which lowered or eliminated school entrance ages. During this time a CEC Policy Statement declared that:

> Provision should be made by government for services which prevent and ameliorate conditions negatively affecting the development and education of children and youth, from preschool programs beginning at birth and continuing through adult education.

Most recently, several congressional acts have given impetus to increased services for the preschool population. Public Law 94-142 passed by President Ford in 1975 has given special encouragement to local and state agencies to begin or to continue providing an education for preschoolers. This act carries a special incentive grant aimed at assisting the states in this venture. Each handicapped child in the State aged three through five who is counted and served will generate a $300. entitlement.

There are probably many reasons for this positive upsurge in interest in the education of preschool children. One of the most important is the result of findings in the current body of research, which seem to indicate that the preschool years are most critical for a child's future development. Some researchers have indicated that modifying a child's environment during his early years can lead to increased intellectual capacity later on. Others have even suggested that a child has already developed 50 percent of his total intellectual capacity as an adult by the age of four.

Much evidence indicates the early developmental years are the most crucial for improving a child's social, emotional, physical and intellectual deficits. The following selections provide a sound rationale for the early identification and education of preschool handicapped youngsters. The trend toward the establishment of preschool programs appears to be accelerating. Hopefully, P.L. 94-142 will eliminate most of the administrative roadblocks such as insufficient funding, inadequate facilities, and poorly trained professionals.

The Rationale for Early Intervention

BETTYE M. CALDWELL

BETTYE M. CALDWELL *is Director, Center for Early Development and Education, College of Education, University of Arkansas, Little Rock.* *The research reported herein was performed in part pursuant to Grant SF-500 with the Children's Bureau, Office of Child Development, US Department of Health, Education, and Welfare.*

Abstract: Antecedents of the current interest in early intervention are traced, with particular attention to the applicability of early intervention for exceptional children. The rationale presented draws inferential support from animal studies concerned with the effects of early experiences, descriptive studies contrasting development in children reared in different social environments, and major conceptual analyses of the importance of early stimulation for development. Empirical support is drawn from current and previous work demonstrating the results associated with early environmental enrichment. Guidelines are suggested for future research and action programs.

ACCORDING to Kessen (1965), scientific interest in the young child was a legacy of the attempt to link psychology with evolutionary biology. The nature of man was to be apprehended by a study of his origins in early infancy rather than by a meticulous analysis of his functioning as an adult. Some of the early publishers of observational biographies (Darwin, 1877; Preyer, 1888) clearly exemplified this point of view. The developing theory of psychoanalysis led Freud (1905) to be concerned with infants, but his method of study—anamnestic recall by adults—precluded direct study of the child during these theoretically important early years. In his only published venture about the application of psychoanalysis to the problems of a child, Freud (1909) did not see the child but worked vicariously through the father.

The most significant early influences came directly from the educational pioneers of Europe—Comenius, Rousseau, Pestalozzi, Froebel, Seguin, Montessori, and Rachel and Margaret McMillan (see Ulich, 1945). The efforts of America's most catholic and catalytic child psychologist, G. Stanley Hall, were instrumented in helping to import the ideas of the kindergarten movement. In 1895 he organized a symposium to be devoted to problems of kindergarten education, and, in a tour de force of nondiplomacy, so angered the participants with his criticisms of Froebel that 33 of the 35 in attendance walked out of the meeting (Hill, 1941). However, the antagonism and activity generated by the meeting had a major impact on educational planners of the era. By the early twenties kindergartens and university based nursery schools were no longer rarities, albeit still stepchildren of formal education. "Preschools" they were called, in a semantic insult even now not eradicated. But these early educa-

"The Rationale For Early Intervention", Bettye M. Caldwell, *Exceptional Children* Vol. 36, No. 10, Summer 1970, © 1970, The Council For Excetional Children

tion programs remained the darlings of a few prestigious departments of child study (i.e., Iowa, California, Minnesota, Vassar), perhaps less because of their presumed benefits to the children than because of the contributions they could make to understanding how children develop. Claims regarding the potential value of such experiences for the intellectual development of young children were ironically associated with their decline in status. Vitriolic attacks upon a series of research investigations that have come to be referred to disparagingly as "the Iowa studies" (see especially McNemar, 1940) eventually caused the preschool advocates to slip silently away to lick their wounds and to dream of apologies for their existence. Programs continued, but those in the universities operated to provide subjects for research studies and to train teachers.

Then suddently in the mid-sixties—probably it can be officially dated as February, 1965, the month when Head Start was born—early childhood was rediscovered. Perhaps early childhood was not so much rediscovered (as countless new book titles announce) as simply no longer overlooked.

Inferential Rationale for the Current Interest in Early Childhood

An inferential rationale is an idea generated in another context, sometimes bearing no apparent relation to early intervention, from which one can infer the importance of early intervention. At least three of these can be identified.

Animal Studies on the Effects of Early Experience

For three or more decades biologists and psychologists have researched the effects of experience upon development. In some instances the studies were not based on any prior conviction about the importance of early experience but rather on an interest in whether and to what extent certain kinds of experience had any effect. Such research is often concerned with the relative effects of maturation and learning (or heredity versus environment). However, in many studies the results directed attention to the timing of as well as the type of experience.

A few illustrative studies will be cited to demonstrate the contribution of this line of research to the current concern with early cognitive stimulation. The studies have used as dependent variables a variety of behaviors, including sensory, perceptual, and motor functions, learning and problem solving, and complex forms of social behavior.

For example, using performance on the Hebb-Williams (1946) tests of animal intelligence, Thompson and Heron (1954) examined the effects of being reared under varying conditions of social deprivation. Working with Scottish terriers, they arranged for three different degrees of deprivation in 13 dogs: two were raised in complete isolation and encountered neither dogs nor humans from weaning until 8 months of age; eight were reared in cages in which they could hear and smell but could not see other dogs or humans and in which they had restricted light; and three were deprived only insofar as any or all laboratory animals are deprived. The 13 animals used as controls were reared as ordinary house pets. On all measures the deprived animals made more errors than the dogs reared as pets, even though the testing was done some 4 months after the termination of deprivation. The two groups of dogs also showed significant differences on problems which required a delayed response and on tasks which required modification of a previously acquired technique of problem solving.

The evidence on the effects of deprivation during early life upon learning ability in primates is not clear cut. In monkeys, for example, Roland (1964) and Mason and Fitz-Gerald (1962) have claimed to find no differences between isolates and controls in discrimination learning tasks. However, in these studies the deprived animals were described as being extremely resistant to placement in the apparatus and as requiring many adaptations before learning studies could proceed. These behaviors themselves represent significant distortions. Beach (1966) found that chimps reared in laboratories tended to be "brighter" than chimpanzees growing up in nature, with "home reared" chimps appearing as geniuses by comparison. The chimpanzee reared by a family almost as though it were another of their own children (Hayes, 1951) tended to outstrip any described performance of chimpanzees either in nature or the laboratory. Such studies suggest that early experience does indeed have a profound effect on primates either in the sense of retarding or accelerating development by the manipulation of certain critical experiences.

The animal literature suggests that the critical time for the manipulation of experiences is during the early infancy of the animals under study. With nonhuman animals, timing may be important because most complex forms of behavior are mediated by intrinsic processes which, when fully developed, are relatively less sensitive to variations in experience. However, data also indicate the importance of experience during the time that neural patterns which form the substrata for all complex forms of behavior are being established.

Developmental Studies of Children Reared in Different Environments

Differences on most cognitive variables can be demonstrated as a function of an early childhood spent in environments presumed to differ in the amount and quality of available stimulation. The most commonly used index of presumed environmental adequacy has been the socioeconomic status (SES) of the family. Computation of an SES index generally involves consideration of some combination of the variables of occupation, income, education, and area of residence. Although a designation of "low" status does not automatically guarantee a less than optimal early experience, at least some conditions inimical to development will be present. Whether measuring by general intelligence, school achievement, or laboratory learning procedures, one can generally demonstrate a deficit in performance associated with lower SES. For purposes of this discussion, the most crucial question is when this deficit appears.

Coleman (1966) found that as early as first grade most groups of children from lower SES backgrounds and most children representing minority groups tended to score significantly lower than the national average on most measures of school achievement and thus lower than children from high SES backgrounds. Deficits increased as children progressed through the typical school experience. This absolute increase in discrepancy between achievement and prediction for grade level led Deutsch (1960) to refer to the typical performance of disadvantaged children as reflecting a cumulative deficit.

But what about younger children? Data based on a large sample (1,409 children) were recently published by Bayley (1965) in the first presentation of information on the standardization of new Scales of Mental and Motor Development. At all assessment points up to 15 months of age, there were no significant differences as a function of sex, birth order, parental education, geographic residence, or race on the Mental Scale. Negro babies tended to score consistently higher than Caucasians on the Motor Scale, with the differences significant at most evaluative points up to 12 months but not significant thereafter. Later data from the larger study of which this standardization was a part will be instrumental in pinpointing the age at which differences begin to appear and the types of tasks on which the differences are most obvious.

A recent study by Golden and Birns (1968) suggested that the difference had not appeared by the age of two on test scores but that the full constellation of test behaviors (similar to those observed by Hertzig, Birch, Thomas, & Mendez, 1968) did reveal differences by that time. Using the Cattell Infant Intelligence Scale (1940) and an experimental procedure designed to assess a child's achievement within the Piaget framework (Escalona & Corman, 1967), Golden and Birns examined three separate groups of Negro children 12, 18, and 24 months old. On neither test were statistically significant differences observed at any of the three age periods. However, the authors reported that children from the lower SES groups were far more difficult to test and often required more than one session to complete the procedures. Had the examiners not worked to get a valid score for each child, significant differences in mean scores might have appeared.

All the research summarized here points to the period of about 18 months to 3 years as the time at which significant differences in cognitive level and style begin to appear between children from relatively privileged and underprivileged backgrounds.

Along with attempts to discover just when in the life span differences associated with social class membership appear, recent research efforts have been devoted to an identification of features in the lower social class environment which might be causative factors. Caldwell (1967) stressed it is as important to measure the environment in which development is occurring as it is to measure the developmental processes themselves. Using an inventory which combines observation and interview to assess the environment, Caldwell (1967) showed that the lower class environment was by no means homogeneous and that magnitude of change in test scores during the first year of life was correlated with amount of support for development found within the home.

In several recent studies concerned with what might be called life styles (Wortis, Bardach, Cutler, & Freedman, 1963; Pavenstedt, 1965; Malone, 1966) the interpersonal and experiential environment of the lower class child has been found to involve disorganization to the point of chaos and hostility or indifference to developmental needs. While the environment did not always indicate lack of parental concern for the children, most of the parents (many of them unwed and with inadequate financial resources) were simply so overwhelmed with other problems that the entire child rearing process had to be subordinated to survival needs. Hess and Shipman (1965) analyzed behavior patterns of lower and middle class mothers and found significant differences in maternal language, in teaching styles in an experimental situation, and in strategies for controlling children who did not respond as expected. Although the damaging effects of physical aspects of the environment have not been ruled out as influential, processes of interpersonal transactions appear to be more potent and damaging (Dave, 1963; Wolf, 1964).

Major Conceptual Analyses of the Role of Experience in Development

Hunt (1961) attempted to survey research on the influence of experience on intelligence since psychology had been dominated too long by a belief in inheritance of fixed intelligence. As he put it, "Evidence from various sources has been forcing a recognition of central processes in intelligence and of the crucial role of life experience in the development of these central processes [p. v]." In his book Hunt presented evidence that would challenge the belief in fixed intelligence and predetermined development and offered a model of information processing which stressed the importance of experience for the development of the central organization of information necessary to solve problems. He also reviewed the thinking and meticulous experimental work of Piaget in terms of the ways in which experiences "program" the development of the human brain. For Hunt the implications were clear: Society should pay greater attention to what takes place in the lives of very young children and should stop leaving things to chance during this period. He stated:

> In the light of these considerations, it appears that the counsel from experts on child-rearing to let children be while they grow and to avoid excessive stimulation was highly unfortunate. . . . The problem for the management of child development is to find out how to govern the encounters that children have with their environments to foster both an optimally rapid rate of intellectual development and a satisfying life.
>
> Further, in the light of these theoretical considerations and the evidence concerning the effects of early experience on adult problem-solving in animals, it is no longer unreasonable to consider that it might be feasible to discover ways to govern the encounters that children have with their environments, especially during the early years of their development, to achieve a substantially faster rate of intellectual development and a substantially higher adult level of intellectual capacity [pp. 362-363].

A second scholar, Bloom (1964), studied all the available data published from a number of major longitudinal studies carried out over the last half century. His chief interest was identifying periods during which the characteristics under study were relatively stable and periods during which they were unstable and showed rapid change. After considering the data found relating to repeated measures of physical and personality characteristics, intelligence and achievement test data, Bloom concluded that "the introduction of the environment as a variable makes a major difference in our ability to predict the mature status of a human characteristic [p. 184]."

In calling attention to the impact of the environment, Bloom suggested that environment will have relatively more impact on a characteristic when that characteristic is undergoing relatively rapid change than when relatively little change is likely. Thus Bloom suggested that "in terms of intelligence measured at age 17, about 50 percent of the development takes place between conception and age 4, about 30 percent between ages 4 and 8, and about 20 percent between ages 8 and 17 [p. 88]."

Again the implications of this analysis are abundantly clear. If the environment can be presumed to have its greatest impact during roughly the first four years of life, careful attention to the development of growth fostering environments during this early period is essential. Furthermore, the analysis suggests that education may well have placed the emphasis at the wrong points in time. Whereas there are elaborate mechanisms providing education for older children, guidance of the growth and development of the very young child has been a casual venture.

This section should not be concluded without reference to the conceptual contribution offered by Bruner (1960). Although in the chronology of events it appeared earlier than the two books already discussed, it has been consciously saved for the final item. This was done because the Bruner book did not so much sound a tocsin about the importance of early experience as it offered encouragement that through education something could be done to improve the proper "environmental encounters" needed by the child. Bruner implied that certain rigidities about the proper age at which to introduce certain subjects had crept into the thinking and that possibly the whole issue of instructional timing and sequencing should be reexamined. One of his generalizations has become an aphorism: "... any subject can be taught effectively in some intellectually honest form to any child at any stage of development [p. 33]." Although possibly misinterpreted and abused by subsequent zealots for early education, Bruner's optimistic formulation provided an encouraging challenge for the educational practitioners who were beginning to respond to the logic of the analyses offered by Hunt and Bloom.

By the middle of the sixties, no thinking person could ignore the importance of the first few years of life for subsequent developmental competence. A social mandate to give careful attention to the development of programs which would foster early cognitive development seemed only a step away.

Empirical Rationale for Early Childhood Education

On the basis of the criterion of frequency of citation in the scientific literature, one would be forced to conclude that two main research projects helped make the transition from the theoretical to the practical. Both projects dealt with exceptional (retarded) children.

Following the discovery that two infants transferred from an overcrowded orphanage to an institution for mentally retarded adolescent girls showed a spurt in development after the transfer. Skeels and Dye (1939) arranged an experiment in which retarded adolescent girls were used as "enrichers" for a larger group of 13 babies who were failing to thrive in the orphanage environment. At the time of transfer the babies were about 19 months old and had a mean IQ of 64. A contrasting group of 12 infants was found, averaging 16.6 months of age at the time of the first assessment of their abilities and having a mean IQ of 86.7. Thus the contrast infants did not appear to be as seriously damaged as the experimental group. After an experimental period of approximately 19 months, the enriched children showed an average IQ gain of 28.5 points, while the contrast group, after an average interval of 30.7 months, lost 26.2 IQ points. Such short term gains are impressive, but a demonstration of some lasting effects would be grounds for jubilation.

After the passage of some 30 years, Skeels (1966) searched out the original subjects to determine whether their progress during the postexperimental period had continued at a rate comparable to that shown during the experimental period. Skeels (1966) described the results as follows:

> The two groups had maintained their divergent patterns of competency into adulthood. All 13 children in the experimental group were self-supporting, and none was a ward of any institution, public or private. In the contrast group of 12 children, one had died in adolescence following continued residence in a state institution for the mentally retarded, and four were still wards of institutions....
>
> In education, disparity between the two groups was striking. The contrast group completed a median of less than the third grade. The experimental group completed a median of the twelfth grade. Four of the subjects had one or more years of college work....
>
> Marked differences in occupational levels were seen in the two groups. In the experimental group all were self-supporting or married and functioning as housewives....In the contrast group, four (36 percent) of the subjects were institutionalized and unemployed....
>
> Eleven of the 13 children in the experimental group were married; nine of the 11 had a total of 28 children, an average of three children per family. On intelligence tests, these second-generation children had IQ's ranging from 86 to 125, with a mean and median IQ of 104. In no instance was there any indication of mental retardation or demonstrable abnormality.
>
> The cost to the state for the contrast group, for whom intervention was essentially limited to custodial care, was approximately five times that of the cost for the experimental group. It seems safe to predict that for at least four of the cases in the contrast group costs to the state will continue at a rate in excess of $200.00 per month each for another 20 to 40 years [Skeels, pp. 54-55].

The second major empirical antecedent which deserves special mention was conducted by Kirk (1958). He studied the development of some 81 retarded children between the ages of 3 and 6, with IQ's ranging from 45 to 80. Of the total group, 28 children living at home with their families attended a special nursery school and 15 children residing in an institution for the retarded attended a nursery school operated in the institution. Two contrast groups were 26 retarded children living at home who did not attend nursery school and 12 institutionalized retarded children for whom no extra enrichment was available. All of these children were followed for several years, with encouraging results. Seventy percent of the children for whom special preschool programs were available showed IQ increments ranging between 10 and 30 points, even though half of the children were classified as organically retarded. The IQ's of the control groups of children declined, with the difference between changes shown by the preschool and control groups being statistically significant. Furthermore, the gains shown by the experimental children during the enrichment period were sustained for several years during the followup period.

In commenting on his own data and the finding of Skeels and Dye (1939) and others who attempted to produce changes in the developmental rate of retarded children, Kirk (1966) suggested that greater gains can be expected if the enrichment is begun earlier. None of the known studies that began enrichment programs as late as age 6 produced gains as large as those of either Skeels and Dye (1939) or Kirk (1958).

Early Education Projects

One of the first projects resulting from increased interest in early childhood education was the Early Training Project (Gray, 1966) in Nashville, Tennessee. In this project a summer preschool program was offered to disadvantaged Negro children, with home visitor contacts provided during the academic year. One group received three summers of this enrichment program, and one received two summers. Two control groups were identified, one living in the same city and another in a city about 25 miles away (to minimize casual diffusion of program ideas). The curriculum was carefully structured and centered around what the authors call aptitudes for achievement, attitudes toward achievement, and careful manipulation of reinforcement for desired behavior. At the end of the summer preschool experience, there were significant differences between the groups that had received the summer preschool plus winter home visiting and the control groups (Gray & Klaus, 1965). At the end of second grade there were differences between the two experimental groups and the two control groups. No superiority for the group that had had three summer preschools over the group that had had only two could be detected.

An enrichment project was established in Syracuse, New York, between 1964 and 1969. (See Caldwell & Richmond, 1964, 1968). The most unique feature of this project was the age range of subjects accepted—6 months to 5 years. As the intervention pattern involved voluntarily sought day care, with enrollment at the convenience of the children and parents rather than at the dictates of precise experimental design, several years were required for the accumulation of the sample. Preliminary results have already been reported, but the final analysis has not yet been completed. At this juncture it can be stated that, like other early intervention programs, this one has produced positive and encouraging results. It has not, however, clearly demonstrated the superiority of beginning enrichment before age 3. For example, 86 children who entered the program prior to their third birthday (most of them between one and two) showed average developmental quotient gains of 14 points across an average interval of 25 months.

Another group of 22 children who entered at an average age of 44 months and had an average of 17 months of day care showed an average increment of 18 points. Both subgroups differed significantly from their controls, but the difference between the magnitude of change shown by the younger and older experimental children was not statistically significant ($t = 1.27$; $p =$ NS). These data are summarized graphically in Figure 1.

One could continue at length to cite data demonstrating that early childhood enrichment produces impressive gains in the intellectual functioning of young children. Similar findings have been obtained by Weikart (1967), Bereiter and Engelmann (1966), Nimnicht and Meier (1967), Karnes (1969), Hodges and Spicker (1967), and many others. The consistency of results with different groups, different pedagogy, and different samples is one of the most persuasive features of this data.

Cognitive changes have been the basis of this discussion. Conventional intelligence tests have been the center of attraction while little has been said about changes in social and emotional functioning. Similarly neglected are achievement data. The first neglect is largely due to the absence of good instrumentation which is appropriate for young children. The second is due to the fact that few of the current projects have reached the level of maturity where conventional achievement tests can be administered to the children.

Discussion

At the risk of belaboring the obvious, one must first say that the main thing needed is more of the same. Early childhood education today would not be having to experience a renaissance if, some thirty years ago, good quality research had been continued. At this point nothing is proven other than that people can become excited about early experience. At least four obligations need to be met if significant progress is to be made from this point on.

Mandatory Followup

Researchers conducting studies dealing with the effects of early intervention are obligated to follow their subjects into subsequent developmental periods. The neat, clean, quick research study is everybody's favorite research style; the prolonged, progressively boring, occasionally discouraging, longitudinal pursuit is the obligation of everyone concerned with change over time—which is what development is all about. In order to determine conclusively the effects of early intervention, such followup is essential, for some change on most assessment instruments is likely to be found any time there is a second assessment. As meaningful control groups are often difficult to obtain, long term followup is mandatory lest before and after results merely reflect increased familiarity with the testing situation or the instrument.

This point can be illustrated with some recent data from Karnes (1969), who has compared gains made during and following three different preschool enrichment programs: ameliorative, direct verbal, and traditional. The ameliorative curriculum stressed verbalization in conjunction with the manipulation of concrete materials as the chief means of remediating language deficiencies measured by a test of linguistic abilities. The direct verbal curriculum was that generally known as the Bereiter-Engelmann (1966) program and it stressed intensive oral drill in verbal, mathematical, and logical patterns. The traditional curriculum employed a goal of promotion in motor, social, and general language development of children. This was accomplished through the medium of play, both indoor and outdoor, with available materials.

The ameliorative curriculum group attended the special preschool for one year. The second year, the children attended kindergarten and received one hour per day of special work. The direct verbal group attended school in its special building following its special curriculum for two years. The traditional group attended preschool the first year and public kindergarten the next year. All three groups attended regular public school in their home community for the third year of the study. All groups showed gains on intelligence tests for the first year; however, the traditional group showed the greatest gains. During the second year, only the children attending the direct verbal program continued to gain. Each of the three groups dropped to similar levels when they entered the public first grade classes. The data point to two increasingly common facts. There is a spurt following preschool enrichment, and there is a decline when the children enter regular educational programs.

Preschool-primary continuity

There must be continuity between preschool enrichment and subsequent educational endeavors. Implications of the followup studies now available are abundantly clear: Gains associated with individualized, carefully planned, meticulously executed preschool programs cannot continue unattenuated unless subsequent educational endeavors are as individualized, carefully planned, and meticulously executed. Thus it seems imperative to link preschool programs with elementary education programs.

Careful program description

The need for more program description cannot be stressed sufficiently. What kind of intervention produces positive effects? What kind of intervention produces what kind of effect or, still better, what kind of intervention produces what kind of effect in what kind of child? These are questions which need answers. The concern is now with curriculum. Weikart (1969) suggested that the magnitude of change associated with different curricula is similar provided a particular staff model is created and teachers are convinced

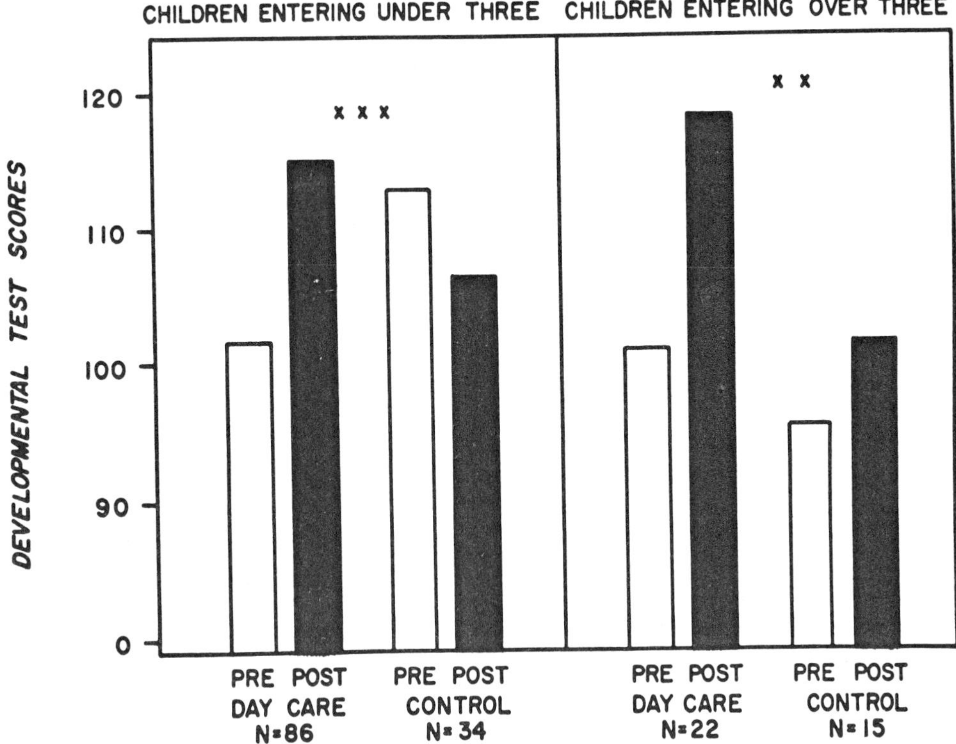

xx Difference between changes significant at .01 level.

xxx Difference between changes significant at .001 level.

that they are using the best method available. The staff model which he advocates is one to which most educators would subscribe–ample planning, team teaching, parent involvement, low teacher pupil ratio, deep staff commitment, and child oriented focus. Until detailed, naturalistic descriptions of minute to minute, person to person, and person to object classroom transactions are available, nothing can be concluded about the effectiveness or even the existence of different curricula.

Assigning priorities

At times of peak excitement about certain ideas, it is easy to campaign for one approach and to seek diversion of funds from one endeavor to another. There seems to be no justification at this time for a strategy that would involve diversion of funds from education of older children into early education. Rather, increased allocations for programs for all ages are needed.

In our enthusiasm for early education, it is easy to promise too much. When too much is promised a little disappointment seems like a lot. The natural sequel to oversell is overkill. It is a fervent hope that in our current enthusiasm for early intervention, we do not try to oversell ourselves to the point where we cannot deliver and thus be forced into another early demise. We do not need another renaissance of interest in early childhood; we only need to make certain that the current interest fulfills its obligation. Instead, the current interest should culminate in practical and effective programs.

A DEVELOPMENTALLY INTEGRATED APPROACH TO EARLY INTERVENTION

DIANE D. BRICKER
WILLIAM A. BRICKER

DIANE D. BRICKER *is Associate Professor of Pediatrics and Educational Psychology, and Administrator, Debbie School, Mailman Center for Child Development, University of Miami, Miami, Florida and* WILLIAM A. BRICKER *is Professor of Special Education, Kent State University, Kent, Ohio.*

Abstract: A rationale is presented for early intervention as a necessary component of sound educational programing for the handicapped child. An early intervention program serving 78 children ranging in age from 5 to 76 months is discussed. This project was composed of an infant unit, toddler unit, preschool unit, and parent education unit. The approach used in the project emphasized early intervention, parental involvement, developmental programing and the integration of normal (nondelayed) and handicapped (delayed) children in the same program.

Early Intervention: A Rationale

Although day care and early intervention programs continue to be discussed from the perspective of whether or not they should exist (Highberger & Teets, 1974), this is clearly not an issue for many parents and professionals. Unless this country undergoes some dramatic reversals, day care and educational programs for preschool children will remain a part of our daily existence for several reasons which cannot be readily changed.

First, statistics clearly indicate that more women are going back to full time employment for money if not simply liberation. The mothers in this working force need child care facilities. Second, much of the literature on the effects of early experience strongly suggests that developmental progress can be enhanced by providing children with a variety of experiences during the formative years (Hunt, 1961; Denenberg, 1970). In order to provide these varied experiences many parents seek out play groups and educational programs for their young children.

Finally, child advocates and handicapped children's parents' groups have brought considerable lobbying and litigation pressure on many states to provide appropriate educational and social services for young handicapped children (Hobbs, 1975). The rationale for much of this legislation is that handicapped youngsters should be entitled to extra services to enable them to become productive, stable, and happy contributors to society. These extra services often entailed providing educational programs from birth onward (Gilhool, 1973).

When one considers the needs of working mothers, current legislative moves in favor of the handicapped, and the desire by many parents for educational programs for their

"A Developmentally Integrated Approach To Early Intervention, Diane Brickner, William A. Brickner, *Education and Training of The Mentally Retarded,* Vol. 12, No. 2, April 1977, © 1977, The Council For Exceptional Children.

preschoolers, the issue becomes not whether, but how to establish quality day care and educational programs for both young handicapped and nonhandicapped children.

The literature on day care and early educational programs is extensive and can be classified into four convenient groups: (a) laboratory school or demonstration programs often situated in colleges and universities, (b) programs for the sensory handicapped child which have generated many training methods and procedures (Haring & Schiefelbusch, 1967), (c) speech therapy and language training for the young speech deficient child which often includes autistic children or children with behavior disorders (Gray & Ryan, 1973; Berry, 1969; Lovaas, 1968) and (d) programs for low-income preschoolers which have been probably the most extensively evaluated (Hodges & Spicker, 1967).

Until recently the literature has contained relatively few descriptions of programs that have concentrated on infants and children under the age of 3 (Horton, 1974; Caldwell & Richmond, 1968). The lack of programs for young developmentally retarded children is particularly noticeable (Honig, 1973).

Almost by default one approach has been available to parents of developmentally retarded or delayed preschool-age children, that of having the child remain at home until the age of 6 when the options of special classes or institutionalization become available. Two classic studies on high risk and/or children with documented problems have suggested the benefit of early intervention with a population of children who have a substantial probability of having moderate to severe learning difficulties (Skeels & Dye, 1939; Kirk, 1958); however, the impact of these and similar investigations has been slow in coming. Only during the past 5 years have parents and professionals begun to recognize the need for early detection and subsequent intervention for developmentally retarded children (Bricker & Bricker, 1974).

Descriptions of early intervention programs for moderately to severely developmentally retarded preschoolers are now beginning to appear in the literature, lending optimism to the once dismal picture of early institutionalization (Shearer & Shearer, 1972; Olshin, 1971; Bricker & Bricker, 1973). The purpose of this article is to discuss an early intervention program that has provided a sizable group of parents and their children with a relatively atypical approach to the education of young normal and developmentally retarded children.

Early Intervention: A developmentally integrated approach

Early in 1970 an early intervention project was begun at the John F. Kennedy Center for Research on Education and Human Development at Peabody College for a number of toddlers who were evidencing developmental problems or who were at high risk for developing such problems (e.g., Down's syndrome, hydrocephalus, prematurity). From the project's inception the staff felt that the program ought to be an innovative approach to the education of young handicapped children. Consequently, several important decisions were implemented which served as the keystones of the project during the four years of our involvement (Bricker & Bricker, 1971; 1972; 1973; 1976). First, although we were convinced that the environment needed to provide more than concerned care for the children, we chose to begin with a relatively undemanding structure knowing that more structure could be imposed as necessary. The form that this structure assumed was developmental programing. Second, like Schaefer (1972) we deemed parental involvement in the project to be critically important. Third, we believed that maximum benefit for handicapped children could be achieved only if they were included in the program before age 2. Finally, we decided to attempt to provide the most normal environment possible for the handicapped children. To accomplish this we proposed an approach which integrated within the same classroom an equal number of normally developing (nondelayed) with children having developmental problems (delayed). The remainder of this article expands and details these four operating tenets with special emphasis on the integration of the delayed and nondelayed children.

The Program of Integration

During the first year of this project, a morning program for 10 children and an afternoon program for the same number of children was offered. This initial group was composed of 11 children with developmental delays, and 9 children who were from all appearances and measures nondelayed. During the initial year of the project it was not easy to find parents of nondelayed children who were willing to place their child in a program that also included handicapped children. Many parents who were eager to have their toddler enrolled in an educational program quickly changed their minds when they learned that handicapped children would be integrated into the same classroom.

We were often asked during that first year why we chose to place delayed and nondelayed children in the same program. Our answers generally covered three areas which are discussed below.

Although mainstreaming is now a somewhat common term in education and special education, in the early 1970's the concept of normalization as described by Wolfensberger (1972) was new. The idea behind normalization is that every child should be entitled to live the most "normal-like" existence possible. That is any child who can function in a regular public school class should remain there. A child who can be maintained in the regular school program by providing a special support teacher should remain in a regular class rather than be isolated in a self-contained classroom. Only children who cannot function appropriately in a regular education program should be removed to self-contained special classes and finally only those few exceptional individuals who cannot be maintained in the community be institutionalized (Hobbs, 1975). The concept of mainstreaming which now has legislative support in many states provides the maximum opportunity for handicapped children to interact with normally developing peers thus providing the atypical child with a more normal environment than programs that only include children with problems. The preschool years would seem to be an ideal time to begin mainstreaming.

Effects of the Program

The integration of delayed and nondelayed children into the same program produced an unexpected outcome. Not only did the children have the opportunity to explore and learn about each other but also the parents of nondelayed youngsters had the chance to interact closely with parents of children who had moderate to severe problems. This interaction has the potential of being an enlightening experience for parents. An often heard comment by mothers in the project as they entered their children in the program was that they had a real fear of or great uncertainty about handicapped children. Their experiences in the project quickly changed fear to calm once they realized that handicapped children, first of all, are children. The close interaction between parents allowed for communication which we believe has been important in terms of educating a wide variety of people about developmental disabilities.

Finally, research by Bandura and others has suggested that children do imitate behavior that produces observable reinforcement from the environment (Bandura, 1967). Perhaps one of the most effective ways for a young delayed child to learn a new functional response is to observe the occurrence of that response in another child. For example, by watching a nondelayed youngster drag a chair to the water fountain to get a drink and succeed, the delayed child may be able to imitate the response. This imitation should result in acquiring the desired drink plus the independence of not having to seek assistance from the teacher or parent. For these reasons, we decided to build a program that would integrate children with a variety of problems and skills without interfering with the developmental progress of any individual child.

To substantiate this approach two methods were used. First, the performance of the nondelayed children in a number of areas such as motor, sensorimotor, and language was assessed. Second, standardized tests of intelligence were administered (Bricker & Bricker, 1971; 1972; 1973). This information has indicated that these normal children did not develop problems as a function of associating with children who have moderate to severe learning difficulties. However, it should be emphasized that the children were not placed into the various classrooms in a random fashion. Indeed we do not recommend that children of widely disparate developmental levels be placed in the same classroom without careful planning. The delayed and nondelayed children included in this program were matched on the basis of developmental level with little attention given to chronological age; consequently, the nondelayed children were generally 1 to 1½ years younger than the delayed children in the same class.

The matching of children on general developmental level was, we believe, extremely important if the class was to function as a group and if the children were to learn from each other. A busy, active 2 year old who is learning to run and to produce sentences may have little to offer a nonambulatory child who has yet to learn how to control his head movements. However, this same 2 year old may be able to serve as an excellent model for and to interact effectively with a 3 year old Down's syndrome child who is also learning to utter words and move about the classroom.

Responses from Parents

The second source of support for the integration of the classroom comes directly from the parents of the children involved in the project. As mentioned previously, finding normal children to participate in the project during the initial year was difficult. At the termination of the first year, all of the parents were asked to fill out a questionnaire concerning the integration of the delayed and nondelayed children. The questionnaire was composed of questions such as "Do you think your nondelayed child suffered any negative effects from interacting with less capable children?" or "Would you place your child in the program again?" All 8 of the parents of the nondelayed children who returned the questionnaire indicated they felt their nondelayed child had not suffered any negative effects from the integration and all were willing to place their child in the program again. All 11 parents of the delayed children responded that they felt the integration had a positive effect and they would choose to place their child in an integrated program over one composed of only delayed children (D. Bricker & W. Bricker, 1971).

Following the termination of the second year of the program, the questionnaires were administered again. Two of the 12 parents of the nondelayed children indicated that perhaps their child had picked up some undesirable response from the delayed children; however, all 12 parents of the nondelayed children requested that their children be allowed to return to the program the following year. We felt that this positive response by parents was important because the success of this approach is largely dependent upon parental willingness to support the concept of integration.

Finding nondelayed children to participate in the project during the third and fourth years was no problem. In fact, we had many more requests by the parents of nondelayed children than we were able to accommodate which suggests that at least locally this project has become an accepted educational program for young children.

Program Components

Initially, a program for toddler-age children seemed to meet the requirements of early intervention but after 2 years of observing young developmentally delayed children we became convinced that intervention for these youngsters should begin in early infancy. Intervention during infancy is particularly appealing if one accepts the developmental position of Piaget (1970):

> The establishment of cognitive or more generally, epistemological relations, which consist neither of a simple copy of external objects nor of a mere unfolding of structure performed inside the subject, but rather involve a set of structure progressively constructed by continuous interaction between the subject and the external world (p. 703).

Piaget has repeatedly discussed two powerful theoretical positions that if accepted would lead naturally to intervention with infants. First, as stated in the above quote the child learns from active interaction with his environment; consequently, the structure of a child's environment is extremely important if that child is to make developmental progress. Often parents at home simply do not know or do not have the confidence to use the appropriate strategies for influencing the developmental growth of a handicapped child. Second, Piaget believes that later more complex forms of behavior are developed from early response forms. In his view earlier processes such as primary and secondary circular reactions are prerequisite to the acquisition of cognitive skills that occur in later stages of the sensorimotor period which in turn are prerequisite to concrete operations from which develop formal operations (Piaget, 1970).

Bricker and Bricker (1974) argue that the sensorimotor period provides the basis for subsequent language development as well as other more complex forms of behavior. If this position can be empirically validated, than early training is crucial to the acquisition of more complex cognitive processes. These two theoretical positions provided the rationale for the development of the three intervention units of this project.

Infant Class

The infant unit contained approximately 23 babies ranging in developmental level from 5 to 16 months as can be seen in Table 1. This unit focused on high risk or children with documented problems, for example, children with Down's syndrome, documented birth injury, genetic abnormalities and at risk children (e.g., baby with a fractured skull at three months, baby from a large family all of whom are educationally retarded). No baby with a normal past history has been included in this unit. This program accommodated babies on either an all day, half day or once a week basis. The primary emphasis was the acquisition of sensorimotor skills in order to prepare the baby to move into the toddler unit.

When possible, the teachers who operated this classroom trained the mother and/or father to work with their baby rather than working directly with the baby themselves. Unfortunately, this was not always possible since many of the children were from low income or middle income backgrounds in which both parents had to work. In other families, the mother had several other preschoolers at home. A few parents

TABLE 1

Demographic Information on Children in the Infant, Toddler and Preschool Research and Intervention Project

	Infant Unit	*Toddler Unit*	*Preschool Unit*	*Total*
N	23	28	27	78
CA (in months)				
Mean	22	36	56	39
Range	5–43	21–50	43–76	5–76
Sex				
Male	9	16	18	43
Female	14	12	9	35
Race				
Black	6	5	9	20
White	16	22	17	55
Other	1	1	1	3
Economic Level[a]				
Upper	1	6	4	11
Middle	8	9	8	25
Lower	14	13	15	42
IQ[b]				
Delayed (N = 33)				
Mean	49 (N = 11)	55 (N = 12)	50 (N = 10)	52
Range	28–64	36–68	32–63	28–68
Nondelayed (N = 41)				
Mean	91 (N = 8)	109 (N = 16)	94 (N = 17)	99
Range	72–119	71–135	70–145	70–145
Etiology[c]				
Down's syndrome	8	8	9	25
Brain injury	3	0	1	4
Suspected genetic disorder	2	1	0	3
General delay	4	2	1	7
Autistic-like	1	1	2	4
Physically handicapped	1	0	0	1
Multiply handicapped	0	0	0	1
Normal—at risk	4	6	5	15
Normal	0	9	9	18

[a] The Upper category refers to families whose income exceeded $12,000 per year. The Middle category refers to families whose income was between $6000 and $12,000 per year. The Lower category refers to families whose income was less than $6000 per year.

[b] The Delayed category refers to children who scored below 70 on standardized intelligence tests. The Nondelayed category refers to children who scored above 70 on a standardized intelligence test. Four infants have not been tested.

[c] Normal—at risk refers to children who scored above 70 on a standardized intelligence test but who had additional factors in their environment that would make educational problems a high probability. General delay refers to children who scored below 70 on a standardized intelligence test but for whom no specific etiology has been isolated.

were extremely limited themselves or unable to work effectively with their moderately to severely developmentally delayed child. Parents with this variety of needs mandated a flexible program.

Parent Program

The parent training program has not always been flexible, but we have learned through a variety of experiences that parents require as much individual programing as children. Treating parents as a homogeneous group when they vary from having advanced academic degrees to those who spent their childhood and youth in one of the state residential facilities for the mentally retarded obviously will not work. During the first two years of the project the parent training and advising was carried out by the research and teaching staff. Although these people were qualified and appropriate for the roles of parent advisors, they were unable to spend adequate time with the parents.

During the third year additional funding supported the creation of a parent advisory unit composed of three full time advisors, a social worker, and a part-time coordinator. The primary responsibilities of this component were: (a) to help parents become effective educational change agents with their child, (b) to assist parents in becoming educated consumers of programs and materials offered as services for their children, (c) to offer services for those families with special needs (e.g., help in acquiring food stamps, obtaining proper medical and dental services for a child, special counseling services), and (d) to coordinate educational activities of the home and the classroom.

The parent education program focused on language, motor, sensorimotor and social areas which also formed the core classroom curriculum. Initially parents were trained in the use of behavior management skills as prerequisite to working in the curriculum areas. Training was generally conducted in small group sessions; however, when a parent had a special or particularly difficult problem, the parent advisor shifted to individual sessions. Videotapes were made of the parent training his child which then served as the focal point for helping the parent improve his training skills. The use of video replay appears to be an effective teaching strategy to employ with parents (Filler, 1974).

Consumer education was carried out by exposing parents to appropriate films, books and other printed matter, informing them about organizations that are concerned with providing education and services for young children and by arranging meetings with local, state, and national personnel who are in decision making positions. For example, the director of the special education department in the local public schools attended two parent meetings expressly to answer questions about what type of services would be available to their children in the future. The parents also had the opportunity to question representatives of the Joseph P. Kennedy, Jr. Foundation, a member of the President's Committee on Mental Retardation, officials of the State Department of Education as well as individuals associated with other early intervention programs.

All of these interactions were designed to provide the parent with knowledge about issues which directly concerned their child's education. Special services were offered through a variety of mechanisms such as evening meetings for fathers who were unable to attend the program during the day to helping a mother learn to read. The primary objective of these special services was to help families move from continuous crisis stricken existences to more stable ones by learning to anticipate trouble-producing events and developing strategies for meeting these events. For example, the family who repeatedly ran out of food was helped to develop a strategy for spacing food usage throughout the month as well as locating other food sources such as government surpluses.

The final responsibility of the parent advisory component was the coordination of training activities conducted in the classroom and at home. The parent advisors and the teaching staff shared information in order for both components to function effectively. The parents should not be working at cross purposes with the classroom program, any more than classroom training should be disrupting parental goals.

Toddler Class

The toddler classroom offered a morning and afternoon program for children who ranged developmentally from approximately 1½ to 3 years. We chose this format for two specific reasons. First, offering two half day programs allowed a well trained staff of educators to serve twice as many children and second, this program avoided activities such as meals and napping that in many instances can be better done at home by the parent. Children who needed day care were bused from this project to neighboring day care centers. We believe this format allowed more functional use of an educational setting which was important since adequate programs for young handicapped children and their parents were scarce.

Half of the 28 toddlers in the project attended the morning session while the remainder came in the afternoon. As seen in Table 1 this population of children included 12 delayed and 16 nondelayed children. The toddler unit was staffed by two teachers with assistance from practicum students. The focus was on programing in the areas of language, social, sensorimotor and motor development. Although the teachers in this unit worked directly with the children, the parents were trained simultaneously by the parent advisors to work on similar skills in order to maximize the generalization of classroom training to the home environments.

Preschool Class

The preschool unit was an upward extension of the toddler unit and the morning and afternoon program format was the same. The children in this classroom ranged developmentally from approximately 3 to 4 years and included 10 delayed and 17 nondelayed children. The program in this classroom imposed more structure on the children than was found in the infant or toddler classes with the emphasis upon the acquisition of appropriate language and social skills. Again this unit was staffed with two teachers plus various practicum students.

The educational curriculum covered the four areas of language, sensorimotor, social, and motor development for all three classroom units. These four areas were mapped out from the beginning stages to the terminal states using the principles of developmental programing. Developmental programing assumes that in the acquisition of a particular skill or process there is a beginning point when the response is not there, a termination point when the response becomes part of the child's repertoire and an in-between sequence of relevant related activities. A second assumption is that most efficient learning will occur if the training between the beginning and termination point follows the appropriate developmental sequence (Bricker, 1970).

Before training a specific skill the child needs to have the prerequisite behavior for acquiring that skill. For example, attempting to train a child in verbal imitation is probably inefficient if he cannot first focus on the face of the trainer for a suitable period of time, imitate gross and fine motor activities, and auditorily discriminate one sound from another. Focusing on the face, motor imitation, and auditory discrimination are probably prerequisite skills to verbal imitation, and the teacher should make sure the child has these skills before beginning training on verbal imitation.

Although we are fully aware that future research may suggest more appropriate training models, we believe that at present the most efficient and effective training sequences are generated using the developmental model. The teaching and research staff have concentrated much effort on building the developmental curriculum used in the infant, toddler, and preschool classrooms, and although we are far from the final solutions to the training of young children, strategies such as developmental programing provide excitement and impetus for future developments in education.

Summary

The purpose of this paper has been to discuss an intervention program based on the rationale of early intervention, integration of delayed and nondelayed children, parental involvement, and developmental programing. One of the primary goals of this project has been to demonstrate that viable alternatives to traditional preschool education exist, especially for young developmentally delayed children. Preschool education has suffered too long from a variety of constrictions that have legislated the type and age of children to be served, teacher approach, and general educational content that is or is not appropriate. Preschool programs for low income children have rocked many of these traditional notions and the field of early childhood education is now ready for a variety of new and exciting approaches.

References

Bandura, A. The role of modeling processes in personality development. In W. Hartup & N. Smothergill (Eds.), *The young child: Reviews of research.* National Association for the Education of Young Children, 1967.

Berry, M. F. *Language disorders of children.* New York: Appleton-Century-Crofts, 1969.

Bricker, D. D., & Bricker, W. A. Toddler Research and Intervention Project Report: Year I. *IMRID Behavioral Science Monograph No. 20,* Institute on Mental Retardation and Intellectual Development, George Peabody College, Nashville, Tenn., 1971.

Bricker, D. D., & Bricker, W. A. Toddler Research and Intervention Project Report: Year II. *IMRID Behavioral Science Monograph No. 21,* Institute on Mental Retardation and Intellectual Development, George Peabody College, Nashville, Tenn., 1972.

Bricker, D. D., & Bricker, W. A. Infant, Toddler and Preschool Research and Intervention Project Report: Year III. *IMRID Behavioral Science Monograph No. 23,* Institute on Mental Retardation and Intellectual Development, George Peabody College, Nashville, Tenn., 1973.

Bricker, W. A. Identifying and modifying behavioral deficits. *American Journal of Mental Deficiency,* 1970, **75,** 16–21.

Bricker, W. A., & Bricker, D. D. Behavior modification programmmes. In P. Mittler (Ed.), *Assessment for learning in the mentally handicapped.* London: Churchill Livingstone, 1973.

Bricker, W. A., & Bricker, D. D. An early language training strategy. In R. Schiefelbusch & L. Lloyd (Eds.), *Language perspectives—acquisition, retardation, and intervention.* Baltimore: University Park Press, 1974.

Bricker, W. A., & Bricker, D. D. The infant, toddler, and preschool research and intervention project. In T. Tjossem (Ed.), *Intervention strategies for risk infants and young children.* Baltimore: University Park Press, 1976.

Caldwell, B. M., & Richmond, J. The Children's Center in Syracuse, New York. In L. Dittman (Ed.), *Early child care—The new perspective.* New York: Atherton Press, 1968.

Denenberg, V. H. (Ed.), *Education of the infant and young child.* New York: Academic Press, 1970.

Filler, J. W. *Modification of the teaching styles of mothers: The effects of task arrangement on the match-to-sample performance of young retarded children.* Doctoral dissertation, George Peabody College for Teachers, Nashville, Tenn., 1974.

Gilhool, T. K. Education: An inalienable right. *Exceptional Children*, 1973, *39,* 597–609.

Gray, B., & Ryan, B. *A language program for the nonlanguage child.* Champaign, Ill.: Research Press, 1973.

Haring, N. G., & Schiefelbusch, R. L. (Eds.). *Methods in special education.* New York: McGraw Hill, 1967.

Highberger, R., & Teets, S. Early schooling: Why not? A reply to Raymond Moore and Dennis Moore. *Young Children*, 1974, *29,* 66–77.

Hobbs, N. *The futures of children: Categories, labels, and their consequences.* Report of the Project on Classification of Exceptional Children. San Francisco: Jossey-Bass, 1975.

Hodges, W. L., & Spicker, H. H. The effects of preschool experiences on culturally deprived children. In W. W. Hartup & N. L. Smothergill (Eds.), *The young child: Reviews of research.* Washington, D.C.: NAEYC, 1967.

Honig, A. S. *Infant education and stimulation (birth to 3 years): A bibliography.* Champaign, Ill.: ERIC Clearinghouse on Early Childhood Education, 1973.

Horton, K. B. Infant intervention and language learning. In R. Schiefelbusch & L. Lloyd (Eds.), *Language perspectives—Acquisition, retardation, and intervention.* Baltimore: University Park Press, 1974.

Hunt, J. McV. *Intelligence and experience.* New York: Ronald Press, 1961.

Kirk, S. A. *Early education of mentally retarded.* Urbana: University of Illinois Press, 1958.

Lovaas, O. I. A program for the establishment of speech in psychotic children. In H. Sloane & B. MacAulay (Eds.), *Operant procedures in remedial speech and language training.* Boston: Houghton Mifflin, 1968.

Olshin, G. S. Model centers for preschool handicapped children—Year II. *Exceptional Children*, 1971, *37,* 665–669.

Piaget, J. Piaget's theory. In P. H. Mussen (Ed.), *Carmichael's manual of child psychology.* Vol. 1 (3rd ed.). New York: John Wiley, 1970.

Schaefer, E. S. Parents as educators: Evidence from cross-sectional, longitudinal, and intervention research. In W. W. Hartup (Ed.), *The young child: Reviews of research*, Vol. 2. Washington, D.C.: NAEYC, 1972.

Shearer, M. S., & Shearer, D. E. The Portage Project: A model for early childhood education. *Exceptional Children*, 1972, *39* (3), 210–17.

Skeels, H. M., & Dye, H. B. A study of the effects of differential stimulation on mentally retarded children. *Proceedings and addresses of the American Association on Mental Deficiency*, 1939, *44*, 114–136.

Wolfensberger, W. *The principle of normalization in human services.* Toronto: National Institute on Mental Retardation, 1972.

A Plea for Early Intervention

Nancy W. Stone

Author: NANCY W. STONE, M.D. Director, Infant Development Project, Gulf Regional MH/MR Center, and Clinical Associate Professor, University of Texas Medical Branch, Galveston.

ABSTRACT. Observations are presented in support of the premise that programming for the biologically handicapped should begin in infancy. The recommendation is made that the goal of early intervention should be to assist the mother to develop special parenting skills which facilitate the development of the handicapped child.

The successful normalization of the biologically handicapped person is contingent on the development of his ability to function in the environment in which he is being normalized. Programs designed to achieve this goal usually begin with the pre-school age child and continue through public school special education to sheltered or semi-sheltered employment and housing. Little attention has been paid to the important early years of the biologically disadvantaged child's life. If special education methods are necessary in the years of formal schooling, it would seem questionable to assume that families intuitively are able to modify their child rearing practices to meet the needs of the biologically handicapped infant.

As there are a wide variety of opinions about the rearing of the biologically normal child, the feasibility of attempting to develop patterns of parenting which are responsive to the needs of the biologically abnormal child may be challenged. However, the fact that there are differences in philosophy and methods in all aspects of education has not resulted in the closing of schools. Theory in the field of child development supports the argument that intervention programs should be developed for handicapped infants.

Theoretical Background

The helplessness of the human infant is such that he requires continuing functional support from a mothering person, long after the structural umbilical cord is cut. A grandparent, the father, or another caretaking person may meet this need of the child. For purposes of discussion in this paper, the relationship will be referred to as the mother-child system.

For many years it was assumed that the mother's role was only to love the infant; to protect him from extremes of termperature and from physican danger; to keep him externally clean and dry, and internally hydrated and fed. Recent studies have identified other responsibilities.

Bruner (1964, 1967), Hunt (1961), and Piaget (1950, 1954) have shown that innumerable transactions between a child and his environment must occur during the course of the child's development. He must establish channels of communication with the human resources in his environment. He must look at, listen to, smell, touch, manipulate, move and consider animate and inanimate objects and their relationships, as a part of the process of learning and developing.

When maternal assistance to the biologically normal child is insufficient, the deprivation leads to retardation of development (Freedman, 1971; Provence & Lipton, 1962). Cognitive, affective, and physical development may be affected. The complex of symptoms occurs in the form of hospitalism, a failure to thrive syndrome, or socio-cultural deprivation, depending on the quality and timing of the deprivation.

Recent studies have clarified aspects of the mother's specific functions in facilitating the child's development. In early infancy, visual attentiveness in the infant appears to be increased by handling (Brody, 1951; White & Held, 1966). Spontaneous vocalizations (Ramey & Ourth, 1971; Weisberg, 1963) and smiling behavior (Wahler, 1969) increase in the presence of an attentive, responsive mothering person. Prescott (1971) suggests that a critical factor in early development is the kinesthetic and tactile stimulation which occur through the mother's handling of the baby.

Through her actions, the mother appears to reinforce the infant's use of the primitive receptor and response systems through which he obtains the sensory nutrients necessary for his early perceptual and motor development. Cuddling, tickling, rocking, smiling, and affectionate verbiage all have their place as effective methods. Optimally, the mother also functions to structure the child's encounters with stimuli in such a way that she helps him to extract information from his experiences. The functioning of this mother-child interactional system is the context in which the infant's early learning takes place.

The importance of a single mother figure as contrasted with multiple caretaking persons is a controversial issue. The term mother-child system is used in this paper to refer to the presence, in physical proximity, of responsive human resources with whom the infant can learn to communicate, and from whom he receives social reinforcement for attending to the external environment. The timing and quality of the human responses appear to be critical. No position is taken regarding the relative merits of fathering, mothering, grandmothering, or day care.

"A Plea For Ealy Intervention", Nancy W. Stone, *Mental Retardation* Vol. 13, No. 5, October 1975, © 1975, American Association on Mental Deficiency.

When a child has a biologically determined impairment in the functioning of his information procession and response systems, assistance from a mothering person is likely to be an especially critical factor in his development. Yet when the child's biological dysfunction affects the feedback, the responses he makes to his mother, their ability to establish a communication channel, may be delayed or prevented. The mother's "doing what comes naturally" may not lead to the establishment of parenting practices which are helpful to the child. The child with a low level of activity can be seen as "good and undemanding" and can be left unstimulated in his crib. The infant who stiffens, and is unable to mold his body to that of the person who is handling him, can alienate the most loving mothe. The need of the blind child for tactile and auditory stimulation, and the communication hurdles of the deaf child are not culturally transmitted information which evokes complementary patterns of parenting.

The mother's recognition of the child's difficulties and of her own inability to help, or even to establish a channel of communication, generates feelings of uncertainty and frustration. Friends and relatives are unlikely to be a useful resource for advice. Their personal experience in child rearing is not applicable, and they often convey the general society's devaluation of the handicapped child. Maternal withdrawal from the infant and the emergence of a mechanical caretaking pattern or an inhibiting protectiveness can follow. When either occurs, this failure to establish a functional mother-child system adds a secondary environmental deprivation to the primary biological disorder in the child.

Approaches to Intervention

Over the past several decades, services offered for the families of biologically disadvantaged children have had the goal of providing emotional support to the parents. In some instances counseling was given about problems which families could expect to encounter as the retarded or physically handicapped child matured. Information also was provided about available program resources for the child.

In recent years, a number of intervention techniques have been reported to be of value to the developmentally delayed child. Among these are perceptual training (Frostig & Horne, 1964), sensorimotor training (Kephart, 1960, 1964), training in focal attention (Santostefano & Stayton, 1967), increasing the child's exposure to a variety of stimuli (Kugel, 1970), and increasing the discriminative aspects of the individual stimulus (Horowitz, 1968). Behavior modification techniques have been reported to be effective in achieving behavioral change, in facilitating learning, and in training for the development of specific skills (Reese & Lipsitt, 1970; Axelrod, 1971; Gardner, 1971).

The infant's need to learn in the context of a mother-child system suggests that psycho-educational intervention in infancy should be directed at the mother-child system itself rather than the child alone. The instruction of parents in the use of special training techniques for pre-school children has been reported (Santostefano & Stayton, 1967). Parents can be helped to develop special parenting skills for the "pre-pre-school" child. The setting for this type of intervention can be the office/clinic of a health care professional or an infant development center staffed by a team of paraprofessionals and professionals.

This psycho-educational programming does not have a primary goal of directly training the child. Its goal is the establishment of a mutually reinforcing mother-child system which can facilitate transactions between the child and his environment.

The training of parents in the use of special educational techniques shifts the focus of intervention from treating the parents' emotional responses to facilitating the development of the child. An observable response to this education for special parenting is the enhancement of mother-child communications and an increase in mutually pleasurable transactions in the mother-child system. There is theoretical support for the expectation that this will have a positive effect on the development of the child.

Summary

Research in the field of child development has demonstrated the importance of mother-child interactions in the development of the very young child. Programming should provide assistance to the mother of the biologically handicapped infant to aid in the development of special parenting skills which are responsive to the particular needs of the child. Theory and practice support the validity of this recommendation.

References

Axelrod, S., Token reinforcement programs in special classes. *Exceptional Children*, 1971, 37, 371-379.

Brody, S. *Patterns of mothering.* New York: International Universities Press, 1951.

Bruner, J. S., The course of cognitive growth. *American Psychologist*, 1964 19, 1-15.

Bruner, J. S., Olver, R., Greenfield, P. and Hornsby, J., Kenney, H., Maccoby, M., Modiano, N., Mosher, F., Olson, D., Potter, M., Reich, L., Sonstroem, A. *Studies in cognitive growth.*, New York: John Wiley and Sons, 1967.

Freedman, C. A., Congenital and prenatal sensory deprivation. Some studies in early development. *American Journal of Psychiatry*, 1971, 27, 1539-1545.

Frostig, M. & Horne, D. *The Frostig program for development of visual perception.* Chicago, Illinois: Follett, 1964.

Gardner, W. I. Behavior modification in mental retardation. Chicago, Illinois: Aldine-Atherton, 1971.

Horowitz, F. D., Infant learning and development: Retrospect and prospect. *Merrill-Palmer Quarterly of Behavior and Development*, 1968, 14, 101-120.

Hunt, J. M. *Intelligence and experience.* New York: Ronald, 1961.

Kephart, N. C. *The slow learner in the classroom.* Columbus, Ohio: Charles E. Merrill, 1960.

Kephart, N. C. Perceptual-motor aspects of learning disabilities. *Exceptional Children*, 1964, 31, 201-206.

Kugel, R. S. Combatting retardation in infants with Down's syndrome. *Children*, 1970, 17, 188-192.

Maloney, M. P., Ball, T. S., & Edgar, C. L. An analysis of the generalizability of sensory-motor training. *American Journal of Mental Deficiency*, 1970, 74(4), 458-469.

Seeking Protection Against Early Childhood Mythology[1]

BETTYE M. CALDWELL

Bettye M. Caldwell is the Director of the Center for Early Development and Education at the University of Arkansas at Little Rock.

This paper is a revised version of one of the keynote addresses at the NAEYC annual conference November 8, 1973, in Seattle, Washington.

In any field of endeavor, a set of myths and beliefs can develop which, in time, are reacted to as though they were hard-core facts. How can we in early childhood protect children and ourselves from the effects of premature and ever-zealous espousal of inadequately tested ideas? If we cannot do this, we will soon have to ask ourselves how to prevent the disillusionment and discouragement that invariably accompany the discovery that what we had accepted and advocated as dogma was, after all, only myth.

Consideration of these issues was my assignment by the NAEYC Program Committee. As I was working on my paper, a little girl named Dawn looked over my shoulder, read the word "myth" and volunteered the following sophisticated definition: "A myth is something that you think explains something until you find out it doesn't." While reflecting on the wisdom of her words, I found myself remembering a few classic myths that bear more than a faint resemblance to our current situation. Then my colleague, Don Crary, and I pretended that we were contemporary Edith Hamiltons and wrote a few modern myths, each of which hopefully illuminates one of our modern problems. Finally, consideration will be given to ways we can protect ourselves against such myths.

---

[1]The author's work is supported by Grant No. SF-500, Office of Child Development, Department of Health, Education, and Welfare, Washington, D.C. The author expresses special appreciation to Mr. Don Crary for his suggestions and help in preparation of the manuscript.

"Seeking Protection Against Early Childhood Mythology", Bettye M. Caldwell, *Young Children,* Vol. 26, No. 6, Septemberr 1974, © 1974 National Association For The Education Of Young Chldrn.

Tantalus

Tantalus, in order to bring upon the gods the horror of being cannibals, had his only son killed, cooked, and served to them. Miraculously, however, the son was restored to life by the gods and his father doomed to eternal punishment. Tantalus was placed into a pool in Hades and given a great thirst and a mighty hunger. Whenever he reached down to quaff a drink of the water, it drained into the ground and receded from his reach, only to return and lap around his knees as he stood up again. Similarly, he was tortured by the presence of a variety of fruit trees growing around the pool in which he stood. But each time he reached for a piece of fruit, the wind tossed the limb of the tree out of reach. Thus he stood doomed for all time — surrounded by all that was necessary to satisfy his hunger and quench his thirst but never able to attain any of the food or water abundantly available.

Certainly we can sympathize with the predicament of Tantalus. Has the field of early childhood not been tantalized mercilessly in recent years? We are, in the United States, surrounded by abundance, much of which could be directed to the task of providing and improving programs for young children. At the 1970 White House Conference on Children, "Comprehensive family-oriented development programs including health services, day care, and early childhood education" received the largest number of votes as the top priority item to which national attention should be given.

During the year that followed the conference, dedicated efforts were made to have legislation drafted that would ensure the availability of such programs for our children — the water level in the pool rose, and the fruit trees growing around the periphery promised an abundant crop. In December of that year, a bill considered exemplary by many legislators and child development specialists passed both houses of Congress, only to be vetoed by President Nixon — and the limbs of the trees were blown back and the waters receded around our feet. Since that time, we have seen a reduction in the availability of funds to support programs for children.

We, unlike Tantalus, however, are not doomed for eternity. Most of us simply failed to take the steps to wade out of the pool. At the time of the veto, Mr. Nixon's mail was said to be "100 to 1" against the Comprehensive Child Development Act. If all 22,000 NAEYC members had written, I wonder what the ratio would have been.

Thus the protection we need against the myth of Tantalus is to refuse to stand by knee-deep in apathy and instead, to work harder as individual citizens and as a professional group. NAEYC's Committee on Legislation Education should help all of us to become more knowledgeable and more active in this area. Refer to the Children's Cause sections of *Young Children*[2] for suggestions on taking appropriate political action in behalf of young children.

Sisyphus

Sisyphus, who was once a King of Corinth, one day noticed a mighty eagle carrying away a beautiful maiden. Knowing the amorous characteristics of the Number One god, Zeus, Sisyphus had some pretty strong suspicions about who the eagle was. Soon along came Asophus, the river god, lamenting that his daughter had been carried away by an eagle; good old Sisyphus confided what he had seen and who he suspected. This act of compassion by Sisyphus drew down the wrath of Zeus. Zeus banished Sisyphus to Hades and condemned him to carry out the eternal job of trying to roll a big rock uphill — which in turn would forever roll back on him and require him to start all over again.

In today's world of early childhood education, the plight of Sisyphus might symbolize programs like Head Start. I consider Head Start one of the most constructive social action pro-

[2]April, June, August, November 1973 and January, March 1974 issues of *Young Children*.

grams ever to have been conceived and made operational. It really started, like Sisyphus, with a big stone at the bottom of a steep hill. Prior to 1965, how many child development theorists paid much attention to the early childhood years? How many states offered public programs for children under the age of six? How many viewed kindergartens as anything other than baby-sitting? How many cared about the education of poor children? How many felt that educational and health programs should be wrapped into the same delivery package? And yet how many children were there needing developmental services, with families interested in cooperating if program monies could be made available? Head Start began to move up a hill — a steep, steep hill — with a big, big rock in front of it.

The legend does not tell us anything about Sisyphus's moaning and groaning as he repeatedly struggled up that hill. Not so with our modern Sisyphus. We boasted all the way to the top: "Look at us! Look at this heavy rock we can move. We're going to take this rock and build the most beautiful castle in the world. It will have room enough in it for all the poor children. Once a child lives in our castle, he will never need another home. Living in our castle will be so wonderful for children that they will always remember their time in our castle and not mind the inadequacies of their environment." We used up so much wind with our boasts that we just barely had the energy to struggle up the hill.

But did that stone ever crush us on the way down! It broke so many bones and elicited so much jeering from the sidelines that some people were not willing to get up and start back up the hill again. Fortunately many were. This time there are more people pushing the stone, and they are boasting less about their prowess.

Again we are more fortunate than the hero of our myth. We are not doomed to repeated defeat by the gods. We can protect ourselves by pushing harder and boasting less. However, it would be to our advantage if we possessed the diligence of Sisyphus and the conviction that getting at least part of the way up the mountain is better than remaining at the bottom.

Pandora

All the gods one day presented Pandora with a lovely box into which each had placed something harmful. None of the items would harm her provided she left them in the box. Pandora's curiosity got the best of her, however, and she opened the box. When she did she released disease, sorrow, misfortune, and tragedy. Pandora noticed the troubles escaping from her box and quickly tried to close it. But by then the misfortunes had escaped, and only hope remained in her box.

Although many national leaders — and parents most of all — have called for greater availability of quality early childhood programs, as in the White House Conference resolution referred to earlier, others seem to see an increase in such programs as the equivalent to opening Pandora's box. At least two "misfortunes" are still widely suspected of lurking in the box opened by early childhood programs: the weakening of family ties and communal childrearing. The best evidence for these suspicions can be found in an excerpt from Mr. Nixon's message when he vetoed the Comprehensive Child Development bill. His message stated in part that the kinds of programs contemplated in the bill would weaken family ties and "commit the vast moral authority of the National Government to the side of communal approaches to child rearing over against the family-centered approach."

As I have dealt extensively with this criticism elsewhere, including this journal (Caldwell 1972), I shall not belabor the mythical nature of this allegation except to offer a few items to prove that early child development programs represent no new invasion of the family domain. Many aspects of family life are already regulated to some extent by the state. Most people would not have it any other way, for the regulations are designed to help and support the family, not hinder it. Yet these regulations could certainly be regarded as intrusion, if one wished to see them in that light. For example, a person must confer with the state before marriage (obtain a license, have a blood test), before beginning employment (Social Security number), upon having children (take out a birth certificate), prior to foreign travel (passport), and must not forget to have someone notify the state when he dies (death certificate). Upon reaching the age of seven he enters into nine years of participation in state-prescribed and authorized schooling. His parents must obtain certain types of medical care for him (immunizations) or be liable to prosecution. This does not shock us, for any type of social organization requires a sharing of responsibility between individual families and the regulative machinery if the rights and interests of the larger group are to be protected.

With reference to the charge that early childhood programs represent a communal approach to childrearing, certainly they are no more communal than elementary schools, Sunday schools, scouting, etc. Along with a healthy "self-concept," we need to facilitate the development of a healthy "other-concept." It is possible that earlier exposure to life in a group can help develop more empathy with others and a healthier appreciation of their needs.

I see as a major goal of the human experience (in families and outside of families) the provision of opportunities for children to enhance their own self-concepts by acceptance of and service to others. I have trouble seeing anything evil in setting up early group experiences that will help children learn to live with one another in love and peace; to accept one another with all our individual differences; to strive to work for the common good. If early childhood is making a contribution toward the achievement of those goals, let us take credit with pride. To me these qualities represent the one good gift left in Pandora's box — hope. Hope for children and for all of us.

Some Myths in the Making

We do not have to go back 3,000 years to discover myths that fit the early childhood scene today; new ones are being formulated all the time. Today we are more sophisticated so that, at least in their more popular form, our myths lack the deification and personification of qualities so characteristic of the ancient ones. Still the ingredients for myth-making — dogmatic statements about issues that affect the welfare of children — are all around us. I have tried to restate some of the dogmatic assertions most often heard in our field in a more mythological form because it might help us in the future to recognize such statements as only myth. In exploring these myths I will try (though probably unsuccessfully) not to reflect my own position in relation to their validity.

The SAGE Myth

Once a very long time ago, more than a decade, several peasants happened upon an enchanted herb while walking through the Forest of Knowledge. This herb, since referred to as SAGE (Salutary Age for General Enrichment), was soon found to possess certain magical properties. Any child in the land who was nourished with this herb prior to his third year, and even more especially if fed continuously from a few months after birth, immediately became possessed of physical health, moral superiority, and the wisdom of the ages.

The raw material for such a myth is easily found in dogmatic statements to the effect that "all children should be enrolled in early childhood programs as soon as possible, ideally during infancy." Proponents of this myth frequently cite a list of distinguished names to support it. Scholars such as Hunt, Bruner, Bloom, and indirectly Piaget provided the theoretical underpinning for the myth, although, in truth, none of them ever directly advocated it. By pointing to the importance of the first three or four years of life for the establishment of proper foundations for cognitive, social, and emotional development, these theorists seemed to be setting the stage for an advocacy of formal educational programs for all children during the infancy period.

A few of us took the ideas literally and began to explore ways of implementing them. Although at the time there was opposition to the idea, it rather quickly gained enough acceptance for a small number of pilot programs to be established. As a result of those programs we can assert that infant education, whether offered through all-day care, short-term group experience, or family-based tutorial activities can be associated with favorable cognitive and social growth in infants (Caldwell 1971). None of these early projects is old enough even at this time to allow us to say anything about long-term effects.

In certain areas we can be a little more specific. Infants from depriving environmental circumstances appear to show gains associated with such experiences that would not be expected without the intervention (Caldwell and Richmond 1968). Children from middle-socioeconomic class homes are not harmed by such experiences (Keister 1970). Attachment to parents is not weakened by these arrangements (Caldwell et al. 1970, Romaine and Teets 1972), and there is no evidence that emotional disturbance is associated with the experience (Braun and Caldwell 1972). Also we know that such programs can be established without causing an increase in illnesses over and above the incidence that would be expected of children of comparable ages in the general population (Glezen et al. 1971).

The important thing to remember, however, is that this is about all we can say at this point. In fact, the statements about attachment have been recently challenged by Blehar (1974). Do not let anybody try to tell you anything more. For if we say more, we'll be writing myth. What we can say is based on perilously few children, and we could be much more comfortable if the research referred to could be replicated on many other groups of children and families before we say anything at all.

It is only fair to state here that most of the people associated with experimental programs for young infants have been cautious in stating their results and in generalizing from their data. Sometimes, however, it is difficult to maintain caution and not slip into dogmatic assertions — and thence into myth.

The KIDNAP Myth

In our land there once resided a number of men and women who had been endowed by the gods with the fearsome combination of knowledge without moral sensitivity. These persons, despite attempts to halt their actions by the chief god of the land, set out to KIDNAP (Keep Intellectual Development and Nurturance Away from Parents), ripping innocent babes from the womb of love and protection which each home in our land was known to be. These persons desperately sought to control all the children of our land and to rear them in large herds away from the constant love, attention, and care which every mother and father in our land continually bestowed upon their offspring.

This myth is also concerned with the timing of education and, indirectly, with the inferred motives of those who plan and promote early childhood services. It might be described as the antithesis of the SAGE myth. Its origins were hinted at in the discussion of Pandora, which implied that the opening of the curiosity box released all kinds of noxious experiences into the otherwise cozy world of children and families. Most disturbing about this myth was the implication that people who were working diligently to increase the availability of early childhood programs for children had some ulterior motive and really sought to break up families and herd children into communal childrearing environments. But opposition to the KIDNAP'ers gradually became depersonalized and focused on the lack of value provided in the services and on the inaccuracy of the idea which suggested that early experience played a crucial role in development. Thus we began to encounter the allegation that all early childhood education outside the home is a waste of time at best and a harmful experience at worst.

One of the better known statements of this position is the one by Moore and Moore (1972) published not in a scientific or professional journal but in *Harper's Magazine* under the title "The Dangers of Early Schooling." The article, while presenting several arguments against early education, offered little documentation aside from very general statements such as "a wealth of research has established" or "many specialists in early childhood now believe."

A more recent article (1973) by the same authors again offers no documentation but refers to an ostensibly more scholarly article published in the *Congressional Record* — a fact mentioned in a footnote on the first page as though publication of the article in the *Record* established its authority. However, absolutely anything can be published in the *Congressional Record,* especially if the article could be used as evidence against an action, like appropriating money for children's programs, that a particular Congressman does not want to support.

It seems worthwhile to note that frequently one potential myth is initiated in order to protect us (and children) from the consequences of accepting as dogma the opposite point of view.

The SCHOOL Myth

Our land has been uniquely blessed by the gods. For in this land, as in no other land in this or any other world ruled by the gods, we have the blessings of SCHOOLS. The name itself was ordained by the gods as conveying both the purpose and nature of these hallowed places: SCHOOLS is an acronym meaning quite simply, Service to Children by a Holy, Omniscient, Omnipotent, Loving Staff. Without this blessing life would most assuredly be deplorable.

I am not really sure how many people who represent education advocate this position, but it is referred to so often in the popular press that it needs to be dealt with as a potential myth. When I talk about the importance of a continuum of services for young children, ranging from home-based programs to school-based efforts, I have had some administrators say to me, "But don't you want to get the poor children out of the homes as much as possible?"

Most of you have probably encountered a seemingly more innocent form of this myth in statements such as:

> "Teachers are trained to teach children, and they know how to do it."
>
> "I don't want parents coming in my room all the time. It always takes me an hour to get the children settled down after they leave."

Or the one which is most popular in schools with a student body primarily from economically disadvantaged families:

> "It is no wonder that this boy acts the way he does when you consider what his home is like."

The greatest danger inherent in this myth is that acceptance of it encourages having the home and the school become isolated entities.

It is difficult to cite data to support the contention that things go better for children if home and school work together. Research touching upon this question was conducted by Gilmer, Miller, and Gray (1970), who compared the effectiveness of what they called a "maximum impact" approach (preschool five days a week plus participation of mothers in the school a half day a week) to an approach which involved only preschool experience and to an approach consisting of home visits once a week. In general it appeared as though more participation of mothers in the educational activities was associated with greater cognitive gains for the target children. However, it was difficult to point to the clear superiority of home-plus-school to extended home intervention by itself or to a carefully planned preschool curriculum without parent involvement. I know of absolutely no research that has been concerned with the impact of father participation in school activities.

Our failure to secure more data on this important issue which has major policy implications is probably due in part to the tendency to think categorically. We either endorse the SCHOOL myth or its opposite (to be discussed in a moment) and seldom collect any information that would permit us to draw inferences about the effects of cooperation between the two.

We have Head Start (school) and Home Start, but not, at least at the policy level, Home and Head Start. We have advocates of home-based programs (Gordon 1968; Madden et al. 1974) and apparent advocates of school-based programs (Caldwell 1973). I know of no advocate of a school-based program who does not urge close liaison with the home; only by unwarranted inference is the intent of such programs interpreted as advocating a separation of home and school. This is perhaps not true of the proponents of the opposite position, for the implication is often made that more can be accomplished (with the added bonus of lower cost) if intervention is offered *only* through the parents (generally the mother) and the child is protected from early group experience. With advocacy of this position, inadequately supported by evidence, another myth is promulgated.

The PARENT Myth

Once when each and every god was at peace with each and every other god (a truly remarkable time) a decision was made which has, to this very moment, yielded blessing upon blessing for the children of our land. The decision made by the gods was that from that time forth, each man and each woman should receive the gifts of perfect wisdom, infinite patience, and inexhaustible love at the moment of their first child's birth — at that moment they would become a PARENT (Parents Are Right, Erring at No Time). The virtues inherent in PARENThood would forevermore be apparent in every interaction with their offspring.

We seem to visualize every household as containing a mother and father and Dick and Jane who live in a white house with a picket fence around it, and have a dog named Spot in the yard. In this myth they live together in total harmony and mutual support. The big people do everything in their power to help the little people, and the little people model their behavior after that of the big people. The big people wipe tears and bind wounds and coach softball and teach words, and the little people love and obey. And nobody gets mad when somebody tracks dirt in on a freshly scrubbed floor.

If this myth were valid in today's world, probably our divorce rate would not be quite so high, thus taking fewer children out of their biological family and depriving them of the opportunity to know both parents. If it were true, "do your own thing" would certainly stop when we become parents.

Most of us strive to make this myth a reality and do the best we can to raise our children to be the kinds of adults we think will be adaptive in tomorrow's world. And this is true whether we are poor or well-to-do, regardless of what ethnic group we belong to or how much education we have had.

But all parents deviate significantly from the myth some of the time, and some parents disprove it most of the time. We are not doing children any favor if we make public statements to the effect that no early childhood program should operate unless it is parent-centered. If such were the case, what about Mae, the daughter of a severely retarded mother and an unknown father who was being cared for by a psychotic grandmother; or Gerston, the subject of chronic abuse from his mother, who went into rages every time he soiled a diaper and lowered him into a tub of scalding water; or Liz, a terribly frightened four-year-old with a speech impediment who was seduced by her mother's boy friend; and for a great many other children. These children are around today because concerned teachers and aides and researchers perceived that they would not make it in life without a great many extra-family supports.

The CHILD Myth

The gods, knowing the extremes of human frailty, and seeing the weakness and ineptitude which comes with age (a decrepitude often beginning as early as 25), soon recognized that much of the trouble and suffering in the land could be eliminated by investing the children rather than the adults with divine attributes. The gods, therefore, agreed that each child should possess both the instinctive will for all that is best for himself and the necessary intelligence to achieve those ends — i.e., that each child should become a CHILD (Children Heed Internal Lessons for Development). Further, each CHILD, if only permitted to do so by the often feeble and misguided adults around him, would naturally progress by himself to the highest levels of human development — both morally and intellectually.

This myth has always held a prominent position for some early childhood educators. Its origin is probably linked to a desire to protect children from the dangers of the two previous myths. Yet this noble effort has the potential for becoming equally destructive. Children are indeed born programmed to some extent to develop their "humanness." But we know that this humanity may assume protean forms, and that there must be some guidance from the adults with whom the child interacts in order to help the child in the process.

Proponents of this myth can sometimes make a teacher who formulates a lesson plan or writes a behavioral objective feel as though he or she is "manipulating" or "controlling" the child. And, to be sure, this is exactly what is happening, just as a parent is "manipulating" the child by encouraging him to talk, to eat with a utensil rather than fingers, and to agree upon times and places for eliminating. All such behaviors are shaped by the culture as well as by the internal programming of the child, and the child needs cues as to acceptable varieties of behavior in order to be able to adapt to the culture in which he lives. Cultures are changing rapidly and we cannot predict which behaviors will truly be adaptive in the culture of the future. Yet this lack of certainty does not permit us to abrogate all guidance, all value training, and to assume that "the child knows best and will find the way."

Children enter life with individual differences and we do well to recognize those differences in planning programs for children. However, this is not the same as suggesting that, because of these inherent characteristics, we should turn over all decision making to the children. In his sensitive novel *Lord of the Flies,* William Golding paints a frightening picture of what happens when children assume all the decision making. We need to exercise caution lest we succumb to the rhetoric of the CHILD myth; it is no less dangerous than any of the others.

To summarize this section, I have suggested that we are surrounded by a number of modern myths about children. We are propagating myths if we imply that early experience is everything, or call people who endorse this position foolish or evil. It is equally a myth to claim that schools *always* know and do what is best for children, that parents *always* know and do what is best for children, or that children *always* know and do what is best for themselves. In short, almost any of our ideas which are heuristic and rational if held as working assumptions become myths if pushed to their categorical limits. Much of our thinking and writing on these topics has been partisan and categorical, not reasoned and open. Perhaps we must search for that elusive point at which the kernels of truth contained in each of these myths intersect, and let that point serve as a basis for evaluating existing programs and for planning others for the future.

Protection against Myth-Making

In seeking protection against this kind of myth-making, I have two fairly simple suggestions. The first is to avoid what I call the *press conference orientation.* Let me facetiously dramatize what I mean. An investigator returns to his office happily clutching a computer print-out; he cannot wait to learn the results of his experiment. Well, his study dealt with 21 experimental and 19 control children and measured their school achievement at grade 5. The experimental children had been enrolled in a prekindergarten program for a year, and some had also been available for kindergarten. No one was in a position to evaluate the quality of the programs for him. Also the children, because of high mobility, had attended a variety of elementary schools. Therefore our experimenter congratulated himself on finding so many who by chance had been given the same achievement test years later. His data reveals no difference between the two groups, thus "proving" that the early childhood experience was unnecessary and of no value.

Now he has to decide what to do with that information. "Well," he muses, "I am not sure one of the journals will publish it, as the size of the sample is really kind of small. And no one here now was around when the children were in the early childhood program, and an editor might get after me for that. And I suppose the value of the group test is kind of questionable. Also, we've had a run on these studies lately. But, we are being asked to appropriate large sums of money for these early childhood programs, and this study proves that they are not worth the money. Since there is a good chance a journal won't take the paper, maybe I should call my congressman. Yeah, that's a good idea. But this is important stuff. Maybe I'd better call a press conference instead."

Needless-to-say, at our fantasied press conference, the researcher freely generalizes from his data, urging that the community take a close look at funding patterns for early childhood programs. And he feels like a good citizen for having translated his scientific work into immediate social action.

I propose that caution on the part of our researchers, and avoidance of this press-conference orientation, would offer significant protection against some of our mythology of early childhood. This admonition leads into my second recommendation for avoiding myth-making: Develop and follow a research paradigm for interpreting research with social policy implications.

Many of the important ideas that have influenced educators have evolved via the same sequence usually followed in the biological sciences. For example, many concepts are derived from animal studies. Most of the workers in the field have shown a modest amount of caution in resisting extrapolation all the way from the mouse to the human. Where there has not been so much caution is when we have extrapolated from the human to humanity, i.e., from small scale, carefully conducted studies to large scale, possibly casually operated and bureaucratically complex programs. A perfect example would be in the area of the effects of infant day care. Virtually all of the data that can be cited come from settings that have been carefully monitored and meticulously evaluated. To extrapolate from such studies to programs not likely to be able to remain constantly on target and to be under careful surveillance is risky indeed.

I have over the last several years been proposing a model schema through which every socially relevant idea must pass, without skipping any steps, before we okay the idea for public consumption. This schema would involve beginning with an animal study (if relevant), following with a small controlled pilot study done with humans. If results warrant, the next step should involve double-blind field testing and replication by an independent group of investigators. This design is not unlike that followed whenever a new drug is developed and is proposed for use with human subjects. If such a design had not been formalized a number of years ago, undoubtedly the thalidomide tragedy would have been repeated many times over. In early childhood there is as great a need today for vigilant people who can be on the qui vive for premature application of inadequately tested ideas as there is for creative people to generate new ideas and institute the routine of pilot study, field test, and replication. Without this approach we may always be using myths as a basis for our actions.

Summary

Now is an exciting time to be part of the field of early childhood education. We can reflect on some of the trends of the last decade and see reenactments of old myths in ways that have touched us all. Myths are made when we do not completely understand something. Once made, they serve as anxiety-reducers for us — it is easier to refer to the myth than to think through the issue and derive an appropriate explanation each time. I have a favorite line from Arthur Koestler's *Darkness at Noon:* "The ultimate truth is penultimately always a falsehood." Or, stated another way, current knowledge always makes the way we previously understood something obsolete, which is much like Dawn's definition of a myth — "something you thought explained something until you found out it didn't."

We *can* protect children from the harmful effects of myths about childhood if we refuse to let ourselves become dogmatic and doctrinaire in our thinking. We can insist on quality research with long-term follow-up and with relevant and significant evaluation. If we adopt this orientation we will not be doomed to relive any of the ancient myths and we will at the same time protect our children and ourselves from the creation of a modern set.

IDENTIFICATION AND ASSESSMENT

Early identification of children with handicapping conditions has received particularly favorable support by most professionals in the field of special education. There is definite evidence for the beginning of intervention early. This rationale, that the sooner intervention begins the greater chance for positive results, is well founded in the literature. Only when the possible detrimental effects of labelling are considered, do individuals question identification of children at an early age. In this case it is not the issue of whether preschool handicapped children should be identified, but which diagnostic measures should be used to determine eligibility in early childhood programs and how the diagnostic results should be reported. There is a need to specify the characteristics of young handicapped children and describe their particular behaviors in a manner that will avoid later deleterious effects. Sophisticated efforts must be made to identify all preschool handicapped children. Traditional methods of screening and locating these children have often been quite effective when the child has a physical handicap or other severe deficits. When children demonstrate less severe speech, hearing, cognitive or motor disorders they are often overlooked, however. Improved pediatric training and concentrated efforts by "child find" programs are two suggestions that may improve this situation.

A major difficulty involved in appropriate assessment and evaluation of preschool youngsters is the limitation of available valid and reliable measurement instruments. While selection and use of suitable commercial and teacher constructed assessment and evaluative devices is advocated, many issues do arise. Should these children be evaluated by standardized tests, or should baseline data be collected in a naturalistic setting over a continuous period of time? When should the effectiveness of a program be measured: at the end of the year, at the conclusion of the preschool program, or in the primary grades? and which variable do you choose as the index for improvement: I.Q., achievement scores, or specific behavioral changes?

Specific guidelines for screening, diagnosing and evaluating the progress of preschool youngsters are offered in the following section. Functional recommendations for program planning are also made.

an early childhood education center with a developmental approach

william j. meyer

In his presentation, Dr. William J. Meyer outlined the general strategy he and his colleagues are using to conduct observational research in an early childhood day care program. The procedures include extensive observations of the children's behaviors, longitudinal analyses of the data, and development of measurement instruments and classroom materials.

Dr. Meyer emphasized the need to delineate the cognitive competencies of a child and match the cognitive demands of the primary grades to these competencies.

"An Early Childhood Education Center With A Developmental Approach", William J. Meyer, *Not All Little Wagons Are Red,* ©1976 Published by The Council For Exceptional Children.

IDENTIFICATION OF EVALUATION NEEDS

□ In our work at the Syracuse University Early Childhood Education Center (SUECEC), we have identified three attributes which seem crucial for meaningful program evaluation and planning:

1. There is a need to reexamine the instruments used for assessing the aptitudes of children and achievement outcomes, and these instruments must be process oriented.
2. Observational research in the naturalistic setting which emphasizes the individual child's encounters is crucial.
3. Indices of cognitive functioning must be related to behaviors in the naturalistic setting, and these relationships must be examined for individuals over time.

This work will provide teachers with the knowledge to identify process variations without having to rely on "tests." In addition, the data will provide teachers from the preschool with clues as to how to proceed with the child.

We need a better understanding of levels of cognitive functioning.

We believe that this work must also extend into the primary grades because we need a better understanding of the changes in levels of cognitive functioning that occur in this important period. In order to evaluate the outcome of the preschool or day care programs, one must be able to delineate the cognitive competencies of the child when in the primary grades and to relate these to his experiences in the primary grades. We are particularly concerned that in a typical elementary school, children are not viewed from a developmental point of view and that a considerable degree of damage can occur to the child, regardless of the success of the preschool or day care program, unless an effort is made to match the cognitive demands of the primary grades to the cognitive competencies of the child.

DAY CARE PROGRAM

□ The Early Childhood Education Center is involved in a day care program for children between the ages of 3 and 6 years. At the present time, approximately 20 of the 40 children had been previously involved in a day care program (The Children's Center Program) from the age of approximately 6 months to 36 months. The Children's Center Program initially was developed by Dr. Bettye Caldwell and is now under the direction of Dr. Ronald Lally. Eventually our program will be expanded in size and will accommodate all "graduates" of Dr. Lally's program.

My purpose in describing our current program is not only to provide you with information about our setting, but also to emphasize the rather unique opportunities available for an extensive program evaluation involving longitudinal data. The children we receive at the Day Care Center arrive with extensive background information, including prenatal data, general medical information, and detailed reports of their early cognitive development. The work on assessing cognitive development involves Piagetian tasks, as well as

Assessing cognitive development involves Piagetian tasks.

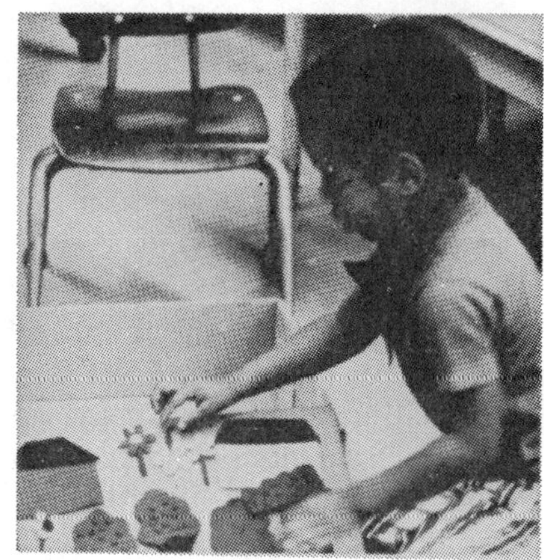

other kinds of age appropriate indices, and is consistent with the theoretical orientation of our program directed by Dr. Margaret Lay and with the assessment procedures we are attempting to develop. Briefly, the Day Care Program (Lay, 1972) provides the children with a relatively free environment that involves three major activity areas:

The program provides three major activity areas.

1. A task area comprised mainly of table activities where the children are expected to be relatively quiet.
2. An expressive area (painting, dress up corner, clay, etc.) where more noise and fewer restrictions are expected.
3. An active area in which noise and active physical movement is permitted.

In addition, there are invitational activities of various kinds, but the children are free to accept or reject an invitation.

Children become involved in those activities where the cognitive and social demands are consistent with competencies.

In a very real sense, our program is an effort to operationalize Hunt's (1961) "match-mismatch" hypothesis, where it is assumed that children become involved in those activities where the cognitive and social demands are consistent with the child's competencies. The theoretical conceptualizations for both program planning and evaluation are consistent with those expressed by Kohlberg (1968) and Flavell and Wohlwill (1969). Specifically, with respect to evaluation, our thinking has been influenced by Wohlwill (1970) and Bereiter (1962). Summarizing these major sources of input, our program evaluation and planning strategies encompass the following features:

1. Extensive (monthly) observations of the children's behaviors in the day care environment.
2. Longitudinal analyses of the observation data and other assessment procedures emphasizing the individual child.
3. The development of instruments which index *processes* as opposed to the use of instruments which are diffuse and less well defined in content.
4. The development of classroom materials and procedures which emphasize *processes* as opposed to products.
5. The integration of objectives 2, 3, and 4, with objective 1 providing a test of our major theoretical formulations, an extensive description of the actual program each child experienced and how it is hoped these experiences covary with child characteristics, and a set of reasonably objective "marker" behaviors that can be used by others with recommendations for modifying specific aspects of the environment in ways that are compatible with the child's competencies.

OBSERVATIONS OF BEHAVIORS

□ The observation schedule (see Figure 1) provides in detail the behaviors which are of concern to us. There are three basic classifications: (a) the frequency with which the children use the various task areas, (b) the frequency and quality of the children's social

Figure 1. Codes for Observations of Children: Initial Format

A. Location. Observer indicates where S is in program setting.

1. Active
2. Expressive
3. Task
4. Outdoors
5. Invitational room # 1
6. Invitational room # 2
7. Rest
8. Snack, lunch
9. Other (lavatory, hallway, etc.)

B. One - 10 names of female children
C. One - 10 names of female children
D. One - three names of female children

} Observer indicates those with whom S has verbal, gestural, tactile contact.

E. One - seven names of male children
F. One - 10 names of male children

} Observer indicates those with whom S has verbal, gestural, tactile contact.

G. Kind of interaction

1. Verbal
2. Gestural
3. Tactile
4. Visual

H. One - 10 names of staff/adults
I. One - two names of staff/adults

} Observer indicates those with whom S has verbal, gestural, tactile contact.

J. Staff/adults

1. Male visitor
2. Female visitor
3. Self (observer)

4.-9. Student teachers' names

} Observer indicates those with whom S has verbal, gestural, tactile contact.

K. Kind of interaction

L. Language use: tells what he's doing

M. Language use: indicates wants

N. Language use: tells others what to do

O. Language use: asks help

P. Language use: asks permission

Q. Language use: asks how to do

R. Language use: asks for name

Children gain in cognitive competency without an increase in task area use.

interactions with both peers and adults, and (c) the frequency of the children's use of language, as opposed to gestures, etc., to communicate.

Initially, we viewed these codes as representing our objectives. We were hopeful the children would be increasingly attracted to the task area, that their social interactions would become more frequent and positive in affect, and that the children would use language as their major form of communication, especially the form of question asking behavior. Our position with respect to items *b* and *c* has not changed, but there is now some uncertainty about the first objective. Specifically, we now suspect that children can gain in level of cognitive competency without a corresponding increase in their use of the task area. The question is still open, however, and further data analyses are now underway. It may be that our initial formulation was not wrong but perhaps too narrow. For example, one analysis indicates that the older children, in general, make greater use of the area. There is also evidence to suggest that, among the older children, those who perform better on our indices of cognitive competency spend more time in the task area. It should be noted that this question has forced us to attack the very difficult problem of assessing the quality of the children's performance in all three of the areas.

I shall describe only the highlights of our observational study. The first conclusion is that despite whatever rubric we use to describe our program—currently it is called a "reactive environment" there is actually a great deal of variation in the nature of the program for individuals.

Table 1 shows the means and standard deviations for the use of the various areas. Clearly, the children prefer the active area, with the expressive and task areas following in that order. Boys use the active area more than girls, girls use the expressive area more than boys, and there are no sex differences with respect to the task area. The frequency of verbal interactions with peers increases over time, and the

Table 1. Means and Standard Deviations on Location in Each of the Six Areas

	Oct-Nov		Dec-Jan		Feb-March		Apr -May		7 Mo.Tot.	
	M	SD	M	SD	M	SD	M	SD	M	SD
Active	33.6	9.9	34.3	12.5	39.9	14.1	33.6	11.1	35.7	9.1
Expressive	20.4	10.0	21.3	7.8	15.2	8.1	15.7	6.6	18.2	5.6
Task	13.0	8.6	12.1	8.7	12.7	9.2	9.0	8.9	11.2	6.2
Snack	12.3	7.0	12.6	7.0	8.8	5.5	8.0	5.8	10.2	4.7
Invitational	3.9	5.2	5.4	3.3	8.9	6.3	11.6	6.6	8.2	2.7
Outdoors	7.3	6.4	4.8	4.3	5.6	5.6	19.8	7.0	10.4	4.1

quality of these interactions improves substantially. There were no sex differences. Finally, there was some increase in the frequency of question asking behavior, but not to the degree anticipated.

The observation schedule provides data about achievement of objectives.

One aspect of this work needs to be stressed. A frequent criticism of evaluation research is that either it is irrelevant to the stated goals of the program, or it contributes little or nothing to program planning. These are all too often valid criticisms, but in this case, neither is valid. First, the observation schedule provides direct data about the achievement of objectives and, second, the data can be (and were) used to make modifications in both materials available to the children and in the quality of invitational activities made available to specific children. Despite the incredible logistics problems involved in this work, not to mention costs, the data base now available permits us to understand the properties of our program and the children.

LONGITUDINAL ANALYSIS

Our objective is to relate behavioral change to initial behavioral and cognitive characteristics.

□ This aspect of our strategy is very much in the infant stage. The report by Lay and Meyer (1971) provides some information about the changes over time of the total group, but our objective is to attempt to relate behavioral change to the initial behavioral characteristics of the children and to certain of their cognitive characteristics. Specifically, our objective here is to focus on the behavioral patterns of individual children over time. Briefly, our procedure will involve the use of cross lagged panel correlations (Holtzman, 1962) which provide information on the degree to which behaviors at various points relate to behaviors at an earlier point in time. These analyses will be run on the observational data where 40 time points will be identified.

COGNITIVE COMPETENCY SCALE

□ The development of this instrument is a major undertaking at our Center and is proving to be a very difficult task with respect to the measurement problems encountered. There are three problems of immediate concern:

1. Identifying the salient cognitive processes.
2. Developing a sufficiently large population of items.
3. Demonstrating that the scales reliably classify the children.

What are the salient cognitive processes?

The first problem is exemplified in a variety of intelligence tests where various levels of cognitive demands are blended in unknown ways (Meyer & Goldstein, 1969). But, neither available theory nor methods presumably related to process are very helpful. The various conservation tasks which we are using appear to require several competencies, but they are difficult to identify. They may prove useful, however, in determining if children rely on perceptual cues (Piaget, 1947), if they can perform transformations, and if they are able to verbalize their cognitive manipulations (this last attribute may not be viewed as critical, depending on how you view the relationship between language and cognition).

The second problem is not so much one of developing items, but rather determining the optimal number of items that can be used before the children become bored or begin to learn. The third problem is closely related to the second because, as everyone knows, reliability is a function of test length. There is, however, an implicit position taken in the third item. Specifically, our objective is to make reliable binary decisions: a child is a conserver or he is not. This strategy, you will recognize, is different from traditional tests which attempt to answer the question of "how much?" and not the question "does he?"

2. IDENTIFICATION

MAJOR TASKS □ Three major tasks are being used: a Classification Task developed by Sigel (Sigel, Anderson, & Shapiro, 1966), Conservation Tasks (the procedures for these tasks were developed by Dr. Vernon Hall at our Center), and the Raven Coloured Progressive Matrices (RCPM) (Raven, 1956).

The Classification Task involves 12 objects familiar to children (top, ball, matches, etc.) which are presented in both object form and pictorial form (life sized color photographs). Each object (picture) is presented, and the child is asked to select other objects (pictures) that go with it and to explain the basis of classification. The use of pictures and objects with the same child is to determine the child's ability to cope with representations. Responses are coded in terms of whether the child uses perceptual properties (form, color), functional categories, or class inclusive categories (see Meyer, 1971, for a detailed report of the procedures and results).

I shall briefly report a study using 108 middle class children tested at IV-2 and again at IV-11. Three findings are of interest:

1. There was a statistically significant difference in the classification scores for objects as opposed to pictures on the pretest, which was not found on the posttest 9 months later.
2. On the pretest there was a significant order effect where it was found that when objects were presented first for classification, there was a significant effect on performance with pictures, but when pictures were presented first, there was no effect on the performance with the objects. This effect was not found 9 months later.
3. On the pretest, the primary basis for the children's classifications were perceptual (form, color, etc.), and with respect to form and color, the children used form slightly more than color. On the posttest, the predominant basis of classification was form, with a significant increase in the number of classifications that were categorized as "functional" (objects grouped together because of some functional relationship among them).

There was no evidence that the children were able to classify on the basis of broader, more inclusive categories. The findings are consistent with Sigel's (1968) "distancing hypothesis" which states that there is a developmental trend in the direction of children becoming better able to cope with representations in comparison with actual objects. Another finding of interest is the fact that there was no improvement in the children's ability to correctly label the objects on the pre- and posttest. This finding suggests that mere labeling does not guarantee that the child has an abstract representation of the features of the object.

CONSERVATION TASKS □ I shall now comment on Conservation Task data. A detailed description of the procedure used in administering the scales is available from the Center. I will focus on a sample of 45 middle class children who are currently in the first grade and who were tested in the month of December with the conservation tasks. These data are important because they provide some indication of the stability of the conservation tasks and point toward the reliability of classification problems alluded to earlier in this paper.

A total of 45 children were administered the task and then were retested within 10 days. Although the scales generate either 4 or 5 points, we decided, on theoretical grounds, that a child had to get all the items correct in order to be a conserver. Any score below a perfect one was not considered to differentiate among children; that

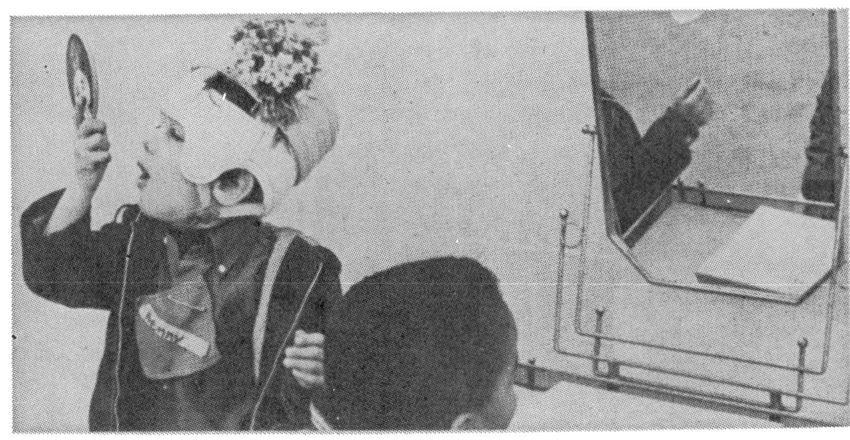

There was no evidence that children were able to classify on the basis of broad, inclusive categories.

is, on a scale from 0-5, a child with a score of 4 was not considered to be in any particular way better than a child with a score of 0 or 1. It is our position that within the Piagetian framework, this is a more defensible position than the one taken by Goldsmith and Bentler (1968), who while talking about conservers and nonconservers nevertheless treat their scales as continuous.

Evaluation of the data indicated a problem in classifying the children on the basis of one administration of the task. There is a general trend for all three tasks for the children to improve on the second administration; and in the case of length, nine children became conservers; in the case of mass, five children became conservers; and in the case of weight, seven children became conservers on the retest.

These data suggest one of two possibilities: (a) our assumption of noncontinuity is, in fact, not valid, or (b) inadvertently some learning occurred on the pretest. In order to determine more precisely what happened, we are examining our procedures carefully to determine if the children were receiving feedback.

RAVEN PROGRESSIVE MATRICES

□ The Raven Coloured Progressive Matrices (RCPM) was administered to the same first grade middle class children as were used in the conservation study. The children were given scales *A*, *Ab*, and *B* and were readministered the test within 10 days.

A test-retest reliability was .80, indicating a reasonably high overall stability of behavior. However, an examination of the reliabilities of the individual scales (*A*, *Ab*, *B*) suggested that although the overall score remained relatively constant, performance within scales shifted significantly.

These data, along with the correlations, suggested the possibility that the two administrations of the task somehow interacted with subject characteristics. An initial exploration of the data suggested that children who used a consistent strategy in answering each of the items, where consistency was defined in terms of the use of the same strategy on four or more occasions on both administrations of the task, may have improved more on the posttest. Detailed statistical data on this study and related studies is available from the Center.

DEVELOPMENT OF CLASSROOM MATERIALS

□ The development of the competency scales has little meaning until the indices are related to more achievement oriented indices. Here again, there is general dissatisfaction with prevailing achievement test measures because of their diffuseness with respect to process demands (see Ginsburg, 1972, for an excellent discussion of the issues). Instead of relying exclusively on standardized tests, we are attempting to develop tasks which teachers can use not only for interesting learning exercise but also to ascertain, on their own, whether or how a child is processing the demands of the tasks. A TV tape is now being edited which shows, among other things, the variations in children's performance characteristics on a puzzle solving task and a balance scale problem. Specifically, the tape attempts to show the importance of looking at the strategies the child employs while working on the problems (whether successful or not), to sensitize teachers to the nuances of the child's behaviors, such as his eye movements, and finally to demonstrate that when a task is overly demanding, the child's main desire is to escape.

A TV tape shows variations in performance.

Also, a student of mine and I are trying to analyze the cognitive demands of the various reading programs to ascertain first if there is truly variation among them, and, given that there is variation, to ascertain the major cognitive demands. Concurrent with this essentially armchair speculation, we are also developing tasks to assess children's strategies in deciphering new words.

Are there truly variations in reading programs' cognitive demands?

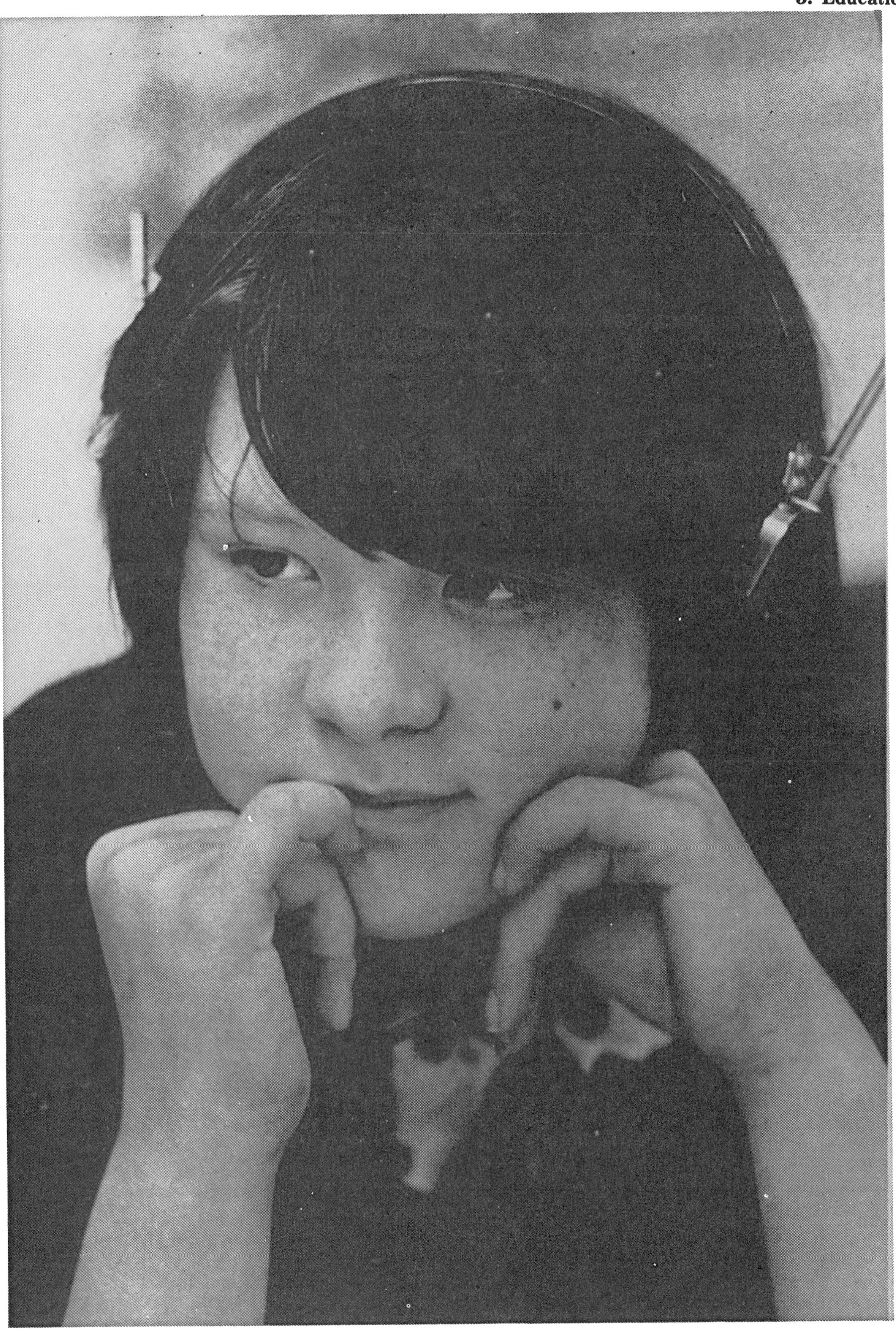

Identifying Developmental Discrepancies at the Preschool Level

Samuel A. Kirk, PhD and John Elkins, PhD

This paper describes a procedure of using the average deviation from the child's mean scaled score on the ITPA to determine significant developmental discrepancies in preschool children. By using this deviation score we found approximately twice as many developmental disabilities in Head Start children as were found in an average population of preschool children.

Children with learning disabilities at the school age level are generally identified as those who have a discrepancy between mental capacity and achievement in one of the academic subjects. A child with average or above average intelligence who is not achieving at a normal or average rate in reading, writing, spelling, arithmetic or language, and who has a significant discrepancy (two years or more) between his mental capacity and achievement, is usually considered to have a learning disability.

At the preschool age level, where academic achievement is not a factor, different criteria must be evolved. Using the same definition of learning disability, a logical extension here would be a discrepancy in growth in motor, cognitive, linguistic and perceptual abilities. The major problem with such a definition is the inability to measure these functions accurately in young children. Different criteria have been used, including discrepancies in verbal and nonverbal abilities found in tests like the Wechsler Preschool and Primary Scale of Intelligence (WPPSI), the Detroit Tests of Learning Abilities, and other similar tests. Discrepancies in abilities on the Illinois Test of Psycholinguistic Abilites (ITPA) have also been used to identify children with learning disabilities at the preschool level.

In using the ITPA, a practical procedure for determining learning disabilities in preschool children is to examine the profile dispersion within a preschool population. Such a criterion has been established in the standardization population of 962 children on the ITPA, by using an average deviation on the subtests from the child's own mean scaled score (Paraskevopoulos & Kirk 1969, p. 141).

The purpose of this report is to describe an operational method of determining developmental discrepancies (learning disabilities) in preschool children using the ITPA average deviation score.

METHOD AND RESULTS

Subjects for this study were 101 children in the Head Start program in a city in the southwestern United States. The children's ages ranged from 3-6 to 6-1. Included in the sample were 34 Anglos, 24 blacks, 38 Mexican-Americans, and 5 children of American Indian

"Identifying Developmental Discrepancies At The Preschool Level", Samuel Kirk, John Elkins, *Journal of Learning Disabilities,* Vol. 8, No. 7, August/September 1975, © 1975 Professional Press, Inc.

and/or Asiatic race.

The ITPA was administered to all the children by an experienced examiner who had been trained in the administration and scoring of the test by one of the authors of the ITPA.

The average deviation – a measure of the extent of discrepancies between abilities and disabilities in psycholinguistic functions – was then determined. For each child, it was calculated by summing the deviations of each subtest from his mean scaled score, disregarding the sign, and dividing by 10. Two examples are presented: one with a deviation markedly below 6.0 and one with an average deviation above 6.0 (see Table I).

TABLE I. Two examples of profiles computed using the ITPA average deviation score.

CASE 1. No significant average deviation. Mean scaled score is 39.			CASE 2. Significant average deviation. Mean scaled score is 38.		
	Scaled Score	Deviation		Scaled Score	Deviation
AR	39	0	AR	32	−6
VR	39	0	VR	44	+6
AA	40	+1	AA	26	−12
VA	38	−1	VA	40	+2
VE	45	+6	VE	47	+9
ME	39	0	ME	42	+4
GC	42	+3	GC	27	−11
VC	50	+11	VC	50	+6
ASM	29	−10	ASM	33	−5
VSM	36	−3	VSM	41	+3
		35			64
Average Deviation		$\frac{35}{10} = 3.5$	Average Deviation		$\frac{64}{10} = 6.4$

Table II presents the cumulative percentage of children with average deviations equal to or exceeding a given value for both the standardization group and for the Head Start group (N = 101). In the Head Start sample, 13% of the children have average deviations greater than 6.0, whereas only 5% of the standardization sample have deviations that high. If we arbitrarily define children with learning disabilities as constituting 3% of a population, then an average deviation of 6.6 could be taken as the cutoff point for a learning disability. According to this criterion, 7% of the Head Start children in our sample have learning disabilities as compared to 3% of an average population. Table II indicates that the prevalence of children with extremely deviant profiles is over twice as great in the Head Start sample as in the standardization group.

TABLE II. Distribution of average deviations on the ITPA for standardization samples and for Head Start.

Average Deviation	Percentage of Children with Average Deviations Greater than or Equal to 6.0	
	Standardization Group for ages 4-7 to 5-1*	Head Start Children
6.9		3
6.8	2	5
6.7	3	6
6.6	3	7
6.5	4	8
6.4	4	9
6.3	5	10
6.2	5	11
6.1	5	12
6.0	5	13

*See Paraskevopoulos & Kirk 1969, p.141.

DISCUSSION

It should be pointed out that the use of an average deviation on the ITPA to identify learning disabilities among preschool children is not foolproof. Of the 13 children in the Head Start population who had a deviation of 6.0 and above, one child who scored at the superior range had a scaled score of 48. His lowest scaled score was 36, or average. Under no circumstance could this child (with an average deviation of 6.8) be considered to have a learning disability, since he had no marked deficits that required remediation. Instead his discrepancies in abilities and his superior scores could classify him as a child with specific learning abilities rather than with a specific learning disability. He is similar to a child who has high musical, artistic or mathematical ability and is average or above average in other abilities. That child would not be considered to have a specific learning disability because he is not highly talented in everything.

On the other hand, it is possible that a child may have a marked deficiency in one function, such as in verbal expression, with relatively average abilities in other functions, rendering an average deviation below 6.0. Such a child could be considered learning disabled and requiring remediation in verbal expression, even though his profile dispersion or average deviation is not great.

Two raters have analyzed the records of the remaining 88 children (not considered learning disabled) in the Head Start group and have found that 2 out of 88 remaining children could be considered learning disabled and requiring remediation, even though their average deviation was below 6.0.

CONCLUSIONS

The procedure of using an average deviation score (the extent of discrepancies between abilities and disabilities) to screen preschool children for learning disabilities is a viable procedure, providing workers check for false positives and false negatives. In this sample of 101 Head Start children, 13 children had an average deviation of 6.0 and above. One, however, was considered to have special learning abilities, rather than a learning disability, even though his deviation was 6.8. Of the 88 remaining children not identified as learning disabled, two were considered to have special deficits requiring remediation, even though their average deviation was below 6.0. In other words, using the procedure of accepting an average deviation of 6.0 and above as a criterion of learning disability, the number of learning disabled children in this group was overestimated by 1, and underestimated by 2. With these cautions in mind the average deviation procedure in identifying learning disabilities in preschool children may be a helpful procedure, provided facilities are available to examine the children – *Department of Special Education, University of Arizona, Tucson, Ariz. 85721.*

REFERENCE

Paraskevopoulos, J., and Kirk, S.A.: The Development and Psychometric Characteristics of the Revised Illinois Test of Psycholinguistic Abilities. Urbana, Ill.: Univ. of Ill. Press, 1969.

Teacher Identification of Hyperactive Children in Preschool Settings

BARBARA BUCHAN
SUSAN SWAP
WALTER SWAP

BARBARA BUCHAN *is an advisor to the Follow-Through Program, Educational Development Center, Newton, Massachusetts;* SUSAN SWAP *is Assistant Professor, Eliot-Pearson Department of Child Study, and* WALTER SWAP *is Assistant Professor, Psychology Department, Tufts University, Medford, Massachusetts.*

Definitions of hyperactivity quite naturally focus on quantity and quality of motor activity (Keogh, 1971). Recent investigators, however, have not consistently found differences in activity level between hyperactive and control children in unstructured or open field situations (Kaspar, Millichap, Backus, Child & Schulman, 1971; Routh, 1975), which is the setting most comparable to a preschool classroom. Teachers are frequently consulted by doctors or parents to judge whether a child is hyperactive in school, but the criteria which teachers use to label a child hyperactive have not been examined empirically. Given the reported inconsistent findings on activity level, it may well be that other factors actually play a critical role in such judgments.

The present study uses an ecological approach to investigate the extent to which inappropriate behaviors and differences in attention span provoke teachers to differentiate between highly active and hyperactive children. Specifically, it was hypothesized that when highly active and hyperactive children were matched on activity level, hyperactive children would be distinguished from their controls by a higher overall frequency of inappropriate behaviors, with more unprovoked disruptive behaviors and more disruptive behaviors occurring both in the presence and absence of the teacher. Further, it was hypothesized that the hyperactive children would display more difficulty in attending to classroom activities for extended periods of time, which would be reflected in a greater frequency of entering classroom subsettings than controls.

Method

Subjects. Six highly active 4 and 5 year old Caucasian boys, consisting of three experimental (labeled by teachers as hyperactive) and three controls (unlabeled), were selected for the study. Because of the focus in this study on the factors which teachers use to identify hyperactive children in the classroom, the teachers decided which of their children should be labeled hyperactive and which highly active. All six children attended a laboratory preschool. Control and experimental children were matched for social class of parents, chronological and developmental age, and activity level. Activity level was assessed by teacher ratings and by periodic monitoring of the intensity and quantity of arm and wrist movement with an actometer.

Procedure. Data collection took place over a period of 5 weeks, during which time each child was observed for 14 hours. The Swap (1971) Pupil-Teacher Disruptive Interaction System (SPTDIS) was modified to assess types of inappropriate behaviors. The teacher's presence or absence, type of subsetting, time spent in each subsetting, and nature of activities were also noted.

Results

Of 13 disruptive behavior categories in the SPTDIS, 10 reflected a higher incidence for the hyperactive children ($p < .05$, sign test). Specifically, the hyperactive children demonstrated more resistance to the teacher ($p < .025$) and tended to engage in more inappropriate behaviors both not involving others

"Teacher Identification of Hyperactive Children in Preschool Settings", Susan Swap and Walter Swap, *Exceptional Children,* Vol. 43, No. 5, February 1977, © 1977 The Council For Exceptional Children.

($p<.06$) and involving others ($p<.10$). The hyperactive children were more likely to respond inappropriately in the absence of provocation ($p<.05$, across all behavior categories), both when the teacher was present ($p<.07$) and absent ($p<.05$). As hypothesized, hyperactive children entered all subsettings with greater frequency than highly active children ($p<.025$).

Discussion

It appears that the preschool teachers in this sample used cues other than a high activity level to determine whether a child should be labeled hyperactive. The children labeled hyperactive differed from their matched controls in being more disruptive and in moving more frequently to different areas of the classroom. Their disturbing behaviors were more highly visible, unpredictable, unprovoked, and not easily controlled by the presence or even intervention of teachers.

There may be other cues apparent in the classroom that separate children labeled hyperactive and highly active. For example, highly active children may be more often focused on socially acceptable, task relevant behaviors. A further study using more subjects is currently in preparation. It seeks to replicate these findings related to disruptive behavior and to evaluate adaptive behaviors of hyperactive children and their controls.

References

Kaspar, J., Millichap, J., Backus, R., Child, P., & Schulman, J. A study of the relationship between neurological evidence of brain damage in children and activity and distractibility. *Journal of Consulting and Clinical Psychology*, 1971, *36*, 329-337.

Keogh, B. Hyperactivity and learning disorders: Review and speculation. *Exceptional Children*, 1971, *38*, 101-109.

Routh, D. The clinical significance of open-field activity in children. *Pediatric Psychology*, 1975, *3*, 3-8.

Swap, S. *An ecological study of disruptive encounters between pupils and teachers*. Unpublished doctoral dissertation, University of Michigan, 1971.

Home Observation for Measurement of the Environment: A Validation Study of Screening Efficiency

ROBERT H. BRADLEY AND BETTYE M. CALDWELL
University of Arkansas at Little Rock

Home environments of 91 6-month-old infants were assessed with the Home Observation for Measurement of the Environment (HOME) Inventory. Multiple discriminant functions composed of the six subscale scores from the HOME Inventory were used to predict whether a child would be low IQ (below 70), low average (70 to 89), or average to superior (90 and above) at age 3 years. The mean vector of HOME Inventory subscales for the three IQ groups was significantly different ($p < .01$). Significant univariate effects were observed for three HOME Inventory subscales: organization of the physical and temporal environment, provision of appropriate play materials, and maternal involvement with child. The discriminant function of HOME Inventory subscale scores correctly predicted 71 percent of all children who scored below 70 IQ. Results attest to the usefulness of the HOME Inventory in a comprehensive program of screening for developmental delay.

The critical importance of developing appropriate preventive experiences for children "at risk" for developmental retardation was dramatically underscored by the recent enactment of the Handicapped Children's Act as amended by Public Law 91-230. This legislation calls for the establishment of preschool and early childhood programs for high risk and handicapped children beginning at birth. A major stumbling block in efforts to implement effective preventive treatment for these children has been the inability to identify precisely which children are most in need of assistance. Generally speaking, the types of screening instruments needed to identify "at risk" children early in life are not available (Gallagher & Bradley, 1972).

Since the extent of developmental delay that will be manifested in a particular child will be influenced by the environment, there is an especially urgent need to produce instruments that can identify environments that pose a risk to infants' development (Bloom, 1964; Caldwell, Bradley, & Elardo, 1975; Heber & Garber, 1975; Meier, 1971). Beginning efforts in this direction have been made, with appreciable success. For example, screening batteries including even such crude measures of environmental quality as socioeconomic status (SES) have demonstrated considerable predictive validity for later child competence (Smith, Flick, Ferriss, & Sellman, 1972; Parmalee, Sigman, Kopp, & Haber, Note 1). However, since measures of the specific "processes" involved in a quality environment (e.g., parental language, maternal reinforcement style, availability of toys) appear to account for more variance than do SES variables (Elardo, Bradley, & Caldwell, 1975; Moore, 1968; Walberg & Marjoribanks, 1973), process measures of environmental quality may prove especially useful in screening for developmental difficulties. Thus, the purpose of this study is to examine the predictive efficiency of a process environmental measure in predicting retardation.

Method

Subjects

Subjects were 91 children and their families who participated in a longitudinal observation study conducted at the Center for Child Development and Education (Lit-

This research was supported in part by a grant from the Carnegie Foundation.

"Home Observation for Measurement of the Environment: A Validation Study of Screening Efficiency", Robert H. Bradley, Bettye M. Caldwell, *American Journal of Mental Deficiency*, Vol. 81, No. 3, March 1977, © 1977 American Association on Mental Deficiency.

tle Rock, Arkansas). A majority of the subjects resided in the relatively poor central section of the city, although some were also obtained from lower-middle- and middle-middle-class sections. The father was absent in 24 families, and 35 families were receiving welfare. Maternal education averaged 12.1 years, paternal education 12.9 years. The range of paternal occupation was wide, but generally fell between skilled labor and sales. Of the 91 children, there were 33 black and 18 white males and 25 black and 15 white females. The mean 6-month Bayley Scale of Infant Development, Mental Development Index score was 100.8, standard deviation (*SD*) = 16.8; the mean 36-month Stanford-Binet Intelligence Scale IQ was 93.4, *SD* = 18.1.

Instruments

Mothers were observed and interviewed at home using the Home Observation for Measurement of the Environment (HOME) Inventory (Caldwell, Heider, & Kaplan, Note 2) when their infants were 6 months old. The Stanford-Binet was administered when the children were 3 years of age.

The HOME Inventory contains 45 items and assesses six categories of stimulation available to the infant in the home: emotional and verbal responsivity of the mother, avoidance of restriction and punishment, organization of the physical and temporal environment, provision of appropriate play materials, maternal involvement with the child, and opportunities for variety in daily activities. All data were collected in the home when the mother and infant were present and the infant was awake. The HOME Inventory requires about 60 minutes to administer and registers a range of scores for families from each SES level. A Kuder–Richardson 20 reliability coefficient for the HOME Inventory was computed at r = .89. Observers were trained to achieve 90 percent agreement on items. Previous researchers indicate that HOME Inventory scores are related to intelligence test scores, language performance, and other general measures of child cognitive competency (Bradley & Caldwell, 1976; Elardo et al., 1975; Wachs, Uzgiris, & Hunt, 1971; Wulbert, Inglis, Kriegsmann, & Mills, 1975). Researchers have also shown that the HOME Inventory differentiates between "normal" and "high risk" homes (Ramey, Mills, Campbell, & O'Brien, 1975) and is sensitive to improvements in child-rearing practices that resulted from training (Hamilton, 1972).

Procedure

To examine the predictive efficiency of the HOME Inventory as a means of early screening for retardation, we placed children into three groups according to their Stanford–Binet IQ (1972 norms) scores: (a) below 70 IQ (low), (b) 70 to 89 IQ (low average), and (c) IQ of 90 and above (average to superior). Of the 91 children tested, 17 had IQs below 70; 34, between 70 and 89; and 40, above 89. A multiple discriminant analysis procedure was used to determine if a reliable discrimination could be made among the three groups on the basis of their 6-month HOME Inventory scores.

To evaluate further the efficiency of the HOME Inventory as a screening instrument, we made a more detailed investigation of the "hit and miss" rate of the discriminant function predictions. Frankenburg (1973) suggested examining the "hit and miss" rate of screening tests using a two-dimensional table. One dimension represents the actual presence or absence of a certain condition for an individual; the second dimension represents the classification of individuals in terms of the probability of their having or not having the condition on the basis of test results. Frankenburg contended that one can judge the usefulness of a screening instrument using two criteria: first, the percentage of people with a condition who are properly classified as having it on the basis of their test scores (test sensitivity); second, the percentage of those classified as having the condition on the basis of their test scores who actually have the condition (test specificity). Since the discriminant function analysis provides a means of classifying individual cases on the basis of the predictor variables used (in this case, HOME Inventory subscale scores), we could compare the predicted cases for each IQ group with the observed cases for each IQ group according to the Frankenburg formula.

Results

The multiple discriminant function analysis was performed in an effort to differentiate among the three IQ groups on the basis of their HOME Inventory scores. More specifically, a discriminant function composed of a vector of six HOME Inventory subscale scores was computed for each group. The analysis revealed that the mean vector of HOME Inventory subscale scores was different for the three IQ groups ($p < .01$). Separate univariate tests showed that the low-IQ group was associated with the poorer organization of the physical and temporal environment ($p < .01$), fewer provisions of appropriate play materials ($p < .01$), and less maternal involvement with child ($p < .01$).

As Table 1 shows, the discriminant function based on 6-month HOME Inventory subscale scores was fairly sensitive in identifying homes of children in the low-IQ group (71 percent correctly identified). It was somewhat less sensitive in identifying homes of children in the average to superior group (62 percent correctly identified). In most cases where the HOME Inventory "missed" in predicting eventual IQ level, however, it did not miss far. For example, none of the children in the low-IQ group were predicted to have an average IQ on the basis of the 6-month HOME Inventory

TABLE 1
Classification of 36-month IQ[a] Using Discriminant Functions Composed of 6-month HOME[b] Inventory Subscale Scores

IQ at 36-months	IQ predicted from 6-month HOME scores 70	70–89	90+
70	12	5	0
70–89	9	14	11
90+	7	8	25

[a] Stanford-Binet Intelligence Scale.
[b] Home Observation for Measurement of the Environment Inventory.

scores; and only 18 percent of the children with average to superior IQs were predicted to have a low IQ. Thus, the HOME Inventory appears sensitive in identifying the types of home environments associated with various levels of intellectual development.

With respect to the specificity with which HOME Inventory classifies home environments, the present data indicate that the number of homes incorrectly identified as being associated with low IQ (the number of false positives) is high. By comparison, the specificity of the HOME Inventory in identifying homes associated with average to superior IQ is quite respectable (70 percent).

Discussion

Findings from this study attest to the utility of the HOME Inventory in screening for mental retardation. Using 6-month HOME Inventory scores, we could predict with reasonable accuracy whether a child would be in the low, low average, or average to superior IQ range at age 3 and, thus, whether some type of early intervention program might be appropriate.

Results from this study are related to those from an earlier study by Elardo et al. (1975). They found a correlation of .54 between 6-month HOME Inventory scores and 36-month IQ scores but a correlation of only .28 between 6-month Bayley Mental Development Index scores and 36-month IQs. Moreover, the HOME Inventory by itself predicts 36-month IQ scores about as well as do a combination of HOME Inventory and Bayley Mental Development Index scores (.54 vs. .55). While these analyses do not permit any causal interpretations, the HOME Inventory apparently measures aspects of the environment that are significantly associated with cognitive development.

In deciding whether a high degree of sensitivity or a high degree of specificity is more desirable for a particular screening test, Gallagher and Bradley (1972) have argued that the cost of failing to identify a person who needs some type of treatment must be weighed against the cost of identifying him. Given the devastating effects of poor mental ability and the need for beginning remediation early, sensitivity would seem more important than specificity when screening for retardation. Thus, the high degree of sensitivity of the HOME Inventory to low IQ (71 percent) relative to its degree of specificity (43 percent) would appear to be acceptable. Of course, cross-validation studies are needed with both different populations and different ranges of IQ scores.

In future investigations of the predictive efficiency of process measures of environmental quality, screening for more specific cognitive deficits might be considered. It might also be useful to examine the predictive efficiency of a screening battery composed of developmental, neurological, and environmental process measures, particularly since many developmental disabilities appear multiply determined. Composite measures including structural measures of environmental quality have shown considerable effectiveness in identifying "at risk" children and provide a basis for most specific intervention.

Early Detection of Learning Problems: Questions, Cautions, and Guidelines

BARBARA K. KEOGH
LAURENCE D. BECKER

***Barbara K. Keogh** is Associate Professor of Special Education, and Director, Special Education Research Program, Department of Education, University of California, Los Angeles; and **Laurence D. Becker** is Assistant Professor, Department of Education, University of California, Riverside.*

Abstract: Assumptions underlying programs of early identification of young children viewed as educationally "at risk" are reviewed in terms of the research literature relevant to questions of validity of identifying or screening techniques, implications of recognition for remediation, and possible compounding negative effects of early identification. Guidelines for development and implementation of programs of early detection are proposed. Recommendations include emphasis upon techniques which are short term and educationally oriented and which are based on functional aspects of children's behavior in classroom settings.

Early identification of children with learning problems has received wide support from medical, psychological, and educational professionals as well as from parents. Reasons for early identification and diagnosis are obvious and unequivocal when applied to children with physical, sensory, and gross developmental problems. Yet, generalization of the emphasis on early identification to children with educational exceptionalities raises some uneasy questions which warrant examination.

Support for the importance of early identification comes from the physical disability or disease model, an approach based on several important assumptions. The condition to be identified is seen as already existent in the child. The recognition or diagnosis carries a specified direction or prescription for treatment. The sooner the treatment is begun, the greater the likelihood of impact of the treatment. Examples of the importance of early diagnosis and treatment are cases of children with disease conditions, congenital sensory disabilities, and limiting physiological or neurological conditions.

A related benefit of early diagnosis is, of course, that treatment may prevent development of other deleterious conditions or may minimize compounding problems. Dietary treatment of phenylketonuria (PKU) is a dramatic example of the prevention of further damage to a child, contingent upon early recognition. Many other secondary compounding problems, for example, disruption of parental and family relationships, confounding emotional conditions, and interpersonal and affective disturbances, are sometimes prevented or at least minimized if recognition and treatment are begun early. Thus, for many conditions of exceptionality, early identification of the condition and implementation of treatment is not only advantageous but critical.

When early identification efforts are applied to exceptionalities of more educational or psychological definition, however, some subtle differences from the physical disability model must be considered. Basic to the question is this: When we seek to identify preschool or kindergarten children whom we fear may become learning failures, we are, in fact, hypothesizing rather than confirming. That is, the conditions which we view as atypical, namely, learning disability and failure in school, have not yet developed. Our concerns are that these conditions will develop. Yet, children who have not been exposed to a reading pro-

"Early Detection of Learning Problems, Cautions, and Guidelines", Barbara Keough, Laurence Becker, *Exceptional Children,* Vol. 40, No. 1, September, 1973, © 1973,The Council For Exceptional Children.

gram cannot really be said to have reading problems: children who have not participated in a first grade program cannot be classified as first grade failures.

Differences between identification or recognition of an "in-child" condition (a condition which is already there) and the hypothesis or prediction that a condition will develop need to be made explicit. This article was written to clarify some problems in the early identification of children with learning problems and to propose guidelines for the implementation of early identification programs.

Problems in Early Identification

Problems in regard to early identification of learning disorders may be grouped about three major questions:

1. How valid are the identifying or predictive measures?
2. What are the implications of diagnostic data for remediation or educational intervention?
3. Do benefits of early identification outweigh possible damaging or negative effects of such recognition?

Validity of Identification Techniques

A critical consideration in validity questions is the definition of outcome goals against which predictions are based. In the case of early identification of physical conditions, treatment goals tend to be specific and objective, for example, control of the level of phenylalanine in the PKU child or amplification of hearing for the hearing impaired child. Educational goals are not always as precise. Are outcomes defined in terms of IQ, standardized achievement test norms, achievement comparable to mental age expectancies, consistency of performance with parental expectancy, or mastery of subject matter? Do we take into account social and affective goals as well as strictly academic ones? Are we concerned with immediate or long term outcomes? Lack of clarity of outcome goals complicates prediction. Yet, validity of particular tests or screening batteries is clearly related to the goals defined.

Closely related to a consideration of outcome measures is the question of the validity of tests used as early predictors. Simply stated, what tests used in the preschool years may be relied upon as valid indicators of future school success or failure? Readiness screening at school entrance or during the kindergarten year has become almost routine in many school districts. Some preschool identification programs are under consideration or actually operational. A variety of screening and readiness tests have been developed to assess facets of children's development assumed to be related to later school achievement, namely, language, cognitive, sensory, perceptual, and physical-motor dimensions (de Hirsch, Jansky, & Langford, 1966; Ilg & Ames, 1964; McGahan & McGahan, 1967; Sprigle & Lanier, 1967; Slingerland, 1964; Pate & Webb, 1966). Reliability and validity of many items for prediction of subject matter achievement is as yet uncertain, however.

Intelligence tests. Historically, tests of intelligence or measures of educational "aptitude" have been the basis for screening, selection, and placement of children into special educational programs. Standard IQ tests have a strong relationship to school achievement across the broad range of intellectual ability, that is, when children with high and low IQ's are included in the range. However, when consideration is limited to children with IQ's which are borderline or above, the relationship to school performance is markedly weakened.

Within the low average to superior range, IQ has only limited relationship to school performance. All classroom teachers have high achieving pupils with only average IQ's or high IQ children who are school failures. These latter pupils are often the ones identified as educationally handicapped or learning disabled. For this group, IQ per se is of limited predictive value. The problem is confounded further for early identification of potential problem learners in that considerable evidence may be interpreted to suggest that intelligence or IQ is malleable in the early years and is not a stable, predetermined trait (Bloom, 1964; Hunt, 1961). In sum, when children with markedly low IQ's are excluded, prediction of school failure on the basis of intelligence test score alone appears tenuous.

Other possible predictors. Other dimensions of child development have been considered as possible indicators of later learning problems, mostly with limited success. Recent review of the literature in regard to medical and physical-motor predictors yielded few child characteristics which provided a solid basis for the prediction of school success or failure (Leydorf, 1970). Longitudinal studies (Keogh, 1965; Keogh & Smith, 1967) based primarily on the *Bender-Gestalt Test,* a perceptual motor measure, demonstrated that although there are consistent statistically significant relationships between Bender scores at kindergarten and later school achievement, caution must be used when making predictions about any particular child. Wedell (1970) added to this the concept that only in cases where severe disability is noted can later development be predicted from early perceptual motor functioning.

In a review of cognitive and language factors in early identification, Faust (1970) emphasized that individual characteristics change as a function of interaction with the environment and that there are, thus, few "inherent, stable traits of the individual [p. 346]" which allow long term prediction. Reading and other school learning tasks are made up of many components and require perceptual, cognitive, and motor skills; child characteristics vary in relation to the learning task and situation. Thus, many facets of the child's development and experience may be directly relevant to tasks to be learned. There are few clear one to one relationships between specific preschool characteristics and specific school learnings.

On the basis of present evidence, it seems reasonable to conclude that relationships between single, specific preschool test findings and later school achievement are too low to allow definitive prediction about individual children. The limited predictive validity for individual cases is, in part at least, a function of the limited range of competencies tapped and the almost total concern with conditions of deficit or disturbance within the child. As argued by Adelman (1970), a substantial number of school learning problems may be attributed to the interaction of child and learning situation. Yet, instructional variables and situational effects are usually not assessed, as the focus of evaluation is on the child. Exclusion of situational variables in the prediction eliminates a significant portion of the variance and thus reduces the accuracy of prediction of particular tests.

A paradox. A methodological paradox deserves attention. If early identification and diagnosis were insightful and remedial implementation successful, the preschool or kindergarten high risk child would receive the kind of attention and help which results in successful school performance. In essence, he would no longer be high risk and would instead be a successful achiever. Predictive validity of the identification instruments would, therefore, be low. In such a case, success with the child would negate accuracy of prediction. Research on development of predictive tools is thus limited by ethical considerations. Having identified a child as high risk, the researcher is obligated to intervene, thus limiting examination of the long term predictive validity of the instruments.

Early Identification and Educational Intervention

In the medical or physical disability model, diagnosis leads directly to remediation. Implementation of a low phenylalanine diet for a child with PKU is implicit in the diagnosis. In contrast, development of preventive educational strategies and remedial programs for children identified as high risk is not so clear cut or direct (Ensminger, 1970; Deno, 1971). Remedial programs reflect a variety of points of view, as for example, Bettleheim (1950); Cruickshank, Bentzen, Ratzeburg, and Tannhauser (1961); Hewett (1968); and Kephart (1960). Each program is successful in varying degrees with various subsets of high risk children. Yet, on the basis of much of the predictive data collected, it is often difficult to match a given child with the appropriate preventive or remedial strategy. In a recent study of 253 children in special public school programs for the educationally handicapped, Hansen (1970b) found that the majority of children were placed with recommendations for individualized instruction in a small class setting, for perceptual training, and for counseling. Similarity of remedial recommendation was startling in light of the diversity of child characteristics represented in this sample. It seems likely that it is not always possible to determine definitely the most optimal remedial intervention for many children. Selection of diagnostic data and educational techniques may be a function of investigator point of view as much as of child characteristics. Assignment of children to a particular intervention may be in large part a matter of program availability, point of view of the diagnostician, intuition, and a little bit of faith.

Prediction and Prophecy

A final matter of concern has to do with effects of identification per se. The term, *self fulfilling prophecy,* used by Rosenthal and Jacobsen (1966) to describe effects of teacher expectancy on pupil performance, may be applicable to the early identification issue. Although the particular study describing the phenomenon has been criticized (Thorndike, 1968; Snow, 1969), the effect must be reckoned with.

When children are identified as high risk, a set of expectancies, anxieties, and differential treatment patterns may develop. Effects may be particularly insidious in that preschool or kindergarten children have not yet developed the deficit conditions for which they were identified. It is important to reiterate that persons dealing with high risk children are, in fact, not identifying; rather, they are hypothesizing about future development from present behavior. Thus, the act of predicting learning problems may, unfortunately, have a built-in expectancy phenomenon. Concern for development of a given child may result in intervention strategies of benefit; however, concern may also lead to overemphasis upon certain abilities or inabilities and result in anxiety which generalizes to affective and motivational aspects of development. Because effects of parent and teacher anxieties upon a child are uncertain and the possibility that the effect of an expectancy involved in prediction may be harmful, the ethical issues relating to programs of early identification require consideration.

Guidelines for Early Identification

On the basis of evidence reviewed thus far, it is possible to suggest that programs of early identification should be discontinued or curtailed. On the contrary, the thesis presented here is that effective early identification is critical and may be accomplished given changes in emphasis and techniques. Specification and clarification of the evidence used for identifying problems, as well as broadening the base of identification data seem promising directions for change.

Specification of Outcomes

A first step in an early identification program involves specification of expected outcomes. One of the operational implications of this approach is that the most efficient and accurate screening measures are those which are close to the criterion or outcome measures in both content and time. Specifically, does the preschool child have the skills and abilities necessary to perform successfully in the kindergarten? Does the kindergarten child have the skills necessary to master the demands of the first grade program? Has the child learned the prereading skills that will enable him to succeed at reading? Task analysis forces one to think in terms of more immediate goals and steps to reach them. Questions of whether the preschool child will be successful in third grade, sixth grade, or high school lack operational meaning.

Validity of early identification is increased when prediction is made to outcomes which are close in time and based on evaluative measures which tap abilities required in the immediate educational program. Attempts to make long term predictions are inherently weak since it is not possible to sample the broad spectrum of skills needed for successful school performance years later. Emphasis in early identification may well be changed from a future orientation to one that is more concerned with what is needed for success in the present or immediate future. The closer the measure and criterion are in content and time, the more likely that the prediction is, in fact, identification.

Focus on Competence

A second step in developing effective early identification programs is recognition of the importance of specification of children's abilities and competencies which might be used to maximize success experiences in educational programs. The purpose of identification or evaluation is not just to document or confirm deficits but rather to provide information which might be used as the basis for prevention of later problems.

Recognition of compensatory abilities and emphasis upon instructional strategies which use them may result in success in educational tasks despite possible delays or deficiencies in some developmental dimensions. A compensatory model of psychoeducational evaluation (Keogh, 1971), when applied to early identification of children with educational problems, may well provide direction for remediation which minimizes anxiety and concern over possible deficit conditions and thus reduces confounding and complicating secondary problems. Many children are high risk in specific abilities yet perform successfully in educational programs. The use of high competence skills may overcome possible effects of high risk conditions.

Inclusion of Task and Situation

A third major guideline is that the basis for early identification must be broadened from the present almost exclusive focus on child data to consideration of task components and situational variables which affect the child's learning (Adelman, 1970). Carroll (1970) and Venezky, Calfee, and Chapman (1970) provided preliminary analyses of components of the reading task, emphasizing that success or failure in reading is a function of child skills and task requirements. Feshbach and Adelman (1971) proposed a "personalized classroom" for identifying child and situational variables of importance and developed a "prediction and prevention" program now in progress (Adelman, Feshbach, & Fuller, in press).

Child characteristics and program characteristics may match or be remarkably discrepant. A given child may well master the social requirements of a kindergarten program but have serious difficulty with the language curriculum the teacher stresses. A child entering the first grade may have sound cognitive development but serious motoric problems which interfere with neatness of handwriting and arithmetic computation, achievements highly valued by the teacher. Questions of which child is "ready," or alternatively which child is "at risk," have little meaning unless considered within the context of the situation in which the child must function and in terms of the expectancies defined for him (Adelman, 1971).

Assessment of School Behavior

A fourth major guideline has to do with the choice of data used for early identification. It seems likely that identification based on standardized quantified test instruments screens out important evaluative information, that is, the child's behavior in the classroom, his problem solving strategies. Keogh (1972) summarized the limitations of the standardized test battery orientation in assessment and called for a process oriented behavioral approach to educational evaluation. Keogh and Chan (1973) delineated psychomotor and affective influences of importance in children's school performance.

A behavioral approach to early identification receives support from a number of independent investigators (Cobb, 1972; Fargo, Roth, & Cade, 1968; Haring & Ridgway, 1967; Lahaderne, 1968; Spivack, Swift, & Prewitt, 1971; Westman, Rice, & Bermann, 1967). Conrad and Tobiessen (1967) defined 13 behavioral dimensions (such as waiting and sharing, level of organization of play, clarity of speech, and use of materials) which they have found useful in screening kindergarten children. Spivack and his colleagues (1971) identified 11 factors derived from the *Devereaux Elementary School Behavior Rating Scale,* including classroom disturbance, impatience, and anxiety, as predictors of school performance. Attwell, Orpet, and Meyers (1967) reported that behaviors as assessed with their Test Behavior Observation Guide were highly related to learning problems in elementary school. Becker (1971), using a retrospective design, found that third grade children with learning problems differed from normally achieving third graders on behavioral measures obtained at kindergarten, especially in attentional skills and ability to work independently.

Forness (1972) observed highly significant differences in school related behaviors between children referred to an outpatient clinic for possible learning and/or behavioral problems and "normal" peers in the same classroom. Differences were noted in attending behavior and in the quantity and quality of interaction with the teacher. The ability of behavioral observation techniques to differentiate between these two groups of children provides support for a method of identifying high risk children based primarily on direct observation of classroom behavior and analysis of children's problem solving styles. It is possible that enthusiasm for standardized test procedures has obscured the importance of other sources of information. How a child approaches a learning task, his strategies for solution, his sensitivity to various kinds of reinforcers, and his ability to sustain attention and persist may all be important indicators of his likelihood of success in school. Systematic observation of children's behavior in the educational setting provides useful data for early identification of educationally high risk children.

Closely related to questions of what data are relevant in early identification is the question of who might best provide that information. Examination of referral patterns of children with school learning problems demonstrates clearly that the classroom teacher is the major initial source of identification and referral (Hansen, 1970a; Keogh, Becker, Kukic, & Kukic, 1972). In recent work Keogh and Tchir (1972) found kindergarten and first grade teachers sensitive to high risk indicators as reflected in classroom behaviors. Fargo and his associates (1968) reported that preschool teachers were more accurate than pediatricians or psychologists in predicting later school achievement of children in their sample. Tobiessen, Duckworth, and Conrad (1971) and Keogh and Smith (1970) demonstrated the effectiveness of teachers' evaluations using kindergarten rating scales, as have Spivack and his colleagues (1971) and Bullock and Brown (1972) for older elementary age children.

Such findings are reasonable, for teachers have the closest and most continuous relationship with the child of anyone in the school programs. It seems likely, too, that teachers recognize behaviors, abilities, and problems which have relevance to the educational setting. Recognizing the potential inaccuracies of the use of teachers' perceptions of children, it is, nevertheless, reasonable to consider systematic inclusion of teacher observations as a source of information about classroom performance. Implications for the preparation of teachers in this role seem obvious.

Identification and Remediation

Finally, a broader approach to early identification directly relates recognition and remediation. Standardized tests often provide little direction to planning an educational program for the high risk child. Engelmann (1967) argued that results of tests like the *Illinois Test of Psycholinguistic Abilities* (ITPA) provide what he called an "inclusive remedy" for the teacher. In essence, this remedy is general and offers little specific as to what to do in an instructional sense. Similarly, other standardized tests which purport to identify children with possible learning problems often include many items lacking in educational relevance.

In contrast, behavioral observation techniques may have a higher probability of pinpointing functional aspects of children's performance which might be used as the basis for instruction. For example, Hewett (1968) identified classroom behaviors and instructional tasks which incorporate preacademic as well as academic skills. Included in his plan are considerations of a child's ability or inability to attend, to respond, to follow directions, and the like—all behaviors which are related to determination of high risk and which can form the target for remedial intervention. Techniques which identify but which provide no educational direction lack power, and techniques which serve as the basis for remedial and preventive programs have obvious advantage.

Conclusions

Programs of early identification will be effective relative to the educational programs which are available to accommodate the child. Identification of a given child as high risk for school learning is in essence a prediction that he will fail or have problems in the existing school program; to place him in the program which has been predefined as failure producing for him without modifying that program puts the child in double jeopardy and maximizes the possibility of a self fulfilling prophecy.

It should be emphasized that program modification and special class placement are not necessarily the same. Support for segregation of children who may develop learning problems into special classes is indeed tenuous. Bloom (1968) proposed that most children are able to perform school tasks at a mastery level given adjustments in time, materials, and teaching strategies, for example. Too often, however, the major portion of time and funds are spent on extensive diagnosis and evaluation so that neither time nor money is left to modify educational programs in light of the identification data. It well may be that focus on effective educational programing per se is a more productive route than is the search for precise measures for early identification of individual children.

Writing of the "sacred cows" of diagnosis as applied to mentally retarded, Wolfensberger (1965) noted that

> Early diagnosis is desirable when it leads to prevention, early treatment, or constructive counseling; it is irrelevant if it is purely academic and does not change the course of events; it is harmful if, in balance, child or family reap more disadvantages than benefits [p. 65].

It seems reasonable that the state of the art of early identification or prediction of learning problems must stand the same tests.

Early Diagnosis of the Deaf Child

. . . how about those families that were told, "Nothing can be done, the child is too young to be tested" or, "He'll outgrow it"?

Sandra Fleishman

Sandra Fleishman, recently elected to serve on the Newton, Massachusetts School Committee, was asked to speak to the New England Pediatric Society about parent-doctor communication. She concentrates on her own experience with her daughter who is hearing impaired. Her remarks raise questions that are of importance to all parents and professionals concerned about the care of children with disabilities.

I am a former member of the Board of Directors of the Massachusetts Parents Association for the Deaf and Hard of Hearing. My husband, Jack, is a past president of the organization and together we serve on a "Hotline" for newly diagnosed families of hearing impaired children. I realize that our story gets longer as Debbie gets older, but I will stick to the first year and a half.

Our daughter, Debbie, now eight years old, is the youngest of three children. At the time of her birth, our son Ken was three and a half and our son David was two. Our family visited the pediatrician regularly. Debbie has always been bright, alert and very charming. There was no reason to suspect that anything should be wrong.

When Debbie was 13 months old, her father remarked that she does not come when called. I remember the time vividly, yet I sloughed it off with, "She is too busy and engrossed in what she is doing." I was worried about the fact that she seemed "slow to talk" and I mentioned it to the pediatrician on our next visit. He replied that, "It is not unusual for the third child in the family to be slow in speech development since everything gets done for her." I accepted that. It seemed perfectly reasonable.

At 16 months of age, my mother stayed with the children for the weekend. Deb cried all weekend. To comfort her, Mother had to be with her constantly. A neighbor and my mother discussed the fact that, "Debbie doesn't come when she is called." Now three people had all separately come to the same conclusion.

On Monday, Deb and I went to see the pediatrician. He examined her ears and used cricket snappers. He then said he could not tell if she was hearing, or was visually alert and did indeed have a hearing loss. He had always asked if she was babbling, repeating syllables and playing pat-a-cake. She did all these things. The pediatrician recommended that we see an otolaryngologist. We were told we had to wait three weeks for an appointment. We were very upset, and we finally got through to speak with the eye, nose and throat (ENT) specialist. He said to me over the phone, "Mrs. Fleishman, you are a selfish woman, nothing has changed for Debbie, only for you." That is one of the most insensitive remarks I have ever heard. Indeed our state of apprehension was evident to all our children, including Debbie. After pushing the doctor to do something, he agreed to make an appointment at Massachusetts Eye and Ear Hospital, where Debbie was finally diagnosed as profoundly deaf in both ears.

Our story is not unique. Rachel's mother suspected a hearing loss and finally at three years of age, really pressed the issue with her pediatrician. After ringing some bells, he reassured

"Early Diagnosis of The Deaf Child", Sandra Fleishman, *Exceptional Parent,* Vol. 8, No. 1, February 1978, © 1978 Psy. Education Corporation.

her that nothing was wrong. He wondered if the child was paying attention. Rachel turned out to have a moderate hearing loss in one ear and a profound loss in the other.

The point is: the parent is saying, "There's a problem here." She is then falsely assured by the pediatrician. Perhaps because mother brings the diagnosis, the pediatrician finds it difficult to accept. Serious time for language development is being lost.

Lest you think these are unusual cases: in 12 years of experience with over 100 families at the Thayer-Lindsley Nursery at Emerson College, in every case it was the families who first diagnosed their child's hearing loss. Many reported stories similar to ours. We were relatively fortunate. When made aware of the strong possibility of a problem, we were immediately referred to an ENT specialist, an audiologist and a program. But how about those families that were told, "Nothing can be done, the child is too young to be tested" or, "He'll outgrow it"? At Thayer-Lindsley Nursery, over 100 families were asked, "Knowing what you know now, did your pediatrician tell you the right thing at first?" 43% said, "No."

Along with diagnosis comes devastation for the parent and the need for emotional support. In most cases parents reported that the pediatrician was nice, though he had very little information about hearing loss and its habilitation. I think it a strange position for pediatrician and parent to be in where the parent quickly learns an enormous amount of information about a profound handicap and the pediatrician has so little knowledge.

In closing I would like to leave you with some thoughts and comments.

1. How much training in ENT does a pediatrician receive in the course of his medical training?

2. When a family is newly diagnosed, what kind of parent intervention takes place? I referred earlier to the devastating effects of diagnosis.

3. Please do not slough off slow language development to maturation. Check it out. Listen to the parents' concerns. If I knew then what I know now, I would have asked that all of my children's hearing be tested routinely very early.

4. Ultimately, what we parents are hoping for is a strengthening of the pediatrican's role in the early detection of hearing loss. Referrals of children who do fall into the high risk categories, as well as those who do not, need to come from you at an earlier date in the child's life.

I am encouraged by your attendance and attention. It has taken us so long to get here — perhaps it is because we never really asked for the opportunity to speak with you.

THE PREDICTABILITY OF INFANT INTELLIGENCE SCALES: A CRITICAL REVIEW AND EVALUATION

Roger P. Hatcher

ABSTRACT. Unlike other tests of this genre, infant scores have repeatedly demonstrated little relationship to later tests or academic performance. It is the purpose of this article to present a critical review of the relevant research literature dealing with infant test predictability. Although the entire field will be reviewed, special attention will be given to studies of predictability in mentally retarded populations.

Reliability Studies

Perhaps the first requirement of any test is that it demonstrates acceptable statistical reliability. Indeed, the predictive usefulness of a test can be no greater than its reliability, and so it is necessary to first examine the reliability studies of infant tests before validity studies can reasonably be discussed.

Thomas (1970) reports that internal reliability (split-half) and test-retest reliability for the Cattell is quite high, rarely falling below .85. Cattell (1940) reports reliability coefficients (split-half) for her scale at 6, 9, and 12 months to be .88, .86, and .89 respectively. Reliability at higher age levels is similarly high. Reliability studies for the Bayley scales have also been favorable (Werner & Bayley, 1966). Interjudge reliability was reported to be .89 for the mental scale and .93 for the motor scale. Test-retest correlations (interval of one week between tests) ranged from .79 to .94 for the mental scale and .57 to .97 for the motor scale. The lowest correlations, as on the Cattell, were found in the first 6 months, with correlation coefficients above .85 thereafter. It seems, therefore, that whatever predictability problems are present with infant intelligence scales cannot be attributed to poor reliability.

Studies of Predictability in Normal Children

Since the pioneer work of Gesell and his colleagues at Yale University (1925), there has been a multitude of studies which have questioned the long-term stability of infant test scores (Furfey & Muehlenbein, 1932; Honzik, 1938; Anderson, 1939; Bayley, 1949; Wittenborn, 1956; Cavanaugh et al., 1957; Drillien, 1961; Lewis & McGurk, 1973). Most of these studies used correlations with school-age tests as criteria for predictive validity of infant scales. Thorndike's (1940) review of the studies in this area prior to 1940 concluded that it does not seem possible to make reliable long-term predictions from infant test scores. Later Bayley (1949) reported a longitudinal study of 54 to 61 children between birth and four years. Test scores from 1 month to 21 months correlated -.16 to +.49 with test scores at 4 years. In another study, Gesell scores obtained at 14 months were correlated with Stanford-Binet scores at 5 to 6 years (Wittenborn, 1956). Again, the correlations were very low, falling to .28 when other sources of variance were partialled out. In a sample of prematurely born infants, Drillien (1961) reported moderate correlations between Stanford-Binet scores at age five and Gesell scores at 6 months (r = .54), 12 months (r = .57), and 24 months (r = .66). Although most of the correlational results reported are statistically significant, they are far too low to justify individual prediction. However, as a sidenote, Drillien reported that all of the 16 infants in his study who scored below 70 also scored in the dull normal or retarded range upon retest.

Several authors (Fishler, Graliker, & Kock, 1965; McCall, Hogarty, & Hurlburt, 1972) have noted that test scores in later infancy are more accurate predictors of later performance than are scores at earlier ages. Fishler et al. (1965) concluded that although accurate prediction of later test scores is not possible before 2 years of age, there is a steady increase past 2 years such that the Gesell test can offer "a valuable source of intellectual estimate by the time the child is four years of age" (p. 515). Although McCall et al. recognized the low agreement between infant and later tests, they also note the presence of two significant trends in correlation studies' findings:

> The first (trend) is that when predicting to any age in childhood, the later the test is given during the infancy period, the higher is the relationship. Second, correlations to IQ after 3-4 years is higher than with IQ scores assessed thereafter (p. 729).

"The Predictability of Infant Intelligence Scales: A Critical Review and Evaluation", Roger Hatcher, *Mental Retardation*, Vol. 14, No. 4, August 1976, © 1976, American Association on Mental Deficiency.

So it seems that although there are several hopeful trends that improve infant test prediction at upper age levels (Fishler, Graliker, & Koch, 1965), and although most of the infant test correlation with later school-age scores are statistically significant (MacRae, 1955; Drillien, 1961), infant test scores are widely considered as invalid measures of future potential. Bayley (1970), in a review of infant test research, summarized the evidence as follows:

> The findings of these early studies of mental development have been repeated sufficiently often so that test scores in the first year or two have relatively little predictive validity (in contrast to tests at school-age or later), although they may have high validity as measures of the child's cognitive abilities at the time (p. 1, 174).

In recent years several authors have attempted to improve infant test predictability through special selection techniques. Thomas (1967, p. 197), for example, has pointed out that "most early studies make use of normal or superior children while several studies of the last decade have attempted to show the diagnostic or predictive usefulness of infant tests if defective or retarded children are included in the sample."

In the same vein, Fishler (1959, p. 400) "ventures the proposition that, because of certain biological and physiological variants, organismic behaviors are predictable in only one segment of the predictor-criterion relationship." In other words, after noting that many physiological and psychological tests (such as the EEG, lumbar puncture, Rorschach test, etc.) demonstrate high accuracy in predicting pathology from positive test findings but poor accuracy in predicting from negative test findings, Fishler suggests that infant tests might be useful predictors only within a defective population.

Studies of Predictability in Subnormal Populations

The English pediatrician Illingworth has staunchly defended infant testing as a means of identifying mental retardation early in life (Illingworth, 1961). He reported a longitudinal study in which 87 children, who were diagnosed as mentally retarded on the Gesell scale in the first year, were retested at school-age. Illingworth notes that 65 of the 87 children demonstrated mental retardation upon retest. However, Illingworth does not give even basic statistical information about his sample, nor does he identify the population characteristics from which his sample was drawn. Many children in the sample suffered significant medical disease since he reports a 28% mortality rate from the original sample of 122. Perhaps the predictability of the Gesell, in this population, did not exceed chance for predicting mental retardation. Drillien (1961) also has reported that slow children can be more accurately identified with the Gesell than average or superior children. However, this study also suffers from methodological problems since only selected Gesell items were used, and items were only presented if the examiner expected the subject to succeed. Using a different test, the Cattell Intelligence Scale, Oppenheimer (1965) identified 34 children below 1 year of age who demonstrated mild retardation (IQ, 50-84). Periodic retesting showed that "it is possible to locate mildly retarded children under the age of three years, even in the absence of medical disease" (p. 849). However, since she did not report detailed sample characteristics or specific test-retest correlations, it is difficult to judge this study. Knobloch and Pasamanick (1967) reported encouraging results on a sample of neurologically defective children tested with the Gesell between 4 months and 1 year. For those with infant test scores below 80, the correlation with Stanford-Binet scores at ages 8 to 10 years was .68. An earlier study by these authors produced a correlation of .74 between low Gesell scores at 40 weeks of age and 3-year Stanford-Binet scores (Knobloch & Pasamanick, 1960).

Erickson (1968) similarly obtained increased predictive validity with the Cattell scale in a group of young mentally retarded children. However, this author noted the limited degree to which she could generalize her study:

> The results of this study gave evidence that the Cattell Infant Intelligence Scale (CIIS) was useful for predicting later IQ scores of children referred to a clinic for possible developmental problems. The predictive validity of the Cattell scale with this sample of children proved to be substantially greater than found for samples restricted to normal children. The children in this sample, however, were also a biased group in that they were deviant to the extent physicians had referred them for more intensive examination. This study, then, offers no predictive validity information on the CIIS for normal children selected by other methods. The value of this study lies in the demonstration of the CIIS in a University medical setting (Erickson, 1968, p. 732).

Most recently, Vanderveer and Schweid (1974) followed a group of 22 children who scored in the retarded range during infancy. Upon follow-up evaluation 1 to 3 years later, all scored significantly below average on later tests. Other encouraging results have been published by workers at Brown University (Holden, 1972). In a field where most studies suffer grave methodological problems, Holden reports a well-run, controlled experiment as part of a broader child development study. A stratified sample of 115 children who had been tested at 8 months, 4 years, and 7 years was chosen as a control group for two experimental groups. The two experimental groups included all children who had scored 1 month or more below age level upon examination with the Bayley Scales of Infant Development at age 8 months. The only difference between the two experimental groups was that one group was retested at age 4 and 7 years, while the other group was only retested at age 4 years. Holden found that the differences between the mean IQ of the control group and both experimental groups upon retesting was statistically significant beyond the .05 level. However, that author noted that the .05 level of probability might not be sufficient to justify the use of the Bayley for prediction of mental retardation in individual cases.

Infant intelligence tests might demonstrate even higher predictive validity if broader categories of mental functioning were used as predictive criteria rather than specific test scores. This hypothesis has been tested by several authors (MacRae, 1955; Simon & Bass, 1956; Escalona & Moriarty, 1961).

2. IDENTIFICATION

MacRae (1955) followed a group of 102 children from infancy to middle childhood (median age at retesting was 9 years, 2 months). He found that the correlation of agreement of the Cattell or Gesell with the WISC or Stanford-Binet was above .55 when children were first tested below 2 years of age and general categories of intellectual functioning were predicted. The categories devised for this study were: mentally deficient, below average, average, above average, and superior. MacRae's results were significant at the .01 level. However, as Thomas (1967) has pointed out, this "grouping" study may be misleading. For example, the correlations reported by MacRae were based on linear regression analysis, but were not corrected for grouping of data. MacRae's results are probably in violation of the basic assumptions of linear regression. Similarly, Simon and Bass (1956), in a *post facto* study, found 56 children who had been tested with the Cattell or Gesell as infants and later evaluated at school-age on the WISC or Stanford-Binet. Using three categories (below average, average, and above average) of mental functioning rather than specific test scores, they report a correlation of .52 between infant and later tests. Additionally, when infant test results were corrected for "non-optimal" testing conditions the correlations rose to .63. However, since the correlations were based on chi square analysis, and since many of the expected frequencies were extremely low (several below one), their findings are "undoubtedly in error" (Thomas, 1967, p. 201). In a related study using only two categories, average and above average, Escalona and Moriarity (1961) reported that neither the Cattell or Gesell scales were able to discriminate between the categories beyond the .1 level of probability.

Multiple Regression Studies

Other researchers have also been able to improve the predictive validity of infant test scores by including additional factors in a multiple regression equation (Knobloch & Pasamanick, 1967; Hindley & Munro, 1970; Ireton, Thwing, and Gravem, 1970; Werner, Honzik, & Smith, 1968). Increased predictability of low infant test scores has been reported by Knobloch and Pasamanick (1967) who were able to raise infant test agreement with later Stanford-Binet scores from .68 to .84 when a multiple correlation technique was used. They found that socio-economic status and persistence of convulsive seizures could significantly improve predictability over test scores alone. Werner, Honzik, and Smith (1968) followed a sample of 639 full-term children who were seen for pediatric and psychological assessment (Cattell scale) at age 20 months, and were later tested at 10 years on the Primary Mental Abilities Test. They report that of 12 infants who scored below normal by both the pediatrician and on the Cattell, 11 scored below normal at age ten. "In sum: the prognosis remained poor for the children who were considered 'below average' in infancy by both psychologists and pediatricians" (p. 1071). For the normal children of this sample the combined psychologic and pediatric rating was correlated .58 with 10-year scores, as compared to a correlation of .49 for the Cattell score alone. Ireton, Thwing, and Gravem (1970) report that infant neurological status and socio-economic status both relate to later test scores on the Stanford-Binet at age four, although for children with infant scores below 85 the test results are the best predictor of later performance. These authors did not combine neurological status, SES, and infant test scores in multiple regression analysis. Hindley and Munro (1970) report multiple correlations for SES and normal infant test scores with Stanford-Binet scores at age eleven. For males, the multiple correlation was .55, while females were slightly more predictable at .62. In a review of these studies, McCall, Hogarty and Hurlburt (1972, p. 733) summarized the separate contributions of infant test scores and socio-economic status to coefficients of predictability as follows:

> The infant test apparently has value in picking out relatively permanent deficits in neuromotor functioning, but socioeconomic status is a better predictor than the infant test for the average infant.

Thus, although SES contributes significantly to the prediction of later childhood test scores in a normal population, its effect is lessened though still present, in a retarded population where infant test scores are the best predictor.

Sex Differences

Some researchers have attempted to identify sex differences in the predictability of infant test scores (Bayley, 1965; Moore, 1967; Werner, Honzik, & Smith, 1968; Goffeney, Henderson, & Butler, 1971; McCall, Hogarty, & Hurlburt, 1972). In general, these attempts have not been successful, although it should be noted that participants for these studies have been chosen only from average or above average populations. Bayley (1965), for example, reports no sex differences on the Griffiths Baby Scale when scores at 6 and 18 months were correlated with Binet scores at 3, 5, and 8 years. In a multiple correlation study cited previously, Werner, Honzik, and Smith (1968) also failed to find correlational disparity due to sex differences. Somewhat more positive findings have been reported by Goffeney, Henderson, and Butler (1971). These authors correlated Bayley scores at 8 months with WISC scores at 7 years, and found higher (but not statistically significant) correlations for girls than boys. Most recently, McCall, Hogarty, and Hurlburt (1972) reported data from the longitudinal studies at Fels Research Institute. The Gesell scale was administered at 6, 12, 18, and 24 months, and test scores were correlated with Stanford-Binet scores at 3, 6, and 10 years. They report that "except for the fact that there is no significant prediction from 6 to 10 years for either sex, the correlations from 6 and 12 months to other childhood ages are all significantly higher for girls than for boys" (p. 731). So although there has been no direct research on subnormal populations, related research in normal groups of children indicates that there might be increased predictability of girls' infant test scores over boys'.

Summary

A number of general statements can be made on the basis of the information presented. First, studies of reliability have been favorable, with split-half and test-retest correlations rarely falling below .85. Second, infant IQ-stability in normal populations is poor, with correlations between infant tests and school-age tests ranging from -.16 to +.49. Third, infant test scores in subnormal populations are more stable than test scores of other children, although correlations between infant and school-age tests are too low for prediction in individual cases. Fourth, other variables used in conjunction with infant scores, such as socio-economic status, might significantly increase the predictability of the infant score alone.

References

Anderson, L. D. The predictive efficiency of infancy tests in relation to intelligence at five years. *Child Development*, 1939, **10**, 203-212.

Bayley, N. Mental growth during the first three years: A developmental study of sixty-one children by repeated tests. *Genetic Psychology Monographs*, 1933, **14**, 1-92.

Bayley, N. Consistency and variability in the growth of intelligence from birth to eighteen years. *Journal of Genetic Psychology*, 1949, **75**, 165-196.

Bayley, N. *Bayley scales of infant development: Birth to two years.* New York: Psychological Corporation, 1969.

Bayley, N. Development of mental abilities. In P.H. Mussen, (Ed.), *Carmichael's manual of child psychology.* Vol. I. New York: Wiley, 1970.

Bayley, N. & Schafer, E. Correlations of maternal and child behavior with the development of mental ability: Data from the Berkeley Growth Study. *Monographs of the society for research in child development*, 1964, **29**, Serial No. 97.

Cattell, P. *The measurement of intelligence in young children.* New York: Psychological Corporation, 1940.

Cavanaugh, M., Cohen, I., Dunphey, D., Ringwell, E., & Goldberg, I. Prediction from the Cattell Infant Intelligence Scale. *Journal of Consulting Psychology*, 1957,**21**, 33-47.

Drillien, C. A longitudinal study of the growth and development of prematurely born children. Part VII: Mental development 2-5 years. *Archives of Diseases in Childhood*, 1961, **36**, 233-240.

Erickson, M. The predictive validity of the Cattell Infant Intelligence Scale for young children. *American Journal of Mental Deficiency*, 1968, 72(6), 728-733.

Erickson, M., Johnson, N., & Campbell, F. Relationships among scores on infant tests for children with developmental problems. *American Journal of Mental Deficiency*, 1970, 75(1), 102-104.

Escalona, S. The predictive value of psychological tests in infancy. *American Psychologist*, 1948, **3**, 281.

Escalona, S. & Moriarty, A. Prediction of school-age intelligence from infant tests. *Child Development*, 1961, 32, 597-605.

Fisher, J. The twisted pear and the prediction of behavior, *Journal of Consulting Psychology*,, 1959, **23**, 400-405.

Fishler, L., Graliker, B., & Koch, R. The predictability of intelligence with Gesell Developmental Scales in mentally retarded infants and young children. *American Journal of Mental Deficiency*, 1965, **69**(5), 515-525.

Furfey, P. & Muehlenbein, J. The validity of infant intelligence tests. *Pedagogical Seminary and the Journal of Genetic Psychology,* 1932, **40**, 219-233.

Gesell, A. *The mental growth of the pre-school child.* New York: MacMillan Co., 1925.

Gesell, A. The ontogenesis of infant behavior. In L. Carmichael, (Ed.), *Manual of child psychology*. New York: Wiley, 1954.

Gesell, A. & Amatruda, C. *Developmental diagnosis.* 2nd ed. New York: Hoeber, 1947.

Goffeney, B., Henderson, N. & Butler, B. Negro-white, male-female, eight month developmental scores compared with seven-year WISC and Bender test scores. *Child Development*, 1971, **42**, 595-604.

Hindley, C. & Munro, J. A factor analytic study of the abilities of infants and predictions of later ability. Cited in McCall et al. Transitions in infant sensorimotor development and the predictions of childhood IQ. *American Psychologist*, 1972, **27**, 728-748.

Holden, R. Prediction of mental retardation in infancy. *Mental Retardation*, 1972, **10**(1), 28-30.

Honzik, M. The constancy of mental test performance during the preschool period. *Journal of Genetic Psychology*, 1938, **52**, 285-302.

Continuous Measurement Of Progress in Infant Intervention Programs

MARCI J. HANSON
G. THOMAS BELLAMY

MARCI J. HANSON *is Coordinator of the Down's Syndrome Infant—Parent Program, and* G. THOMAS BELLAMY *is Research Coordinator, Center on Human Development, University of Oregon.* *This research was supported by BEH Special Project Grant No. G007402775.*

Several demonstration and research programs have been conducted during the last few years to accelerate the development of infants at risk for developmental disabilities (Hayden & Dmitriev, 1975; Ramey & Smith, Note 1). In these programs systematic treatment has typically involved both professional workers and parents, and treatment effects have been evaluated by periodically administering standardized assessment instruments. By accelerating the development of skills measured by these instruments, the programs have done much to argue the case for early intervention in special education. As a result, service programs for handicapped infants are increasingly available.

As effective as standardized instruments were in demonstrating the possible impact of early intervention, it seems unlikely that they will serve the current generation of service programs as well. In these programs decisions must be made which require data not provided by standardized instruments. For example, a parent or treatment consultant must decide whether specific intervention techniques are having their intended effect. Similarly, they must determine whether a specific set of steps is in fact leading toward a defined objective. For these decisions, data are needed which are more immediate and more specifically related to the procedures used.

The purpose of this paper is to argue for the use of measurement systems in which infants' daily performance of targeted skills is recorded. The discussion is intended specifically for the many professionals and paraprofessionals who are now charged with implementing infant intervention programs, and whose procedures involve parents in the treatment program. A simple method of continuous measurement will be described along with the benefits which accrue with its use. Discussion and illustration will center on experiences from a parent implemented research program for Down's syndrome infants at the University of Oregon, in which a consultant assists parents in designing individual treatments.

Measures—Selection and Uses

What kinds of continuous measures are useful? The measurement system described here presupposes that specific developmental objectives have been defined for the infant, steps toward these objectives specified, and criterion levels of performance defined for progression through each step. As treatment procedures are implemented, infant responses to defined cues are recorded so that progress toward the criterion can be monitored. Progress toward different kinds of criteria is measured differently. For example, one step in an independent sitting program might be the child sitting supported by his arms with his hands on the floor in front of him. The performance criterion for progression to a next step involving less support could be the ability to maintain that posture for

"Continuous Measurement of Progress in Infant Intervention Programs", Marci J. Hanson, G. Thomas Bellamy, *Education and Training of The Mentally Retarded* Vol. 12, No. 1, February 1977, © 1977, The Council for Excepltional Children.

an average of 60 seconds on 10 training trials for 3 days. Continuous measures of performance would thus involve the amount of time, or *duration*, the infant sat with the specified support.

A somewhat different measurement strategy is necessary for other criteria. In a crawling program, it could be useful to record the percent of correct responses to a defined cue, e.g., the percentage of trials on which the child responds correctly and crawls the criterion distance of 12 inches when given a foot prompt. After the infant begins to perform a defined behavior, useful measures often focus on the frequency with which it is performed or on response latency, the time between cue presentation and the infant's response.

Whichever measure is appropriate for the criterion, several benefits accrue when continuous measures of infant behaviors are used in programs in which parents and professionals are jointly involved. Although these benefits have occasioned some comment in other reports, they are discussed specifically here to facilitate the work of parent trainers or treatment consultants in infant intervention programs.

Continuous measurement facilitates individual programing. For most treatment objectives in infant development, the parent and consultant may choose among a variety of possible task analyses and intervention approaches. That is, several possible sequences of steps often exist which could lead to the objective. After a particular sequence is selected, several treatment approaches are also possible to improve performance on each step. Continuous measurement of infant progress provides a check on such decisions about sequencing and treatment, insuring that they are appropriate to the individual infant.

To illustrate, a convenient system used in the University of Oregon program is an adaptation of the data recording method of Saunders and Koplik (1975). In one program, parents were asked to perform 10 trials per day on a crawling program in which the infant was expected to crawl independently, foot prompts having been faded out. Parents recorded infant performance by placing a "+" over the number of each trial on which the infant responded correctly and a "−" over the number of each incorrect trial (See Figure 1). The number of correct responses was then counted and the total circled, indicating the frequency of correct responses over trials in one day. Circles on subsequent days were then connected, forming a graphic representation of the child's progress through the program. As can be seen in Figure 1, the infant crawled the criterion distance of 6 inches on 50 percent of the trials the first day, 70 percent the second, 80 percent on the third and fourth, and 90 percent on the fifth day. The parent then moved to the next step in the program which required the child to crawl 8 inches. Modifications of this system also can be used to gather other kinds of data, such as frequency or duration counts.

This system gives the parents and treatment consultant a quick overview of progress without demanding much additional time for either data collection or graphing. With this overview, a number of treatment decisions can be made to individualize programing. When the data show lack of progress on a given step, the treatment procedures (reinforcers, cues, time of day of administration, etc.) might be changed. If progress is not then noted, attention could be turned to the sequence of steps. "Branching" or adding a number of smaller steps may then facilitate progress.

Continuous measurement facilitates communication and increases parents' role in program decision making. The measurement system described also serves as a system of communication between parents and the treatment consultant. With it communication is focused on the actual performance of the child in prescribed activities, and thus the effectiveness of the consultant's suggestions can be communicated clearly during periodic visits.

Perhaps one of the most important products of the daily measurement system is its effect on the relative roles of parent and treatment consultant. With objective measures of their infant's progress parents can become informed consumers of consultant services. The ability to communicate objectively the exact result of previous treatment suggestions allows the parent to play a major role in the infant program. Further, by using a daily data system, a parent can readily see when a program change should occur. Thus, parents can advance their child through steps in a program at a rate appropriate to each child, without waiting for professional consultation to proceed in the program. Therefore, the data serve to increase the role of the parent in the overall decision making for individual program planning.

Continuous measurement allows for analysis of treatment effects. Persons responsible for infant intervention programs often have considerable difficulty in establishing the benefits of their program. Rapid behavioral changes occur in infancy simply as a result of growth and maturation. Unless

2. IDENTIFICATION

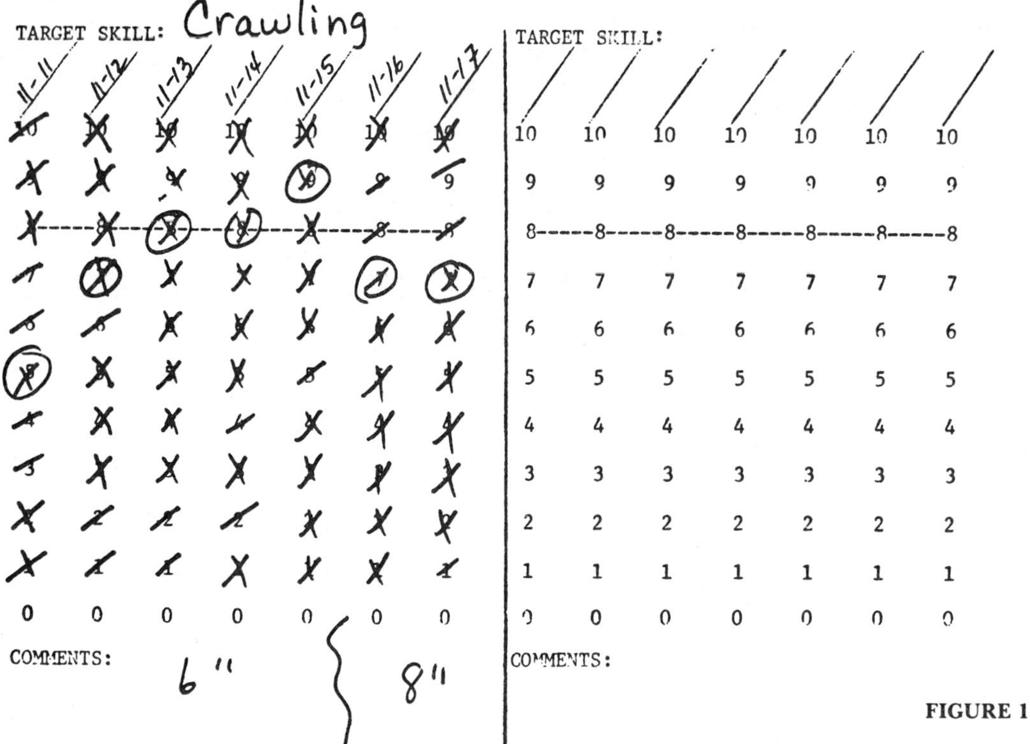

FIGURE 1. Sample data collection sheet.

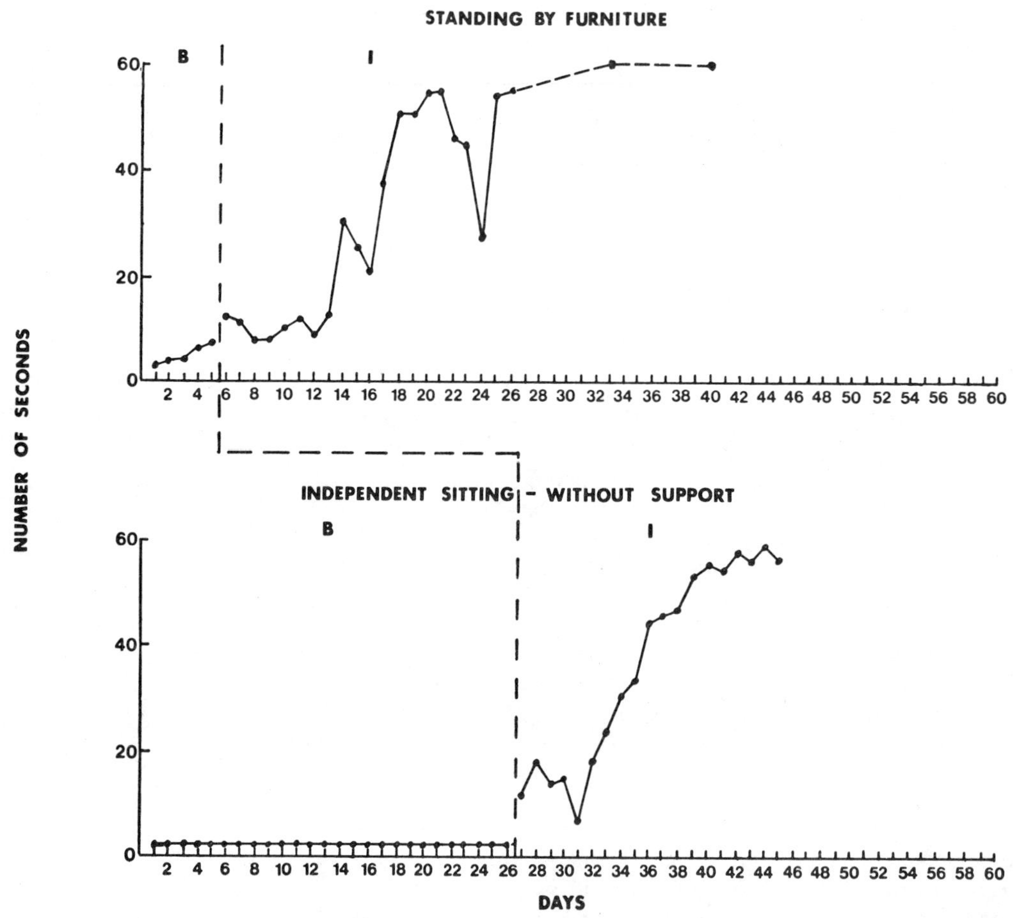

FIGURE 2. Number of seconds infant maintained the positions of standing by furniture and sitting independently during baseline and intervention conditions.

Self Feeding Program

Steps	Levels of Independence	1 (baseline)	2	3	4	5	6	7	8	9	10	11	12	13	14	15	16	17	18	19	20
Returns spoon to bowl, Step 5	independent - no prompt																			80	100
	elbow guide																	80	80		
	forearm prompt																				
	wrist prompt																				
	full hand prompt																				
Scoops food, Step 4	independent - no prompt													100	70	80	100				
	elbow guide							80	40	40	40	100	100								
	forearm prompt																				
	wrist prompt					80	80														
	full hand prompt																				
Brings spoon to mouth, Step 3	independent - no prompt																				
	elbow guide	25	70	80	100																
	forearm prompt																				
	wrist prompt																				
	full hand prompt																				
Removes food from spoon, Step 2	independent - no prompt																				
	elbow guide																				
	forearm prompt																				
	wrist prompt																				
	full hand prompt																				
Grasps spoon, Step 1	independent - no prompt																				
	elbow guide																				
	forearm prompt																				
	wrist prompt																				
	full hand prompt																				

Days

Figure III

FIGURE 3. Levels of independence of an infant on steps of a self feeding program. Numerals indicate the percent of correct responses on 10 training trials for the level and step being taught on each day. Shaded areas represent correct responses on nonconsequated probe trials.

some behavioral changes can be specifically attributed to the intervention procedures, the value of the program is difficult to establish. For this reason, measurement designs which provide evidence of a functional relationship between treatment procedures and behavioral changes can be quite useful. Two such designs seem particularly applicable to infant intervention programs. Each can be used with little modification of the measurement strategy described earlier.

In one of these, the multiple baseline design (Hall, Cristler, Cranston, & Tucker, 1970), baselines are established on two or more independent behaviors. Intervention is then begun on each, one at a time. Evidence for a functional relationship between the intervention procedures and behavior changes is provided if changes do occur in each behavior when and only when the intervention is implemented. Variations of the design include establishing baselines on several behaviors for the same individual, on the same behavior of several individuals, and on the same behavior across several situations.

The use of a multiple baseline design to evaluate one treatment used in the University of Oregon program is illustrated in Figure 2. Baselines were obtained on two behaviors of one 5½ month old Down's syndrome infant: standing by furniture (defined as child standing, bearing weight on feet, holding on to furniture for support) and independent sitting (defined as child sitting in an erect position on flat surface with no support). Performance on both behaviors was recorded daily on 10 trials which occurred throughout the day. During Days 1 through 5 (Baseline) the infant averaged less than 7 seconds for standing by furniture and did not exhibit independent sitting on any opportunity. Treatment was begun on standing by furniture on Day 6, while baseline was continued for sitting. Treatment involved the parent providing presumed social and material reinforcers for approximations of the behavior. By Day 25 the infant was standing by furniture for an average of approximately 60 seconds, which was the defined criterion for completion of that training program. Periodic assessments of standing by furniture were taken on subsequent days, showing that the infant was able to stand for more than 60 seconds.

Independent sitting did not occur until treatment was begun on Day 27. At that point the average number of seconds the infant could sit independently began to increase until the infant was able to sit independently for an average of nearly 60 seconds on Days 40–45. Again treatment involved the parent providing presumed social and material reinforcers for approximations of the behavior. These two behaviors, standing by furniture and independent sitting, increased to criterion levels when and only when intervention was begun. Thus, the design argues strongly for the interpretation that infant gains were functionally related to the training procedures employed.

A second convenient design which can be used to evaluate the effects of training procedures is the changing criterion design. In this design behavioral criteria for consequation are set and sequentially changed when each criterion is met. This design, like the multiple baseline design, supports the interpretation that infant behavior changes are functionally linked to intervention procedures.

The use of a changing criterion design to evaluate a self-feeding program is illustrated in Figure 3. In the program an 18 month old infant was taught to feed herself independently with a spoon in the following sequence of steps: (a) grasps spoon, (b) removes food from spoon in mouth, (c) brings spoon to mouth, (d) scoops food with spoon, (e) returns spoon to bowl. Infant performance on each of these steps was assessed during one daily probe trial in which the infant was given the opportunity to demonstrate the highest level of independence on each step without teaching. Levels of independence were recorded using the following five categories: (a) performs behavior with a full hand prompt from parent, (b) performs behavior with a wrist prompt from parent, (c) performs behavior with a forearm prompt from parent, (d) performs behavior with an elbow guide from parent, (e) performs behavior independently with no prompts from parent.

Baseline was established on four probe trials on Day 1. As can be seen from Figure 3, the infant was able to grasp the spoon and remove the food from the spoon independently. In addition, she performed bringing spoon to mouth (Step 3) with a full hand prompt, wrist prompt, and forearm prompt 100 percent of the time. However, with prompting faded to only an elbow guide, she accomplished the behavior on only 25 percent of the opportunities given. Therefore, treatment was begun on Step 3 using an elbow guide for training. Treatment was limited to one step and independence level each day and involved the parents providing presumed reinforcing consequences for the behavior on each of 10 daily training trials. Treatment was advanced to the next level in the series when a criterion of 80 percent or more correct responses was reached for 2 successive days. When probe trials showed a correct performance on 80 percent or more of the probes on a given level, training on that level was skipped and the next level in the series was taught. For example, on Day 17, several steps were skipped and the program advanced to the elbow guide level for Step 5 because probes indicated the child had advanced to this level. Her rapid progress on the final Step 5 may have been due to the effect of similar training on the previous steps. Levels reached on probes are indicated in Figure 3 by the shaded areas; data points from training are listed numerically by the percent of correct responses per day (example: 70).

Figure 3 illustrates that the child's performance during both training and probe situations specifically reflects the step on which training was implemented. As can be seen, criterion on most steps was reached only when training was implemented. This increases the confidence of the treatment consultant that a functional relationship exists between training procedures and infant skill development.

Discussion

This paper has argued that periodic administration of standardized assessment instruments will provide insufficient data for making program decisions in the many infant intervention programs which are now available. Instead, a method of continuous measurement has been proposed, which utilizes a recording format suggested by Saunders and Koplik (1975). In this system, infant responses to specific treatment cues or situations are recorded daily by noting their frequency, duration, latency, or percent correct.

Several benefits accrue when such a data system is used. It is possible for treatment programs to be individualized for each infant; parents participate more completely in the decision making concerned with their child's program; and continuous measurement can facilitate the evaluation of program effectiveness by identifying functional relationships between procedures and infant behavioral changes. Convenient measurement systems thus can be employed in a parent program with little disruption to ongoing training practices and no significant commitment of additional time by parents or professional treatment consultants.

References

Hall, R. V., Cristler, C., Cranston, S. S., & Tucker, B. Teachers and parents as researchers using multiple baseline designs. *Journal of Applied Behavior Analysis*, 1970, *3*, 247–255.

Hayden, A. H., & Dmitriev, V. The multidisciplinary preschool program for Down's syndrome children at the University of Washington Model Preschool Center. In B. Z. Friedlander, G. M. Sterritt, & G. E. Kirk (Eds.), *Exceptional infant: Assessment and intervention* (Vol. 3). New York: Bruner/Mazel, 1975.

Saunders, R. R., & Koplik, K. A multi-purpose data sheet for recording and graphing in the classroom. *American Association for the Education of the Severely/Profoundly Handicapped Review*, 1975, *1*, 1–8.

Reference Note

1. Ramey, C. J., & Smith, B. J. *Learning and intelligence in disadvantaged infants: Effects of early intervention*. Paper presented at the annual meeting of The Council for Exceptional Children, Chicago, Illinois, April 1976.

PROGRAMS FOR THE PRESCHOOL HANDICAPPED CHILD

Legislation has spawned a plethora of studies to investigate model programs and the effectiveness of early childhood programs in general. We need to conscientiously investigate whether the positive results of early intervention prevail over time, for some research concludes that only when the environment in the critical years is relatively consistent for a minimum of five years, can effective learning be stabilized. As we examine environmental conditions, we may find that the poverty of one generation by virtue of its circumstances becomes the incompetence of the next generation which results in restricted growth and development. There remains the sensitive issue that children who live in poverty live lives of intellectual and physical depression; and, without home environmental change, any gains from early compensatory programs will diminish. "Minor disorders" in perception, cognition, impulsivity and delayed academic function will become permanent educational handicaps for these children in an educational setting. Longitudinal studies support the contention that without the continued effort of educators, families and communities, the benefits of early intervention will decrease or disappear. To maintain more lasting effects, programs for young handicapped children need ongoing and continued evaluation and appropriate prescription changes to meet the change and maturation of the individual children involved.

Proponents of early childhood education programs for the handicapped have refuted these pessimistic findings and questioned the efficacy of the studies, citing questionable research design and evaluation. They questioned what constituted a measure of effectiveness for this population. A change in I.Q. score? Increased achievement scores?'More supportive and understanding families? Another issue emerged: at what point or period in time should effectiveness be measured? After six months? One year? At the conclusion of the preschool years? In the primary grades? Adulthood?

Despite the emergence of the myriad questions, theoretical work in the behavioral sciences proposed that the development of highly susceptible young children was influenced by positive intervention stimulation and education in the young years. Special education in particular renewed interest and investigation into previous research which indicated that long range effects of intervention programs for mentally retarded children were beneficial.

Some research indicates that the earlier the intervention for high risk children, the more positive the results. Investigation on nursery schooling for socially disadvantaged children in Britain and the United States suggested that early intervention with high risk children produce increased effective language development. Language increased and a more positive self-image was established as a result of child-parent programs. School/home learning programs for young handicapped children paved the way for more successful kindergarten mainstreaming. Orthopedically handicapped infants placed in a developmental/educational day care center indicated a significant decrease in crying as a result of supervised adult-infant interaction. Likewise, Child Development/Day Care resource projects offer information to assist parents and the community in working with and teaching the control and the effect on the development of cognitive and social skills. There is variation of approach and philosophy. Some feel that stimulation must begin during a "critical period", namely, early infancy. Others postulate the existence of a "sensitive period", a developmental phase when learning is most easily accomplished because the organism is ready to receive. Despite the conflict in philosophical learnings, classroom programs, camp programs, language stimulation and mainstreaming programs have emerged with new vigor, knowledgeable and trained personnel, and the acceptance, encouragement and partnership of family and educator. Longitudinal studies, investigation of appropriate materials and methods, still need to be explored. Yet, one must give credence to support of and hope that the young handicapped child of today will live a better tomorrow.

BETTER EARLY THAN NEVER

Dr. Barbara Flood, Dir. Early Childhood programs West Islip P.S.S., N.Y.

The need for the early identification of children who require special intervention to achieve their right to an education has become recognized by our nation's schools. The advent of P.L. 94-142, Education for All Handicapped Children Act, documents this area of concern as a national priority. Furthermore, the direction of identification toward treatment and intervention rather than identification alone has gained momentum in the U.S. Appropriate educational services for handicapped children must be immediately forthcoming, especially for those in the early, critical years of development – those in the preschool years.

Legislative Commitment

Despite various state laws in the past – such as Vermont's 1971 law directing that every child be provided with special education from birth if needed, and the 1972 Massachusetts 'Comprehensive Special Education Law' mandating schools to deal with the special education problems of the Commonwealth's children between 3 and 21 – it is only with the passage of P.L. 94-142 that we have demonstrated a full and significant commitment by Congress and the American people to the education of all handicapped children in our nation.

Critical Early Years

The first opportunity for screening and intervention presently occurs at age 5 or 6 with kindergarten or first grade registration. Dr. Burton L. White, director of the Harvard Preschool Project and a developer of the Brookline Early Education Project regards 5 as hopelessly late. According to Dr. White, serious deficits are already visible at 3. The importance of early childhood experiences for appropriate

"Better Early Than Never", Dr. Barbara Flood, *Special Children* Vol. 3, No. 3, Spring 1977, ©1977.

cognitive, social, and personality development of the human being is of general acceptance among most educators today. With the realization and support, philosophically and fiscally, that sequential, appropriate, and optimal intervention can affect the success of our young children, our efforts will be more substantial, more effective than that which has resulted from our "let's wait and see" attitude of the past.

First Steps

A program of treatment which responded to these concerns was evolved by the West Islip Public Schools (West Islip, NY) with the assistance of title VI-B funding (Education of the Handicapped Act) through the Division for Handicapped Children of the New York State Education Department. Project Providing Enriching Experiences for Preschoolers (PEEP) is based on the belief that the longer detection and amelioration is delayed, the deeper the frustration and damage to the self-concept of the child, and, the longer and more difficult – if not impossible – remediation becomes. This program was established to provide every child with meaningful experiences which relate to his/her own functioning levels of personal and academic success.

Components of this project include 1) a district-wide screening-re-screening process, 2) the intervention of educational, prescriptive treatment in a specially designed classroom, 3) cooperative interaction between a preschool teacher and parents in the home setting to plan, arrange, and evaluate stimulating activities which are responsive to each child's special needs, 4) parent seminar sessions, and 5) the availability of ancillary personnel (speech therapist, psychologist, social worker) for participating children and their families.

Child-Find Activities

Initially a child-find program, this preschool project focused on identification of developmental discrepancies handicapping conditions among 750 preschool children ages 3-5 in the Spring of 1976. An assessment of each child's relative educational abilities was made using a locally developed instrument with particular attention to four major developmental areas: Language Development, Perceptual–Motor Development, Cognitive Development, and Social-Emotional Development.

The screening phase of this project constituted date collection for pre-assessment of the target population. Preschool children born between December 2, 1970, and January 1, 1973, were eligible to participate in the Screening Program of this project. Child-find activities were undertaken to reach the target population.

a. introductory letters to parents of 3, 4, and 5 year old children
b. descriptive posters displayed in local shopping centers
c. announcements on local radio stations
d. articles in local newspapers
e. sibling-in-school notices
f. follow-up letters to parents
g. PTA assistance
h. cooperation of civic and community organizations
i. contacts through local pediatric clinics
j. contacts through local specialized medical practitioners
k. cooperation of local churches
l. announcements in local nursery schools, day care centers
m. video announcement on local cable TV channel

Preschool Screening

Screening took place during a three day period at each of nine district neighborhood schools. Parents brought their children according to an arranged alphabetical schedule for two visits of one half hour each. The parent and child were greeted by a teacher aide and escorted through the screening stations. Every effort was made to allay the child's discomfort or anxiety in the Screening Program. Parents were requested to accompany their children through each screening station. Acuities in hearing and color perception were examined by a school nurse. PTA volunteers performed amblioypia testing. A social and developmental history interview with parents was also conducted by a school nurse. School psychologists and speech therapists administered a locally developed psychoeducational survey. Those children who demonstrated deficits during Screeming were given a complete evaluation by a school psychologist at a later time before the initiation of program services. Upon completion of the Screening visit, the parent had a brief, private conference with a staff member who summarized the screening process and preschool project. Letters were sent to the parents of all children who participated in the Screening program to express appreciation for parental cooperation.

Those children who were diagnosed as having special learning needs as a result of final evaluation were offered educational intervention 1) in the preschool classroom setting in which children fully interact with the instructional program and available resources through the coordination of a teacher and teacher aide, 2) in their home environments as a teacher works cooperatively with parents in the home setting to design and implement activities pertinent to an individual child's specific needs, or 3) referral to an outside agency. The type of project service was selected on the basis of the child's special needs.

Intervention Services

A center for the educational intervention service was established in an available first floor classroom of a district elementary building. Two sessions (one AM and one PM) operate daily. A prescriptive program for each child is coordinated accordingly. Children attend sessions on individual schedules. At the present time, 24 children attend the Center program. According to the special learning needs of each individual child, performance objectives are selected, focusing on sequential stages of child development and correlating to each major developmental area (Language, Perceptual-Motor, Cognitive, Social-Emotional). These areas and sample corresponding performance objectives were developed by the University of Virginia for a Performance-Based Early Childhood / Special Education Teacher Preparation Program (OEG-0-7104153 603) and are identified as follows:

Developmental Area	Performance Area
Language	**Expressive:** To develop the ability to ask questions as a means of seeking and gaining information.
	Receptive: To identify the discriminate degree of sound.
Perceptual-Motor	**Gross Motor:** To use postural adjustments.
	Fine Motor: To integrate the movements of fingers, hands, and wrists into a purposeful, synchronized pattern. a. manual dexterity b. finger dexterity
Social-Emotional	**Self Help Skills:** To clothe oneself. a. dressing/undressing b. zippering/unzippering c. buttoning/unbuttoning d. lacing/unlacing e. tying/untying f. buckling/unbuckling
	Individuation: To objectively describe physical self (body, size, strength, etc.).
	Behavioral Adjustment: To form relationships with peers.
Cognitive	**Classification:** To develop descriptive discrimination (size, shape, etc.).
	Spatial Relations: To develop the ability to perceive direction in space (to, from).
	Temporal Relations: To develop the concept of time in terms of periods having a beginning and an end.

Types of handicapping conditions among participating children include speech impairment, emotional disturbance, hearing impairment, orthopedic handicap, and specific learning disabilities. Personalized, prescriptive educational programs are coordinated according to each child's handicapping condition(s). The project's focus addresses a descriptive analysis of child deficits and assets and precise planning for each child follows. A daily evaluative session about each child's progess in his/her prescriptive program takes place between the preschool teacher and aide.

Detailed record-keeping of each child's progress is maintained. Recorded data is discussed and consequent tasks for each child which are appropriate to his/her level, interest, and needs are determined at this time. Learner Accomplishment Records (LAR) are compiled summarily for each child at the end of 10 week program cycles. This process of record-keeping is also maintained by the At-Home Teacher.

Home intervention services are conducted by a preschool teacher in the home setting for 10 children and visited by the At-Home Teacher once each week. The purposes of this unique service are to build on the strength of the family unit and to involve the family in the special needs of the child. It is clear that parents become involved in educational programs for their children if they are approached appropriately and if they are involved appropriately. This has been the experience of this project.

Children participating in Project PEEP receive ongoing diagnosis and remediation of learning and/or behavior problems through project staff, including services of a speech therapist and a psychologist who are designated for 50% and 20% professional time respectively. These specialists contribute both formal and informal services to participating students, while also sharing recommendations with other staff members and parents.

Parental Involvement

Parent seminar sessions are provided for parents whose children receive project services. On a biweekly basis, a school social worker directs the sessions for the purposes of 1) building the skills of the parent, 2) enabling the parent to optimize the intellectual, social and physical development of their young children, and 3) increasing parental confidence in working with the schools and with his/her child. Topics solicited from parents range from implementing positive guidance techniques to selecting suitable reward systems.

During the current project year, program activities have focused on the refinement of classroom programming both in the Center and At-Home service components, the improved coordination of staff roles, and the dissemination of project events to the district teaching staff. Parenting skill workshops are planned for the future to be available to local residents who are parents of preschool children.

A Must for Our Third Century

Our current priorities – attending to preventive early childhood education, investigating and developing new programs for young children with special needs – seem likely to remain priorities for this decade. The continuing realization of educational opportunities for the handicapped at the Federal, State, and local levels, a succession of court decisions attesting to the rights of the handicapped, and landmark new Federal legislation have produced a stable foundation for further progress. The crucial issue is really not in pedagogical practices, nor research, nor funding. The central issue is a matter attitude. Our progress of the past 200 years will be meaningful when handicapped people achieve their rightful place not only in "regular" schools, but also in "regular" society, to be judged not on the basis of their deficits, but rather on the basis of their value as human beings. That struggle has really just begun.

Head Start for the Handicapped-What's Been Accomplished?

Jean Nazarro, CEC Information Center

The HEW Report

A little over a year has gone by since Head Start received the legislative mandate to enroll handicapped children into their programs. In April 1974 the US Department of Health, Education, and Welfare presented its second annual report on services provided to handicapped children in Project Head Start to the US Congress. The report stated:

> To date, children professionally diagnosed as handicapped account for at least 10.1 percent of the children enrolled in full year programs. In addition, 3.1 percent of children enrolled in Full Year programs are either partially diagnosed or reported as possibly handicapped. The distribution of handicapped children by category of handicap is as follows: 35 percent speech impaired, 20 percent health or developmentally impaired, 12.2 percent seriously emotionally disturbed, 9.4 percent physically handicapped, 7.9 percent hearing impaired, 7.4 percent mentally retarded, 6.6 percent visually impaired, 1 percent deaf, and 0.5 percent blind [p. iii].

The summary statement went on to say, "For the purposes of this annual report, only professionally diagnosed children are reported [p. iii]."

Other highlights of the report specify that "90 percent of the Head Start programs are serving at least 1 handicapped child, and one out of every 5 handicapped children in Head Start has multiple handicaps [p. iv]."

The accomplishments summarized in this report were for the most part gathered by December 1973 and therefore reflect the status of programs that were in the beginning phases of implementing the legislative mandate. The information was gathered by a mailout census sent to all Head Start projects and delegate agencies, followup telephone interviews made to programs that did not respond to the census, and visits made by a team of skilled observers.

In almost all cases, according to the HEW report, handicapped children have been fully integrated with other Head Start children. Modifications have been made to existing physical facilities in order to accommodate special needs of the physically handicapped. Inservice training for Head Start personnel has been conducted in order to prepare staff to better integrate handicapped children into their programs. Professional diagnostic services have been used to identify handicapped children. Parents of 41.1 percent of the enrolled handicapped children received some counseling related to the child's handicap; 38.2 percent of the children were receiving planned special experiences to increase adjustment skills related to their handicap; 36.1 percent of the children were provided with individual counseling; 20 percent were given speech or physical therapy; 9.8 percent had received medication or drug therapy; 5.4 percent had been provided with prosthetic devices; and 5.1 percent received some other special service. These special services were either provided directly or were arranged through the Head Start program.

Congress' Response

On May 15, 1974, the House Education and Labor Committee formally responded to the claims summarized in the Head Start annual report. The Committee's report stated:

"Head Start For The Handicapped--What's Been Accomplished?", Dr. Barbara Flood, *Exceptional Children,* Vol. 41, No. 2, October, 1974, © 1974, Council For Exceptional Children.

It appears that in the desire to meet the Congressional mandate, considerable "over reporting" of children has occurred and, in fact, many children who normally have been recipients of the Head Start program, because they have "handicapping conditions" are now being classified *improperly* as "handicapped." The concern is that these children in all probability will outgrow their problems and the Committee does not want to see them stigmatized or labelled for life because of the need to meet the Congressional quota. The reason why children are being improperly classified suggested to the Committee is for the sake of bureaucratic convenience or the need to meet statistical levels [p. 14].

The problem seems to lie in the discrepancy between the definition of "handicapping conditions" and the term "handicapped":

A child who has a "handicapping condition" but does not require special education or related services is one who may need eyeglasses, has a minor hearing loss, a mild emotional problem, asthma, anemia, or slight or delayed speech. These children with "handicapping conditions" have traditionally been served by the Head Start program, but until this year have *not* been classified as handicapped. The Committee recognizes that OCD already has guidelines requiring that children be certified by professionals. Yet in spite of the fact, children are still being improperly classified [p. 14].

The House has ordered the following: (a) that the Office of Child Development take immediate steps to guarantee that no child is included in the count under the 10 percent requirement unless he or she truly has a certified handicap, (b) that greater efforts be made to bring the more severely handicapped child into Head Start, and (c) that the 10 percent enrollment criterion be met by each state enrollment, rather than by overall national or regional enrollments. The mandate, in present form, provides that 10 percent of the national Head Start enrollment opportunities must be filled by handicapped children.

The Syracuse Report

An Interim Report on the Assessment of Handicapped Effort in Experimental and Selected Other Head Start Programs Serving the Handicapped ("the Syracuse report") was prepared by the Division of Special Education and Rehabilitation at Syracuse University and submitted to OCD by Policy Research Incorporated in February 1974.

The report reflects a sensitivity to the problems encountered by Head Start staff, which goes beyond the political-bureaucratic battles taking place in Washington. They first deal with the discrepancy between the census figures reporting the prevalence of handicapped children in Head Start programs compared to the number of handicapped children observed during the site visits. The census reported that the number of handicapped children in Head Start programs approximately doubled following the 1972 legislative mandate, as compared to the year before. The onsite observers indicated that "the increase in handicapped children was only modestly changed during the 73-74 school year [p. 100]." In trying to explain this discrepancy, the Syracuse report stated:

. . . a clue in understanding both sets of data, other than to dismiss one or the other as inaccurate, is embedded in the frequent remark we heard from Head Start teachers, supervisors, and directors, "in retrospect we have always had handicapped children in our Head Start program." Now, however, these youngsters are being labelled as "mentally retarded" or "emotionally disturbed" or "speech impaired." The very significant increase reported in the census questionnaire, juxtaposed with the modest increase noted during observations of classes and discussions with teachers, may be most helpfully illuminated by an examination of the hypothesis that Head Start programs have always served the handicapped, but today, more than heretofore, children are labelled as handicapped [p. 100].

One of the real dangers of labeling children as handicapped comes when the child moves into regular school programs. A child may have been physically and psychologically integrated into the heterogeneous Head Start program, but if he has been labeled as handicapped, the chances are great that when he moves into a public school situation,

. . . if he continues to be viewed as handicapped he will receive his education essentially in a segregated school or class. Stated another way, special segregated Head Start classes and centers are so rare as to be virtually nonexistent; on the other hand, fully integrated public school special education programs, are, conversely, not presently a viable option [p. 101].

Greater Inclusion Without Unnecessary Labeling

How may the 1972 mandate both encourage the greater inclusion of the handicapped yet discourage the unnecessary labelling of children whose needs have not been served by being classified as handicapped [Interim Report . . . , 1974, p. 101]?

This question gets at the problem of including the severely and multiply handicapped child who continues to be unserved by Head Start projects. Somehow the children who have always been included in Head Start must be eliminated from the number identified as handicapped and those who have not yet been accepted because of the severity of their disabling conditions must be added.

> Head Start staffs have been confused by the very concepts of handicap itself, and especially by the different categories and degrees subsumed in this generic label. Probably in self defense, and logically because of functional need, the staffs of the various programs develop their own definitions of the various handicaps, if for no other reason than to provide a mechanism for reporting to the various central offices, and thus continue the funding necessary to keep their programs alive [Interim Report . . ., 1974, p. 103].

The Syracuse project staff of visiting observers has suggested that the claim that 10 percent of all children are handicapped is far too high. "If such an estimate continues to be a target to be served, many thousands of children will be mislabelled and unnecessarily burdened with one more form of social stigma to contend with [p. 103]." It was the impression of the site visitors that

> . . . the 1972 mandate will be realized in many more important ways if the target population is recast as one that is, first, severely and multiply handicapped, and secondly, representative of approximately 3 or 4 percent of the preschool child population. The continuation of the current 10 percent target goal will lead to the unfortunate and unnecessary labelling of very mildly different children, on the one hand, and the deliberate exclusion or neglect of those severely handicapped who are now the truly unserved [p. 104].

In spite of this recommendation the US House Education and Labor Committee (1974) has retained the 10 percent handicapped enrollment figure but has reemphasized the original intent of the Congress that "only children with substantial handicaps that require special education and related services are to be counted for the purpose [p. 15]." The Syracuse team felt that "most of the programs observed have the resources and capabilities to adequately serve the minimally and moderately handicapped and, although less well or frequently, some severely impaired children [p. 104]." These observers felt that Head Start programs are attempting to meet the special needs of these children and by and large are doing rather well.

> Head Start staffs express considerable reluctance to label children unnecessarily, and do so with both anxiety about the future for certain children and a mixture of guilt and fear that the 10 percent quota will or will not be met. Sometimes they feel that they can't win no matter how, or if, they label children [p. 107].

Parent Involvement

> Because so many of those identified as handicapped enrolled in Head Start are mildly or moderately disabled and because the community—teachers and family alike—do not truly view those children as handicapped, involvements of parents of handicapped in Head Start are little different from those enjoyed by parents of typical children. Possibly, the parents of the handicapped are a bit more involved with the Head Start centers, and, possibly, parents of the handicapped are a bit more responsive to the general needs of the centers. Parents are pleased that the handicapped receive opportunities in Head Start and express pleasure that the inclusion of these children in regular Head Start settings enrich the experiences of all the preschoolers enrolled. Parents of severely impaired children are especially pleased and grateful for the impact Head Start efforts have made, not only on the lives of their children, but on all members of their families [Interim Report . . ., 1974, p. 110].

In some cases, where children were designated as handicapped after they were enrolled in the program, a number of parents did not know that their children had been so identified. "Some staffs expressed concerns over the parents' knowing that their children were so designated [Interim Report . . ., p. 53]." This situation is potentially explosive if those children continue to carry a label into regular elementary school.

Staff Training and Technical Assistance

> The general staff continually expressed strong needs for specialized training. They want practical experiences under supervised conditions, juxtaposed with didactic courses concerned with handling children with special problems. They wish to become more familiar with the process of identification and evaluation. They need feedback, consultation, and positive and facilitating supervision [Interim Report . . ., 1974, p. 113].

Among the recommendations presented in the Syracuse report is this basic challenge to the Office of Child Development:

> With national leadership from OCD, a long range strategy should be developed to infuse the general public with a conception of child

variance as a natural aspect of the human condition, rather than, as is more commonly believed in our schools and agencies, as problems that are insoluble, unpleasant, and impossible to contend with in ordinary settings. The Head Start movement is the most promising force available today to reverse the trend in the United States towards greater and greater segregation of the weak, the elderly, and people with special needs [p. 120].

References

Interim report on assessment of the handicapped effort in experimental and selected other Head Start programs serving the handicapped. Syracuse University, Division of Special Education and Rehabilitation. Submitted to the US Department of Health, Education, and Welfare, Office of Child Development, by Policy Research Inc., February 1974.

US Department of Health, Education, and Welfare, Office of Child Development. *Head Start services to handicapped children.* Second annual report to the US Congress. Washington, D.C.: HEW, OCD, 1974.

US House Education and Labor Committee. *Community Services Act of 1974.* Report No. 93-1043 to US House of Representatives, May 15, 1974.

Assessing the Intellectual Consequences of Early Intervention with High-Risk Infants

CRAIG T. RAMEY AND BARBARA J. SMITH
University of North Carolina at Chapel Hill

Infants at-risk for mental retardation were divided into a group that received early day-care intervention and a matched control group that did not. The purpose of the intervention was to prevent sociocultural retardation. Children were tested at 7 and 18 months on a simple two-choice visual-discrimination task and on the Bayley Scales of Infant Development to assess the impact of the intervention program on their development. Analyses revealed that the experimental group's performance was reliably superior to that of the control group on both measures and that experimental subjects scoring high on the Bayley Scales reached criterion on the discrimination task on fewer trials than low Bayley scorers. The relationship was particularly strong at 18 months.

Children who are reared in economically impoverished homes are especially at risk for socioculturally caused mental retardation. Heber, Dever, and Conry (1968) have reported IQ results that support the contention that there is a progressive decline from initial normality in the most severely disadvantaged children. Within the past decade numerous early educational intervention programs have been developed to remediate or to prevent this waste of intellectual potential. Early intervention programs have recently received independent review by Bronfenbrenner (Note 1) and by Stedman, Anastasiow, Dokecki, Gordon, and Parker (in press). These reviewers concluded that early intervention can be effective in changing the young child's intellectual status. However, they criticized intervention programs for relying almost exclusively upon standardized measures of intelligence, such as intelligence tests, as the primary means of evaluating program effectiveness.

Because standardized measures of intelligence administered in early childhood are primarily summative descriptions of intellectual performance, they offer limited insight into the rates at which children can solve new problems or learn new concepts. Further, standardized tests of intelligence are almost always administered in a setting that is unfamiliar to the child and, hence, may not correlate with the young child's learning performance in his typical, everyday environment. The present project was conducted as part of a larger early intervention project. We sought to accomplish two major goals: first, to determine if the intervention was affecting intellectual development as assessed by a traditional standardized test of development (Bayley Scales of Infant Development) and second, to determine if a simple two-choice visual-discrimination task used with young infants in their typical environments would indicate performance differences associated with the intervention process. The discrimination-learning task was used as a first step in developing assessment procedures that are *process* oriented in nature. Such procedures might eventually be used to supplement the information obtained from standardized tests of development to determine more precisely what aspects of a child's performance have been affected by systematic intervention. Finally, a secondary goal was to determine if a statistically reliable relationship would be found between discrimination-learning performance and the Mental Development Index of the Bayley Scales.

This research was supported by Grants No. HD-03110 and HD-00424-02 from the National Institute of Child Health and Human Development.

"Assessing the Intellectual Consequences of Early Instruction With High-Risk Infants", Craig T. Ramey and Barbara J. Smith, *American Journal of Mental Deficiency,* Vol. 81, No. 4, January 1977, © 1977, A. A.M.D.

Method

Subjects

The subjects were 47 infants from lower socioeconomic homes participating in an early day-care intervention program designed to prevent developmental retardation. Twenty-three of the infants were 7 months of age, and 24 were 18 months of age at the time of their participation in the experimental part of the assessment program. The identification of potentially eligible infants and their families began during the last trimester of the mother's pregnancy. The two major referral sources for families were the prenatal clinics at a local University hospital and the County Department of Social Services. A series of interviews was begun after identification of an expectant mother likely to bear a child who would be eligible for the project.

One purpose of these interviews was to rate the family on an experimental version High-Risk Index, which is shown in Table 1. Because there are relatively few systematic epidemiological data concerning the social, economic, and family factors associated with nonorganic developmental retardation, it was impossible to assign empirically derived weights to each factor. Therefore, weights were assigned to the various factors based upon our best guess of their relative importance. The infants were pair-matched at birth on maternal IQ, number of siblings, and sex of the infant and were randomly assigned to either an experimental or a control group. There were 25 experimental- and 22 control-group children.

The unequal numbers of children between the experimental and the control group is accounted for by two infant deaths in the older age groups and the unavailability of one younger control-group infant at the time of testing. Table 2 presents a summary of the background characteristics of the infants by groups and ages. It is important to note that the mean income of the families is extremely low. The income figures cited represent the total amount of cash income earned by these families; it excludes the income of those receiving public assistance. One partial explanation for the extremely low income level is that many of these children and their mothers were being cared for in an extended family context. What is included in Table 1 is the reported earned cash available to the child's immediate family or to the child's mother if the family had no father present. It is noteworthy that although most of the families would qualify for public assistance, many refused to have any contact with the relevant public agencies because those agencies were perceived as threatening and punitive.

TABLE 1
HIGH-RISK INDEX[a]

Factor	Weight
Mother's educational level (last grade completed)	
6	8
7	7
8	6
9	3
10	2
11	1
12	0
Father's educational level (last grade completed)	
6	8
7	7
8	6
9	3
10	2
11	1
12	0
Family income (per year)	
1,000	8
1,001-2,000	7
2,001-3,000	6
3,001-4,000	5
4,001-5,000	4
5,001-6,000	0
Father absent for reasons other than health or death	3
Absence of maternal relatives in local area (i.e., parents, grandparents, or brothers or sisters of majority age)	3
Siblings of school age who are one or more grades behind age-appropriate grade or who score equivalently low on school administered achievement tests	3
Payments received from welfare agencies within past 3 years	3
Record of father's work indicates unstable and unskilled or semiskilled labor	3
Records of mother's or father's IQ indicates scores of 90 or below	3
Records of sibling's IQ indicates scores of 90 or below	3
Relevant social agencies in the community indicate that the family is in need of assistance	3
One or more members of the family has sought counseling or professional help in the past 3 years	1
Special circumstances not included in any of the above that are likely contributors to cultural or social disadvantage	1

[a] Criterion for inclusion in high-risk sample was a score of more than 11.

Intervention Program Content

In any intervention program that attempts to be comprehensive in its efforts, it is very difficult to be sure that all significant factors except the ones to be manipulated have been adequately controlled. In the present intervention program, both for experimental and control subjects, three gen-

TABLE 2
BACKGROUND CHARACTERISTICS OF EXPERIMENTAL AND CONTROL SUBJECTS

Characteristic/Age of children	Group	
	Experimental	Control
Mean maternal IQ[a]		
7 months	86.42	85.09
18 months	78.77	77.27
Mean number of siblings		
7 months	.33	.45
18 months	.92	1.64
Mean maternal education[b]		
7 months	10.33	10.36
18 months	10.46	10.45
Mean family income[c]		
7 months	$458.00	$1181.00
18 months	$1192.00	$1363.00

[a] Wechsler Adult Intelligence Scale, Full-Scale IQ.
[b] In years.
[c] Per year.

eral classes of variables were thought to be potentially important enough to require control.

Family support social work services. Upon request from parents and on the basis of periodic visits to all families, the project staff sought to provide families with guidance in such areas as obtaining legal aid, food, clothing, housing, and other goods and services. These services were provided with the intention of keeping the families intact if that was their desire. Further, because both the experimental and control-group families received these services, it was hoped that this procedure would help to diminish the so-called "Hawthorne effect," which might be more pronounced if only the experimental group received this attention.

Nutritional supplements. Each child in the experimental group received the bulk of his nutrition at the day-care center. Breakfast, lunch, and an afternoon snack were served each day. To diminish the potential nutritional differences between the experimental and control groups, the project staff provided the control-group children with an unlimited supply of free formula for as long as they used it. When the present experiment was conducted, all but one of the control children tested were still receiving formula.

Medical care. Complete medical care for the experimental-group children was provided by project staff. Medical care for the control-group children was arranged through the project and delivered at a local University hospital.

One major difference between the experimental and control groups was that the experimental-group children attended an educational day-care center approximately 8 hours per day, 5 days a week while the control-group children remained at home. The format for the daily operation of this center has recently been described by Ramey, Holmberg, Sparling, and Collier (Note 2).

Two locations for the education and care of the center-attending children were maintained. A suite of four adjoining rooms and a large hallway made up the teaching-learning environment for infants up to walking age. Two rooms were playrooms, and two rooms were bedrooms. Fourteen infants were typically in this area, which was staffed by five teachers.

On another floor in the building, a large area was divided into classes for 1 and 2 year olds and for 1, 2, and 3 year olds. These two classes were set up to accommodate 29 children. One group had 14 children with 4 teachers; a second group, 15 children with 5 teachers.

All experimental-group children began attending the center between 6 and 12 weeks of age. The curriculum within the center is individually prescribed for children and is designed to encourage development in the areas of perception and cognition, language, social development, and motor development. A description of the development and specific content of the infants' curriculum has recently been presented by Sparling (Note 3), and by Ramey, Collier, Sparling, Loda, Campbell, Ingram, and Finkelstein (1976).

Apparatus

The apparatus for the discrimination-learning task consisted of a simple wooden box approximately 33.02 cm long, 10.16 cm high, and 10.16 cm wide. One end of the box was left open. A small slot was cut along the top of the box. Onto this slot were placed two wooden geometric shapes, a square and a triangle. Each of these shapes had a base of 5.08 cm, a height of 5.08 cm, and was 3.81 cm thick. Either of the stimuli could be attached to a pedestal that fitted through the slot and prevented the form from being removed from the top of the box.

Procedure

Each child was tested on a two-choice visual-discrimination task in a context that was familiar to him. The center-attending children were tested on this task in their classrooms, whereas the home-reared children were tested in their homes. These settings were chosen because one purpose of this experiment was to examine the children's learning performance in the settings where most waking time was spent each day; i.e., the procedure was designed to measure the child's rate of acquisition in his typical daily environment.

Each child was seated on the lap of a familiar adult (teacher or mother) facing the apparatus and the examiner who was equally unfamiliar to all the children. For one-half of the children, the square was the correct stimulus and for the other half, the triangle was correct. Left–right position of the stimulus pairs over trials was randomized using the Gellerman (1933) series. The correct stimulus was coated with a sweetened water solution and was removable from the box. Thus, reinforcement was available if the child brought the shape to his mouth. This procedure is similar to one described by Ling (1941). If the child did not put the correct stimulus into his mouth, he was reinforced with sugar-coated cereal. On all correct trials, verbal praise was also used. A trial was defined by the child's first touch or grasp of one and only one of the stimuli. Between trials the experimenter rearranged the stimuli behind a screen designed to simulate a modified Wisconsin General Test Apparatus. The criterion performance was 5 consecutive correct responses. The probability of 5 consecutive correct responses by chance alone is .03. The procedure was terminated if the child did not reach criterion within 70 trials.

For the younger subjects in this experiment, the Bayley Scales of Infant Development were administered when the infants were 6 months of age in a standard laboratory setting equally unfamiliar to experimental and control subjects. For the older subjects, the Bayley Scales were administered in the same setting at 18 months. These assessments were made by an individual not associated with the collection of the discrimination-learning data. All Bayley Scales were administered with the child's mother present.

We hypothesized that children receiving the early educational program would, in comparison to a control group: (a) learn the discrimination task in fewer trials than the control children, (b) require fewer trials to criterion at 18 months than at 7 months, (c) have higher scores on the Mental Development Index of the Bayley Scales at 6 and 18 months of age, (d) score more superiorly to the control group on the Bayley Scales at 18 than at 6 months, and (e) that fewer trials–to–criterion would be required for children who scored higher on the Bayley Scales.

The basic rationale for hypotheses a through d is that the day-care curriculum's emphasis on cognitive skills will have begun to have a positive effect on center-attending children in the first year of life. The positive effect will take the form of preventing intellectual decline and cognitive deficit from occurring. The control group, on the other hand, will begin to differ from the experimental group during the first year of life due to insufficient environmental supports to sustain a "normal" intellectual growth rate. We further hypothesized that the difference between the two groups will become larger during the second year because the control group will fall even further behind the experimental group. The rationale for hypothesis e is simply that there is a positive relationship between general developmental status as assessed by the Bayley Scales and the rate of acquisition of a simple discrimination in a novel learning task.

Results

Preliminary Analyses for the Effects of Nutrition

Because quality of nutrition has been associated with brain development (Coursin, 1972), it becomes important to demonstrate that nutritional differences between the experimental and control children are minimal if one wants to argue, as we do, that other components of the intervention program are responsible for the differences between the experimental and control groups on the Mental Development Index and in the discrimination-learning task. Data relevant to this question were obtained by comparing the Bayley Scale scores and discrimination-learning trials–to–criterion of children who were either above or below the 25th percentile for weight when the children were 1 year of age. First, overall comparisons on the Bayley Scale performance and trials–to–criterion were made by dichotomizing children into two groups: (a) above the 25th percentile for weight at 12 months of age and (b) below the 25th percentile. Second, the scores on the same two measures were compared for experimental- and control-group children who were below the 25th percentile for weight at 12 months of age.

The rationale for these comparisons is that if children were suffering from serious malnourishment, this would be reflected by low weight for age. Further, if nutrition were a factor that was contributing to the *differential* performance of the experimental and control groups then there should be a difference in the number of children who fell below the 25th percentile in those two groups with the control group containing more of those children.

The results revealed that for the discrimination-learning performance, there was no indirect evidence from the children's weights and task performance that seems to implicate nutritional differences as a plausible explanatory factor for treatment-group differences. Further, although there was an association between weight for age and Bayley performance, this finding does not appear to affect differentially the experimental and control group in the discrimination task.

Discrimination-Learning Task Results

Table 3 presents the means and standard deviations (*SD*s) of the trials-to-criterion by groups and ages. These data were analyzed using a 2 (Group) × 2 (Age) analysis of variance. The results of that analysis revealed a significant group main effect ($F = 5.70$, 1/43 *df*, $p < .02$), indicating that the experimental group reached criterion in fewer trials than did the control group. The main effect for age was not significant nor was the Age × Group interaction. Thus, the significant group main effect supports the first hypothesis concerning the relative superiority of the experimental group. However, the nonsignificant Age × Group interaction failed to support the second hypothesis that experimental-group children would perform even better at 18 months relative to the control-group children than they had at 7 months. From Table 3 it can be seen that the trend, while in the predicted direction, is not significant.

TABLE 3
MEANS AND STANDARD DEVIATIONS (*SD*s) OF TRIALS-TO-CRITERION ON DISCRIMINATION-LEARNING TASK

Group/Age of children	Trials-to-criterion	
	Mean	*SD*
Experimental[a]		
7 months	27.08	18.36
18 months	19.15	18.61
Control[b]		
7 months	37.18	25.49
18 months	38.36	21.94

[a] $N = 12$ for 7 month olds, 13 for 18 month olds.
[b] $N = 11$ for both age groups.

Bayley Scale Results

The results from the Bayley Scales suggest that the intervention program is being successful in preventing the anticipated decline in intellectual performance. Table 4 presents the means and *SD*s for the experimental and control subjects at 6 and 18 months of age.

TABLE 4
MEANS AND STANDARD DEVIATIONS (*SD*s) OF THE CHILDREN'S MENTAL DEVELOPMENT INDEX SCORES OF THE BAYLEY SCALES OF INFANT DEVELOPMENT

Group/Age of children	Score	
	Mean	*SD*
Experimental[a]		
6 months	106.00	19.99
18 months	101.82	12.36
Control[b]		
6 months	104.08	15.79
18 months	85.82	10.42

[a] $N = 12$ for 6 month olds, 13 for 18 month olds.
[b] $N = 11$ for both age groups.

Differences between the Bayley Mental Development Index means were analyzed using a 2 (Group) × 2 (Age) analysis of variance. Results of that analysis revealed a significant main effect for group ($F = 6.29$, 1/43 *df*, $p < .02$). An examination of Table 4 reveals a mean Mental Development Index difference of 1.92 points, favoring the experimental group at 6 months of age. Both means, however, are well within the normal range. At 18 months the mean Mental Development Index difference was 16.00 points, favoring the experimental group. Further, the control group at this point was performing at a level that causes concern about their overall developmental status. Although this would seem to indicate that the control group was trending downward over time, the Group × Age interaction failed to reach traditional levels of statistical significance. Further, the main effect for age approached but did not reach significance either. Thus, these findings support hypothesis c but fail to offer strong support for hypothesis d, although the trend was in the predicted direction. Nevertheless, it is clear that the experimental group generally was performing at a superior level relative to the control group on the Mental Development Index of the Bayley Scales.

Correlations among Measures

The trials-to-criterion performance for each subject was correlated with his Bayley Scale Mental Development Index. The Bayley Scales had been administered when the child was either 6 or 18 months of age. Separate correlations were calculated for each age group. The 6-month Bayley scores were unrelated to learning performance at 7 months; however, at 18 months there was a significant correlation ($r = -.49$, 22 *df*, $p < .02$), indicating that infants with higher Mental Development Index scores reached criterion in fewer trials. To examine this relationship more closely, we computed separate correlations for experimental and control children at 18 months. These analyses revealed no statistically reliable relationship between measures for the control group. A moderately strong relationship obtained for experimental subjects ($r = -.71$, 11 *df*, $p < .01$). Thus, these results support hypothesis e concerning the relationship between Bayley Scores and trials-to-criterion but suggest that the relationship is stronger at 18 months of age and for experimental group subjects who scored higher on both measures.

Discussion

The results from both the Bayley Scales and from the discrimination-learning task are provocative. It is noteworthy that early child-centered educational intervention has resulted in measurable intellectual performance differences in the first 18 months of life for severely disadvantaged infants. These differences emerged both in the standardized test data and in the more process-oriented discrimination-learning data. Although the group main effects were significant in both analyses, suggesting that there tended to be significant differences at both measurement ages, the predicted Group × Age interactions failed to reach significance, although the means for the anticipated trends across ages were in predicted directions.

Because analyses of both the standardized-test data and the discrimination-learning data revealed very similar results, there is not adequate evidence at this time to conclude that one measure is more sensitive to performance differences than the other.

The correlation between performance on the Bayley Scales and performance on the discrimination-learning task indicate that although there is considerable overlap in the two measures they are far from redundant. Further, the discrepancy between the correlations for the experimental and control groups is puzzling: a significant correlation between the two measures existed only at 18 months of age and only for the experimental-group subjects who tended to score better than control-group subjects on both measures. One possible explanation for this finding is that the more developmentally advanced experimental-group children have learned through their various curriculum experiences how to react to situations that require a problem-solving set. Thus, not only are they intellectually more advanced generally but their history of preacademic experiences allows them to make better use of their intelligence in a problem-solving situation. If this explanation concerning better use of intellectual abilities is valid, then one might expect a higher relationship between the two tasks for the experimental group.

Reference Notes

1. Bronfenbrenner, U. *Is early intervention effective?* Paper presented at the biennial meeting of the Society for Research in Child Development, Philadelphia, March 1973.
2. Ramey, C. T., Holmberg, M. C., Sparling, J. J., & Collier, A. M. An introduction to the Carolina Abecedarian Project. In B. M. Caldwell (Ed.), *Infant education* (Monograph). Frank Porter Graham Child Development Center, Chapel Hill, NC, 1976.
3. Sparling, J. Carolina infant curriculum. In C. Heriza (Ed.), *Proceedings of a conference on the comprehensive management of infants at risk for CNS deficits.* School of Medicine, University of North Carolina, Chapel Hill, 1975.

References

Coursin, D. B. Nutrition and brain development in infants. *Merrill-Palmer Quarterly,* 1972, 18, 177-202.

Gellerman, L. W. Chance orders of alternating stimuli in visual discrimination experiments. *Journal of Genetic Psychology,* 1933, 42, 206-208.

Heber, R. F., Dever, R. B., & Conry, J. The influence of environmental and genetic variables on intellectual development. In H. S. Prehm, L. A. Hamerlynck, & J. E. Crossman (Eds.), *Behavioral research in mental retardation.* Eugene: University of Oregon Press, 1968.

Ling, B. C. Form discrimination as a learning cue in infants. *Comparative Psychology Monographs,* 1941, 17, No. 86.

Ramey, C. T., Collier, A. M., Sparling, J. J., Loda, R. A., Campbell, F. A., Ingram, D. L., & Finkelstein, N. W. The Carolina Abecedarian Project: A longitudinal and multidisciplinary approach to the prevention of developmental retardation. In T. Tjossem (Ed.), *Intervention strategies for high-risk infants and young children.* Baltimore: University Park Press, 1976.

Stedman, D., Anastasiow, N., Dokecki, P., Gordon, I., & Parker, R. How can effective early intervention programs be delivered to potentially retarded children. *Monographs of Council on Exceptional Children,* in press.

child development/ day care resources project–new materials to aid day care programs

ronald k. parker

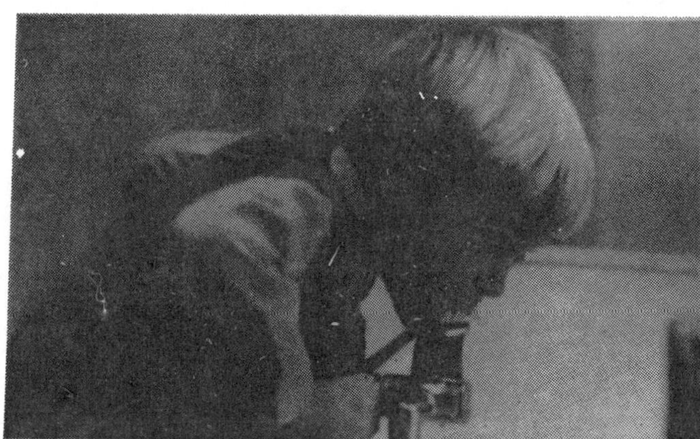

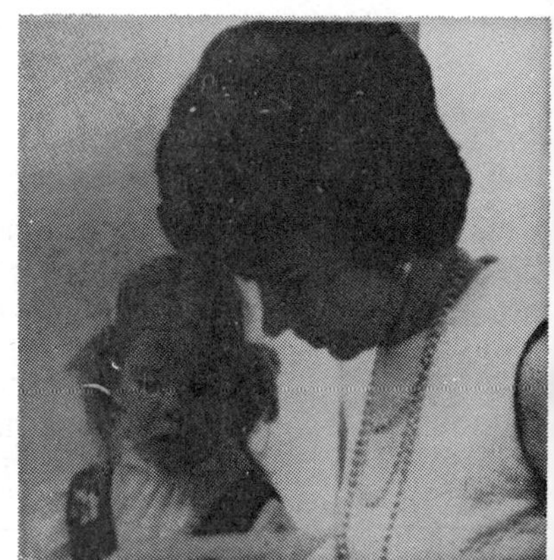

Over 200 national experts were involved in developing resources to help ensure quality day care programs for the nation. A review of day care resources on training and staff development, programs, and curricular and resource materials, by Ronald K. Parker, revealed a need to provide a national structure for interdisciplinary child development projects and broad scale delivery systems.

"Child Development/Day Care Resources Project--New Materials To Aid Day Care Programs", Ronald K. Parker, *Not All Little Wagons Are Red,* 1973, published by The Council for Exceptional Childrn.

THE IMPORTANCE OF ADEQUATE PREPARATION

□ One of the problems with large scale federal programs is that they often appear full blown without the necessary background work having been done. In the human resources area, the results of such a lack of preparation can be disastrous—not only in terms of wasting funds but, more importantly, of also failing to mount good programs for social betterment. If we take Head Start as an example, it is easy to see in retrospect that a better program would have been inaugurated in 1965 if more careful planning had been done prior to the appropriation of operational funds. Unfortunately, the end result of inadequate preparation can be that many potentially good human resource programs go through a fatal three stage cycle: (a) they are started too hastily and so do not rest on solid foundations, (b) subsequent evaluations reveal—sometimes too late—that they are seriously lacking in a number of important respects, and (c) as a consequence, the nation becomes disillusioned, and the programs lose the crucial support of the federal government.

Ill prepared programs are often found lacking, and ultimately lose public and governmental support.

A PROJECT TO INVESTIGATE DAY CARE SERVICES

□ Recognizing that day care would probably expand at a very rapid rate during the present decade, the Office of Economic Opportunity and the Office of Child Development in June, 1970, agreed to fund a project (Grant H 9708) with the avowed purpose of summarizing everything known about how to provide good day care services for children of all ages. The rationale for this decision was a desire to avoid the launching of yet another huge federal program in the human resources area in which the necessary previous steps in planning and preparation had not been satisfactorily worked out. In fact, as early as August, 1969, the original impetus for what was eventually to become this jointly backed venture was given by the education committee of the President's Science Advisory Committee in a recommendation to the President that the above type of undertaking be carried out on a relatively small scale. Additional impetus was supplied by the fact that several pieces of federal legislation were pending which, if passed, would provide millions of dollars for day care programs. The one thing lacking was the availability of child development and day care resources to ensure that program operators could take advantage of current knowledge before day care expanded nationally.

The Child Development/Day Care Resources Project represented a major step by the federal government to ensure this. The government's aim in funding the project was twofold: (a) to use nonfederal talent in developing a series of materials demonstrating quality day care programs and (b) to make these materials available to those persons affected by a rapid expansion of day care in the United States.

FOUR MAJOR OBJECTIVES

□ The Child Development/Day Care Resources Project, directed by Ronald K. Parker, had the following objectives:

1. To develop a statement of principles that can serve as a useful guideline to the operation of day care programs.
2. To develop a set of handbooks that describe the features common to good child development and education programs for use in day care and to include effective curriculum models from current practice.
3. To develop an additional set of handbooks that deal with day care administration, parent involvement, health services, and training.
4. To modify current resources in child development, early education, and day care in order to help improve existing programs and to aid in the spread of good day care services throughout the nation.

These day care resources were developed to aid program operators both within and outside the context of day care settings. In a word, practical resources were developed for parents and professionals interested in child development. Finally, the principles underlying these resources make them applicable to all children, including those from various socioeconomic backgrounds and children with various degrees of special problems. These materials then should be of special importance to the membership of The Council for Exceptional Children.

The project resources were produced by three groups: consultants at a summer workshop, experts in curriculum development working on subcontracts, and the full time staff of the project. The project resources may be classified into the following categories: principles statement,[1] handbooks,[1] child development resources,[2] and reviews.[2]

A principles statement was to serve as guideline.

A *Statement of Principles* was prepared under the chairmanship of Urie Brofenbrenner for presentation to the 1970 White House Conference on Children. The contents of this document can be summarized as follows:

- The basic needs of the child (health and nutrition, security, freedom, structure, compassion, developmental differences, challenge).
- The implications of needs for programing (knowledge of child development, comprehensiveness, health care, cognitive development, esteem for self and others, freedom within structure, identification of children with special problems, importance of parental involvement, importance of familiar people, role of

[1]Available from the US Government Printing Office, Washington, D. C. 20402.

[2]Available from the individual authors.

older children in the development of the young, programs appropriate to older children, family day care programs).

- Economic and social change (child development services as a right, day care and the industrial world, continuity with the child's cultural background, program control, the role of the community, day care as a social institution).
- Administration (the "open" day care setting, diversity in programs, coordination, physical facilities and equipment, selection of personnel, training).

Handbooks were developed to detail the features of good day care programs . . .

Seven handbooks[3] were written to help program operators provide high quality day care. Three of the handbooks were on the subject of child development and dealt, respectively, with the fields of infancy, preschool, and school age. Each handbook presents the salient features of good program practice with a strong emphasis on how to put these good features into practice. The preschool handbook included a second volume profiling effective program models that can either be adopted in their entirety or adapted by child development personnel to local needs. The three handbooks are: *Child Development/Day Care: Serving Infants* (Huntington, D. S., Provence, S., & Parker, R. K. [Eds.], 1971), *Child Development/Day Care: Serving Preschool Children* (Parker, R. K., & Ambron, S. R. [Eds.], Vols. I & II, 1972), *Child Development/Day Care: Serving School Age Children* (Cohen, D., Parker, R. K., Host, M. S., & Richards, C. [Eds.], 1972).

The other four handbooks were on the subjects of training, administration, parental involvement, and health. They include: *Child Development/Day Care: Staff Training* (Parker, R. K., & Dittmann, L. [Eds.], 1972), *Child Development/Day Care: Administration* (Host, M. S., & Heller, P. B. [Eds.], 1972), *Parent Participation in Day Care: Principles and Programs* (Hoffman, D., Jordan, J., Moore, B., & McCormick, F. [Eds.], 1971),[4] and *Child Development/Day Care Health Services: A Guide for Project Directors and Health Personnel* (North, A. F., Jr. [Ed.], 1972).

The project engendered child development resources to aid in the improvement of existing programs and to expand new services.

More than two dozen monographs, books, manuals, and curricula were developed to meet the fourth objective of the project: "to modify current resources in child development, early education, and day care in order to improve existing programs and to aid in the spread of good day care services throughout the nation."

Day care resources may be classified into three areas: (a) training and staff development, (b) day care programs and curricula, and (c) day care resource materials.

Infancy.

Infancy. Irving Lazar of Cornell University completed a lengthy manual which had been written in draft form prior to the inception of this project. Appearing under the title of *An Infant Care Training Manual,* it includes the general information on various facets of training caregivers.

Alice S. Honig and J. Ronald Lally of Syracuse University developed a manual which capitalized on the work done in the Huntington, Provence, and Parker infancy handbook and in Lazar's infant care training manual. The unique contribution of the Honig &

[3] *Child Development/Day Care: Serving Special Children* was added to this series in 1972 by the Office of Child Development.

[4] Available only from Avatar Press, P. O. Box 7727, Atlanta, Georgia 30309.

Lally publication, entitled *Infancy Caregiving: A Training Handbook,* is that it offers infant caregivers a single theoretical framework (Piagetian) within which to operate.

Preschool.

Preschool. Ronald K. Parker edited a series of over 70 booklets to be used in day care and staff development programs. The series as a whole appears under the title of *Day Care Staff Development and Training Program.*[5] Each booklet is about 1,000 words in length, focusing on a single topic in child development and written at a high school English level.

William C. Sheppard, Steven B. Shank, and Darla Wilson of the University of Oregon wrote a manual, *How to Be a Good Teacher,* designed to meet a special need—namely, helping teachers to understand the principles of learning and the modification of behavior.

Merle Karnes, University of Illinois, prepared a monograph entitled *How to Implement the Karnes Curriculum,* within the context of a preschool day care setting.

Shari Nedler, University of Texas, produced the following three monographs designed to help train day care operators and early childhood educators: *Behavioral Objectives: Instructor's Manual, Creating a Learning Environment,* and *Teacher Expectations.*

Family Day Care.

Family Day Care. Esther Cole, New York City Day Care Council, served as editor and coordinator of *The New York City Family Day Care Careers Program Manual.* The manual recounts not only what happened to this program, but how it happened. In so doing, it covers the following topics: history; administrative structure and funding; work of the policy advisory committee; homefinding, licensing, and supervision; job development and training (for career mothers); health and education; and evaluation and research.

Day care programs and curricula

Subcontracts were awarded to program developers who, in the judgment of the advisory committee, had developed effective program/curriculum models even though their materials were not yet ready for national distribution. The explicit purpose of the subcontracts was to make these resources available more quickly to everyone who could use them. In the typical case, many years and large sums of money had already gone into the development of such material; however, with the impetus of a project subcontract, the developer was enabled to write up a detailed description of his program/curriculum for almost immediate use.

A qualifying statement should be made here. The rationale for the awarding of subcontracts was not that the programs involved were necessarily considered to have the best ongoing curricula. Actually, many good programs were available for national distribution when this project was initiated. Rather, the purpose was to bring apparently effective programs that were in an ongoing stage to quick fruition. This may also help to explain why other programs of equal merit were not chosen for subcontracting. Simply stated, they were not yet in a state to be written up in final form at the time when project subcontracts were awarded.

Infancy.

Infancy. Earl S. Schaefer, University of North Carolina, and Father Paul H. Furfey, Catholic University, received the necessary support to detail their program for infancy, *Infant Curriculum: Ages One to Three.*

In *A Day Care Instructor's Manual and Preschool Training Curriculum,* Francis H. Palmer, State University of New York at

[5]Available from Curriculum Development, 144 W. 125 Street, New York, New York 10027.

Stony Brook, developed a cognitive curriculum for 2 and 3 year old children.

Preschool.

Preschool. Barbara Biber, Edna Shapiro, David Wickens, and Elizabeth Gilkeson have described one aspect of the Bank Street approach to early education in a monograph entitled *Promoting Cognitive Growth from a Developmental-Interaction Point of View.*

Robert P. Boger, Michigan State University, provided two publications on child development and education—the first dealing with classification, the second with socialization: *The Adaptation of Classification and Attention Training Lessons for Day Care Programming* and *The Adaptation of Socialization Inputs for Day Care Programming (Parts I and II).*

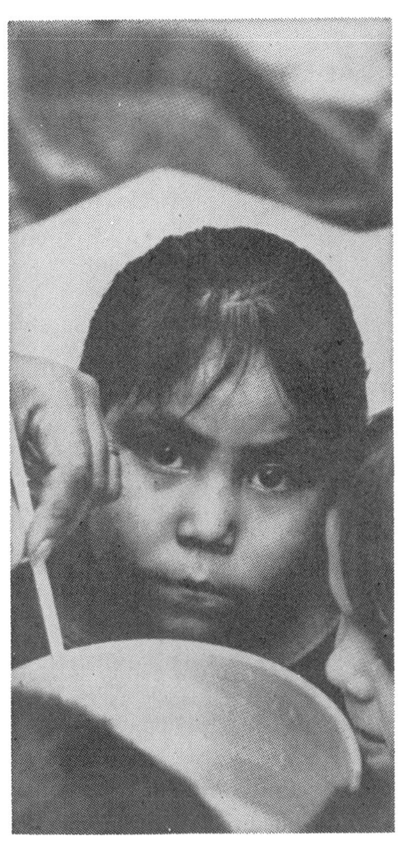

In a monograph entitled *The Use of the Black Experience by the Day Care Center: Enhancing Individual and Family Functioning,* Manuel L. Jackson (Chicago, Illinois) described how the "black experience" can be used productively by a day care center with respect to the child as well as to his parents.

Merle B. Karnes' products describe all facets of the Karnes curriculum developed at the University of Illinois in Champaign. These publications cover the fields of art, cognitive (Guilford) activities, language, mathematics, music, directed play, science, and social studies.

In a publication entitled *The Mother-Child Program,* Phyllis Levenstein (30 Albany Avenue, Freeport, New York 11520) modified her parent involvement program so that it would be better suited for use in day care.

Shari Nedler, University of Texas, described the Southwest Educational Development Laboratory's curriculum in a volume entitled *All about the Early Childhood Program.*

Glen P. Nimnicht and his colleagues—Edna Brown, Stan Johnson, and Bertha Addison—at the Far West Laboratory for Educational Research and Development described a program for parent involvement in *The Parent/Child Toy-Lending Library.* Its content included a large sampling of games, toys, and equipment.

Herbert A. Sprigle, Jacksonville, Florida, received project support that enabled him to extend his Learning to Learn Program downward to meet the needs of younger children. His publication was entitled *Discovering How to Learn.*

School Age.

School Age. The following two publications describe approaches to school age day care: *Proposal for Work-Oriented Program for School Age Children* by William Van der Does and *A School Age Day Care Activity Program for Five-to Ten-Year Old Children* by Docia C. Zavitkovsky.

Audiovisual.

Resource materials

Audiovisual. Ira J. Gordon, University of Florida, produced four videotape prototypes of training operations which demonstrate ways to teach a paraprofessional to train surrogate mothers using presently existing curricula. The tape series is entitled *Infant Education in a Family Day Care Home: Some Prototypes.*

Frank S. Joseph and Robert Clayton (Children's Hospital, Washington, D. C.) developed for audiovisual presentation three series of tape cassettes with accompanying scripts on health care for various ages in a day care setting. The length is approximately 20 minutes each.

Shari Nedler produced three filmstrips with accompanying audiotapes which were designed to implement her early childhood program. They are *Behavioral Objectives–Early Childhood* (9 minutes), *Environment for Learning* (15 minutes), and *Two and*

After (20 minutes).

Research for Better Schools, Inc. of Philadelphia developed a slide and tape presentation entitled *Child Care Outlook for the Seventies,* which presents an overview of future day care needs in this country and some of the avenues open to program developers and operators for meeting these needs.

Reviews. *Reviews.* Bettye M. Caldwell, University of Arkansas, produced a monograph which reviews on a nationwide basis current standards for day care. It is entitled *Day Care Standards: A National Survey.*

In *Day Care and Intervention Programs for Infants,* Marshall M. Haith reviewed and critiqued all of the infant day care programs currently in operation. His publication served as background work for the Infant Committee of the summer workshop.[6]

Jennifer Howse, Florida State University, surveyed how mobile facilities can be used in preschool instruction. The basic purpose of her publication, *Preschool Instruction in Mobile Facilities: Description and Analysis,*[7] was to suggest the means for delivering day care to isolated rural children.

Robert E. LaCrosse, Jr., Pacific Oaks College, wrote a monograph to provide HEW/OCD with a frame of reference on day care. Entitled *Day Care: Effects and Affects,* his report focused on program accountability and cost/benefit factors.

Ronald K. Parker and Jane Knitzer prepared a comprehensive publication for the White House Conference on Children. Entitled *Day Care and Preschool Services: Trends in the Nineteen-Sixties and Issues for the Nineteen-Seventies,*[8] it focused on the following subjects:

1. An Assessment — past and current practice (rationale for an early childhood focus), child care arrangements, day care and preschool capacity, enrollment patterns, caste and class, quality of existing programs and models, the role of the US government.
2. Planning for the Seventies — issues and options (child care services: for whom?), financing child care service, the question of auspices, the challenge of quality, coordination and linkage.
3. Summary and Conclusions—agenda for the seventies.

Texts. *Texts.* Bettye M. Caldwell, University of Arkansas, received partial project support for the preparation of two texts on child care. They are *Educational Day Care for Infants and Young Children* and *Readings on Day Care.*

Stanley Coopersmith, University of California, Davis, compiled and edited a collection of articles that were written especially for this project. It is entitled *The Affective Component in Early Education: Developing Motivation in Young Children.*

A number of action recommendations should be given high priority by the federal government in its ventures into the field of child development and day care. These recommendations apply to three interrelated areas of need—programs and components, training and delivery systems, and a national institute of child development.

[6]Available from Avatar Press, P. O. Box 7727, Atlanta, Georgia 30309.

[7]Available only from Southeastern Educational Laboratory, 1750 Old Springhouse Lane, Atlanta, Georgia 30341.

[8]Available from Avatar Press, P. O. Box 7727, Atlanta, Georgia 30309.

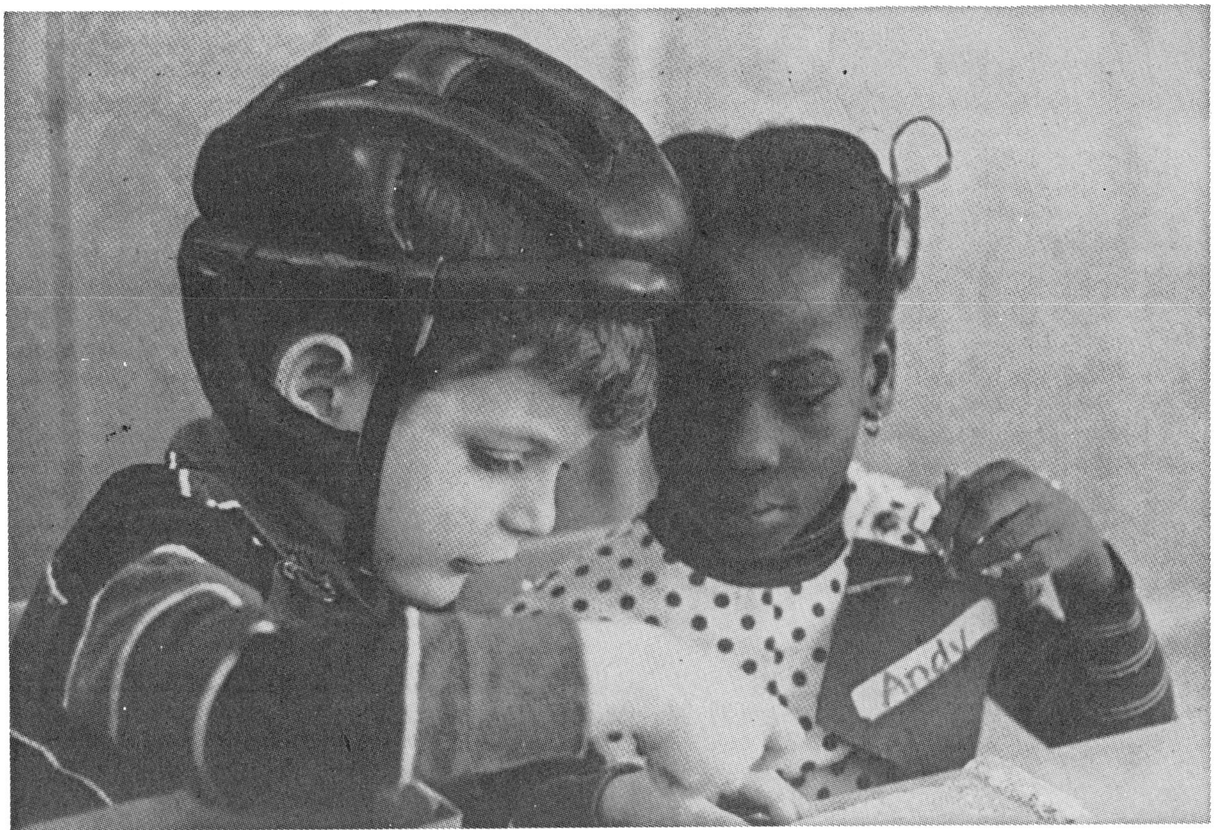

PROGRAMS AND COMPONENTS

□ After an indepth survey of current practices in day care, the project leaders identified two key areas where developmental efforts should take place as soon as possible. First, high quality school age day care programs are almost nonexistent in this country. Funds should therefore be supplied to create a fresh approach to this particular area of day care which goes well beyond the custodial or recreational thrust usually associated with such efforts. Second, the Minority/Parent Committee sensitized the summer workshop to the need for, and importance of, ethnic components as an integral part of day care programs. The development of these components offers the surest guarantee that minority children will come to feel a greater sense of pride in their cultural heritage and ethnic background. Although this need exists among all ethnic and racial groups, it is particularly acute in the case of Black, Chicano, Puerto Rican, and American Indian children. Programs offering bilingual and multilingual components help not only the minority child but also children from the dominant culture to understand, appreciate, and accept cultural and ethnic differences.

. . . and teach children from the dominant culture to understand and appreciate cultural and ethnic differences.

TRAINING AND DELIVERY SYSTEMS

□ While the Parker & Dittman training handbook offers a conceptual overview of training areas, practical resources are still needed to provide pre- and inservice training to day care professionals. The materials edited by Ronald K. Parker in the series entitled *Day Care Staff Development and Training Program* represent a step in the right direction, but they need to be expanded upon. This can be done by the inclusion of more topics, additional media, and individual microteaching and roleplaying units.

Also of importance is the fact that appropriate resources have not been developed which can deliver day care services to the consumer on a broad scale. Most of the work in this field has focused on the question of how to operate an individual center. Plans must be instituted to design, install, and maintain day care systems so that

Plans must be instituted to design total delivery day care systems.

children of all ages can be serviced, be they of urban or rural origin. In setting up such total delivery systems, operators must address themselves to the following considerations: site selection, construction or renovation, management, quality control through the monitoring of all program components, and accountability to suppliers of funds and to recipients of services.

A NATIONAL INSTITUTE OF CHILD DEVELOPMENT

□ In our view, a national institute of child development needs to be established for the purpose of providing a national structure for interdisciplinary projects in child development. This institute, which should operate as a nonprofit corporation *outside* the federal government, could quickly mobilize talent from all parts of the country to meet a variety of national, state, and city needs.

The success of our project has demonstrated the value in breaking down traditional institutional and agency barriers in order to get a job done. This is probably even more the case if the job happens to be, as ours was, complex and wideranging. Three current needs can be cited by way of illustrating the kinds of projects that such an institute might undertake.

An interdisciplinary effort needs to be made to provide every mother, every day care worker, and every nursery school teacher with an understanding of all facets of infant and early childhood development.

First, an interdisciplinary effort needs to be made to provide every mother, every day care worker, and every nursery school teacher with an understanding of all facets of infant and early childhood development. This can be done effectively through the medium of television. *Sesame Street* has already pointed the way by its success in capturing a large audience of children. Using similar techniques, a similarly large (if not larger) audience of mothers, day care workers, and other concerned individuals can be given the training they need in making the home a more meaningful

educational environment for young children. Operating on a nationwide basis, the cost of such programs would be minimal and, once developed, could have a tremendous impact on Western culture and the future lives of the young.

Within the organizational framework, a national institute of child development should function similarly to the current Child Development/Day Care Resources Project by having an advisory board whose membership would be composed of leading figures in the fields of psychology, education, health, and communications. The initial task of the board would be to set up a number of interdisciplinary advisory committees, comprised of expert consultants in all facets of child development, whose role would be to provide guidance in the development of resource materials. Terminal resource products would include TV color films and backup printed materials in the form of guides. The latter would not only serve as a record of the films' contents but would also suggest practical ways in which the principles and ideas portrayed might best be applied.

To advance our knowledge in child development, a project should be undertaken to organize objectives for early education and to then assess their attainment.

Second, in order to advance our knowledge in applied child development and early education, a project should be undertaken to organize a comprehensive taxonomy of objectives for early education and child development beginning at infancy and continuing through the age of 6 years and to organize sets of dependent measures to assess the degree to which the objectives are attained (recommended to the Office of Child Development in November, 1970).

The purpose of a comprehensive taxonomy would be to help preschool educators in selecting whatever objectives they might be interested in as a first step toward the organization of a comprehensive education program. Many of the curricula that are currently available fail to meet local needs and, as a consequence, many of the curricula that are adopted by new program operators are either unplanned or poorly organized.

As far as a comprehensive battery of developmental dependent measures is concerned, its usefulness would be that it could enable one to *profile* a child's developmental levels rather than to be forced to rely on only a single index of development. Additionally, the child's progress could be monitored across time in all areas of development. In short, such a battery of measures would make possible a standard method of recording child development and behavior, a method of providing program content leads, and a sensitive method of evaluating early education programs.

Third, a national institute of child development could be responsible for the periodic revisions of all the child development and education handbooks produced by this project. The question of revisions is a major consideration in terms of systematically updating the present material to include new information and program models as they become available for national distribution.

Teaching Skills in Early Childhood Programs

NICHOLAS J. ANASTASIOW
GILBERT P. MANSERGH

Abstract: The recent growth of preschool programs for handicapped children has caused a search for models by which to construct total classroom programs. This article explores three models: behavior modification, normal developmental, and cognitive developmental. Similarities among the programs are drawn. Particularly, distinctions are made as to the necessary steps to meet the requirements of each approach.

***Nicholas J. Anastasiow** is Director and **Gilbert P. Mansergh** is Research Assistant, Institute for Child Study, Indiana University, Bloomington.* *Portions of this work were supported by Grant No. USOE-OE6-0-71-1079 from the US Office of Education, with Richard L. Turner the principal investigator.*

The role of early childhood education has taken on new meaning, particularly in special education, with the establishment of over 150 preschool model centers for the handicapped child. This article explores the same basic premise upon which early childhood programs are based and the major differences among three dominant philosophies of education.

One can define teacher skillfulness in early childhood education in many ways, and each set of descriptors has some advantages and disadvantages. Commonly, the usefulness of early childhood approaches has been evaluated by a prospective consumer on the child oriented versus teacher oriented dimensions. The advocates of child oriented programs typically have assumed that the child has control of his own learning in an environment where the teacher acts as a facilitator or stimulator of pupil development. On the other hand, the advocates of an extreme teacher oriented position have assumed that the child must receive training in an environment in which the teacher directs, leads, or instructs. Here, the teacher is perceived as the one who makes input into the child by the manner in which "lessons" are conducted.

Although much heat has been generated over the efficacy of these two extremes, few if any exemplars of either the child or teacher oriented approach exist. Bank Street and the University of California at Los Angeles demonstration school probably come the closest to the child oriented approach, and the school district kindergarten in most areas of the United States comes closest to the teacher oriented approach. Most American education consists of the cultural transmission of knowledge but varies on the dimension of how to transmit that knowledge.

"Teaching Skills In Early Childhood Programs:", Nicholas J. Anastasiow, Gilbert P. Mansersh, *Exceptional Children,* Vol. 41, No. 5, February 1975, © 1975 The Council For Exceptional Children.

Program Diversities and Similarities

The curriculum materials or teacher guides available in early childhood centers reveal great similarities in content among supposedly diverse schools of thought. Most early childhood education programs are primarily concerned with the learning of appropriate school behavior and attitudes—taking turns, standing in line, sitting in groups, raising hands, responding to questions, completing tasks—as well as the learning of concept pairs (such as up-down, in-out, over-under, right-left) and the names of objects. Regardless of the philosophy of the program, most teacher guides contain a list of concepts to be attained (names of colors being almost universal), self help skills, and some comments about motor, language, emotional, and cognitive development. Further, in most every program, movable floor toys and paints and puzzles can be found, along with a climbing apparatus and an outdoor playground.

It is in the manner in which the toys and equipment are used for instruction that the programs vary the most. At one extreme, the toy is presented to the child by the teacher, who asks him to identify it. At the other extreme, the child is encouraged to manipulate or play with the toys to "discover" their properties. In addition, major differences exist among educators in the amount of play recommended and the use of small or large group instructional patterns.

The point to be made is that our analyses of early childhood programs reveal that there is high agreement on the instructional content and materials to be used. Where early childhood educators differ is in the techniques they select to "teach" children.

The critical continuum along which to determine differences among early childhood programs is how the child is perceived as a learner. We propose that this hypothetical continuum ranges from one extreme of those who perceive the child as a passive receptor (a behavioristic program which would use drill and small step procedures) to the other extreme of those who perceive the child as the active transactor (a program which would use discovery or guided discovery). At one end of the continuum we place the behaviorally oriented programs and at the other end, the cognitive developmentalists. We have chosen the term *cognitive developmental* because the word *cognitive* implies a desire by some educators to make inferences about the internal life of the child (i.e., the actions of the brain).

It should be pointed out that there are many types of developmental theorists. There are the traditional age-stage descriptions of McGraw, Gesell, Spock, Shirley, and Hilgard. These developmentalists have provided, usually from observations of children, lists of when young children can accomplish skills, such as buttoning a coat, riding a bicycle, or cutting with scissors. Educators who have derived programs from these developmentalists suggest that teaching in the main should introduce an activity as near as possible to the time when most children can accomplish the skill involved. However, developmental psychology and proponents of cognitive developmental programs basically claim to have derived their curriculum from a Piagetian point of view rather than from Gesell and the earlier developmentalists.

Differences between Behaviorism and Cognitive Developmentalism

The major differences between the behaviorist and the cognitive developmental positions are in how they (a) describe the child as a learner on the active-passive dimension and (b) view cognitive hierarchies, i.e., the behaviorally oriented learning theorist Gagne views the hierarchies to be developed through instruction, and developmental theorist Piaget believes the child constructs his own hierarchies. Further, the cognitive approach deviates most sharply from the behaviorist in the cognitive developmentalist's hypothesis that there are internal, innate mechanisms available for thought.

Use of Reinforcement and Social Learning Principles

Mistakenly, the behaviorist and cognitive developmentalist have appeared to differ concerning the efficacy of reinforcement and social learning principles (imitation, modeling, and rewards). We believe that this is not a "real" issue, as the cognitive developmentalist uses positive social reinforcement and provides models for imitation.

Rather, it is in the manner of sequencing reinforcement and the use of primary natural reinforcers that the behaviorist and cognitive developmentalist differ. The cognitive developmentalist appears to have incorporated into his theory (sometimes unknowingly) the basic tenets of behaviorism or social learning theory. Largely, the cognitive developmentalist has used principles of behavior modification to enable the developing child to master the specific content of the culture into which he is born (for example, English rather than French). The critical difference between the two theoretical approaches is how much beyond the behaviorist the cognitive developmentalist wishes to speculate about the internal life of the child.

BELMONT COLLEGE LIBRARY

Structure in Planning

Given the above distinctions between the theories, it should be clear that the major differences in how the theories are translated into practice lie in the nature of the "structure" the teacher is to provide in daily classroom activities and in the amount of structure.

In our opinion, there has been great confusion and misunderstanding over the use of structure as it applies to a teacher's activity. All early childhood programs that qualify as programs and not as babysitting arrangements have some structure. The behaviorist teacher has a highly structured set of lesson plans, specifying goals and objectives for each child. The behaviorist view requires the teacher to structure lessons into small sequential steps. These lessons cover social management as well as concept attainment. Likewise, the cognitive developmental program requires that the teacher highly structure his plans for implementing the program. For instance, rooms must be arranged with the appropriate areas and materials so the child may transact with the environment in such a way as to develop, for example, the concept of conservation (conservation of mass or volume). Teachers are required to be skillful observers and must frequently plan and rearrange the environment based on how a child plays.

Where the two approaches differ is in what teachers do during instruction, not in the amount of planning and structuring the teachers engage in before instruction. Too often, we believe, the term *structure* has been confused with the term *authoritarian*, or amount of teacher control. Clearly, in the sense used here, structure relates to the degree to which the teacher must plan. Thus, it is proposed that early childhood programs of quite different philosophical and psychological orientations vary more on the dimension of how they perceive the child as a learner than they do on how much structure is required to carry out the program's goals.

Three Approaches along the Continuum

So far, we have discussed the two extremes of one continuum. Clearly many programs fall in between. We see what Evans (1971) refered to as "typical" or "traditional" preschool or kindergarten programs as falling in the middle ground. A typical classroom has preplanned curriculum, for example, a unit on the school, animals, or plants. While teachers are required to plan and set up the environment, this is not done with the same degree of structure as the behaviorist or developmentalist. Learning is predicted by the traditionalist to occur as a result of instruction, but teachers are not required to individualize or attempt to control (be responsible for) a child's mastery of concepts or social skills. To the traditionalist, most children will learn as a result of instruction. Those children who do not progress are said to be "not ready" or "emotionally insecure" or "from a difficult family."

For the purposes of this article one program of each type has been selected to represent the ends and middle point of the continuum. At one extreme we have placed the behavior modification groups. We have based our examples on the observations of the Nashville Regional Intervention Program project and the Contemporary School of Education in McLean, Virginia, as well as the work of Bandura (1971) and Hayden and her co-workers (Haring, Hayden, & Allen, 1961). For the normative developmental group, we have based our examples on our numerous observations of programs across the country and specifically the senior author's participation in the analyses of over 35 high risk intervention projects during the 1972 year (Stedman, Anastasiow, Dokecki, Gordon, & Parker, 1972). For the descriptions of the cognitive developmentalist group, we have been somewhat limited for few if any old "progressive" classes exist and few programs currently exist which have been adequately derived from Piaget.

The British open school approach bears a strong resemblance to the "progressive movement" which was popular in the United States during the 1920's and 1930's. As Dowley (1973) suggested, the teacher in the activity-type schools described by Dewey, Kilpatrick, and Hill and the teacher in the British open schools walks a narrow line between maintaining control over the curriculum and management of the classroom and allowing children to follow their own interests and develop in their own unique ways.

One characteristic the "good" progressive schools had in common was that the teacher, not the children, was always in charge. Without structure from the teacher, chaos resulted. We have, therefore, drawn what we feel to be reasonable goals in teacher training for anyone who would develop such a program and recognize that these goals may be a strong reflection of our own bias. We present a tentative grouping of some current examples of each group (see Table 1).

Behavior Modification Approach

The following is a description of those elements of the theory necessary to understand a behavior modification early childhood educational program. It is, of necessity, not all inclusive.

The behavior modification classroom approach is based on the premise that the child's skills development is dependent upon the nature of the environment and on a trainer. Environments are comprised of objects, places, and persons (or trainers). Trainers are any individuals such as parents, children, or teachers who attempt to shape or influence the child's adoption of a behavior. The behavior of children (or people in general) is perceived to be a direct result of training. In other words, all behavior is learned behavior, including such constructs as friendliness and cooperation as well as easily observable behaviors such as walking or sitting in a chair.

Behavior is defined as all those observable events emitted by a person. All nonobservable events such as motives, needs, and drives are not acceptable constructs in the theory. Frequently practitioners of behavior theory may draw upon "needs" or "reasons" in hypothesizing how to modify or shape a pupil's performance. However, these are not legitimate aspects of the theory and are perceived to be idiosyncratic features of a trainer's hypothesis making.

Further, of major importance to the theory is the hypothesis that all skills and complex behaviors of people are culturally determined. No innate structures are hypothesized and no internal structures are perceived to be available to the child prior to training. The only exceptions to this principle are the four survival motor mechanisms available to the child at birth: sucking, thrashing, head turning, and head lifting. In addition, perceptual abilities in primitive forms are available to process environmental input (hearing, seeing, touching, and tasting). Behavior is neither "good" nor "bad." It is culturally relevant in a dimension of its acceptability or desirability.

Assessment of Skill Level

Children are perceived to arrive at school with some degree of skill development in the areas of motor, socioemotional, language, and cognitive development. A teacher's prime responsibility is to be able to assess where on a continuum of skill development the child is operating. This diagnosis is based on a prior analysis of all skills into their smallest component parts. Each discrete step within skill development serves as a basis for diagnosis as well as a guide to teaching. That is, diagnosing where a child is on a continuum provides the teacher with the basis of determining where to begin instruction.

Thus, diagnosis and instruction are integrally related in the behavior modification approach. Each discrete step following the child's current attainment is to be taught sequentially and directly to the child at a pace at which the child can experience success according to a predescribed criterion. Usually the teacher will attempt to provide stimuli so that the child emits responses at a success rate that reaches 80% to 90% correct within a given lesson.

Reinforcement of Behavior

A reinforcer or reward is to be administered to a child who successfully masters the desired behavior set by the teacher. The primary reinforcer, in the theory, is food. All other rewards, such as social rewards, are perceived to be secondary rewards which are developed through interactions with previous trainers such as parents.

Following the child's response to the teacher's demands (e.g., "Hand me the red cup"), the teacher will administer an appropriate reward previously determined to be reinforcing to the child. A reinforcing condition is said to exist when the child models his behavior or emits the desired response following the presentation of the stimuli and contingent upon the reward. All rewards are provided to the child contingent upon the child's correct response based on a rate predetermined by the teacher as an acceptable criterion performance (e.g., hands teacher red cup four out of five times upon verbal request to do so). Competing responses emitted by the child (nonattentiveness, running away, laughing) are ignored during lessons, and natural reinforcers (such as play) are used as modes of instruction to establish learning sets in children.

Reinforcers are predicted to increase a child's performance of a skill and are basically feedback mechanisms. Punishment, another feedback mechanism, is used only in extreme cases to decrease the appearance of strong negative behaviors (hitting, destroying property).

Once learned, all behaviors are perceived to be possibly emitted under rewarding conditions. Thus, ignoring undesirable behaviors is perceived to extinguish behaviors not culturally appropriate. However, once an extinguished behavior is rewarded it may reappear as a part of the child's behavior.

All rewards are established in relation to food, and secondary rewards grow out of the interpersonal relation established between the trainer who administers the rewards and the child. In addition, the child is perceived to model and imitate the trainer in order to secure both primary and secondary rewards. Thus, modeling, imitating, and responding to verbal commands are response patterns developed by the child from interactions with trainers.

Curriculum and Success Criteria

The subject matter which comprises the

curriculum of early childhood classes is all those behaviors and skills deemed important by the culture. These skills include number concepts, concept formation, language development, socioemotional conformity and growth, and eventually, abstract reasoning.

Future teachers are trained under conditions in which basic behavior principles are used. Modeling, imitation, feedback, and rewards are used to shape the teacher's behavior to meet the criterion set by the trainer. Fundamentally, the criterion performance of a teacher is the appropriateness and correctness of the responses the teacher is able to have children emit.

All descriptions of children's or teachers' behaviors are based on data. Relevant data are the number of times the teacher performs a procedure and the resulting number of times a child emits a correct or incorrect response. Of prime importance is that, following training, teachers or children will establish independent rates of emitting desirable behaviors under conditions of self reward schedules or intermittent trainer reward schedules.

The behavior modification lesson is a tightly integrated whole in which no one segment may be eliminated without serious damage to the total lesson. Therefore, a minimum lesson includes the following conditions: Objectives must be specified based on individual pupil behaviors; feedback in some form of reward schedule must be administered contingent upon pupil behavior indicating correct response; discrete steps in the analyses of tasks must be determined and administered with appropriate materials in appropriate settings; and data must be collected upon which to evaluate the children's and teachers' performance and to plan the next phase of instruction.

Normal Developmental Approach

Historically, early childhood education programs have been developed without the aid of a single or dominant philosophy. Thus, unlike the behavior modification or cognitive developmental approach, one is hard pressed to identify a single spokesman or group of educators readily identified with the traditional early childhood classrooms. These programs, however, might best be described as prototypes of the "readiness for school" concept, preschools, or public school kindergartens. While both the behavior modification and cognitive developmentalist groups also share the readiness goal, both of these extreme groups more readily modify their programs to accommodate idiosyncratic behavior patterns of individual children. This is not to say that the normal developmental programs do not try to meet individual differences. However, the nature of the typical nursery or preschool normal developmental program is large or small group oriented and focuses on teacher oriented activities to prepare children for formal school, usually first grade.

Emphasis on Age and Developmental Norms

The normal developmental approach draws upon the field of child development for the basic stock of knowledge about children. This knowledge is usually found in the descriptions of what typical normal children can accomplish in the motor, socioemotional, and cognitive areas of development at certain ages. Thus, age is a critical dimension. For example, the Berkeley Growth and Developmental Scale, Bayley's Scales of Infant Development, the Denver Developmental Screening Test, and the Preschool Attainment Record all have used age as a reference point to assess children's functioning. In addition, most of the widely used intelligence scales used age as the reference point to assess intellectual functioning.

Normal developmental early childhood education has been much influenced by the work of the developmental psychologists Gesell, Shirley, and Hilgard, as well as Lee and Lee, who prepared lists of skills to be accomplished by. a certain age. At one point during the 1950's, inservice training was dominated by an age-stage philosophy, and films such as the "Terrible Two's," "Trusting Three's," and "Frustrated Four's" were shown to parents and teachers.

An analysis of normal developmental programs today indicates a similar influence of age of the child as the determining variable upon which classroom experiences are built. Curriculum specialists in normal developmental programs have generated long lists of skills to be attained by the child at an appropriate age. Curriculum experiences and materials are selected which are said to reflect child growth and development principles. For example, a child's ability to button his coat by himself, to tie his shoes independently, and to use scissors with ease are preceived as typical accomplishments of the 5 to 6 year old. Thus, these skills would be taught in the kindergarten as part of the academic program. Many toy manufacturers, influenced by this philosophy, indicate the age level to which the toy will appeal.

Behaviors Necessary for School Success

Of major importance in normal developmental programs are those behaviors perceived as necessary for school success. These would include such behaviors as standing in

TABLE 1
Structure, View of Child, and Proponents of Three Approaches to Early Childhood Education

Variables and proponents	*Behavioristic approach*	*Normal developmental approach*	*Cognitive developmental approach*
Degree of structure	High	Medium high	High
View of child	Child is a responder	Child is a mediating interactor	Child is a transactor
Proponents and practitioners	Bear Bijou Williams & Sibley (McLean VA) Lindsey Ora & Wiegerink Bereiter & Englemann Becker & Englemann	Karnes Clauss & Gray Caldwell Gordon McCandless, Spicker, & Hodges	Kamii Kohlberg Weikert (new program) Anastasiow, Stedman, & Spaulding Bank Street College UCLA Open education (English school variety)

line, taking turns, sitting in groups, raising hands, and asking and answering questions. Thus, long lists of behaviors assumed to be associated with first grade success have been generated to describe how a child must act. Typically, the lists reflect behaviors of the average first grade classroom, which contains large and some small group instruction. Small group instruction usually is restricted to the area of reading.

Normal developmental programs emphasize those concept pairs thought to be necessary for school success such as right-left, up-down, over-under, and in-out, as well as color names, the concept of number ("You can count things"), the concept of writing ("Those marks on the board say your name"), and the concept of reading ("The books contain stories and I can read them"). Again, long lists of skills perceived to be related to academic success (reading, numbers, and science) have been generated.

Emotional Growth

Another major area of emphasis in normal developmental programs is on socioemotional development. This area is probably the least well developed area of the program if one evaluates the traditional school on lists of skills associated with emotional growth. Statements as to developing "the whole child," "a healthy self concept," "a positive attitude towards self and others," and "a positive attitude towards school" are typical examples. In general, emotional growth is assessed by the intuitions of the teacher. The normal developmentalist makes a major assertion that the emotional development of the child underlies his cognitive development and hence, is instrumental to school success. Interestingly, those behaviors that the normal developmentalist asserts indicate socioemotional development are largely ones that reflect conformity to school rules and interest in school related events rather than independence and self assertiveness.

A Unit Curriculum

Given the emphases or goals just stated, the normal developmentalist therefore constructs classroom experiences into "units" of work (such as a study of animals or the circus) in which the child can learn how to act in school, master the school related concepts and participate in school related tasks. Thus, the term *preschool* is very descriptive of the aim of the normal developmental early childhood educational classroom.

Cognitive Developmental Approach

The cognitive developmental approach is an outgrowth of Deweyan philosophy, Piagetian theory, and techniques and procedures of the traditional school.

Basically, the cognitive developmentalist assumes that all children go through a series of stages of development. The stages are invariant, sequential, and hierarchically arranged, and they roughly follow the child's age periods. The stages or periods commonly accepted are the sensorimotor (0 to 2 years of age), preoperational (2 to 5 years of age), concrete operations (5 to 12 years of age), and abstract reasoning (12 to maturity). Piaget (Piaget & Inhelder, 1969; Piaget, 1971) has maintained that the child has available to him at birth innate structures by which he can act on the environment to internalize representations of the environment. As the child "takes in" objects by the process of assimilation, he constructs a model of the world. When the child must revise his construction of the world through new experiences, according to Piaget the child does so by the process of accommodation. A further process of equilibration is hypothesized to account for a mechanism which provides a motive for the balance between the processes of assimilation and accommodation.

Like Dewey before him, Piaget has posited that the child acts on the environment and that the nature of the child's acts provides the material by which the child constructs his own intelligence. Thus, the richness of the environment influences what the child can construct but does not provide the input. The child is the agent of his own experiences. In a less rich or less structured environment, the child will be delayed in his cognitive development, not because of lack of training but because of a lack of opportunities to experience.

The actions of the child are fundamental to the theory. These actions are both observable motor acts and unobservable internal acts such as occur in thinking. The child acts on the environment through his physical movements, manipulation of objects, experimentation with objects, and the internalization of symbolic representations of the objects which alter his mode of thought. The child is said to learn about the physical nature of the world (the laws of physics, chemistry and causality, as well as time and space) through play, drawing, and symbol manipulation and later through language development and reading.

Kamii (1973) perceived the basic difference between Piagetian approaches and other developmental programs, such as Bank Street College, in Piaget's distinction of how children master knowledge. Whereas both Bank Street and a Piagetian program emphasize the use of free play as a learning device, Kamii believed the Bank Street program is based on the teacher's intuitive notion of how children learn. A Piagetian program, in contrast, makes distinctions among the various kinds of knowledge children master.

Piagetian Types of Knowledge and Teacher Orientations

The Piagetian types of knowledge were proposed by Kamii as physical, logicomathematical, and social knowledge. Each type requires a different orientation on the part of the teacher.

Physical knowledge is knowledge of objects, shapes, texture, function, action, and response to action. These knowledges in the Piagetian view only can be obtained by the child's own actions on objects. It is therefore crucial for the teacher to provide objects for the child to act upon. Social knowledges are those arbitrary symbols or names given to objects, for example, *apple*. Piagetian oriented teachers are free to supply the name *apple* for the child's mastery of social knowledge of the name *apple,* but they would also provide an apple for the child to encounter and experience the physical knowledge of the taste, smell, texture, color, and shape.

Logicomathematical knowledge (e.g., numbers) is hypothesized to be obtained by the child through his own actions and his curiosity in being interested in finding out how things work. Children are believed to learn how to classify not because they want to learn how to classify but as a result of discovery through experimentation with objects. A teacher in the Piagetian classroom is encouraged to ask children questions which will focus the child's attention on the logicomathematical properties and to provide the vocabulary for relationships and comparisons. Questions such as "Do you think this is more, less, or the same?" and "Do you think this is longer, shorter, wider?" help the child engage in examining the underlying process of the mathematical properties of the environment.

Teachers also will develop materials to engage children in examining, and thereby developing, notions of classification, seriation number, spatial and temporal reasoning, and representation. In general, the sequence of experiences provided by the teacher begins with presentation of the object, then provides a model of how the object is used ("You saw with a saw"), next allows the child to use the object to discover its properties, and finally through questioning procedures encourages the child to examine the process and underlying properties of the results of his actions ("A board sawed in half is two pieces but is as long as the original board").

Both the Piagetians and the child developmentalists emphasize the socioemotional development of the child. Piaget and Inhelder (1969) have stated that the need to be accepted and to express love may be the fundamental need and motivation for all learning. Acceptance of the child is crucial if the child is to feel free to explore.

Of major importance to the Piagetian orientation is the allowance of the child to fail. Piaget has stated that failure is critical to learning: It is only when the child is wrong in his hypothesis making that he comes to discover and must accommodate new knowledge.

Dependency on Cognitive Development

Many other areas of development are perceived to be dependent upon the degree of the child's cognitive development. For instance, in language development, developmentalists believe that the child only develops language to the degree to which he is able to think in the mode that the language form represents. For example, it is hypothesized that a child is not able to use the if-then construction accurately until 12 to 14 years of age, the time when the child is able to think in abstractions. Language is said to have advantages in thinking over other symbol systems, particularly in its efficiency of categorizing concepts.

Thus, in strong contradistinction to the behavior modificationist, the pure cognitive developmentalist would not teach the child basic concepts but would provide the conditions and materials by which the child can discover (or uncover) the basic operations of the world. For example, Piagetians would maintain you cannot teach a child before 5 to 7 years of age about conservation of matter; however, by 5 to 7 years of age most normal children will have mastered the concept.

Ideally, the cognitive developmentalist will try to provide a rich classroom environment and an underlying structure which is appropriate to the child's stage of development. However, the structure is apparent only to the teacher; the child must seek and discover the structure for learning to take place. In Piagetian theory, premature structuring cannot occur since the child is unable to form structures before he is at that stage of development.

The cognitive developmentalists do not have a well developed theory of affect development but assert that it is probably fundamental to healthy cognitive functioning. Piaget has proposed a concept of decentration, which is the process of the child's development of a concept of self by the continuous process of learning which aspects of the environment are separate from the self. This, to Piaget, is a lifelong process.

Concluding Comments

Early childhood programs for handicapped children have drawn on the models described in this article. The behavior modification approach has become very popular among the programs; however, most preschool programs for handicapped children draw upon some notions of the normal developmental approach in addition to prescribing treatment programs. Based on children's overt behaviors, the Technical Assistance Developmental Systems (TADS) at North Carolina describes programs that combine sections of behavior modification and normal developmental programs as developmental prescriptive. In our opinion, few Piagetian programs currently exist. We hope that the discussion provided in this article will assist future directors of preschools in developing programs that are internally consistent and draw upon a philosophy of education that matches the goals and objectives of the model center.

References

Bandura, A. Analyses of modeling processes. In A. Bandura (Ed.), *Psychological modeling.* Chicago: Aldial-Atherton, 1971.

Dowley, E. Personal communication, 1973.

Evans, E. D. *Contemporary influences in early childhood education.* New York: Holt, Rinehart, & Winston, 1971.

Haring, N. G., Hayden, A. H., & Allen, K. E. Intervention in early childhood. *Educational Technology,* 1961, 52-61.

Kamii, C. A Piagetian contrasts three educational approaches. *Dimensions,* 1973, *1* (2), 17-19, 30-33.

Piaget, J. *Biology and knowledge.* Chicago: The University of Chicago Press, 1971.

Piaget, J., & Inhelder, B. *The psychology of the child,* New York: Basic Books, 1969.

Stedman, D. J., Anastasiow, N. J., Dokecki, P. R., Gordon, I. J., & Parker, R. K. How can effective early intervention programs be delivered to potentially retarded children? Report No. OS-72-305-DHEW for the Office of the Secretary of the Department of Health, Education, and Welfare. October, 1972.

ENLARGING THE CIRCLE

The Parent-Infant Program at United Cerebral Palsy

Berta Rafael is Director of
Early Education and Day Care
at United Cerebral Palsy
of New York City, Inc.

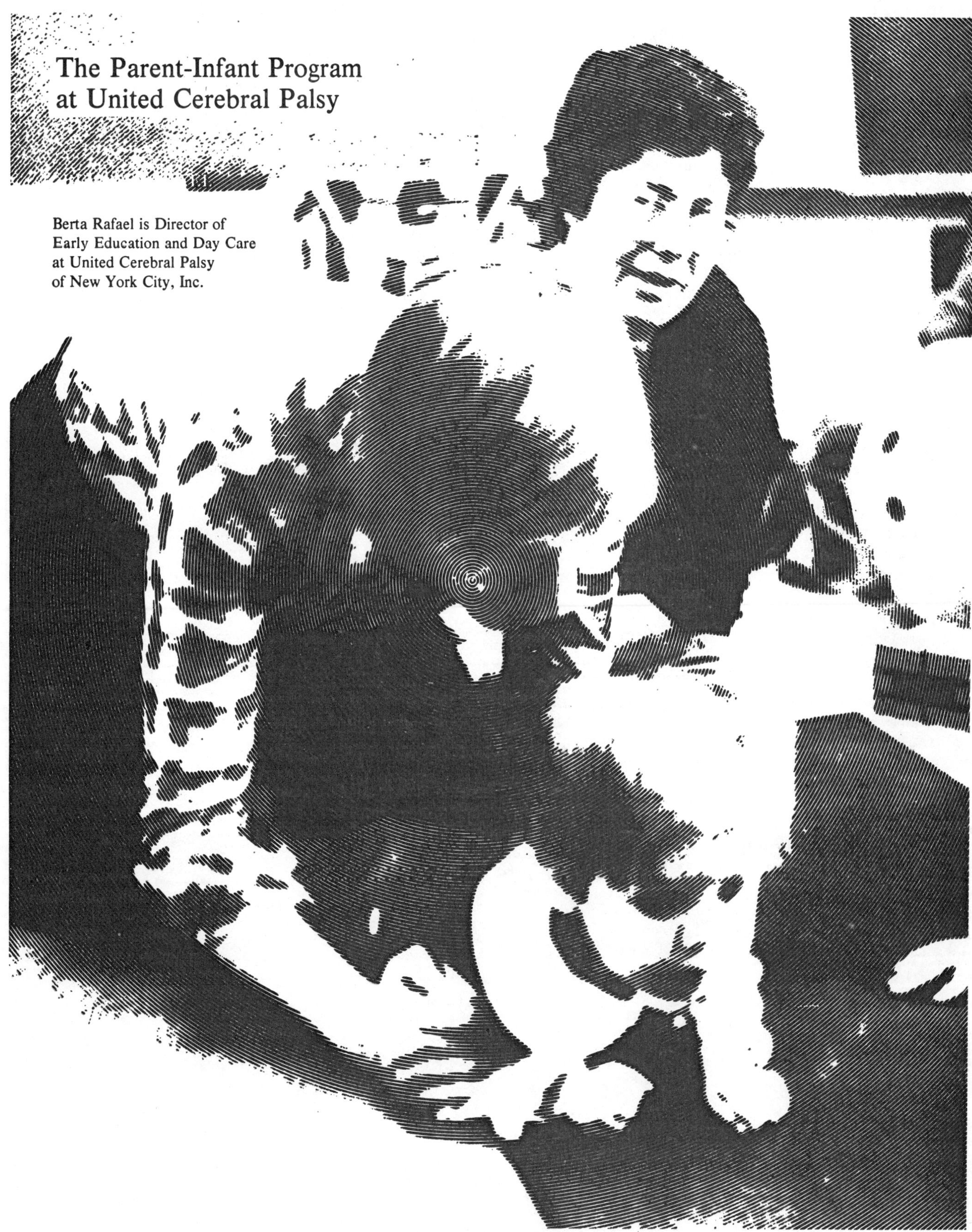

"Enlarging the Circle-The Parent-Infant Program At United Cereral Palsy,",Berta Rafael, *Teaching Exceptional Children,* Vol. 9, No. 3, Spring 1977, © 1977 The Council For Exceptional Children.

Carrying an infant for 9 months and then finding the baby develops differently from other infants is a frightening, lonely, and disheartening experience. Many parents report that no one will answer their many questions, because it is not always possible to diagnose atypical development in a young infant.

United Cerebral Palsy of New York City, Inc., in 1971, undertook the responsibility for providing services to parents of infants with atypical development. The Parent Infant Program was originally part of the Early Education Project partially funded by the Bureau of Education for the Handicapped Children's Early Education Assistance Act (Public Law 90-538). The purpose of the program was to provide the earliest possible educational services for those infants who are diagnosed or suspected of atypical development and the families of these infants.

The program was created because it was believed that:

1 The earlier intervention begins the greater the success in developing the child's maximal functioning.
2 Parents can become skilled in the management of their child through guidance and thereby contribute to the child's increased functioning.
3 Parents need to be educated toward a better understanding of the organic, psychological, genetic, and educational factors related to the handicap.
4 Parents need ongoing support toward coping with the shock, pain, and guilt, as well as the "aloneness" when first confronted with the fact that they have an impaired child.
5 The more guidelines parents receive in the education of their impaired child while young, the more accepting they become of the child's and their own needs.
6 Parents experience relief and hope when they are guided toward helping their child.

INFANTS

Infants are selected from those considered high risk or impaired, based on medical information and family history, and are accepted into the program from about 3 months to 2 years of age. Infants are grouped according to ability in groups of not more than four. Between the ages of 2 or 3 years the children are transferred into the nursery classes at United Cerebral Palsy or referred to another agency.

PARENTS

Admission is based on the commitment of one or both parents, or a substitute caregiver (this may be a grandparent, aunt, or guardian), to the philosophy of the program and to working within it. Parents must be willing to attend the program once or twice a week with their infant. At a preliminary screening interview, the social worker explains the program to parents, while other staff members observe and evaluate the infant's functioning. Thereafter, members of the team meet to discuss whether or not parents and child can benefit from the program. Admission is based on this decision.

The delivery system emphasizes the parent as the "learner and doer." This means that, in addition to observation, parents participate directly in all the activities related to their child's development.

STAFF

The staff members are, to a large measure, the special ingredients of the service delivery system. The best planned curriculum is of little value without a highly skilled and harmonious staff. Staff members are selected by the following criteria:

Individual expertise in their own discipline.
Willingness to work as part of a team.
Willingness and ability to share their own skills and knowledge with colleagues from other disciplines.
Ability to develop a framework which creates an atmosphere that supports growth.
Enthusiasm and ability to motivate parents.
Willingness to accept parental feelings even if they are hostile and angry.
Willingness to share with parents their knowledge about the learning and functioning of the infant and at the same time to learn from parents the many insights and skills that they have developed in the management of their child.
Ability to communicate, to explain, to give reason, to deal in specifics, and to stay away from ambiguities, sweeping generalizations, and stereotypes.
Patience and willingness to wait for success.

The staff at the United Cerebral Palsy Parent Infant Program consists of a physical therapist and/or occupational therapist, a speech therapist (who is also an expert in feeding techniques), an early childhood teacher, a psychologist, a social worker, and the director of early education. A medical consultant is available when needed.

ASSESSMENT

In order to develop an organized, appropriate, and yet flexible program for each infant, a careful assessment of the child's strengths and weaknesses is made by team members. This assessment is based on medical referral material and is made in consultation with each child's physician.

The assessment is carried out in the presence of the parents or designated substitute caregiver. Reports of home behavior are important components of the assessment. Based on the developmental status of the infant at the time of assessment, objectives are set and strategies developed to reach these objectives. The strategies form the curriculum for each child.

The objectives and strategies are based on fine task analysis so that success can easily be obtained. The joy and satisfaction of reaching an objective becomes the reinforcement for child, parents, and staff. When a set of objectives has been reached, a new one is developed. If an infant does not reach an objective as planned, a review is made to determine if (a) the objective was set incorrectly; (b) the strategies were at fault; (c) parental cooperation is missing; or (d) other variables, such as illness, interfered with achievement. New modified objectives and strategies are then developed with some of the possible reasons for failure in mind.

THE PROGRAM

The staff works in close harmony with the family to plan appropriate intervention techniques for each infant. They observe the rate and quality of the child's development and work toward normalization. The program is based on principles of child development, which include the belief that children learn through play. To facilitate this learning the environment is adapted to the physical needs of each child.

Physical Therapist's Role

Each staff member has a variety of responsibilities. The role of the physical therapist is to teach and share with staff and parents the physical management of the child. Parents are taught a variety of skills which include:

1. Lifting and carrying the baby.
2. Positioning the baby—prone, side lying, side sitting, and so forth.
   Achieving correct sitting, if possible (proper seat belts, foot rests, arm rests, special chairs).
   Positioning for dressing (so the baby can see body parts being dressed and actually participate in the process).
   Positioning for toileting (if ready).

Speech Therapist's Role

The speech therapist's role is to reach and share with all staff and parents skills such as:

1. *Feeding techniques:* Checks maturity and normalcy of the baby's sucking, biting, chewing, and swallowing functions. If necessary, normalizes oral functioning or recommends the next developmental stage, that is, weaning from nipple to cup or straw; progressing from strained foods to thicker textures, then to finger food, then to utensils.
   Vocalization: Checks to see if baby is vocalizing. Is baby imitating sounds? differentiating sounds? babbling? If not, makes appropriate recommendations, including proper motivation or better positioning.
   Language development: Teaches parents to speak to the baby appropriately (few words repeated often), and sees that the infant learns from himself out. Therefore, emphasis should proceed from body parts to familiar people and objects, action, and then descriptive words. The idea that an object is present and then may disappear and reappear is an important concept in language development, and parents are shown how to incorporate that into play with their child.

Teacher's Role

Teachers share with all staff and parents the concept that educational interventions are based on developmentally appropriate activities, with much care given to the right amount of stimulation. The teacher assists parents in establishing a trust relationship between themselves and their child through adequate cuddling, cooing, and comforting. This may be especially difficult when an infant is seriously impaired and therefore responds to affection in very limited ways. The teacher helps parents and other staff select appropriate toys, with emphasis on one toy or educational material at a time, and stresses focusing the child's attention on this material in order to provide a successful experience.

The most important area around which the teacher builds curriculum is the five senses or modalities. Two purposes are accomplished: first, evaluation of the efficiency of the child's senses; and second, use of all channels for learning. At the infant stage, unless we know for sure that the infant is blind or deaf or that the taste organs are impaired, we do not accept sensory loss as irreversible and therefore stimulate all senses. Such stimulation will lay the foundation for sensory motor, perceptual, and cognitive learning.

Social Worker's Role

Due to the isolation of most parents of young handicapped children, parent discussion groups have been developed under the leadership of a trained psychiatric social worker. In these group meetings parents can help each other by relating their own experiences, or they can turn to staff for education and support. Many parents find that their family and friends rarely recognize the suffering and pain experienced when first confronted with the awareness that they have an impaired infant. Support from the social worker and other parents will help develop the coping behavior necessary to bear such a burden.

The social worker also provides individual counseling as indicated. An important function of the social worker is to provide for interaction and liaison between hospitals, referral sources, other agencies, and all people involved in the child's care. The social worker assists the family members in their relationship to each other and to the handicapped child. He assists in obtaining equipment necessary for easier living, in finding more suitable housing, and many other needs of the family.

Psychologist's Role

The psychologist helps evaluate the infant's level of functioning through observation and the use of various screening inventories, such as the Denver Developmental Screening Test and the Bayley Infant Scale. Depending on the severity of the impairment, one of the many developmental checklists is used. The infants are periodically retested and reevaluated to help measure their progress. Emphasis is placed on the gains the infants make relative to their own rate of development. The psychologist works in cooperation with the teacher and assists in developing ongoing objectives and strategies to enhance the infant's cognitive, sensory, and perceptual-motor development.

Supportive counseling and guidance are also given to the parents to help them understand the expectations and limitations of their child's impairment. For example, many parents of Down's syndrome infants do not expect their children to learn at all and have to be convinced that learning is possible. Many parents progress and feel encouraged when this is pointed out to them.

The psychologist also helps the parents understand the effects of their behavior on the infant's development. Often the emotional interchange between parent and child is colored by the impact of the atypical development. Thus the parents may react with greater intensity, with more protection and less freedom for the infant, or they may react in a negative fashion, making undue demands or neglecting the child. Parents are made aware of the most productive way they can interact with their child and they are guided toward this end.

HOME VISITS

At the United Cerebral Palsy Center parents are guided in the management and education of their infant. They need to carry this learning into their home environment. To facilitate this, home visits are made by one or two of the team members. These staff members help parents with feeding, dressing, bathing, and toileting of the infant. They may make suggestions regarding toys, transportation, or positioning the child for participation in family activities. The home visit is also designed to assist parents in budgeting their time between the care of the handicapped infant and the needs of the rest of the family.

CONCLUDING COMMENTS

Overall, the Parent Infant Program is built on mutual respect among staff members and between staff and parents. Everyone appreciates the uniqueness of each child in all areas of development. An atmosphere of joy in achievement (however small) and focus on each child's success is maintained throughout the program.

The Portage Project: A Model for Early Childhood Education

MARSHA S. SHEARER
DAVID E. SHEARER

Marsha S. Shearer is Staff Training Coordinator and David E. Shearer is Project Director, The Portage Project, Cooperative Educational Service Agency No. 12, Portage, Wisconsin. *The project reported herein was funded by the Education of The Handicapped Act, P. L. 91-230, Title VI, ESEA, Part C.*

Abstract: This article describes an intervention program serving 75 preschool multiply handicapped children living in a rural area. Ages of the children ranged from birth to 6 years. All instruction took place in the child's home. Individualized curriculum was prescribed and demonstrated by a home teacher who visited each parent and child 1 day per week for 1½ hours. During the week, the parents taught the prescribed curriculum and recorded the child's resultant behavior on a daily basis. The results of the project indicate that handicapped children can progress above their expected developmental rate and that parents can initiate, observe, and accurately record this change.

The growth of programs for preschool children has been paralleled by an increased involvement of parents in the education of their children. During recent years there has been a concerted effort by Federal funding sources, such as the Office of Child Development and the Bureau for the Education of the Handicapped, to fund programs that involve the parents of the children being served. This parental involvement could occur at various levels of program development. For instance, including parents on an advisory council, having parents work as classroom aides, and counseling parents could be methods of involving parents in a program.

The Portage Project, a home teaching program, is an attempt to directly involve parents in the education of their children by teaching parents what to teach, what to reinforce, and how to observe and record behavior.

There are several advantages in teaching parents in their homes to be effective agents of behavioral change. First, learning is occurring in the parent and child's natural environment; therefore, the problem of transferring to the home what has been learned in a classroom or clinic does not occur. Second, there is direct and constant access to behavior as it occurs naturally. Third, the maintenance of desired behavior will likely be enhanced if the behaviors have been learned in the natural environment. Fourth, the training of parents, who already are natural reinforcing agents, will provide them with the skills necessary to deal with new behaviors when they occur.

Children Served

The Portage Project presently serves 75 handicapped children from birth to 6 years of age. The children live within the Cooperative Educational Service Agency No. 12 area in south-central rural Wisconsin.

"The Portage Project: A Model For Early Childhood Education", Marsha S. Shearer, Daid E. Shearer, *Exceptional Children,* Vol. 39, No. 9, November 1972, © 1972 The Council For Exceptional Children.

The project serves children who have been previously diagnosed as having behavioral problems or as being emotionally disturbed, mentally retarded, physically handicapped, vision impaired, hearing impaired, culturally deprived, or handicapped in the area of speech or language. The project also serves children with any combination of these disabilities.

Referral Sources

The children are referred to the project by local physicians, social workers, county health nurses, public schools, local guidance clinics, and speech therapists. Public service announcements on local radio stations and newspaper articles describing the project have brought additional referrals, many from parents themselves.

Of the 150 parents contacted regarding the project, only 6 (approximately 1 percent) refused to enroll their child. Of the 150 children referred, 30 were found not to need an early intervention program. Four of the 75 parents and children enrolled in the project withdrew after the home visits began. Of these 4, 2 children were in families who moved from the area, 1 child was placed in a state hospital, and 1 parent was dissatisfied with the project.

Rationale for the Home Teaching Model

During the planning phase, as children were being identified, it was evident that a classroom situation could not be provided. The intermediate agency serves 23 school districts and covers a geographical area of 3,600 square miles. To transport these preschool handicapped children to one central location would not have been either practical or possible. Even when several children had been identified within a smaller area, i.e. one school district, their handicaps and/or their chronological ages varied so greatly that it was not to the children's advantage to place them in a group.

The project's administrative staff decided that, due to these problems, a home teaching model would be the most feasible delivery system to provide educational services. An educator–a home teacher–was provided to each child and his family 1 day per week for 1½ hours for a period of 9½ months. This schedule of home visits was met 92 percent of the time, which takes into account cancellations due to inclement weather, illness, family vacations, and hospitalizations. During the 6 days the home teacher was not present, the parents served as the child's teachers by implementing prescribed curriculum and recording the child's progress.

Assessment of the Children

After a child had been referred to the project, a home teacher assessed the child to determine if he needed an early intervention program. The project does not serve children functioning at or near their chronological age in the developmental areas. However, the project has never refused service because a child had too many handicaps or had handicaps of too great a degree.

The assessment instruments used have included the Developmental Skill Age Inventory, experimental edition (Alpern & Boll, 1969), the *Stanford-Binet Intelligence Scale*, Form L-M (Terman & Merrill, 1960, the *Cattell Infant Scale* (Cattell, 1940), the *Peabody Picture Vocabulary Test* (Dunn, 1965), and the *Slossen Intelligence Test for Children and Adults* (Slossen, 1963).

The developmental scales and intelligence tests were administered in order to provide objective data concerning gains in mental age and IQ; however, the teaching staff was not concerned with labels or IQ scores. The concern was the behavior of the individual child. Knowing that a child is a mongoloid or has an IQ of 50 or is brain damaged does not tell a teacher what the child can already do, what next to teach, nor how to teach it. Each child was provided with an individualized curriculum based on his present behavior, not his disability label.

Staff

Four certified special education teachers and three paraprofessionals were hired and trained to serve as home teachers. Certified personnel served an average of 12 children; the paraprofessionals had an assigned caseload of 10 children. Preservice training included instruction in child development, assessment techniques, precision teaching, and behavior modification (Shearer, 1971). Pre- and posttests were given after each instructional period to evaluate the instruction itself. Inservice meetings for the entire staff were held 1 day per week and home visits were not scheduled on that day. These sessions provided the individual staff member with needed reinforcement and help with specific problems encountered during the week.

During a specific 2 hour staffing period, each home teacher presented problems causing concern. The group reacted by making suggestions and finally by establishing a prescriptive goal which the home teacher implemented the following week. Data on this prescription was collected, and at the next inservice meeting the home teacher reported either success or failure. If the goal was not achieved, the staff modified the reinforcer, changed the reinforcement schedule, or divided the goal into smaller segments.

The paraprofessional home teachers met with the staff training coordinator one additional half day per week to review the previous week's data and to help in planning prescriptions for the coming week.

The home teacher accompanied the parent and child on clinic appointments and suggestions were sought from outside professionals at this time and throughout the year as problems arose.

Curriculum Planning

To facilitate planning for individual children, the project staff devised an Early Childhood Curriculum Guide (Shearer, Billingsley, Frohman, Hilliard, Johnson, & Shearer, 1970). The guide is in two parts: (a) a Developmental Sequence Checklist, which lists sequential behaviors from birth to 5 years of age in five developmental areas–cognitive, language, self help, motor, and socialization; (b) a set of Curriculum Cards to match each of the 450 behaviors stated on the Checklist, using behavioral objectives to describe the skill and suggesting materials and curriculum ideas to teach each of these 450 behaviors.

The Checklist is used to pinpoint the behaviors the child already exhibits in the five developmental areas. This is considered initial baseline behavior. Based on this data, the home teacher can then prescribe the next behavior on the Checklist, often dividing this behavior, which is called a long term goal, into smaller segments. Thus, the child is assigned a goal he will achieve within 1 week regardless of the severity of the handicap.

As the parents experienced success and gained confidence in their ability to teach their child and record his behavior, the initial one or two prescriptions per week were increased to three or four prescriptions. These activities were in several areas of development. For instance, the parents might have been working on buttoning, reducing tantrums, and counting objects all within the same week.

The parents were encouraged to contribute to the planning and implementation of the curriculum and these suggestions were absorbed into the prescriptions during the home visit. The parents were shown how to record their child's behavior on the prescribed curriculum tasks, and as the parents taught their child during the week, they recorded the behavior as it increased, decreased, or remained the same.

Recording behaviors was new and somewhat threatening to some of the parents, so the home teachers initiated just one prescription during the first week. The home teachers showed the parents how to record and the parents practiced during the home visit. This initial goal was chosen so that it would be helpful to the family (i.e., the child will put on coat without help) and be at a level that the home teacher believed would be achieved within 1 week. This helped guarantee the parent and child immediate success.

Thirty percent of the parents did not record during the first month. Praise and sometimes more tangible reinforcers were used in some situations to initiate recording behavior. However, once the parent began recording, tangible reinforcers were no longer necessary; seeing the behavior of the child change became a reinforcer in itself. The overall rate of daily recording by the 75 families in the project was 92 percent.

Home Training Process

The home teacher entered each child's home with the average of three to four prescriptions per week and any materials needed to carry out these activities. First the home teacher took postbaseline data on the previous week's activities. Based on this data, the home teacher altered these prescriptions or introduced new activities. Baseline data was then collected on each new task. Such collection is important since it is necessary to first discover how close the child is to achieving the prescription. For instance, a prescription might have been for hopping on one foot in place without support, 5 times per trial, 3 trials per day. If baseline data had indicated that success on this activity was not likely to be achieved in 1 week, the home teacher would have changed the prescription, gone back to a prerequisite skill, and prescribed hopping on one foot in place with support, 5 times per trial, 3 trials per day.

As baseline data was collected on each new prescription, the task was demonstrated to the

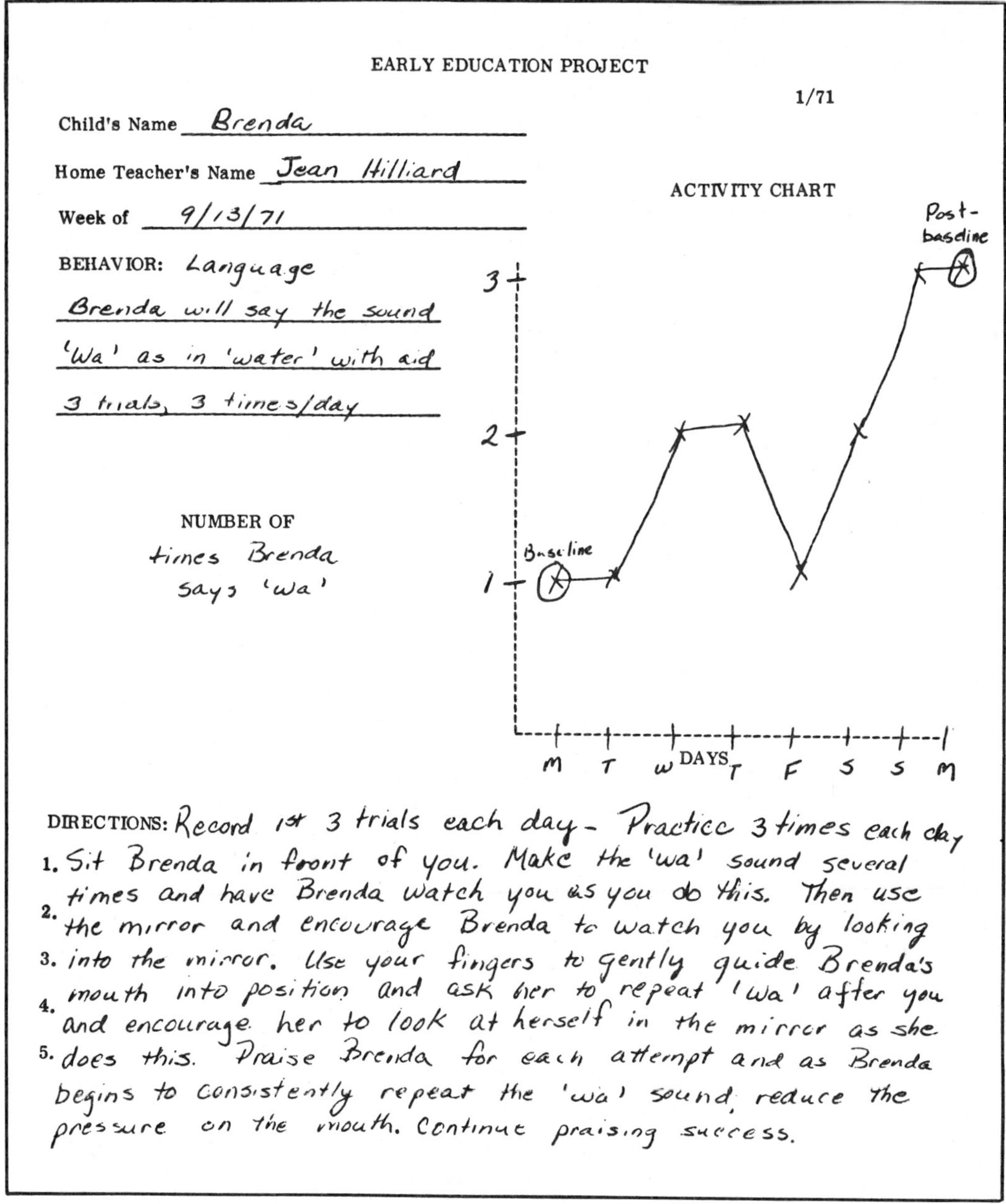

EARLY EDUCATION PROJECT

1/71

Child's Name Brenda

Home Teacher's Name Jean Hilliard

Week of 9/13/71

ACTIVITY CHART

BEHAVIOR: Language
Brenda will say the sound
'Wa' as in 'water' with aid
3 trials, 3 times/day

NUMBER OF
times Brenda
says 'wa'

DIRECTIONS: Record 1st 3 trials each day - Practice 3 times each day
1. Sit Brenda in front of you. Make the 'wa' sound several
times and have Brenda watch you as you do this. Then use
2. the mirror and encourage Brenda to watch you by looking
3. into the mirror. Use your fingers to gently guide Brenda's
mouth into position and ask her to repeat 'wa' after you
4. and encourage her to look at herself in the mirror as she
5. does this. Praise Brenda for each attempt and as Brenda
begins to consistently repeat the 'wa' sound, reduce the
pressure on the mouth. Continue praising success.

FIGURE 1. Sample activity chart.

parent as the home teacher worked with the child. The home teacher then observed the parent working with the child on the prescription. Often the home teacher supplied the parent with additional teaching information, such as, "How about increasing the amount of praise and see if he will perform better," or "You are giving too many clues to Johnny. Look, you are holding your hand in front of the colored block you have asked Johnny to give you. Place your hand between the two blocks." The parent is expected to stay with the child and the home teacher during the session because this visit is designed to teach the parents how to teach, how to record, and how to reinforce the prescribed behavior for the coming week.

An activity chart for each prescription was left with the parent (see Figure 1). This chart described in behavioral terms what goal was to be accomplished, how often the skill was to be practiced, what behavior was to be reinforced,

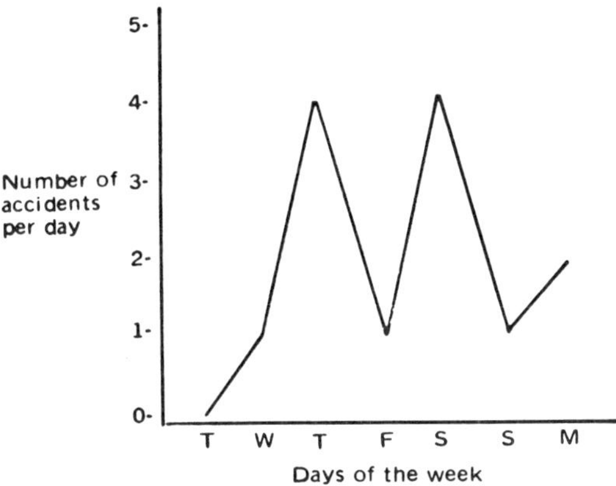

FIGURE 2. Baseline data on the frequency of Donovan's toileting accidents.

and how it was to be reinforced. The directions were specific and the parents had the activity chart to refer to during the week. The parent was instructed to record on the activity chart the child's behavior each day on each prescription. Recording proved to be reinforcing to the parents because they could see the daily changes in their child's rate of appropriate responses. When the home teacher returned the following week, he recorded postbaseline data on the previous week's activities. This helped the home teacher validate the accuracy of the parents' recording.

Examples of Behavioral Change

The presentation of typical behavioral changes that have occurred may further aid in describing the techniques and processes of the Portage Project.

Donovan

Donovan was 4 years old when referred to the project by the county health nurse. He was born with club feet and was strabismic. Donovan had been hospitalized several times for surgery on his eyes and legs, and in between hospitalizations his mother had begun the toilet training process. After each hospital stay, the training regressed. There had never been consistent success in toilet training, and even though the last surgery had occurred 8 months prior, toilet training had not been reinstated.

During the first phase of the toilet training procedure, Donovan's mother was instructed to check him every hour and to record on a chart when he went (time) where he went (pants or toilet), and what he did (bowel movement or urination). This information revealed that Donovan did not defecate or urinate for 3 hour stretches, that he had one bowel movement a day at about the same time each day, and that he averaged two accidents per day but with great fluctuation.

Donovan's chart (Figure 2) indicates that he was already having some toileting success, and in fact, the first time his mother recorded, Donovan had a perfect day. The home teacher hypothesized that if Donovan recorded his own behavior, his rate of success would increase. Figure 3 describes Donovan's rate of progress over the next 2 weeks using self recording.

During the time these data were collected, Donovan was receiving praise and, in addition, was recording his own successful behavior by

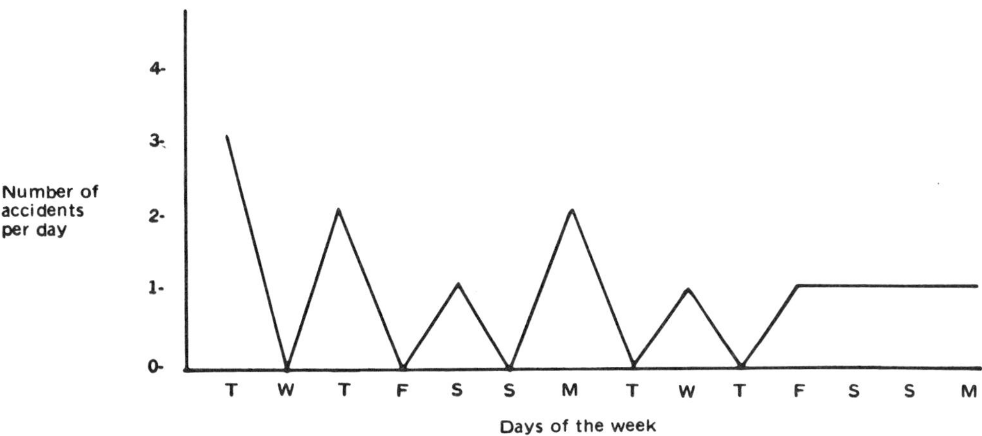

FIGURE 3. Frequency of Donovan's toileting accidents when he was given praise and Snoopy sticker for each success and when accidents were ignored.

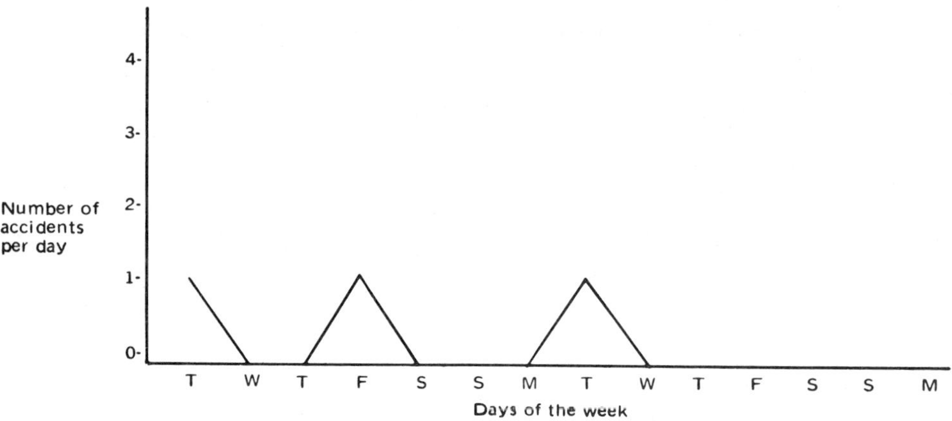

FIGURE 4. Frequency of Donovan's toileting accidents when he was given praise and a happy face sticker was applied to the bathroom door for a perfect day

pasting a Snoopy sticker on his toileting chart for each success in the bathroom. Accidents were ignored (except for parental charting), and Donovan had to change his own clothing and do whatever cleanup was necessary.

As the third week of recording ended, Donovan was having an average of 1 accident per day, and this was a bowel movement. The home teacher and parent altered the frequency of the reinforcer, and the reinforcer itself changed. The payoff for success was now a happy face sticker which Donovan applied to the bathroom door only if he had a successful day, i.e., no accidents. Figure 4 describes Donovan's change in behavior.

After several more days of success, the stickers were faded out. Donovan's behavior continued to remain consistent. Fading occurred as Donovan noticed that the supply of stickers was running low and he suggested that he did not need to have one every day.

Penny

Penny was 13 months old when she was enrolled in the project. She was born with Moebius Syndrome, a congenital anomaly which resulted in bilateral facial paralysis, strabismus, and gross motor retardation. Socialization skills were also below normal as measured by the Alpern-Boll Developmental Skills Age Inventory and the Sequential Checklist. Penny did not engage in typical imitative behaviors common to her peers. Because imitation is thought to be a necessary prerequisite needed to learn new behaviors, the home teacher prescribed a series of activities to teach Penny a new behavior through shaping and rewarding closer approximations to the final behavioral goal, i.e., clapping hands in imitation.

Since this was a behavior that was not in Penny's present repertoire, it was necessary to provide maximum physical assistance, i.e., her mother took Penny's hands, clapped them together, and said "pat-a-cake" with each movement. Penny was given a fruit loop and praise after each successful trial. Because Penny was receiving help to accomplish the task, success for both Penny and her mother was built into the activity. As the first week progressed, her mother applied less pressure to Penny's hands.

Beginning with the second week, the prescription was for clapping hands in imitation without physical help. A food reward was still given immediately if Penny imitated her mother. If Penny did not perform, her mother provided help, but no food reward was given.

The final prescription was the completion of the long term goal—clapping hands in imitation without help or food reward. Penny continued to perform successfully even though no food reward was provided (see Figure 5). The social reward (attention and praise) was a sufficient reinforcer for Penny to continue to perform the new behavior.

Evaluation

Evaluation was an ongoing process. The parent recorded her child's performance on the prescription daily. The home trainer evaluated weekly by comparing baseline and postbaseline data, and a complete evaluation was undertaken twice a year using the IQ tests and developmental scales described earlier.

The weekly assessment of the child's behavior was also an assessment of the home teacher's ability to prescribe appropriate curriculum. If the child had not succeeded on a task within a given length of time, then it was not assumed to be the child's fault. The failure was likely to be the home teacher's, perhaps because the appropriate task had not been prescribed for the child or the parents had not been given adequate directions. Unlike most teachers, the home teacher knows this within a week, and the prescription can be modified.

If the parent had not been able to work effectively with the child during the week, the home teacher might need to modify the prescriptions (perhaps there were too many) or give the parent additional reinforcement.

A log was kept on each child listing each behavior prescribed, the date the curriculum was initiated, the date the behavior was achieved, and the developmental area the behavior is assumed under, i.e., self help, language, cognitive, socialization, or motor. This log provided information concerning the specific behaviors each child had learned, the date he learned them, and the duration of each prescription. In addition, data concerning the percentage of success on tasks was also available.

Penny and her mother performing the exercise of clapping hands in imitation.

Results

The average IQ of the children in the project was 75 as determined by the *Cattell Infant Test* and the *Stanford-Binet Intelligence Test*. Therefore, it would be expected that on the average, the normal rate of growth would be 75 percent of that of the child with normal intelligence. Using mental ages, one would expect that the average gain would be about 6 months in an 8 month period of time. The average child in the project gained 13 months in an 8 month period; he gained 60 percent more than his counterpart with a normal intelligence.

Children who, because of age, remained in the project after 1 year were retested in September, and these test results were compared to the scores achieved the previous June. Although it would be expected that some regression would occur, there was no significant difference in the scores. This may indicate that the parents continued to work with and reinforce behaviors even though the home teacher was no longer making visits.

An average of 128 prescriptions were written per child. The children were successful on 91 percent of the prescriptions written by professional and paraprofessional staff.

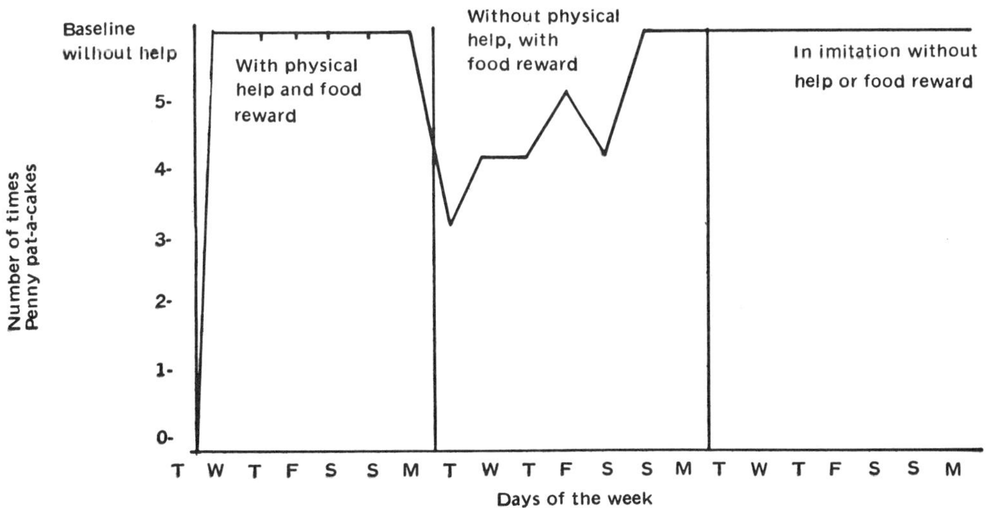

FIGURE 5. Frequency of Penny's imitative behavior.

An experimental study was conducted involving randomly selected children from the Portage Project and randomly selected children attending local classroom programs for culturally and economically disadvantaged preschool children. The *Stanford-Binet Intelligence Scale*, the Cattell Infant Scale, and the Alpern-Boll Developmental Skills Age Inventory were given as pre- and posttests to both groups. In addition, the *Gesell Developmental Schedule* was given as a posttest to both groups. Multiple analysis of covariance was used to control for IQ, practice effect, and age. The greater gains made by the Portage Project children in the areas of mental age, IQ, language, academic development, and socialization were statistically significant, as compared to the group receiving classroom instruction (Peniston, 1972).

Using the children as their own control, test results and behavioral gains were compared and measured. The mean gain in IQ scores on the Alpern-Boll Developmental Skills Age Inventory was 13.5 and was statistically significant beyond the .01 level. The mean gain in IQ scores on the Stanford-Binet was 18.3 and was statistically significant beyond the .01 level.

A Catalyst for Parent Involvement

There is a growing concern for more parental involvement in education and in the provision of good educational services to handicapped children in rural areas. This model indicates that parents can effectively teach their children and that their children can, indeed, learn. All parents have the major responsibility for decision making, rearing, and teaching their children. Parents of handicapped children often have this responsibility for a much longer period of time and are in greater need of parenting skills and knowledge concerning methods of teaching and child development.

Educators have been guilty of relieving the parents of the responsibility of education. Yet, a child's poor classroom performance is often blamed on the "inadequate parent syndrome." Parents of handicapped children need guidance, but more importantly, they need the experience, satisfaction, and the pleasure of working with their children and seeing them succeed as a result of their own efforts. Most parents of handicapped children want to be able to be at least partially responsible for the progress of their child and do not want to be told that the teaching can only be done by somebody else. Home based programs involving individualized instruction through precision teaching is the catalyst which can provide this service to parents and their children.

References

Alpern, G., & Boll, T. Developmental Skill Age Inventory. Unpublished manuscript, Indiana University Medical Center, 1969.

Cattell, P. *Cattell Infant Scale*. New York: The Psychological Corporation, 1940.

Dunn, L. M. *Peabody Picture Vocabulary Test*. Minneapolis, Minn.: American Guidance Service, 1965.

Peniston, E. An Evaluation of the Portage Project. Unpublished manuscript, The Portage Project, Cooperative Educational Service Agency, No. 12, Portage, Wisconsin, 1972.

Shearer, D., Billingsley, J., Frohman, S., Hilliard, J., Johnson, F., & Shearer, M. Developmental Sequential Checklist. Unpublished manuscript, The Portage Project, Cooperative Educational Agency No. 12, Portage, Wisconsin, 1970.

Shearer, M. Staff and parent training program of the Portage Project. Unpublished manuscript, The Portage Project, Cooperative Educational Agency No. 12, Portage, Wisconsin, 1971.

Slossen, R. *Slossen Intelligence Test for Children and Adults*. New York: Slossen Educational Corporation, 1963.

Terman, L., & Merrill, M. *Stanford-Binet Intelligence Scale*. (3rd rev.) Form L-M. New York: Houghton Mifflin, 1960.

Teacher-Mom Intervention with Academic High-Risk Preschool Children

John C. Abbott/David A.Sabatino

*John C. **Abbott** is Assistant Professor of Special Education, and **David A. Sabatino** is Associate Professor of School Psychology, Department of Special Education, The Pennsylvania State University, University Park.* *This investigation was supported by U.S. Office of Education, Bureau of Education for the Handicapped Grant No. OEG-0-72-4509, Title VI-G, Model Learning Disabilities Systems, Tyrone, Pennsylvania.* *A more inclusive and detailed manuscript may be obtained by writing David A. Sabatino, 207 Cedar Building, University Park, Pennsylvania 16802.*

The relative value of preschool programs for handicapped children appears to be closely associated with efficient and effective delivery of these services. The current financial picture and the recognition that professional manpower limitations are realistic considerations have forced special educators to search for alternatives to the delivery of specialized services, especially those associated with early childhood education. The purpose of this study was to measure the effectiveness of having mothers function as teachers for their own preschool academic high risk children, using the *Frostig Program for the Development of Visual Perception.* It was postulated that if such a teacher-mom intervention program was successful, schools would be able to use parents more fully as direct intervention strategists.

A review of the research literature (Gordon, 1971) reveals that only three of seven model programs in compensatory education involved parents in direct teaching. The remaining programs had the parents helping develop materials, observing classes, making home visits to other parents, or volunteering to help in the classroom. This finding reflects the general attitude that educators have a preconceived role for parents in the educative process, and it is not one involving direct intervention.

Method

Subjects. An initial sample of 50 perceptually handicapped children was drawn from a racially balanced early childhood center in an inner city school district serving children aged 4 and 5 years. The children who were selected as subjects all demonstrated visual-perceptual deficits of at least one and one-half developmental years as measured by the *Beery-Buktenica Developmental Test of Visual-Motor Integration* (DTVMI).

The experimental group was composed of 12 four year old and 13 five year old children with a mean age of 5.7 years. Twelve boys and 13 girls were in this group. The control group consisted of 9 four year olds and 16 five year olds with a mean age of 5.6 years. Sixteen boys and 9 girls were in this group.

The mean mental age of all the children was 4 years 6 months. The standard deviation was 1 year and 2 months, with a month difference between the mean mental age of the experimental and control groups.

All the mothers of these children volunteered to work 20 minutes a day with their children and were randomly assigned to the experimental or control group.

The mean age of the mothers was 28 years, and the mean number of years of school completed was 11.1 years.

Ten households were headed by mothers and the remaining 15 had both parents present. Seventeen of the 25 heads of households were employed as skilled or unskilled laborers. The mean number of children under 18 years of age in the home was 3.8 and the mean number of rooms in the home was six. Only four of the mothers reported that their children had designated study areas with appropriate lighting and limited traffic.

Procedure. Following three one hour preintervention parent training sessions, the experimental program began with the mothers administering daily work sessions of 20 minutes, 5 days per week. The mean number

"Teacher-Mom Intervention With Academic High-Risk Preschool Children", John C. Abbott, David A. Sabatino, *Exceptional Children,* Vol. 41, No. 4, January 1975, © The Council For Exceptional Children.

of minutes spent in the parent-child work sessions for the experimental group was 525 minutes.

There was no attempt to modify the curriculum at the early childhood center, except to exclude the Frostig program and control for other perceptual stimulation activities.

A continuous inservice program of weekly one hour training sessions was held with the parents for the duration of the 10 week teacher-mom intervention. In addition to the dissemination of Frostig materials, a discussion concerning parent-child interactions was conducted at that time.

Results

The results of a 2 × 2 × 2 completely randomized factorial analysis of variance (Myers, 1966) with treatment conditions, age, and sex as main effects revealed one significant F ratio for the experimental-control groups on the treatment main effect. This finding indicates that the experimental group demonstrated significant gains ($p < .05$, $df=1/42$, $F=4.97$) on the *Frostig Developmental Test of Visual Perception* in comparison with the control group.

An analysis of the reports of tutorial sessions revealed that a mean of 525 minutes was spent by the experimental group mothers on the Frostig program work sessions. The experimental subjects were divided on the mean number of minutes of training received to investigate possible differences in performance based on time spent in the training sessions. Those subjects who spent more than the mean amount of time in intervention activities evidenced statistically significant differences in gain scores over those subjects who spent less than the mean amount of time. This supported the observation that the degree of parental involvement is evidenced by the amount of time spent in parent-child interaction.

The parents would have liked to proceed faster with more work. However, we do not agree with these parental observations. We do agree with an overwhelming majority of parents who suggested starting at an earlier age with the children, scheduling meetings between the preschool teachers and parents, and increasing the number of information sessions to at least twice a week.

The parents were asked what improvements, if any, they had noticed in their child over the 10 week intervention period. Beginning with the most prevalent responses, they were: (a) the child has more confidence; (b) the child listens more closely and is better able to follow directions; and (c) the child is now prepared for homework in elementary school.

A final question dealt with the parents' willingness to participate in similar programs in the future. Twenty-one of the 25 parents stated that they would be extremely willing to participate. This attitude is consistent with Riessman's (1964) position that lower class families are not turned off by education but rather by the way they are excluded from the schools' activities.

References

Gordon, I. J. *Parent involvement in compensatory Education.* Champaign: University of Illinois Press, 1971.

Myers, J. L. *Fundamentals of experimental design.* Boston: Allyn & Bacon, 1966.

Riessman, F. The overlooked position of disadvantaged groups. *Journal of Negro Education,* 1964, **33,** 225-231.

TIPS FOR PARENTS WHEN BUYING TOYS AND GAMES FOR YOUNG HANDICAPPED CHILDREN

Alfred L. Lazar
Patricia E. Lazar
Robert A.Stodden

Alfred L. Lazar, Professor
Dept. of Educational Psychology
California State Univ., Long Beach
Patricia E. Lazar, Reading Resource Specialist
Palos Verdes Peninsular Unified S.D.,
Rolling Hills, Calif.
Robert A. Stodden, Ass't Professor
Dept. of Special Ed. & Rehabilitation
Boston College, Mass.

Mom and Dad are often puzzled when it comes time to make toy and game selections for their handicapped child. Like all parents they must consider such emotional factors as safety, suitability of the age and sex of their child along with pure fun and educational value. Another serious and stressful consideration involves the nature and degree of the child's disability and/ or handicapping condition. It is this latter factor that often makes the parents seek the advice and counsel of the special class teacher, administrator, or school psychologist.

TOYS, PLAY, AND LEARNING

Toys and games are serious vehicles for play and fun. Effective play and fun leads to wholesome learning and human development. It is for this reason that parents and educators must give serious consideration to numerous questions when selecting a toy or game for their handicapped child. The impact a new toy or game can have on a young handicapped child could range from positive and joyful on one end of a continuum to negative and hurtful at the other end. Children's reactions will vary from strong affective registration in one case to a strong silence of disappointment with no overt evidence of affective registration.

It has only been within the past decade that serious educational and sociological research is being conducted about children's play and toys. A recent anthology by Bruner, Jolly, and Sylva provides a comprehensive treatment of play and its role in child development and social evolution. It looks at play with objects and tools; play in the social world – cooperation, competition, and the learning of sex roles; play with symbols – language, imagination, and creativity; factors inhibiting play; the use of play as cultural indoctrination and problem solving. This anthology is a must for special educators interested in early childhood development and exceptionality.

To assist parents and special class teachers concerning the selection of toys for young handicapped children, a checklist with 22 questions has been developed. The authors feel that the number of questions are just a start, and that parents and teachers should add other items appropriate to their unique locations and needs. Hopefully, this checklist will serve to stimulate special educators and parents to consideration as to the importance of toy and game selection, especially as related to the nature and degree of handicap and disability.

A TOY SELECTION CHECKLIST

The purpose of this checklist is to help Mom and Dad answer some basic questions before buying a toy for their handicapped child. Answer YES or NO for each question.

"Tips for Parents When Buying Toys and Games For Young Handicapped Children", Alfred L. Lazar, Patricia E. Lazar, Robert A. Stodden, *Special Children,* Vol. 4, No. 2, 1978, © 1978.

3. PROGRAMS

1. Have you prepared a list of the toys that your child has at the present time?
2. Does your child show an interest or a desire for certain type of toys or games?
3. In reviewing the list prepared for item 1, are there any toys in need of serious repair or replacement?
4. Has your child indicated an interest or desire for a specific toy or game during the past few weeks?
5. Will your child have the physical strength and abilities to use the toy or game?
6. Will your child have the mental ability and educational level of achievement to enjoy and use the toy or game effectively?
7. Will your child have fun with the toy?
8. Does the manufacturer recommend this toy for children in a specific age group? Is your child in this age group?
9. Does the toy or game have any sharp or dangerous edges?
10. Do the instructions indicate that the toy or game is nonflammable?
11. Can any part of the toy or game be swollowed? Is that part sharp or toxic?
12. Has any lead based paint been used in making this product?
13. Will the manufacturer replace lost or missing and broken parts?
14. Can the toy package be used as a storage container?
15. Will the toy or game make excessive noise?
16. Can the toy or game be used out of doors?
17. Can the toy or game be used in doors?
18. Can the child play and enjoy this toy or game without constant supervision?
19. Can the toy be played with the child alone?
20. Do you feel that all your safety factors for toys has been met?
21. Do both Mom and Dad agree that this is the most appropriate toy to buy?
22. Can the toy be played with by several people?

Additional blank spaces can be left for parents or teachers to add items unique to their needs and situation.

SUMMARY

Toy and game buying by Mom and Dad for their young handicapped child can be a difficult task. Toys and games are important instruments for play, fun, and learning. To help parents and teachers in planning and buying toys, a checklist containing 22 items has been provided, along with blank spaces for additional items to be inserted by the parents or teacher. It was suggested that the check list was only a start.

A Home Safety Inventory for Parents of Preschool Handicapped Children

GLORIA F. WOLINSKY
SYLVIA WALKER

Gloria F. Wolinsky is Professor of Education, Hunter College, City University of New York, New York.

Sylvia Walker is Assistant Special Education Coordinator, Center for Multiply Handicapped, New York City Board of Education, New York.

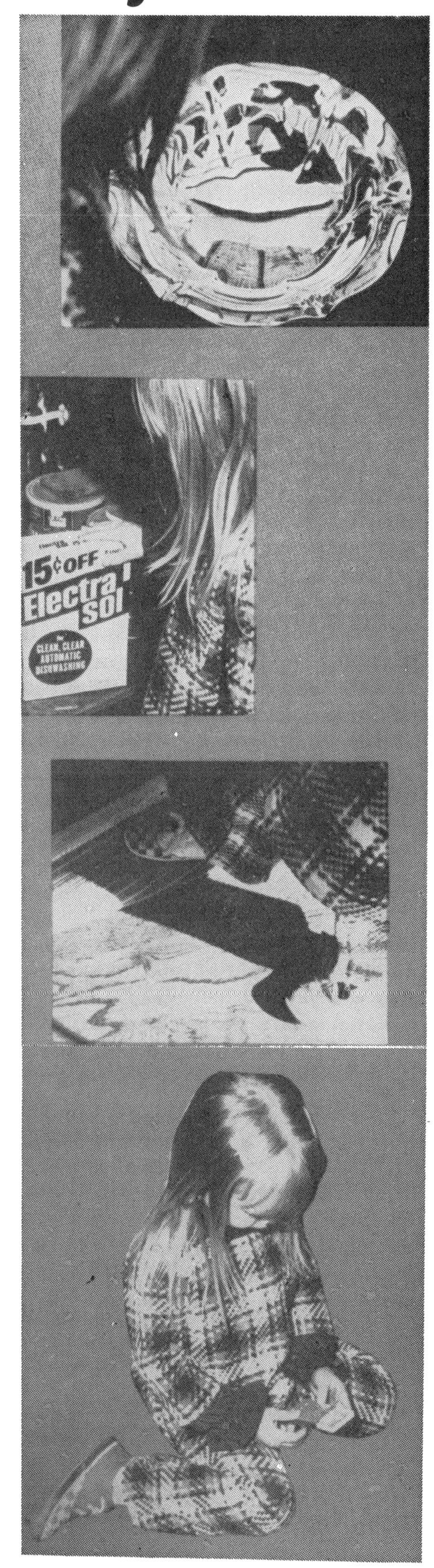

■ One of the axioms of providing experiences for preschool handicapped children is the involvement of parents in programing and planning. This holds when the experiences take place in a formalized setting out of the home but especially when they take place in the home. This involvement should also extend to the entire family.

Quite typically, the objectives of these experiences concern cognitive and affective understanding of the problems of the young handicapped child. This understanding is the knowledge, acceptance, and developmental component presented in various guises in prospectuses for programs, curriculum guides, and sometimes in the description of the intervention process itself. This approach is a logical extension of the meshing of the philosophic aspects of dynamic psychology, descriptive information about the nature of the problem, traditional laboratory experiments, and observations on certain behavioral aspects of growth and development.

However, what becomes apparent in working with the children and their fam-

"A Home Safety Inventory For Parents Of Preschool Handicapped Children", Gloria F. Wolinsky, Sylvia Walker, *Teaching Exceptional Children*, Vol. 7, No. 3, Spring 1975, © 1975 by The Council For Exceptional Children.

ilies is that there does exist in their lives a particular existential reality that interacts in a most fundamental way with many of these objectives. This reality, perhaps because of its apparent and necessary existence, is one that all too often is overlooked in planning. It is simply the particular environmental situation that is home, the physical properties that comprise the domicile of the family.

MOVEMENT WITHIN THE HOME ENVIRONMENT

How does the home environment affect the very young handicapped child? A typical objective or task for the very young is fostering the ability to move in a meaningful way in the environment. All types of activities, from rolling and grasping to bicycling, are to be found in the literature as potential desired goals for a particular handicapped child. Parents are instructed in how to teach their children basic motor skills. The current literature contains an abundance of discussions about self concepts, overprotection, rejection, and feelings. Parents are told that insight, patience, and training will bring about results. If the stated criteria of movement are met, the child has achieved mastery.

Within this process attitudes and behaviors are frequently noted which more often than not are described by the professional staff with terms such as *resistance, overprotection,* and *failure to understand* on the part of the mother and various members of the family.

Resistance often occurs or becomes more pronounced when the family, particularly the mother, realizes that the handicapped child is approaching a degree of independence where he is going to be at danger in a familiar and seemingly safe environment. It is similar to the problems that mothers have when the infant becomes a crawler or walker. It is too often the time for the playpen or other restrictive devices. The home environment is not specifically designed for the child whose function is often limited. The problem of safety and protection of a vulnerable child is compounded dramatically when the parents begin to falter either in training or, perhaps even more importantly, in follow-through. For the vast majority of parents this is a problem that can be resolved on the operational level with relatively simple techniques.

A HOME SAFETY INVENTORY

One simple technique to use is a home inventory which implies no absolute condemnation of the physical properties of a home environment but is rather an analysis of its separate components in relationship to the family's needs. These needs relate to items such as family composition, spatial arrangements, patterns of domestic routine, and life style which interact with the specific problems encountered as the exceptional child begins to actively engage the home environment.

There are parents who face fundamental problems of child safety. Working in what is basically a sheltered situation, professionals, in their concern for the normative experience and potential for normal participation by the handicapped child, frequently overlook the dangerous situations which the child encounters within his own home. Furthermore, parents may be unwilling to verbalize their difficulty in coping with seemingly mundane problems when faced with the overwhelming mass of expertise that is foisted upon them in terms of the needs of a particular young child.

The cerebral palsied child, for example, experiences many random involuntary movements. What does this mean in a household where there is a considerable collection of bric-a-brac? A child who walks with the aid of crutches may easily slip and fall. What does one do to minimize the potential impact of sharp kitchen counter corners? The brain injured child may experience among other things confused spatial orientation. What does one do with decorative bowls that reflect light? The retarded child, like all children, is curious. There is the ever present allure of cleaning powder in attractively boxed containers.

All children have an eagerness to explore their environment. This environment should be conducive to exploration. Active exploration and interaction is a basis for cognitive growth. How does one resolve a seemingly paradoxical situation?

DEVELOPING THE HOME INVENTORY

The inventory which has been devel-

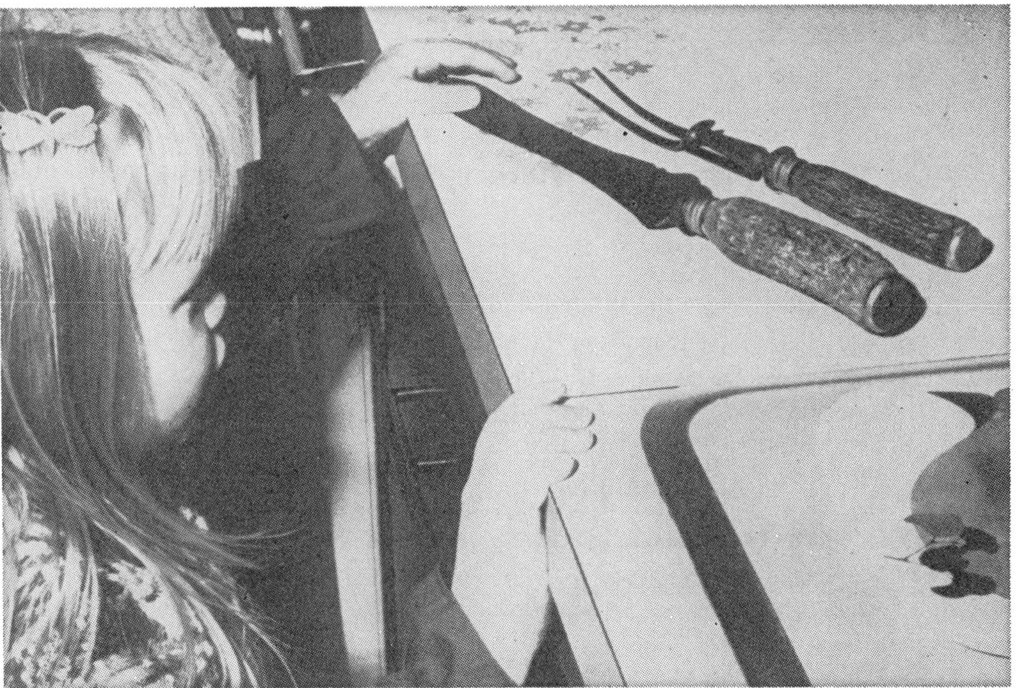

oped to assist with this problem results from a class assignment designed to alert prospective teachers of the handicapped to situational problems within the home. The assignment was to use one's own home or apartment, to choose one child that the student worked with in a field situation, and to list the hazards in the house for their child and suggestions for alleviating the problem.

Each home inventory was discussed in class. Additions were made and a composite list was developed for use as an inventory or checklist. The list itself refers to physical surroundings which range from living quarters in lower class urban tenements to affluent middle class suburban homes. The children used as models were:

- A 6 year old wheelchair bound, cerebral palsied child who was able to use both arms and hands without difficulty.
- A 6 year old rubella boy who was blind and autistic, with neurological impairments.
- A 3 year old totally blind child.
- A 5 year old cerebral palsied deaf child who had little muscle control and was subject to random involuntary movements. He was confined to a wheelchair most of the time, with the exception of occasional play periods when he was allowed to move around on the floor.
- A 3 year old boy diagnosed as cerebral palsied, with other handicapping conditions in the lower and upper extremities. He was ambulatory with assistance.
- A 5 year old cerebral palsied girl who walked with the aid of crutches and had poor motor coordination.
- A 4 year old athetoid cerebral palsied boy with involuntary movements of the body parts and gross and fine athetoid movements of all limbs.

Apparently pots, pans, gas jets, and scatter rugs are fairly universal home items. Glass picture windows present a problem in certain housing, while leaded paint, broken glass, and roach powder are particular dangers in other environments. The inventory functions as a device to alert parents to dangers within their home and stimulates discussion of ways of coping with the problem.

USING THE HOME INVENTORY

How can this inventory best be used? Since it does not concern itself with absolutes, it can vary with the specific problems of the parents and may be used on an individual or group basis. It can be used as a checklist, or it can be used to answer such questions as:

- Are these observations realistic to you?
- Are they problematic?
- What are the specific problems in your home?
- What are other techniques for modifications?

3. PROGRAMS

- Do these modifications mean a problem for your family?
- Is there another way of doing it?
- Is modification for my family realistic?

It can be collated in a booklet, discussed, acted upon, and referred to at subsequent meetings to see if a developing youngster presents different problems in terms of a safe environment. The variations are as numerous as the parents, children, and situations presented. The ultimate aim is to provide an environment which enhances a child's ability to function.

KITCHEN – Safety Level

QUESTION	Yes	No	Sometimes	Easily Remedied	Problem
1. When you are cooking, do handles extend over edge of stove so that pots and pans may be tipped over?	____	____	____	____	____
2. Are your matches easily accessible?	____	____	____	____	____
3. Do your cabinets have sharp corners on which your child might bump his/her head?	____	____	____	____	____
4. Are your kitchen utensils (such as carving knives and forks)					
a. Displayed on racks within the reach of the child?	____	____	____	____	____
b. Stored in drawers or cabinets easily accessible to the child?	____	____	____	____	____
c. Left lying around when not in use?	____	____	____	____	____
5. Can knobs on kitchen range be turned on easily?	____	____	____	____	____
6. Is your kitchen floor waxed to a high gloss (which makes it slippery)?	____	____	____	____	____
7. Are your pots and pans stored in such a manner that they will fall when a cabinet is opened?	____	____	____	____	____
8. Are your detergents and other household cleaners stored in an area where they are quite accessible to children?	____	____	____	____	____
9. Are breakable items, such as glass mixing bowls, within the easy reach of young children?	____	____	____	____	____
10. Are your toasters, bakers, broilers, ovens, blenders, mixer, etc., displayed near your counter edges so that:					
a. They will/may fall if hit by extraneous movement?	____	____	____	____	____
b. They can be pulled down by their cords?	____	____	____	____	____
11. Are your cabinet doors closed when not in use?	____	____	____	____	____
12. Are your tables and chairs sturdy and in good condition so that they:					
a. Will not tip over easily?	____	____	____	____	____
b. Can be used for support by a child who needs such support in order to get from one area (of a room, house, or apartment) to another?	____	____	____	____	____
13. What are some potential hazards in your kitchen?					
BATHROOM – Safety Level					
1. Are your medicines and toiletries stored in areas inaccessible to children?	____	____	____	____	____
2. Is your bathtub skidproof?	____	____	____	____	____
3. Is your bathroom floor slippery?	____	____	____	____	____
4. Can your bathroom door be easily locked from the inside?	____	____	____	____	____
5. Is something left out that should have been included?					
GENERAL – Safety Level (living room, bedroom, etc.)					
1. Are scatter rugs secured to prevent a child from tripping?	____	____	____	____	____
2. Have you secured large rugs and carpets to prevent a child (or other family member) from tripping over corners and edges?	____	____	____	____	____
3. Are your lamps, statuettes, and other such objects likely to topple if they are touched by a child?	____	____	____	____	____
4. Are objects such as vases, plants, glass ashtrays, or knickknacks an invitation for little hands?	____	____	____	____	____
5. Are appliances such as radios, stereos, and portable television sets positioned in a way which will prevent them from falling?	____	____	____	____	____

	Yes	No	Some-times	Easily Remedied	Problem
6. Are electrical cords placed so that:					
a. They will not be tripped over?					
b. The appliance cannot be pulled down by its cord?					
c. They are anchored to prevent dangling wires?					
7. Do your closet doors open easily to allow a child to crawl into the closet and close the door behind him?					
8. Are objects arranged so that they do not fall when closet is opened?					
9. Are there exposed outlets?					
10. Are windows inaccessible to a child?					
11. Are doors leading outside or to basement areas locked securely?					
12. Are all steps guarded to prevent a child from falling?					
13. Do all stairways have railings?					
14. Are floors in all rooms uncluttered to eliminate tripping?					
15. Are your chairs and other furniture so arranged that they may be used as ladders or step stools to dangerous items such as glass framed pictures or wall plaques?					
16. Do your radiators have protective covers?					
17. Does much of your furniture have sharp edges?					
18. Can your child reach a dangling venetian blind cord?					
19. Does your child have easy access to discarded poisonous bottles and containers?					

20. Is there something you would like to add to the list?

DO THESE MODIFICATIONS SOUND RIGHT FOR YOUR HOME?

Sometimes suggestions for improving the environment offer another approach to home inventory. The suggestions can be discussed in terms of feasibility, practicality, further modificaton, and feedback.

A similar checklist format is presented here. Again the ultimate use and modification is dependent on the situation.

KITCHEN

	Feasible In My Home	Practical	Additional Modification
Turn handles of pots and pans away from stove edge.			
Place matches in a secure place. Use safety matches.			
Cover cabinet corners with foam rubber padding (may be glued on).			
Place kitchen utensils in a securely closed drawer (out of reach of children).			
Remove range knobs when stove is not in use.			
Use nonskid wax or, still better, don't wax.			
Store pots and pans neatly in low cabinets.			
Store household cleaners and breakable items on high shelves.			
Place electric appliances away from counter edges.			
Fold cords out of reach when appliances are not in use.			
Check tables and chairs to see that they are in good condition.			
Repair or replace faulty furniture.			
Use placemats (except for special occasions) instead of tablecloth on table, to prevent child from pulling cloth off table.			
Place a gate at the kitchen door to restrict child's entrance during times when kitchen area is highly dangerous (e.g., hot oven door).			

BATHROOM	Feasible In My Home	Practical	Additional Modification
Transfer medicines to safe storage area.	______	______	______
Install rubberized mat.	______	______	______
Install (removable)railing on bathtub.	______	______	______
Place soft, plush, rubberized mat on bathroom floor.	______	______	______
Fit the toilet with a collapsible training pot with raised sides to give security.	______	______	______
Mark the hot water faucet with colored tape.	______	______	______
Remove or disengage low lock. Install hook or other locking device near the top of the door.	______	______	______
GENERAL			
Replace or modify scatter rugs (e.g., sew rubber stripping to underside).	______	______	______
Use carpet tacks to secure large rugs to floor.	______	______	______
Relocate fragile vases, plants, etc.	______	______	______
Use nonbreakable knickknacks.	______	______	______
Place radios, etc., as near to wall and as close to outlet as possible.	______	______	______
Anchor cords to appliances or to floor by using colored Mystik or masking tape.	______	______	______
Arrange furniture to allow for the least exposure of electric wires.	______	______	______
Place a hook near the top of the closet door, above child's reach.	______	______	______
Plug up electrical outlets with plastic protectors.	______	______	______
Install window guards or window locks for low windows.	______	______	______
Place hooks near the top of doors leading to restricted areas such as the basement.	______	______	______
Install radiator covers or screens.	______	______	______
Cover sharp corners with foam rubber.	______	______	______
Install hooks near venetian blinds near the top of a window. The cord may be folded and attached to the hook.	______	______	______
Cover garbage pail, and store in a secure place.	______	______	______
Bend, weight, or otherwise adjust eating utensils such as spoons to better fit the child's hand in order to provide more secure grasp.	______	______	______
Provide a safe secure area where child may have freedom to play.	______	______	______
Use plastic tumblers, plates, etc., when possible.	______	______	______

What other suggestions can you add to this list?

■ The authors wish to thank the following students who helped in the initial listing of the items used in this inventory: R. Amira, C. Behan, G. Benedetto, O. Cromer, L. Guttilla, N. Koehler, J. Levy, J. Malizia, R. Mallison, B. Marterer, J. Reisman, E. Resnick, A. Semelmacher, B. Tetenbaum, A. Zuckerman.

A Multimodality Language Program For Retarded Preschoolers

JUDITH M. WOLF
MARY LYNNE McALONIE

Abstract: Eight retarded preschool children placed in a day activity center setting were selected for inclusion in a multimodality receptive language program. The program is described and teacher training procedures are discussed. Results indicate that all children made gains in receptive language skills and half of the children showed advances in expressive language functioning.

One of the important new trends in the education of handicapped children has been the early identification and treatment of language based deficiencies, recognizing that language development is an essential facet of a child's overall cognitive functioning. More traditional language development programs for the preschool aged child have been concerned primarily with language production rather than comprehension. Two exceptions to this emphasis have been reported in the Infant, Toddler and Preschool Intervention Project (Bricker & Bricker, 1972) and the EDGE Project (Rynders & Horrobin, 1975).

Wolf and Rynders (1975) suggested that the severe expressive language delay common in the preschool retarded child is one of the factors that later complicates the deriving of an accurate educational placement decision. They recommend that one solution should be the consideration of language training strategies for young retarded children that allow for nonverbal response and provide greater stress on receptive stimulation.

Other investigators (Schaffer & Goehl, 1974) have also recognized the need for receptive language programing for young retarded children. They point out that a program offering manual as well as psycholinguistic approaches may be most desirable for the severely language delayed child. This interest in manual language strategies, more specifically the use of American Sign Language, has been apparent in the work of several special educators in programing for the retarded individual. Hoffmeister and Farmer (1972) suggest the use of sign language as a strategy to promote functional communication skills in deaf retarded individuals. Hollis and Carrier (1975) report similar evidence that many severely retarded children can and do learn parts of a communication system when using a nonspeech response mode.

The Study Setting

The language training approach employed in the present study represents a pilot of a multimodality receptive language program with retarded hearing children in a preschool setting. The goals or purposes of this project were to increase receptive language development and to stimulate verbal (expressive) language behavior. The Minnesota Early Language Development Sequence—MELDS (Clark, Moores, & Woodcock, 1975) curriculum was selected as the intervention treatment. MELDS emphasizes the repetition of concrete vocabulary as a learning strategy. It offers a program of structured lessons being used presently by teachers and parents to facilitate the development of language skills in young hearing impaired children who have little or no language. The program

"A Multimodality Language Program For Retarded Preschoolers", Judith M. Walk and Mary Lynne McAlouice, *Education and Training of the Mentally Retarded,* Vol. 12, No. 3, October 1977, © 1977, Council For Exceptional Children.

TABLE 1

Descriptive Data on MELDS Project Children Characteristics

Subject Number	*CA*	*Gesell Developmental Quotient*	*Residence*	*Etiology*	*Other Handicaps*
1	2.2	50	Natural	D.S.*	None
2	2.4	60	Natural	D.S.	None
3	3.9	73	Natural	D.S.	Nystagmus
4	2.3	57	Natural	D.S.	Congenital heart defect
5	3.0	68	Foster	D.S.	None
6	3.1	63	Natural	D.S.	Muscular eye weakness
7	3.7	63	Foster	D.S.	Congenital heart defect
8	3.2	47	Natural	Unknown	Extreme distractibility

* Down's syndrome.

combines two visual language systems, rebuses (picture words) and the vocabulary of American Sign Language (ASL). Materials used in the program include a teacher's manual and lesson guide, rebus cards, sentence cards, and a glossary of signs and rebuses.

The teaching procedure recommended is that rebuses be put into a pocket chart and the teacher use them in combination with signs and spoken language to label words or form sentences. In addition, the fact that MELDS is primarily an input program is consistent with existing literature suggesting that receptive language development precedes expressive language development in children (Myklebust, 1960).

Method

Subjects

Following initial referral by the teacher for inclusion in the project, all prospective subjects were seen by the language consultant and observed for level of sensory and motor ability, receptive and expressive language functioning, and responsiveness to instruction. Letters were then sent to parents explaining the project and the cooperation of the speech clinician or language teacher in each Day Activity Center (DAC) was requested.

Eight retarded preschoolers were subsequently selected to participate in the experimental multimodality language program called MELDS. Criteria of selection included: a delay in the comprehension of language as judged by the child's preschool teacher; an ability and willingness to vocalize (i.e., no hearing loss, no gross physiological or neurological damage, no emotional disturbance); an ability to maintain minimal eye contact; an ability to point to objects and/or pictures; and a pattern of nonverbal behavior which indicated early sensorimotor skills. Children ranged in age from 26 months to 37 months at the beginning of the project. Children selected for the study were attending five different day activity centers for the preschool retarded, which are part of the East Metropolitan Day Activity Center Council (EMDACC) in St. Paul, Minnesota. Table 1 displays descriptive data of the group.

Procedure

Initially an attempt was made to locate 20 children to participate in the project, of whom 10 would be randomly assigned to a MELDS group and 10 randomly assigned to a general language stimulation group. Project limitations prevented this procedure due to an inability to identify and maintain a program for 20 children on a continuous basis. As a result, 8 children were selected according to the criteria mentioned and all were enrolled in the MELDS project. It must be recognized that this decision makes the study a descriptive one rather than adhering to experimental design.

Each child was administered a pretest designed to sample receptive and expressive language ability. Children were tested individually by the language consultant in the therapy room designated by each DAC. A test was designed using vocabulary taken from the first 20 lessons of the MELDS manual. This test consisted of every third noun, five common verbs and one preposition, totaling 18 test items. Consideration was also given to the feasibility of picturing the item in question. Pictures were developed for each item and nonproject children of similar CA were pilot tested using the pictures. Pictures were done in black pen and ink and drawn on 5″ × 5″ cards. Foils (distractor items) were common vocabulary items not drawn from the MELDS manual. Stimulus and foil items were randomly placed on each plate in an attempt to control for position bias. The receptive portion of the test required that the child "point to" the appropriate item, and included both semantic (label) and syntactic (verb, preposition) vocabulary. The expressive portion of the test, requiring that the child name the item, included only pictures depicting a semantic item.

The sequence inherent in the MELDS program prescribed the nature of the language stimulation offered each child. The same individual administered the MELDS program to a given child for the entire 20 week period except in one instance where the child transferred from one DAC to another and continued the MELDS program with a previously trained teacher in the new DAC setting. Children received training three times weekly for approximately 15 minutes each session. Children were generally seen on a one-to-one basis (in one case on a one-to-two basis). Most children were able to complete the first 20 lessons of the MELDS program during 20 weeks although two children completed only 18 lessons.

Participating teachers were pretrained by the investigators in the use of the MELDS materials. Teachers were required to use response sheets for each lesson, summarizing pointing, sign, and verbal behaviors occurring during the session. In addition, one-hour monthly observations were conducted alternately by each of the investigators in the participating centers on each of the project children. The goal of the observation visit was to ensure as much as possible, that each child was receiving the same exposure to intervention. Response opportunities and stimulus offerings were counted for each teacher with each of the project children. Also, six memoranda were sent to the teachers to inform them of changes made in the program, to give them feedback on observations and to provide them with necessary information.

The details of intervention were as follows:

- Teachers presented the MELDS lessons to project children each Monday, Wednesday and Friday morning for approximately 15 minutes, individually or in groups of two.
- Teachers were instructed to present each section of a lesson several times. For example, lesson #1 introduces the words "table," "chair," and "box."
- Using real objects, the teacher pointed to the object, showed the rebus for that object, signed the word, said the word, matched rebus, object and sign to one another (always verbalizing the label), and then asked the child for a receptive response, e.g., "point to box" (real or rebus). This sequence would be repeated for each vocabulary item in a lesson and was referred to as a "loop."
- Teachers were encouraged to do at least three loops for each item in a lesson.

TABLE 2

Total Number of Responses During 11 MELDS Lessons

Subject Number	*Pointed to Object or Rebus*	*Performed Motor Action*	*Signed*	*Said Word*
1	326	27	172	566
2	317	10	340	8
3	348	33	302	360
4	329	45	77	36
5	235	53	190	253
6	118	None	107	117
7	540	45	1431	2030
8	452	89	407	335

In the initial lessons, receptive responses were encouraged from the children and no demand was made for an expressive response. As the lessons progressed, an expressive branch was added to the input portion of each session. This branch provided opportunities for the child to sign for an object, action or rebus, or verbalize the word. The desired outcome of the expressive branch was for the child to offer spontaneously the appropriate verbal label for the object or rebus. Teachers reviewed the rebus cards from the previous two lessons at the beginning of each lesson. This procedure served to orient the children to the situation.

Results

Pre- and posttest scores earned by program children on receptive and expressive portions of the test are shown in Figures 1 and 2. Due to the small N, usual tests of significance were not applied to the data. In terms of the goals of the project, to increase receptive language development and to stimulate verbal behavior, the 8 project children show clear gains in meeting at least the first goal. As is shown in Figure 1, all children made substantial change on receptive test items from November to May. Becuase MELDS is primarily an input program, receptive language gains such as these shown in 8 retarded language-delayed young children would seem to offer support for use of such an approach.

Expressive language results, shown in Figure 2, are not conclusive. No child demonstrated verbal behavior on verbal test items in November. By May, on posttest, 4 children (50 percent) verbalized substantially and

FIGURE 1

Responses of children in MELDS Program to Receptive Language Test Items, Pre- and Posttest Scores

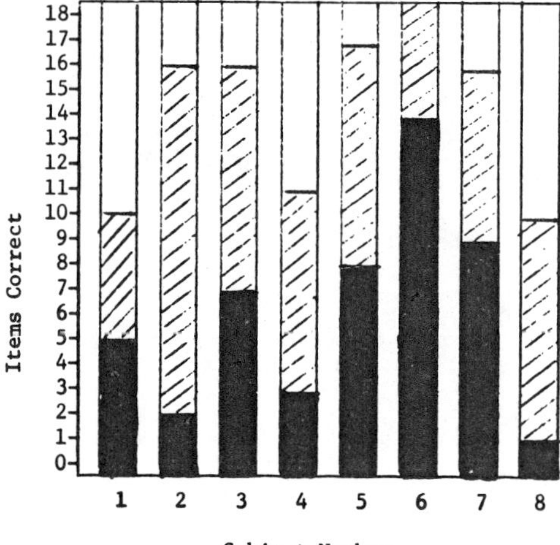

were also noted to have signed responses to several items. One other child signed several of the items, but did not verbalize. The remaining three children demonstrated no evidence of correct verbal response, although, in each case the number of "no responses" decreased and the number of "incorrect responses" increased. It would appcar that the expectation for a verbal response was present, but the child could not or did not produce an intelligible word.

Data were also collected from observation/count sheets filled out by the teachers. During Lessons 1 through 9, teachers were required to count the receptive responses of the child. Children, in general, were reported to respond to verbal guidance and manual guidance. (These data should not be regarded as extremely reliable because it seemed to require several weeks before teachers could comfortably count and instruct simultaneously. Data were therefore not tabled for Lessons 1 through 9.) In terms of expressive responses, teachers recorded verbal responses of children during Lessons 10 through 20. Total number of verbal responses for the 11 lessons ranged from 2,030 responses recorded for subject number 7 to 8 verbal responses recorded for subject number 2. Data collected during the last 11 lessons, including total number of pointing responses per subject, total number of action responses, total number of signed responses, and total number of words, appear in Table 2. It seems clear that the range of performance within each facet of expressive behavior and total expressive responses of children during MELDS lessons 10 through 20 was extensive, as were opportunities for response and number of stimulus offerings recorded by the investigators during teacher observation. The number of stimulus offerings made by teachers during a lesson observation ranged from 17 to 231 offerings, with a mean of 89 offerings. The number of opportunities for response ranged from 12 to 95 with a mean of 56 opportunities.

Summary and Discussion

It is assumed by many special educators that a language training program for retarded preschoolers should emphasize direct manipulation of vocal-verbal output in order to modify expressive language functioning. This study was designed to pilot a language program, MELDS, which provides rich input experiences in an attempt to stimulate the development of expressive language ability as well as expand language comprehension.

Eight retarded preschoolers were placed in the MELDS program for 7 months. Day activity center teachers worked with these children three times weekly using the MELDS vocabulary, i.e., real objects, rebuses, signs, and words representing the MELDS vocabulary. Data suggest that these

FIGURE 2

Responses of Children in MELDS Program to Expressive Language Test Items, Pre- and Posttest Scores

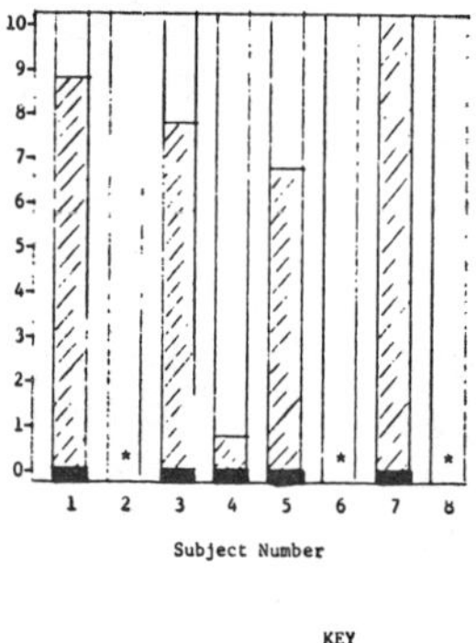

8 children were able to make substantial gains in receptive language over the 7-month period. In addition, considering the nonverbal characteristics of the population at the onset of the study, notable expressive language gains were made by the end of the study by at least 4 of the 8 subjects.

The results of the study offer tentative support for the usefulness of a multimodality receptive language program for stimulating language in severely language retarded preschool children. Results also suggest that nonverbal (manual) communication may precede and facilitate the acquisition of the first spoken words in a child's language development. Early programing emphasizing input but with every expectation of an expressive response on the part of the child seems to be a valid approach. These results must be regarded within the limitations of a descriptive study.

References

Bricker, D. D., & Bricker, W. A. (Eds.). *Toddler research and intervention project report year II, IMRID: Behavioral Science Monograph No. 21.* Nashville, Tenn.: George Peabody College, 1972.

Clark, C. R., Moores, D. F., & Woodcock, R. W. The Minnesota Early Language Development Sequence, Development Kits #1 and #2. Minneapolis: Research, Development and Demonstration Center, University of Minnesota, 1975.

Hoffmeister, R., & Farmer, A. The development of manual sign language in mentally retarded deaf individuals. *Journal of Rehabilitation of the Deaf*, 1972, 19–26.

Hollis, J., & Carrier, J. Research implications for communication deficiencies. *Exceptional Children*, 1975, *41*, 405–412.

Myklebust, J. *The psychology of deafness*. New York: Grune & Stratton, 1960.

Rynders, J., & Horrobin, M. Project EDGE: The University of Minnesota's communication stimulation program for Down's syndrome infants, 1974. In B. Z. Friedlander, G. Sterritt, and G. Kirk (Eds.), *Exceptional infant assessment and intervention* (Vol. 3). New York: Bruner/Mazel Inc., 1975.

Schaffer, T., & Goehl, H. The alinguistic child. *Mental Retardation*, 1974, *12*, 3–6.

Reference Note

Wolf, J., & Rynders, J. *Problems in estimating the educational promise of preschool Down's syndrome*

PARENTS

Society perpetuates myths; one pertinent myth is that from a blissful marriage union come children who are physically and mentally beautiful and perfect. No parent is ever prepared to be the parent of a handicapped child. No matter when the parent discovers that his or her child has a handicap, the realization is a "blow" and few parents adjust immediately. Initial reaction to the handicapped child contains almost universal aggrieved emotions and attitudes. Some repress reality or are unable to grasp the significance of the happening. Feelings of numbness, disbelief and withdrawal successively emerge and the intense disappointment may be accompanied by affective and physical symptoms. Guilt, feelings of helplessness and anger, resentment and rejection are other common emotions. Counseling, guidance and education are needed to help parents recognize these feeling, accept the facts and mobilize strengths to work more effectively with the handicapped child within the family unit.

Transition to any new role necessitates learning new ways of behaving and new socialization patterns. Two broad categories can be considered in differentiating this unplanned for position of parents of a handicapped child. One aspect of this role is that of instrumental or technical facilitator. An example of some instrumental aspects include the parent learning specific ways to help develop visual perception skills, monitor degrees of movement or mobility, establish special ways of home management including precise programs for stimulation, self care, vocalization or verbalization and play activities. The other aspect to be learned is the expressive or emotional; how to cope with the temptation either to overprotect or underprotect the child, how to accept one's own emotional reactions, how to respond to the grief or denial from relatives, friends or community, and how to adjust one's days and life to include the needs of the special child as part of the family pattern. These instrumental and expressive components are not necessarily separate; they mesh together. Emotional or expressive aspects are part of every instrumental endeavor. The parents ability to weld successfully the feelings and the tasks to be done, will be the effective force.

Attitudes toward parental involvement in the education and socialization of their handicapped children have run the gamut from total disassociation to active participation. Today special educators, school personnel and professionals encourage active participation and commitment from the parents. The current parent training movement in special education is a relatively recent condition resulting from several societal trends - parent advocacy groups, parent lobbies, psychological research on parent/child interactions and now the importance and strength of parental voice and opinion as a result of PL 94-142. Specialists and experts for every nuance of special education have developed programs for school and home training, guidance for appropriate toys and materials and checklists of suggestions for household structuring.

Early intervention and parent training programs have proven viable and productive. They have contributed to positive change in attitudes and assisted parents in ways to sucessfully help foster growth and development for their handicapped child.

Parenting, Teaching, and Child Development

Ira J. Gordon

Ira J. Gordon, Ed.D., is Graduate Research Professor, Foundations of Education, and Director of the Institute for the Development of Human Resources at the University of Florida in Gainesville. His areas of experience include counseling and guidance, teacher education, research in human development, early family influences, and home-school relationships.

The processes of parenting and teaching have much in common. Based on what we know about child development, we can specify good teaching and help prepare people for more effective parenthood.

What we do as teachers and parents, as adults, makes a difference in what happens to children. The common view now is that development equals learning, not that the development and learning are parallel and do not meet, but it wasn't many years ago that parents were told there was very little connection between development and learning. If you were a parent, you were supposed to buy Gesell (1941), which was the standard "bible" and had a maturational orientation. If you had a two-year-old, you turned to the right page in Gesell and checked out your child. If he or she were behaving like a two-year-old, you sighed with relief; if the child was behaving like a one-year-old, you locked the child in the back room. But you did not do anything about it.

Today, our view is that the parent is a primary teacher of the child. What we do, both as parents and teachers, makes a considerable difference, not only in children's learning of facts but in their total development, self-concept, intellectual development, in all areas of their life. How do parents as the primary teachers teach their children? They teach essentially the way teachers teach. They provide a learning environment, model behavior, and engage in direct instruction with the child. These three means are common to parents and teachers.

An old custom that originates in the Rabbinic oral tradition is the use of the alphabet as a way of remembering the order of things. The following discussion of those three will be handled by an alphabetical device. There are five "P's," four "R's," and the old reliable "TLC."

"Parenting, Teaching, and Child Development", Ira J. Gordon, *Young Children,* Vol. 31, No. 3, March 1976. ©1976 National Association for the Education of Young Children.

The Five "P's"

The first "P" is the **provision of the learning environment.** We have now a body of literature from a variety of places, not simply in the United States but from around the world, concerning the relationship between the learning environment in the home and the achievement of the child in school. The findings transcend nationality and social class. There seem to be conditions that occur throughout the western world; the following examples, however, come from recent United States research. Elardo, Bradley, and Caldwell (1975) observed in a number of homes in Arkansas when children were six months old, and tested these children on the Stanford-Binet at age three. They reported that there were many ways in which what they saw in the home at three months could be related to the performance of the children at three years of age. The two main factors, in terms of the provision of the learning environment, are (1) opportunities for variety of stimulation and (2) the organization of the environment, the arrangement and order in the home.

In a study in Illinois by Wachs, Uzgiris, and Hunt (1971), homes of children below the age of one were observed. The parents' competence was measured by the Uzgiris-Hunt scales, based on Piaget. They indicated one very positive and one very negative characteristic on this first "P." The positive characteristic was simply the presence in the home and the availability of magazines to the child at nine months of age. You know nine-month-old children really do not read these magazines, but just having them around and being able to feel them, touch them, taste them, smell them seemed to make a difference with these nine-month-olds. The negative factor was noise: Higher levels of noise in a home seemed to specifically affect, in a negative way, the development of the child.

In some of our own work (Gordon and Guinagh 1974), we have gathered information on homes of a number of primarily low-income families in Florida. We gathered information, beginning at three months of age, again at three years of age, and we now can relate this to child performance at age six after a year of kindergarten. In this respect it is different from the other studies, since we can see how long home effects last, and how they affect performance when the child has already been exposed to school. The most important provision of learning experience is out-of-home experience—the planning and use by the family of the environment outside the home for learning. That environment can be broadly defined. The experience can be a car ride, a trip to the supermarket, zoo, library, or museum. It does not have to be cultural, as in terms of the Metropolitan Opera. It can be planning for and using many of the natural kinds of experiences that could go on in any family. For the boys in our study, the presence of reading material in the home at age six related positively to Stanford-Binet scores *within* the experimental group. If the parent made an issue out of reading itself, this had a positive effect on the girls. There are similar findings in North Carolina (Landsberger 1973).

If we look at day care centers, we can find some similar provisions of learning environment as important criteria in child development. The work especially of Prescott, Jones, and Kritchevsky (1972) in California indicates that significant variables are the organization of space, staff, and time, and whether they are integrated.

Kritchevsky concluded that the poor use of space led to tired and irritable teachers and obviously such tired and irritable teachers can do little about creating an affectionate relationship with children. What do they agree are good spatial arrangements? (1) Sub areas for different activities not lined up in a row, (2) opportunities for activities for the single child (a swing for example), as well as (3) ar-

> rangements for privacy [not everything is a great big open space], (4) division of space by the type of activity and the noise level (quiet—noisy, clean—dirty), (5) mixtures of man-made and natural materials (a whole is to dig), (6) one which allows the child to explore in safety, (7) that allows the child to try new things but also to continue to play with old, and (8) an uncluttered environment, but one with much diversity. [How do you keep it both uncluttered and diverse?] (Gordon 1975, p. 148)

One of our problems in some of our parent education work, with both the parent educators and with mothers, is the check off system. You know, the children played with the toy, now on to the next, without recognizing that they need to do what Murphy called "mess and manipulate" (Murphy 1958). They need to go back to the old, familiar, and dog-eared object and enjoy it all over again, and perhaps enjoy it in some new way. There needs to be space in which children can play with new things, but also to go back to the old familiar.

Staffing guidelines, as part of the learning environment, are not so much just the adult-child ratio as the use of staff.

> Infants and young children need continuity of care. This means that the same adult should be with the same children for long enough periods of time so that a bond can develop. Just to have a 1 to 5 ratio in a center with 30 or so children does not guarantee this. (Gordon 1975, p. 148)

We have some kindergartens that have the appropriate ratio 1 to 10, but there are 120 children in a huge room and 12 adults roaming around. Although a ratio is important, assignment and organization will determine if there is the provision of an adequate learning environment.

> Time is a third factor. Children's own energy needs, own rhythms, own sleep needs are highly individual. Centers even more so than homes often override these needs by imposing standard time. It is difficult to organize around individual rhythms, and it is possible for children to learn the schedule. The point here is the awareness of individuality within a scheduled day. Every child does not need the same amount of sleep. If space is arranged properly, some can take longer naps, while others engage in noisy play. Some take longer to eat, and need more help than others. With adequate space arrangements, and staff, it should be possible for them to have this time and help while another toddler is finished and goes off to play. (Gordon 1975, p. 148)

All these are combined—space, staff, time—in the first "P."

The second "P" is **predictability.** There are varied studies that show the need of young children, if not indeed of all of us, for some sense of order and system. Children need to know what is happening. They need to know that behavior allowed today will not lead to punishment tomorrow; behavior approved by mom is also approved by dad. They need the comfort that parents do not operate from whim, but from some sense of consistency, both within the individual parent and between the parents.

We see this also in schools. Kounin (1970) observed Detroit classrooms to find out why it was that in some classrooms the child who had been labeled disturbed was really climbing the walls, and when the bell rang and periods changed, the child moved into the next classroom and could not be located apart from anybody else. As Kounin checked into this, he uncovered two elements that relate to predictability. One of them is transition. How smoothly do you, as either a parent or a teacher, move a child from one activity to another? I know that one of my own faults as a college teacher is making bad transitions. I will start on a new topic, and then remember that there was something more to say about the old, and shift back to it. That may be fine for 21-year-olds; they can handle it, but young children cannot. They need to know what the arrangements

"Children need to know what is happening. They need to know that behavior allowed today will not lead to punishment tomorrow; . . ."

are and are influenced by the smoothness with which the things flow. The second element Kounin called thrusting—interruption of the child's on-going activities because it suits adult needs at the moment. Who among us has not been guilty of this?

An example is the typical three reading group situation, groups B and C are busy while the teacher is with group A. Right in the middle of A's activity, the teacher looks at the clock and says, "11:00: Group B come up." Everything goes to pot. We do a lot of thrusting, because we have time schedules that do not match the learning experiences and the timing of children. They need to know when to shift, but it can be handled in rather simple ways.

You can use what Soar has called gentle control (Soar 1974, p. 7). He defines this as suggesting changes in behavior or giving feedback on pupil behavior in fairly gentle and noncoercive ways. You could say, "We have 5 minutes to wrap that up." This does not mean their 5 minutes matches your 5 minutes, but it does mean that they have some signal to begin to taper off, and move on to something else. It sounds like common sense; unfortunately, it is not very common.

Predictability relates to the amount of control. It's one thing to say that children need order and system. It is another to find that magic line between too much and too little Soar has observed in classrooms all over the United States, from kindergarten through third grade, and up to fifth and sixth grade. Not only has he come up with this notion of gentle control, but he has also examined the whole point about how you can tell the differences in amount of control in classrooms.

> One of the major ways in which classrooms differ from each other, is in the extent to which the activities in the classroom emanate from the teacher rather than from the pupil. [The same thing applies to parent-child.] At one extreme the teacher sets the problem, directs the activities in which pupils are engaged, monitors and reinforces the work of pupils and evaluates the results of their efforts. Pupils have little choice about what they do, how they do it, or the basis on which they will be evaluated. They have little or no wiggle room. At the other end of the scale, pupils have a high degree of freedom to choose the activity on which they will work, with whom, how long, and decision as to which it was useful may be theirs, if the question occurs at all. The teacher is available as a resource, may set the outer limits to the behavior which is permitted, but even these are likely to be broad. Of course, these are extremes of a dimension along which classrooms scale, with most classrooms somewhere in-between. . . . In four sets of data the finding has emerged that when classrooms were rank ordered, from those in which the pupils have least freedom, to those in which pupils have most freedom, gains increased. But this was only true up to a point, and beyond that point as pupil freedom increased, gain no longer increased but began to decrease. That is, there is an optimum point, a balance, between teacher control, and pupil freedom at which the greatest pupil subject matter growth occurred. (Soar 1974, p. 6)

It is fine to discover this fact, but the problem is that it does not help us to find out, in our classrooms and homes, where that "magic" line is. Baumrind (1970) describes the parent who is authoritative, as distinct from the authoritarian parent. The authoritative parent sets limits, has standards, and conveys them with reasoning and explanation. This is another aspect of predictability. Children need to know not only what is expected, but why it is expected.

In studying teacher-pupil relations and parent-child situations we found three other "P's." These come primarily out of our infant work (Gordon and Jester 1972). We videotaped 128 families every 6 weeks beginning when the baby was 13 weeks old until he or she was 49 weeks old. We measured the youngsters on the Bayley scale at age one. The first of these three "P's" is a very positive "P"; it is called **ping-pong** because it looks like a ping-pong game. I do something, you do something, I do something, you do something. It can be related to reinforcement concepts, but also to concepts described by White (1972) and Escalona and Corman (1973, 1974). For example, Escalona and Corman observe for sustained reciprocal social interaction. Our shorthand is ping-pong. There is a new study by Kaye

"Children need to know not only what is expected, but why it is expected."

(1975) in which ping-pong is begun and controlled by the children through their gazing techniques. They get busy in something, the mothers watch; when they gaze away, mothers know it is time to get back into the act again. White and Watts (1973) indicate that ping-pong is often initiated by the child, and is not necessarily a very long volley. Odd moments in natural situations are optimum times for parent-infant ping-pong.

The second positive variable is **persistence.** The child gets interested in an activity and is permitted and encouraged to continue it. The parent or teacher needs to learn when to step aside and leave the child alone. I saw two examples of this recently. One was in a day care center in Haarlem, The Netherlands, where they were trying to involve parents. Parents were asked to model on the teachers. At the time I observed, the children, who were all four years old, were doing jigsaw puzzles. Everytime a child got stuck on a puzzle, five adults would descend. If the child needed help, surely not that much help was needed! The adults did not know how to get themselves out of it again, and it turned into a dependency relationship in which they were cuing the child, practically handing the child the right piece to fit in.

"The parent or teacher needs to learn when to step aside and leave the child alone."

The other situation was in the United States. The project is based on the notion that if mothers watch their children being tested, they will learn good child stimulation techniques and apply these at home. However, if you have watched a Bayley test being given, you know that as soon as the child performs, the item is scored and the child goes on to the next task. So it may be that parents were seeing a disruption of persistence rather than the encouragement of persistence. We need to know how to start a child and back out when too much is too much.

We also uncovered a pattern that was a poor teaching pattern—the label is **professor.** This behavior is talking followed by talking followed by talking, without paying any attention whatsoever to whether anybody is tuned in, responding, or attending.

These three patterns, *ping-pong, persistence*, and *professor* are observable not only in the first year of life but also in the preschool, the primary grades, and all the way through formal education.

Ping-pong is a successful form of social as well as learning interaction and professor is not, yet we persist in professing to young children. One of the reasons people have made that error in infant work may be that we kept telling them how important language was. We kept saying you have to surround the child with a language envelope. And they did. They stuck them inside the envelope and sealed it up.

Since it is painful and I do not wish to profess, let us turn to the four "R's" and leave the five "P's." These four "R's" bear no resemblance to the traditional three R's at all.

The Four "R's"

The first of these is **responsiveness** to the child's initiative and the child's needs. Many parents have been told by some learning theorists that when children cry, the most effective technique is to ignore the inappropriate behavior. We now have some very good studies in Baltimore by Ainsworth and Bell (1974) that demonstrate that when the mother is responsive to the child's crying between three months and six months of age, this leads to a lessening of crying between six months and nine months. Responsiveness to the six- to nine-month-old leads to a reduction in crying from nine to twelve months. My hypothesis is that this occurs because the child knows his or her needs are being attended to and moves on to superior and other ways of communicating. The child leaves the most primitive way because it is not needed anymore. There is a close relationship between responsiveness and ping-pong.

We also need to learn to be far more responsive to children's rhythms, to their built-in biological clocks. This applies not only in day care centers, but also we need to make arrangements even in schools and certainly at home. Husbands and wives do not necessarily have the same rhythm. One may be a morning person and the other an evening person. They learn, somehow, to find noontime. Likewise, we need to observe the child's rhythm and to find when we can communicate most effectively, rather than insisting that simply because this is an industrial world and the child may eventually have to live too by the clock, that he or she must live by the clock at age two.

There is another technique that indicates responsiveness, which has its origins in some elementary science work by Rowe (1973). She calls the variable "wait time." She counts the amount of time between when a teacher asks a question and how long, if the child does not answer it, before the teacher either asks the next child or asks another question. The average, believe it or not, in elementary science classrooms, is one second! What is even more devastating is that the brighter the child, the longer the wait time; the slower the child, the shorter the wait time. This is probably just the opposite of what it ought to be. Further, Rowe found that if she trains teachers to hold off for three seconds, the tenor of that whole classroom shifts in terms of the level of responses, the type of questions the children ask, and the level of questions the teachers ask. They move away from the single right word answer type question to more elaborated response and open-ended questions. We need to learn to give children time before we make our demands. Both at home and in school we need to learn to be more patient.

The other kind of responsiveness is the "deliver us from temptation" responsiveness. It is related to the organization of the environment, and is based on understanding what a child is like. I visited one of our home learning centers during 3 o'clock snacktime. There were six two-year-olds, and the staff had decided that each child was entitled to one cookie. However, the plate had more cookies than there were children, and they left the cookies out after each child had one. Then they wondered why the children were doing everything to get more cookies, not understanding that the simplest procedure was to avoid the temptation. We do a lot of this. We take toys out and say, "Do not play with them." My son went to a kindergarten that was fully equipped but he was not allowed to touch anything because the materials could get dirty. We need to match our expectations to the children, not the other way around.

The next "R's" are **reasoning** and **rationality,** which represents giving the child the "because." Miller (1971) analyzed a number of studies in England. He found that those children who did well in English schools came from homes which he could identify as allowing for and encouraging independent thinking and freedom of discussion.

"We need to match our expectations to the children, not the other way around."

Reasoning and rationality also represent accompanying our control with explanation. This is something that Baumrind (1970) pointed out in her work. Soar (1974) found that there are three kinds of control going on in the classroom, and most teachers do not differentiate among them: One is the control of the behavior, the second is the control of thought, and the third is the control of subject matter. He found that if behavior is tightly controlled in a classroom, the chances are very good that the teacher also controls the thought processes and the choice of subject matter. If one is free, all are likely to be free, but he suggests that the effects of freedom of behavior may be different from those of freedom of thought. For example, in looking at classrooms reflecting both the Becker-Engelman and British Infant School Follow Through programs, there was a positive relationship between free but orderly teacher-pupil interaction (in which children were free to think but there was both wait time and ping-pong) and children's gains in creativity. However, if children were simply physically free to roam around the room, this was negatively related to gains not only in creativity but also in regular academic skills.

The last "R" is **reading.**

In our longitudinal study (Gordon and Guinagh 1974), we found sex differences between home environment and Stanford-Binet scores at age six. Provision of reading materials seemed to be important for boys and reading press seemed to be important for girls. The work of Wachs et al. (1971), Elardo et al. (1975), and the earlier work of Bloom's students (Dave 1963, Wolf 1964) all indicate that the modeling behavior of the home is a critical element in reading for young children. If parents do not read, if children do not see parents reading, then this is a poor beginning when they come into school. Moreover when parents read to their children this seems to be positive, but we are learning to go beyond the symptoms or beyond the simple overt behavior and look a little further. One can read to children in a way that would make them never want to read again, or one can read to them in a way that would make them climb back into one's lap and ask for more.

In keeping with what we are learning about language development, reading to the child needs to be the responsive, highly personalized dialogue encouraging reading. There also should be a good deal of repetition. People do not automatically know how to read to a child. When a teacher of preschoolers says to parents, "I would like you to read to your children," that is a very inadequate message.

Guinagh and Jester (1972) studied parent reading skills in Appalachia and in rural and urban areas. They gave a book to a mother of a two-year-old. It was a delightful book emphasizing sounds. They found that rarely did the mothers do anything with the possibilities of the sounds. Some mothers would simply point to the picture and say, "Cat, say cat." Some, from the same income group, maybe even a next-door neighbor, would say, "Do you remember when that cat came by, and what kind of sound does a cat make?" Such a mother would have a nice dialogue going between her and the child.

We need to work harder not on the formal teaching of reading but on the real beginnings which are the interpersonal, social, warm experiences wrapped around reading. We want responsive reading. There are as many different ways to do that as there are different children. I would like to present to you one of my few orthodoxies: When in the face of orthodoxy, run as far as you can the other way. So if somebody tries to sell you the perfect reading package, run.

So much for those "R's." Let us come to "TLC" (tender loving care).

TLC

It does not help the child if you have provided for a stimulating material environment, played some barren form of ping-pong, reasoned with your child, responded in certain kinds of ways, set up rules and so forth, if all this was done without **warmth**. We have known this for a long time. But there are a lot of people in the last ten years who have tried to separate affect and cognition, who have tried to talk about stimulation as though you are stimulating a portion of the brain and paying no attention to the heart and the gut. There is considerable evidence to suggest that they are wrong.

We can easily identify, even within the first few weeks of the child's life, parents who can be placed on scales from warm to hostile, from involved to noninvolved. Schaefer (1969) pointed out that the hostile, noninvolved mother could not only be found, but also was not very effective as a mother in enabling children to grow. Ainsworth and Bell's (1974) study of advantaged parents indicated that 43 percent of them, almost half of them, were not responsive to the cues the children were giving them.

"We need to work harder not on the formal teaching of reading but on the real beginnings which are the interpersonal, social, warm experiences wrapped around reading."

Responsiveness in a warm fashion does a variety of things for children. It influences more than personality development; it has definite effects on intellectual development as well. In one of our infant studies (Gordon 1974), we found that while ping-pong was good for both boys and girls, what seemed to be more predictive for boys was the affective behavior of the type that Escalona and Corman (1974) measured. Parent and child gazing lovingly into each other's eyes, observed as early as 13 and 19 weeks of age, predicted the child's greater language development and general intellectual development at age one.

"Affection should be shown when you feel it and the child feels it and when it is natural. Children know the difference."

Erikson (1963) taught us the importance of building basic trust; Bowlby (1969) taught us about attachment. Burlingham and Freud (1944) indicated that children need three important things in these early years: a close transaction in an affectional way, a stimulating environment, and consistency of care. The one they place first is the affectional relationship. Children need to know that we care deeply for them. It takes a hug, a pat, a smile. It is not scheduled behavior. You do not pull out your schedule and say, "What's the baseline? Joe gets three pats today and Anne gets two." Affection should be shown when you feel it and the child feels it and when it is natural. Children know the difference.

Conclusion

I have tried to indicate from a variety of research and viewpoints, with my obvious biases, that we do indeed know a good deal about effective parenting, teaching, and child development for young children. Although we still have much to learn, we are past simply sloganizing that the parent is a teacher. We can specify good teaching and we can prepare people for parenthood, as well as helping present parents. Further, the good learning environment needs to be matched to the child. This is what Hunt (1961) called the problem of the match. What we know about good parenting applies equally well to good teaching. The processes are common. They reflect respect for the individual, understanding of children's needs, and a faith that what we do indeed does count. It really is more than rhetoric to say that the future is in your hands.

References

Ainsworth, M., and Bell, S. "Mother-Infant Interaction and the Development of Competence." In *The Growth of Competence*, edited by K. Connolly and J. Bruner, pp. 97-118. London: Academic Press, 1974.

Baumrind, D. "Socialization and Instrumental Competence in Young Children." *Young Children* 26 (1970): 104-119.

Bowlby, J. *Attachment and Loss, Vol. 1: Attachment*. London: Hogarth Press, 1969.

Burlingham, D., and Freud, A. *Infants Without Families*. London: George Allen and Unwin, 1944.

Dave, R. H. "The Identification and Measurement of Environmental Process Variables That Are Related to Education Achievement." Doctoral dissertation, University of Chicago, 1963.

Elardo, R.; Bradley, R.; and Caldwell, B. "The Relation of Infant's Home Environments to Mental Test Performance from Six to Thirty-six Months: A Longitudinal Analysis." *Child Development* 46, no. 11 (1975): 71-76.

Erikson, E. *Childhood and Society*. Second Edition. New York: W. W. Norton, 1963.

Escalona, S. K. "Basic Modes of Social Interaction: Their Emergence and Patterning During the First Two Years of Life." *Merrill-Palmer Quarterly* 19 (1973): 205-232.

Escalona, S., and Corman, H. "Early Life Experience and the Development of Competence." *International Review of Psycho-Analysis*, 1974, pp. 151-168.

Gesell, A. *The First Five Years of Life*. New York: Harper, 1941.

Gordon, I. J. "An Investigation into the Social Roots of Competence." Final Report to NIMH on Project No. 1 R01 MH 22724. Gainesville, Fla.: University of Florida, Institute for Development of Human Resources, October 1974.

Gordon, I. J. *The Infant Experience*. Columbus, Ohio: Charles E. Merrill Co., 1975.

Gordon, I. J., and Guinagh, B. "A Home Learning Center Approach to Early Stimulation." Final Report on Project No. R01 MH 16037-04. Gainesville, Fla.: University of Florida, Institute for Development of Human Resources, November 1974.

Gordon, I. J., and Jester, R. E. "Instructional Strategies in Infant Stimulation." *Catalog of Selected Documents in Psychology* 2 (1972): 122 (Journal Supplemental Abstract Service).

Guinagh, B. J., and Jester, R. E. "How Parents Read to Children." *Theory Into Practice* 11, no. 3 (June 1972).

Hunt, J. McV. *Intelligence and Experience*. New York: Ronald, 1961.

Kaye, K. "Gaze Direction as the Infant's Way of Controlling His Mother's Teaching Behavior." Symposium paper presented at the Biennial Meeting of the Society for Research in Child Development, April 1975, Denver, Colorado.

Kounin, J. *Discipline and Group Management in Classrooms*. New York: Holt, Rinehart & Winston, 1970.

Landsberger, B. Home Environment and School Performance: "The North Carolina Experience." *Children Today* 2 (1973): 10-14.

Miller, G. W. *Educational Opportunity and the Home*. London, England: Longman, 1971.

Murphy, G. *Human Potentialities*. New York: Basic Books, 1958.

Prescott, E.; Jones, E.; and Kritchevsky, S. *Day Care as a Child Rearing Environment*. Washington, D.C.: National Association for the Education of Young Children, 1972.

White, B. L.; Watts, J. C.; et al. *Experience and Environment*. Englewood Cliffs, N.J.: Prentice-Hall, 1973.

Wolf, R. "The Identification and Measurement of Environmental Process Variables Related to Intelligence." Doctoral dissertation, University of Chicago, 1964.

Matching Families and Services

MERLE B. KARNES
R. REID ZEHRBACH

Merle B. Karnes *is Professor, and* ***R. Reid Zehrbach*** *is Associate Professor, Institute for Research on Exceptional Children, University of Illinois, Champaign-Urbana.*

Family involvement has been recognized as a critical component of any educational program—from a legal, ethical, and educational point of view. Lawyers have focused on the legal aspects of family involvement. Teachers have tried to work with parents toward implementing educational goals. Social workers, guidance counselors, and psychologists have been preoccupied with social-emotional problems and/or different communication styles that interfere with parent-child relationships. However, little thought has been given to a *systematic* approach to this involvement.

This article attempts to provide such an approach to involving parents in programs. The basic assumptions reflected in the model include the following: (a) staff should adopt a positive developmental view of children and their families, (b) parents should be involved at the decision making level, (c) parents should have access to viable alternatives when they involve themselves, and (d) staff working with parents should view their role as consultative. Although the approach of this presentation is to concentrate on the parts of the system, the underlying assumption is that all of these parts are important only as they relate to the whole. The basic purpose is to "get the *system* working reasonably well, not perfectly" (Hobbs, 1975, p. 114).

Conceptualization of the Family Involvement Process

To cope with the multiplicity of problems and issues associated with the development and evaluation of a family involvement program, it seems most fruitful to describe a model process which highlights specific target activities and illustrates the interrelationships of all the parts. An 11 stage model is outlined here.

In stage 1, a careful total assessment is made of the child's actual functioning in critical areas—social-emotional, physical, cognitive-language, and intellectual. At stage 2, the assessment is continued by establishing specific goals and objectives for the child based on estimates of his potential. During stage 3, the discrepancies between where the child is and where he is capable of being are carefully scrutinized to determine his unmet needs. At stage 4, an attempt is made to determine what the home is capable of providing *without* the *intervention* of other than simple suggestions or recommendations. In stage 5, an assessment is made to determine the difference between the child's unmet needs and what the family is able to provide. Stage 6 is an entry level item designed to indicate that some person or agency must have a broad background of knowledge of alternative programs for involving parents. This knowledge is compared with the unmet needs of the child and parents during stage 7 to identify appropriate alternatives for meeting these needs. At stage 8, family members choose among the alternatives presented by the liaison worker—selecting the one(s) that they wish to follow to reach the child's unmet needs. In stage 9, the difference between the child's needs and what the family can provide must be determined. During stage 10, the agencies involved with the family assess their capabilities and responsibilities and decide whether or not they are willing and able to work with the parents toward the parents' selected goals. Also, they decide whether they will work with the child toward the same goal and/or provide the child with additional

"Matching Families And Servies, Merle B. Karnes, R. Reid Zehrbach, *Exceptional Children*, Vol. 41, No. 8, May 1975, © 1975 by The Council For Exceptional Children.

services not available to or through the parents. At stage 11a, the chosen plans are implemented. At stage 11b, continuous evaluations and reassessments are conducted at preplanned intervals with new planned actions established when progress is made toward the needs that have been given prime attention. Concomitantly at stage 11c, records are maintained of the unplanned for, unmet needs. These records must be continually reviewed as progress is made toward the higher priority needs so that provisions for unmet needs can be added to the planning when resources and time permit.

Application of the FIP model

1	2
Describe functional level of child	Define potential goals and objectives for child
a. Is able to hear 60 db sounds or louder	a. Improved hearing with aid
b. Speaks in one word sentences	b. Speaks in 2 word sentences
c. Responds to familiar faces	c. Play at parallel play level
d. Runs, walks	d. 1. Experience grocery store 2. Experience bus ride
	e. Learn to swim
3	**4**
Determine difference between 1 and 2 (unmet needs)	Identify what family is able to provide without intervention
a. Hearing aid	a. Provide hearing aid
b. Language stimulation	b. Limited ability
c. Socialization in groups	c. Limited ability
d. Broadening travel experiences	d. Not able to provide
e. Train in swimming	e. Not now
5	**6**
Determine difference between child's unmet needs and what family is able to provide	Agency staff knowledgeable about wide variety of programs
a. (Met)	
b. Same as 3b	In preparation for selecting alternatives need list of all possible alternatives
c. Same as 3c	
d. Same as 3d	
e. Same as 3e	

(continued on next page)

Interpretation of the Model

An outline of a decision making process oriented family involvement process (FIP) model has been presented. How the model might work is illustrated here.

In stage 1, the functional level of the child has been briefly characterized in objective positive statements. For example, the statement that the child is able to hear 60 db sounds or louder presents a child's ability to hear in as positive a light as possible. On the other hand, it should be obvious to a knowledgeable individual that the child has a hearing problem and needs special attention, although no such implication is drawn at this stage. One criterion is that the items listed here have no age referent. For example, the child is not described as speaking like a 2 year old, but rather as speaking in one word sentences. A much longer list would obviously be needed to clearly explicate the abilities of the child but such a list would tend to follow the general categories of physical functioning, social-emotional functioning, intellectual functioning, cognitive-language functioning, interests, and special abilities.

In stage 2, staff members attempt to delineate the child's potential level of functioning in terms of both broad long range goals and short term objectives. For example, a goal might be to improve the child's ability to learn through the auditory channel. This might, or might not, be quickly enhanced through the provision of a hearing aid. Again, a fairly extensive list of long term goals and related immediate objectives might be developed for the child.

At stage 3, a comparison is made between the child's needs and functional level, and a list of unmet needs is developed which parallels the lists developed at the first and second stages.

It can be seen in stage 4 that the family's abilities to resolve the unmet needs is minimal at this time. They are only able to provide a hearing aid. It does not, however, imply that they could not benefit from participation in an appropriate family program.

At stage 5, it is clear that the family has essentially met the child's hearing aid needs but is unable to provide the language stimulation, socialization, broadening experience, and swimming opportunities that have been identified as desirable. Thus, intervention by an agency seems imperative to help the parents acquire the knowledge and skills essential for meeting the child's needs.

Stage 6 refers to the activities of agency

(FIP Model cont.)

7

Agency/liaison worker develops list of alternative goals–programs

a. (Met)

b. 1. Parent training program (Karnes)

2. Language based preschool program

c. Preschool

d. 1. Parent program "enhancing travel experience"

2. Preschool

3. Student volunteer

e. Winter swimming program

8

Family chooses alternatives to help unmet needs

a. (Met)

b. 1. Yes

2. Yes

c. Yes

d. 1. No

2. Yes

3. Yes

e. Later

9

Determine difference between child needs and what family agrees to provide

All plans agreed to except d1: attend parent program on "enhancing travel experience" and to delay entrance into "swimming" program

10

Agencies determine to:

a. work with parents toward their choices, and/or

b. Choose to work with child in some other area(s)

a. (Met)

b. 1. Agree to enroll in Karnes based parent training program

2. Enroll in language based program

c. Same as b2

d. 1. No action—put on need list

2. Same as b2

3. No volunteer available—put on wait list

e. Put on wait list

11a

Continue action toward selected goals

a. (Met)

b. 1. Parent started program March 1, 1974

2. Child started program April 1, 1974

c. Same as b2

d. 2. Same as b2

11b

Reassess at stated intervals and replan adding unmet needs

a. (Met)

b. 1. Review programs April 1, May 15, 6 week intervals

b. 2., c, d. 2. Internal evaluation and 9 week interim review and yearly total review

11c

Unmet and unplanned for needs remain until resolved or added to plan

d. 1. No action. Review need and possible reschedule of parents into "enhancing travel" program in 3 months.

3. Put on wait list for volunteers

e. Schedule for summer swimming lessons

staff required to help them become knowledgeable about the characteristics of various programs for family members. Later in this article, a procedure will be described for assessing family involvement programs in a systematic manner so that the development of the knowledge base needed to identify alternatives and make appropriate decisions can be facilitated.

During stage 7, the agency and/or liaison worker develops a list of alternative approaches designed to meet the specific unmet needs of this illustrative child. Participation in a program designed to teach parents how to stimulate and reinforce the language development of their child, as developed by Karnes (1968), has been identified as one alternative. Another is to enroll the child in a language based preschool program, which is consistent with the goals and procedures of the parent program. Similarly, a parent program has been identified which will provide the parents with assistance in using simple travel experiences to broaden their child's experiential background.

At stage 8, family members are presented with the list of alternatives and they decide which one(s) they would like to pursue. They chose to accept all the alternatives with the exception of participating in the family program on enhancing travel experiences. This was due to a lack of transportation. They also decided to postpone the swimming arrangement until summer.

At stage 9, the difference(s) between the child's needs and the alternatives agreed to by the parents are determined. In the example the parents agreed to all programs except "enhancing travel experiences" and the immediate swimming program.

At stage 10, the agency reviews the program and decides how and to what degree they are able to interact with the system. In the example, the agency was able to interact as planned, with the exception that it placed providing a volunteer on a waiting list.

At stage 11a the planned actions started on March and April, 1974, while at 11b the associated plans for evaluation and review were established. In 11c, the activities that have been established as appropriate for the child but for which no appropriate actions have been planned are listed.

The FIP model provides for the sequential planning of activities and alternatives and involves the family members both at the planning and action stages. On the other hand, analysis of the model reveals several critical points that have not been fully described in related literature.

Problem Areas of the Model

While information is widely available on some of the topic areas in the model, lack of information is judged to occur at stages 4, 6, 7, 8, and 10.

At stage 4, the basic problem is to identify the family's ability to meet needs with minimal intervention. In the example provided earlier, the child had a hearing loss that could be ameliorated with a hearing aid. A simple explanation of the problem to a family member of a higher income level who has no personal objection to the child's using the aid may be all that is required. They would make the necessary appointments and quickly obtain the aid. Another family, however, might lack the economic resources or resist the ideas of a young child wearing the aid. Thus, it would be judged that considerable effort would be required to meet the need; this would be listed at stage 5 as an unmet need.

One of the critical problems at stage 4 would seem to be the need to keep efforts to assess the family's abilities directed toward areas relevant to the child's needs. If the child needs a hearing aid, then the assessment procedures should focus on the economic, time, personal, social, and intellectual factors relevant to the provision of a hearing aid. Automatic digression to assessing the family's ability to stimulate the child intellectually is unwarranted. On the other hand, if, as a result of the hearing loss, the child has a need to develop language facility, then the family members' abilities to meet these needs should be assessed.

One of the benefits of the above procedure is that it reduces the amount of time and resources required to assess specific needs. Another is that it keeps the privacy of the family intact in those areas that do not directly impinge on the needs of the child. Such a procedure is obviously beneficial when the agency, such as a school, is concerned with meeting certain delimited needs of children. If the program is more broadly oriented as suggested by Hobbs (1975), then a broader perspective would need to be taken to define the needs of the child as a member of the system.

Some of the dimensions that need to be considered are (a) administrative considerations such as cost, time, space, and transportation; (b) parents' considerations such as cultural, intellectual, knowledge, skills, and attitudes; and (c) child considerations such as social, physical, motoric, intellectual, and cultural. It may not be necessary to consider all areas for every problem, but a checklist might be devised to insure that the possibility of need in each of these areas is at least explored.

The next problem area in the model is at stage 6, wherein agency and/or individuals need to develop the ability to implement a variety of programs rather than just one or two. The broad underlying philosophy is one of carefully planned eclecticism. Available programs can be analyzed and used as a reference when decisions need to be made about a specific family. One important aspect of this analysis should be to reveal those programs useful to the clients.

At stage 7, the agency and/or selected individuals are assigned the task of identifying multiple alternative programs which meet the needs of children through the training of family members. Development of the background information for the preceding step should reduce the time required to make decisions and, at the same time, insure a more relevant provision of programs and use of staff.

Stage 8 is concerned with the all important problem of providing for, and encouraging, family input into the decision making process. Too frequently families are left out or excluded until after all decisions are made. A social worker surveying the potential of a family will certainly include as a part of the assessment process determining if a family will agree to participate in certain types of suggested activities. In this way, parents' decisions will be anticipated early.

Focusing recommendations for alternative programs on the unmet needs of the child may help parents understand the specific decisions that they have to make. Further, it should be easier to make a decision among two or three alternatives rather than be forced to accept or reject only one. During the discussion, compromise solutions may develop to suggest additional alternatives.

Once the family has decided, the problem reverts to the agency to make certain that it can interact with the family. It may lack the trained personnel, the funds, or the time to complete the activities. Most frequently, these decisions will have been made before the family is approached so that false hopes are not raised by the alternatives presented to them. Action should begin as soon as possible. If some needs cannot be met, then most likely the list of the child's unmet needs would be expanded to include those areas the agency cannot serve.

References

Hobbs, N. *The futures of children.* San Fancisco: Jossey-Bass Publishers, 1975.

Karnes, M. B., Studley, W. M., Wright, W. R., & Hodgins, A. S. An approach for working with mothers of disadvantaged preschool children. *Merrill-Palmer Quarterly of Behavior and Development,* 1968, *14* (2), 174-184.

HOME START: Partnership with Parents

by RUTH ANN O'KEEFE

Ruth Ann O'Keefe, Ed.D., is Director, Home Start, OCD.

In Alaska, a home visitor and a housewife coordinate menu-planning with newspaper food ads.

Home Start, the new three-year Head Start demonstration program designed to bring comprehensive child development services to children and families in their own homes, does so by helping parents provide many of the same services Head Start offers children in centers. Thus, although Home Start includes the same nutrition, health, education and social and psychological services in its program, and reaches children in the same 3- to 5-year-old age group as Head Start, it concentrates on the role of parents in the growth and development of their children.

"I see Home Start as an indicator that we care what happens to family life in America, and that we realize that it's the parents and family who are the most important determinants, especially in the early years of the child's life, of what the child will become," Dr. Edward Zigler, former Director of the Office of Child Development, told participants at a Home Start planning conference in October 1971.

Several factors and considerations influenced the decision to launch a major national demonstration of home-based child development services. First, a number of home-based programs had already evolved in recent years, and the evidence available indicated that such programs were economically feasible, as well as highly beneficial.[1]

The realization that often Head Start and other center-based programs provide only indirect or minimal benefits to other children in the families served, who are not enrolled in a program, was a second consideration, while the vast number of families without access to any preschool child development center was a third.

Another consideration was the fact that the overall Head Start program was encouraging local projects to develop variations, shaped to

"Home Start: Patnership With Parents,", Ruth Ann O'Keefe, *Children Today*, Vol. 2, No. 1, January-February 1973, © U.S. Department of Health, Education and Welfare.

meet local needs, of its standard center program. Home-based demonstration programs, then, could eventually serve as models and resources for other Head Start projects interested in this approach and its heavy emphasis on parental education and involvement.

Within the broad goals of demonstrating and evaluating home-based programs which involve parents directly and help strengthen their ability to facilitate the growth and development of their children, each Home Start project has been encouraged to develop its own specific objectives.

The Sixteen Projects

There are currently 16 OCD-funded Home Start demonstration projects which serve about 2,500 children. Each program receives approximately $100,000 for a 12-month period, and reaches about 80 families, many of whom have two or more preschool children. A wide variety of ethnic and cultural backgrounds are represented among the projects, which are serving white and black, and Eskimo, Navajo, migrant, Spanish-speaking and Chinese families, in urban and rural areas.

Each project has administrative personnel and a staff of trained home visitors who usually serve between eight and 15 families each. The majority of the visitors are paraprofessional women who live near the families they serve. While the projects organize and conduct some group sessions for parents, the home visits are the backbone of the program.

Like Head Start, Home Start is much more than a preschool educational program for it emphasizes children's health and mental health as well as education.

Nutrition Component

The nutritional services are aimed primarily at helping parents make the best use of existing food resources, through improved food planning, buying, and cooking. However, when a family does not have needed food, Home Start makes every effort both to provide it, and also to put the family in touch with whatever community organization can help on a regular basis. Foods that are a regular part of the family's diet, and which reflect cultural backgrounds and preferences, are a major focal point of all nutrition education. Nutritional objectives may include the following:

■ To assess the nutritional needs of each family member and provide direct services and referrals where appropriate.

■ To provide information on such aspects of nutrition as the feeding of young children, the purchase and preparation of food, and food handling and storage.

■ To call attention, when possible, to consumer newsletters and food cooperatives.

During her visit, for example, the home visitor may read and evaluate newspaper food ads with the mother, help her make a shopping list, or accompany mother and child while they shop for food. She may also help a mother prepare supper while she shows her how her young child can be involved in the work—by noting colors, textures and shapes of food and kitchen equipment, by counting eggs, spoons and other items, and in conversation. The home visitor may also help the family take the steps necessary to obtain donated or commodity foods, or arrange for local home economists to demonstrate preparation of inexpensive but nourishing foods to small groups of mothers.

Health Component

In seeing that Home Start children receive the same health services as other Head Start children, staff efforts are directed toward securing such services, by referral and follow-up, through existing Federal, state or local resources. Parents are involved throughout these processes and so learn through practice how they can obtain such services.

Individual program health objectives may include the following:

■ Identification of health problems of children and their families

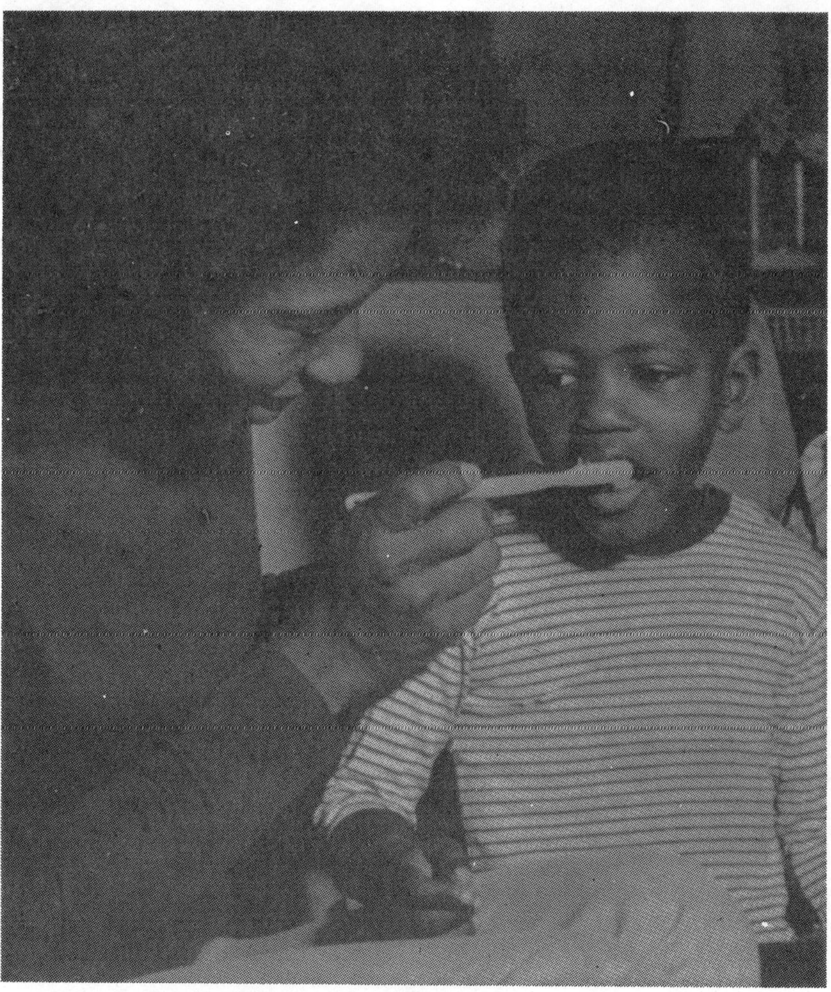

Good health habits begin in this Huntsville, Alabama home.

and referral of family members to appropriate services.

■ Provision of information on family planning and birth control clinics to interested parents.

■ Helping to improve home sanitation and safety.

■ Helping to provide immunizations to children and, where appropriate, other members of their families.

■ Establishment and maintenance of health records.

The home visitor may implement health objectives by accompanying the mother and child during the child's physical and dental examinations and by arranging for the mother's check-up at a free clinic. She may also make sure that all follow-up care is provided for identified health needs, which may include making arrangements with a hospital to provide family health and counseling services at nominal or no cost.

The visitor may also call on local doctors to tell them about Home Start and enlist their help, set up first aid training courses for Home Start staff and parents, and help parents assess such potentially dangerous hazards in the home as exposed poisons, electrical outlets and lead paint, and help them take safety precautions. She may also read health columns in local newspapers with the mother and show her how to check her children's growth and health, by showing her how to mark the height of each child on the wall periodically or, when necessary, how to check children for worms. She may also provide toothbrushing kits and instruction for each family member.

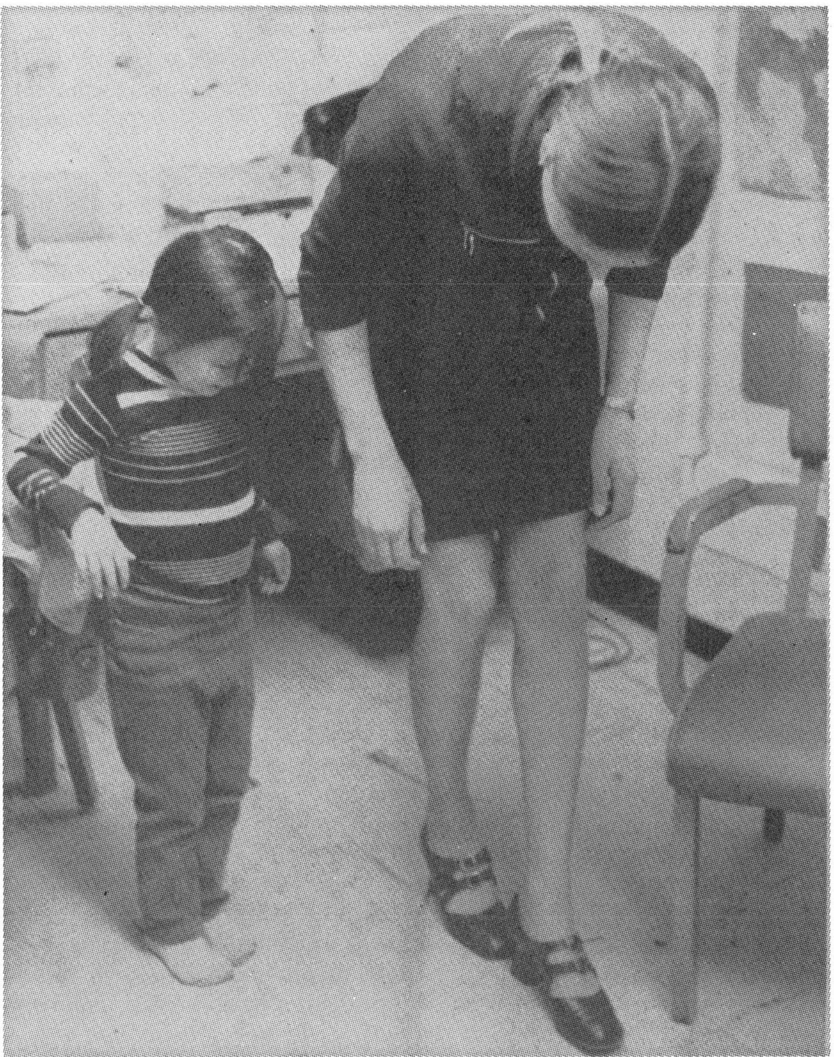

Child development testing techniques are fun for this child in Fairbanks.

Psychological and Social Services

Again making every effort to identify and use existing community services, Home Start provides social and psychological services that parents need and want for their children. These may encompass the following objectives:

■ To help parents identify their own needs and be aware of existing services available to them, such as employment counseling, diagnostic testing, job training, drug counseling, psychotherapy, and housing.

■ To locate and help facilitate transportation to these resources.

■ To help provide much-needed social outlets for families in isolated communities.

The home visitor may help by showing the mother how to use the telephone book as a directory of resources, by escorting the mother or parents through the entire process of going to the resource facility for the first time, or by helping families arrange carpools with neighbors or relatives. She may also organize picnics and other social activities for parents and families.

Intellectual and Physical Development

Deeply embedded in the Home Start concept is the idea that the parents are properly the first and the most influential educators and "enablers" of their own children. Thus, Home Start aims to help parents as the *major* means of directly enhancing the intellectual and physical development of all their children, and particularly those of preschool age, whereas Head Start involves parents as *one* means of directly helping the children who attend the center. Typical educational objectives of a local program may be:

■ To help enhance parents' knowledge and understanding of early childhood development, by providing them with information and material on how to become better educators of their children.

■ To point out materials in the home that can be used as educational toys and games and to develop toy-lending libraries.

■ To help parents reinforce their children's positive behavior.

■ To help parents help their children become better prepared for school, by improving their language ability and understanding of such basic concepts as colors and numbers.

The home visitor's role in educational activities may include taking parents to the library and helping them locate books on subjects of particular interest to them, arranging for interested parents and Home Start staff to take a course on child-rearing or to view a film on child development, or holding mothers' group meetings to encourage them to help each other in working out solutions to child-rearing problems.

Home visitors also help parents make up games that involve classifying, counting, or identifying objects, and help them locate tools and scrap materials—such as plywood—so that fathers and older brothers and sisters can make wagons, puzzles, storage chests, bookshelves and other items for their families.

Home Visitors

There is still much to be learned about selecting persons who will, with good training, make excellent home visitors. In general, emphasis has been placed on the friendly attitudes and suitability of cultural and language background of those who serve, as well as their successful experiences as parents, rather than on academic credentials.

The training and preparation of home visitors have varied from program to program but in general have been practical and broad-based. Preservice training is usually limited to three to four weeks, with emphasis placed on continuing, in-service training. Under the direction of Rose Margosian, of the Gloucester Massachusetts Home Start Program, for example, home visitors began to work with small groups of families after only three weeks of training. The staff got together often to compare notes and assist each other in developing plans for and with each family. Gradually each home visitor increased the number of families she served.

In most cases, the home visitor is a sympathetic listener, a helper, adviser and *friend* to the entire family being served. Some of the things she does are mainly for the purpose of gaining the confidence and cooperation, as well as friendship, of the parents. Others are more directly related to building parents' knowledge and skills. On any particular visit, the home visitor may do one or more of the following:

> **The Home Start Projects**
>
> The 16 Home Start projects are located in 15 states: Huntsville, Alabama; Fairbanks, Alaska; Dardanelle, Arkansas; Fort Defiance, Arizona; San Diego, California; Wichita, Kansas; Gloucester, Massachusetts; Reno, Nevada; Binghamton, New York; Franklin, North Carolina; Cleveland, Ohio; Harrogate, Tennessee; Houston and Laredo, Texas; Logan, Utah, and Parkersburg, West Virginia.

- Introduce a toy or book or creative experience that will involve the parent in a developmental experience with the child. The home visitor will often leave the item at the home, and encourage the mother to use it with the child during the week.
- Help the mother make home-made developmental toys improvised from household items, such as filling and sealing cans containing pebbles, buttons or paper clips to make shaking toys, stacking measuring cups, pans, or mixing bowls for nesting toys, and creating building blocks from empty milk cartons.
- Talk with the mother about each child and what she is doing to further his or her development, praising her for gains made and making occasional suggestions.
- Introduce activities that encourage older children to work with and help their younger brothers and sisters.

Overall, home visitors must see themselves as supporting, not substituting for, the family's role, as Dr. J. Ronald Lally, director of Syracuse University's Children's Center, said at an April 1972 conference launching the Home Start program. Some of the ways in which home visitors might unintentionally stray from Home Start goals, he warned, include working too much with the preschool child rather than with the parents and being too rigid in setting up formal activities and using structured cognitive materials with the children, rather than allowing for more informal give-and-take situations.

The home visitor must also guard against encouraging families to depend too much on her, instead of helping parents become more self-sufficient. She should also be wary of defining her role too narrowly, and of relying on a stereotyped middle-class model of child-rearing, rather than sizing up the situation—and strengths—of each family.

Using Community Resources

All of the Home Start programs try to utilize existing community educational services and resources.

Some programs have enlisted the cooperation of local colleges to sponsor both credit and non-credit courses for Home Start staff. For example, the intensive 2-week (80-hour) Home Start training session for the Huntsville (TARCOG), Alabama Home Start program, under the direction of Dr. Kyo Jhin, carried 3 college credits and was given at little cost to the program.

Some Home Start programs are systematically incorporating television into their educational component and have obtained the cooperation of both local stations and the producers of the shows, including the producers of *Around the Bend* (Appalachia Educational Laboratory), *Captain Kangaroo* (CBS) and *Sesame Street* (Children's Television Workshop).

Helen Skinnell of the Clinch-Powell Home Start program in Harrogate, Tennessee, for example, prepares a weekly guide for parents to use in conjunction with the *Captain Kangaroo* program. The guide is aimed at making television-watching more active for children.

In addition, the programs in Alabama and Tennessee are integrated into Regional Council of Government planning in a broad multi-county support network.

Evaluation

The primary purpose of the Home Start demonstration program is to obtain information on various

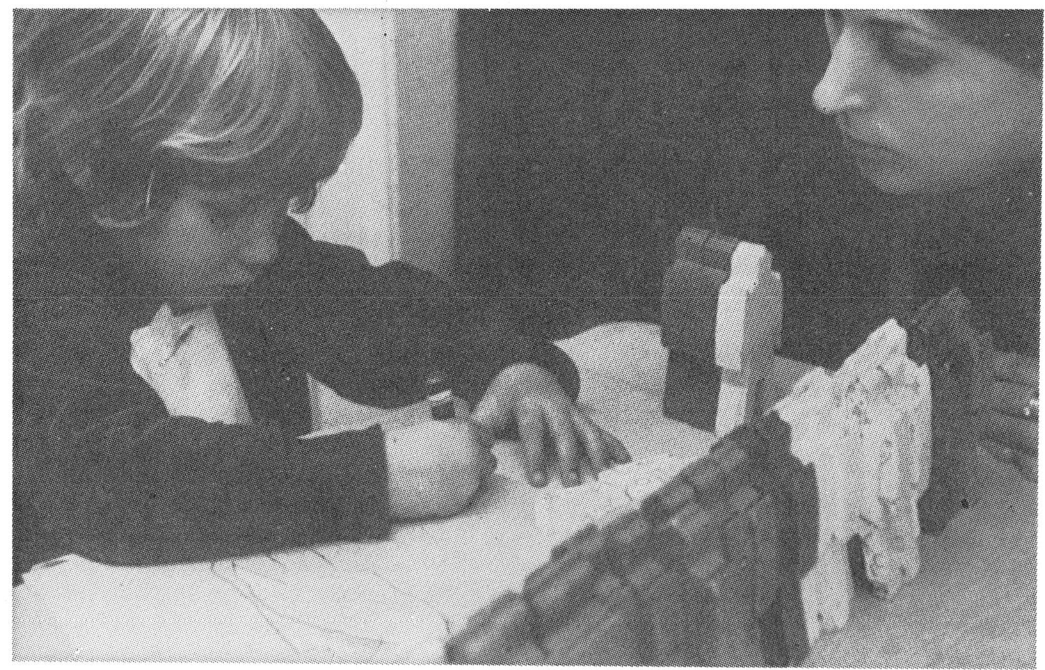

Games are part of this child development test in the Fairbanks, Alaska Home Start project.

approaches to and operational variations within home-based services. These data are expected to be of critical importance in assessing the cost/effectiveness of a home-based approach to child development services.

The program is being independently evaluated by the High/Scope Educational Research Foundation of Ypsilanti, Michigan; Abt Associates, Cambridge, Massachusetts; and Development Associates, Washington, D.C. The evaluation, which will include studies of the Home Start projects and the families and children served, is being coordinated by Dr. Esther Kresh, Acting Director of Research and Evaluation, OCD. A limited amount of formal, standardized testing of children will also be conducted. Assessment techniques have been identified for all areas of national and local program objectives and will be used on a regular basis.

Although the Home Start demonstration program is still in its first year of operation, two important conclusions have already emerged:

■ Many families in a wide variety of locales, and with different ethnic and cultural backgrounds, are willing and often eager to welcome a home visitor into their homes. They *want* to be part of a program which supports their own relationship with their children.

■ Within a relatively short period of time paraprofessionals can be trained to work with sensitivity and skill in a comprehensive home-based child development program.

Further growth of the Home Start concept within OCD will be through many existing Head Start programs which will be encouraged to incorporate some aspects of the home-based projects into their programs. What is needed now is continuing opportunity to develop and evaluate a variety of programs and systems to serve all parents and families who feel the need, either continuously or from time to time, for such support.

Teaching Styles of Mothers and the Match–to–Sample Performance of their Retarded Preschool-Age Children

JOHN W. FILLER, JR. AND WILLIAM A. BRICKER
George Peabody College for Teachers

Twenty-one mothers and their preschool-age retarded children were observed during three structured teaching sessions. Each session was rated for various forms of maternal preresponse and postresponse activity as well as performance of the children. The results indicated that the most frequent forms of maternal behavior were preresponse verbal directions and instructions; however, the best predictor of children's correct performance was postresponse positive feedback. Patterns of intercorrelations among maternal measures were generally consistent with those reported by Hess and Shipman (1965). The hypothesis was advanced that maternal postresponse feedback may occur as the result of correct responding which, in turn, is more directly affected by other aspects of teaching style.

The importance of a careful consideration of the potentially functional relationship between activities of mothers (preresponse and postresponse, verbal and nonverbal) and the performance of their preschool-age children has been pointed out recently by Hess, Shipman, Brophy, and Bear (1971). Summarizing data obtained in their laboratory (Brophy, 1970; Hess & Shipman, 1965; Olim, 1970; Brophy, Hess, & Shipman, Note 1; Olim, Hess, & Shipman, Note 2), Hess and his colleagues have indicated that certain aspects of the teaching styles of mothers tend to covary with socioeconomic status. In addition, preresponse measures of maternal teaching style (verbal and nonverbal forms of communication which primarily precede children's responses) correlate with each other and with measures of children's performance on sorting tasks. Measures of the postresponse reactive aspects of teaching style (e.g., reward, praise, and promise of reward) were also found to relate to children's performance. Thus, it would seem that the successful mother is one who employs elaborate linguistic codes, makes extensive use of nonverbal cues, and praises her child for responding correctly.

The purpose of this study was to provide information relevant to several questions concerning the behavior of mothers and performance of their retarded preschool-age children as exhibited during a situation in which the mother is instructed to teach her child a defined task. Which forms of the behavior of mothers seem to occur most frequently? Which forms of maternal behavior best predict children's performance? Are those forms of maternal behavior which relate to children's performance primarily verbal or nonverbal, preresponse or postresponse?

Method

Subjects

The subjects were 21 retarded preschool-age children (mean chronological age [CA] = 42.8 months, range 20 to 64 months) and their mothers. Each child was enrolled in the Infant, Toddler, and Preschool Research and Intervention Project at the Kennedy

This study is based upon a dissertation submitted by the first author to the Department of Psychology, George Peabody College for Teachers, in partial fulfillment of the requirements for the PhD degree. This and other aspects of the research were supported by National Institute of Child Health and Human Development Grants No. HD07073 and HD00043. Preparation of the manuscript was supported by the Illinois Institute for Developmental Disabilities.

The first author is now at the Illinois Institute for Developmental Disabilities. The second author is at the Mailman Center for Child Development, University of Miami.

"Teaching Styles of Mothers and The Match-To-Sample Performance of Their Retarded Preschool Age Children", John W. Filler, William A. Bricker, *American Journal of Mental Deficiency*, Vol. 80, No. 5, March 1976, © 1976, American Association on Mental Deficiency.

Center for Research on Education and Human Development of George Peabody College for Teachers. The children's IQs ranged from 39 to 80 (mean = 59.2) as indicated from scores on individual tests (Cattel or Stanford-Binet, Form L-M) administered no more than 30 days prior to inclusion in the study. Ten of the children were diagnosed as having Down's syndrome, and two had arrested hydrocephalus. The etiological conditions associated with the retardation of the remaining 9 children were unknown. Thirteen males and 8 females were included in the sample. Mothers of the children ranged in age from 19 to 49 years (mean = 31.8) and had received from 9 to 18 years of formal education (mean = 12.6). Family incomes ranged from $3,200 to $15,000 (mean = $7,757.80).

Match–to–Sample Task

Each mother taught her child one of six match–to–sample tasks. Four picture blocks were to be matched with four identical pictures printed side–by–side on a single card. This stimulus card was mounted on a wooden frame which had slots to accommodate the four blocks. It was the mother's task to teach her child to place each picture block in the correct slot such that a match would be made between the picture on the block and the picture immediately above on the stimulus card.

The stimulus pictures were selected from a pool of six sets which varied in difficulty to ensure that the task taught was not one which the child could already perform. Three sets of pictures were taken directly from the Leiter (1969) International Performance Scale. These were: colors (red, green, blue, and yellow); pictures (elephant, chair, doll, and wagon); and forms (cross, circle, square, and star). Three additional sets of pictures were created from stimulus materials contained in the Leiter Scale. These involved matching according to number and were: matching stars (one, two, three, and four stars); matching sunbursts (four circles with either six, seven, eight, or ten lines drawn perpendicular to the circumferences); and matching wheels (four wagon wheels with either five, six, eight, or ten spokes).

Recording Equipment

Each training session took place at the Kennedy Center Experimental School, a place generally familiar to all of the children and their mothers. All sessions were recorded on videotape. Two Sony AVC 3200 cameras were positioned in the experimental room. One, fitted with a Canon 25-100 mm fl.8 zoom lens, was mounted in the ceiling directly above the table at which the mother and child worked. The other camera fitted with a Cosmicar 8.5 mm fl.5 lens, provided a wide-angle view of the mother and child. Signals from the two cameras were fed simultaneously into a Sony SEG-1 special effects generator such that the image from the wide-angle camera and that from the close-up camera appeared together on a Motorola program monitor. These synchronized images were then taped on a Sony AV3650 Video Recorder. Sound was supplied through two Sony cardiod microphones, one suspended from the ceiling and the other mounted on the table. A Wollensak T-1500 Magnetic Tape Recorder was used to supply a series of audio signals (beep plus segment number) which were superimposed on the videotape. These signals, which were used during the tape analysis, were not heard by the mother or child. All equipment, except the two cameras and microphones, was located in an adjacent room.

Rating Procedure

Tapes of each mother–child training session were rated in a fashion similar to that described by Robinson and Filler (Note 3). Audio signals (described above) were used to divide each tape into 36 10-second epochs for ease of rating. Raters viewed the tapes and rated each of the 12 categories of mother and child behavior as it occurred. In general, the categories occurred frequently, and in no case did 10 seconds elapse with no behavior rated.

Seven categories were used to refer to behavior of the mother that occurred prior to a child's response and constituted efforts to elicit a response from the child. They were:

1. *Verbal directions and/or instructions.* The mother verbally directed the child to place a block (e.g., "Put it in"), provided relevant information to the child while directing him to place a block (e.g., "Put the red circle with the other red circle"), or provided information without directing him to place a block (e.g., "This is a red circle and over there is another red circle"). If a direction were given which contained no information, a talley was entered in the appropriate time segment in the column on the scoring sheet labeled Verbal Directions. However, if a direction were given which contained information or if the mother merely supplied the child with information without requesting a response, the letter *X* was entered.

2. *Cue.* The mother presented the block in a way that suggested the correct match. For example, she placed the block directly in front of the appropriate slot.

3. *Opportunity.* The mother presented a block in a position roughly equidistant from each slot.

4. *Choices limited.* The mother restricted the number of potential placement positions, thereby

increasing the probability of a correct response. There were a number of ways in which a mother could limit choices, e.g., by covering some of the positions or leaving correctly placed blocks in the slots. The exact manner in which choices were limited was recorded.

5. *Points.* The mother pointed to the materials in an effort to emphasize critical aspects of the stimuli.

6. *Guidance.* The mother established physical contact with the child and assisted him in making a task-relevant response.

7. *Demonstration.* Demonstration was indicated when the mother modeled the required response. Demonstration could occur as an aspect of postresponse feedback as well.

The two categories of children's responses were:

1. *Correct response.* A child placed the block, picture side up, either directly in front of the correct slot or inserted it in the correct slot.

2. *Incorrect response.* The child placed the block either in an incorrect slot or in front of an incorrect slot. Incorrect response was also scored when the block was placed with picture side not showing.

The categories of mothers' behavior which occurred after children's response and constituted feedback were:

1. *Verbal feedback.* The mother gave a verbal response to the child's behavior. Positive verbal feedback was scored when the mother provided a potentially reinforcing response (e.g., "Good," "That's right,") to a child's response; negative verbal feedback was indicated by the occurrence of a potentially punishing verbalization (e.g., "No!" "You're wrong!").

2. *Physical feedback.* The mother responded to her child's behavior by touching the child. Physical feedback could be either positive (e.g., a potentially reinforcing physical response such as hugging) or negative (e.g., a potentially punishing physical response such as hitting or restraining).

3. *Rewards.* As a consequence of a response, the mother provided the child with rewards such as edibles or toys.

A research assistant who was unfamiliar with the purpose and design of the study rated each videotaped session. The ratings were used exclusively in all subsequent analyses of the interaction sessions. A second observer independently rated 50 percent of the total number of sessions. Reliability checks were distributed across all sessions and mother–child dyads. Complete agreement was obtained between raters for the assignment of individual kinds of behavior to categories. That is, given that both noted the occurrence of a specific act, there was agreement as to category assignment. However, raters disagreed more frequently concerning the actual occurrence of a behavior. For this reason, and because data were to be represented as averaged frequencies in the analyses, Pearson product-moment correlations were computed between observations of raters for the frequency of occurrence of each category of behavior. The obtained correlations ranged from .88 to 1.00. The mean correlations across categories was found to be .99 (Fisher's Z).

Procedure

Prior to the first phase of the study (pretest), it was carefully determined that all children could perform the motor act of inserting blocks into slots. Test and interaction sessions took place in a small experimental room where the child was seated at a lowered table.

In the pretest, a 16-trial test on each of the six iconic tasks described earlier was administered to each child for a total of 96 trials. For all children the sequence of task presentation was: colors, pictures, forms, stars, sunbursts, and wheels. The order of presentation of individual picture blocks within each task was predetermined randomly and remained constant across children. Each block for each task was presented by placing it on a standard reference point, and the child was asked to "Put it where it goes." Each block was removed before the next was presented. Two observers independently scored each child's responses, with complete agreement by raters. Although each child received verbal praise and an edible for correct responses, no evidence of learning across presentations was noted. The first task in the sequence on which a 25 percent level of correct performance (chance) was obtained was selected as the training task. (Multiple correlated *t* test comparisons of the average percentage correct scores obtained by the children on six problems revealed that, with the exception of colors, the first task presented, significantly higher scores were obtained on the noncounting iconic tasks than were obtained on the counting tasks. Differences between individual noncounting tasks, as well as between individual counting tasks, were not significant.) When the child did not perform at chance level on any task, the task with the score closest to 25 percent correct was selected for training. Thus, although the level of task difficulty may have differed slightly across subjects, each child was initially performing at approximately chance level. On the task selected for training, no child obtained a 25 percent score by responding consistently correctly to a single picture.

During the second phase of the study (training), each mother was asked to work alone with her child for a total of 3 periods of 6 minutes each. These 3 teaching periods took place on 3 consecutive days. On the day preceding the first training session, each mother was shown the task which had been selected. She was told, "*Your job is to teach your child to insert each of these four blocks in its appropriate slot such that the picture printed on the block is at the top and directly under the appropriate picture on the stimulus card.*" The experimenter then demonstrated the correct placement of the blocks, removing each before placing another. Next, the mother was asked to place the blocks and was corrected if mismatches were made. Each mother was encouraged to use any method and/or any additional materials she chose to teach her child the task. No specific methods were suggested. Although juice and other edibles were readily available as rewards, they were not used during training, since none of the 21 mothers requested them. After being told that all sessions would be recorded on a videotape and that the tapes would be erased following the completion of the study, each mother was asked to return with her child at a specific time on the next school day for the first session. Across sessions, the position of stimuli on the stimulus card was randomly varied.

The third phase of the study (posttest) took place on the day following the third training session. It consisted of a repetition of the pretest with the modification that only the training task and two additional tasks on which the child had not been trained and which had been included in the pretest were presented. The additional tasks were selected on the basis of pretest scores with performance approximately equivalent to pretest performance on the training tasks. For each child one of the nontrained tasks was selected from the same group of tasks to which the trained task belonged (noncounting or counting iconic tasks). This task constituted a test for possible generalization to a *similar* but nontrained iconic match-to-sample problem. Whenever possible, the second nontrained task was chosen from the group of tasks on which the child had not been trained and was termed the *dissimilar* task. Each child received a 16-trial test on the training task and each of the other two tasks for a total of 48 trials.

Results

Frequency Measures of Mothers' Behavior and Children's Performance

Table 1 contains the average frequencies and standard deviations (*SD*s) for each form of mothers' pre- and postresponse behavior during training. Correlated t test comparisons indicated that the average frequencies

TABLE 1
MEANS AND STANDARD DEVIATIONS (*SD*s) FOR EACH CATEGORY OF MOTHERS' BEHAVIOR DURING TRAINING

Category	Mean	*SD*
Preresponse		
Information-containing verbal directions	27.16	26.34
Information-devoid verbal directions	67.95	25.16
Opportunity placements	22.21	7.20
Cue placements	3.59	4.00
Limited choice presentations	12.30	4.76
Points	13.65	7.47
Guidance	0.71	1.81
Demonstrations	0.77	1.39
Postresponse		
Postive verbal feedback	18.05	11.34
Negative verbal feedback	8.75	6.72
Positive physical feedback	6.14	7.16
Negative physical feedback	0.03	0.14
Reward	0.00	0.00

of all measures except points did not differ across training sessions. More instances of pointing occurred during the third training session than during the second ($t = 2.56, p < .05$).

As can be seen from Table 1, the two forms of preresponse verbalization occurred more frequently than any other behavior. Information-containing and information-devoid verbal directions together accounted for 53 percent of all preresponse behavior. The average frequency of information-devoid verbal directions was significantly greater than the average frequency of information-containing verbal directions ($t = 4.01, p < .01$). Positive verbal feedback occurred more often than negative verbal feedback ($t = 3.81, p < .05$), and positive physical feedback was the most frequent form of nonverbal postresponse behavior. Seventy percent of all positive physical feedback was accompanied by positive verbal feedback. The average frequency of children's correct responses was 14.44, and the average frequency of children's incorrect responses was 14.50.

Correlations among Measures of Mothers' Behavior and their Children's Performance

For all correlational analyses, measures of the behavior of mothers and performance of children were expressed as averages. However, three measures of the preresponse behavior of mothers were converted from frequency measures to percentages. They were: percentage of verbal directions or instructions which contained stimulus-specific information, percentage of block presentations which provided cues, and percentage of block presentations when choices available for a response by the child were less than four. Three measures of children's performance were included in each analysis. They were: percentage of correct responses during training, percentage of correct responses on the trained task during posttest, percentage of correct responses on the similar task during posttest. Because many of the children (12) obtained scores significantly above the 25 percent level during pretest on dissimilar tasks, posttest performance on these tasks was not represented in these analyses. Maternal reward, negative physical feedback, guidance, and demonstrations occurred infrequently and were deleted from the analyses.

The Pearson product-moment correlation coefficients obtained among the various measures of mothers' and children's behavior during training are presented in Table 2. Consistent with the findings of Hess and Shipman (1965), measures of the preresponse activities of mothers generally tended to correlate positively with each other and with children's performance. However, only percentage of limited choice presentations was significantly related to performance scores. The two measures of positive postresponse feedback (positive verbal feedback and positive physical feedback) were highly related and each was positively correlated with percentage of correct responses during training. None of the measures of mothers' behavior correlated significantly with trained task and similar task scores on the test administered after training.

An additional set of correlation coefficients related mothers' behavior and children's performance to the nature of the task employed during training. Each of the six iconic match–to–sample tasks was assigned a score of either one or zero, depending upon the group to which it belonged. The three noncounting tasks (colors, pictures, forms) were represented by zeros, and the three counting tasks (stars, sunbursts, wheels) were represented as ones. Thus, a binary vector was created which indicated the type of task taught by each of the 21 mothers. Only percentage of information-containing verbal instructions was found to correlate significantly with task ($r = -.81, p < .01$), indicating that mothers who taught counting tasks tended to use proportionately fewer task-specific verbal directions than did mothers who taught noncounting tasks.

In order to determine which of the seven measures of mothers' behavior best predicted the performance of children, we performed two multiple linear regression analyses, one with percentage of correct responses during training as the criterion and one with percentage of correct responses on the trained task during posttest. The fundamentals of this procedure have been described by Ward and Jennings (1973).

The results of the regression procedure in which we employed the percentage of children's correct responses during training as the criterion are presented in Table 3. The total proportion of variance associated with the linear combination of the seven predictor variables was found to be .68 ($p < .05$). Positive physical feedback contributed most to the predictive power of the full model ($R^2 = .43$, $p < .01$). Since positive physical

TABLE 2
CORRELATIONS AMONG MEASURES OF THE BEHAVIOR OF MOTHERS AND PERFORMANCE OF CHILDREN DURING TRAINING

	Correlation							
Measure	1	2	3	4	5	6	7	8
1. Percentage information verbal directions	—	.45*	.36	.51*	.08	−.01	.01	.07
2. Percentage cue placements		—	.21	.64**	−.07	−.17	−.13	.26
3. Percentage choices limited			—	.07	.28	−.24	.27	.44*
4. Points				—	−.06	.17	−.14	.23
5. Positive verbal feedback					—	.32	.90**	.60**
6. Negative verbal feedback						—	.13	−.06
7. Positive physical feedback							—	.66**
8. Percentage correct responses during training								—

* $p < .05$.
** $p < .01$.

TABLE 3
SUMMARY OF THE RESULTS OF THE MULTIPLE REGRESSION PROCEDURE WITH PERFORMANCE OF CHILDREN DURING TRAINING AS THE CRITERION AND MEASURES OF THE BEHAVIOR OF MOTHERS AS PREDICTORS

Predictor	r	R	R^2	Beta weight
Positive physical feedback	.66**	.66	.43**	0.6552
Percentage cue placements	.26	.35	.12*	0.3546
Points	.23	.23	.05	0.3188
Percentage choices limited	.44*	.19	.04	0.2021
Percentage information verbal directions	.07	.17	.03	−0.1994
Negative verbal feedback	−.06	.08	.01	−0.1078
Positive verbal feedback	.60**	.00	.00	0.0728

* $p < .05$.
** $p < .01$.

feedback and positive verbal feedback correlated highly and the correlation between positive physical feedback and children's performance was greater than the correlation between positive verbal feedback and children's performance, only physical feedback emerged as a significant predictor. Given these relationships, one can consider positive feedback as a single dimension which consists of both physical and verbal feedback and is significantly related to children's performance during training.

Only one of the measures of the mothers' preresponse behavior—percentage of cue placements—contributed to the predictive power of the full model. Although the simple correlation between the percentage of limited choice presentations and children's performance was significant, the associated *R* square derived from the regression procedure was not significant. Similarly, none of the mothers' preresponse behavior contributed significantly to the prediction of training session performance scores. When the trained task scores and similar task scores on the posttest were used as criteria, none of the seven measures of the behavior of mothers emerged as significant predictors.

The final set of analyses consisted of correlated *t* tests which were performed to determine, first, whether or not test scores on the trained task differed significantly and, second, whether or not test scores on the similar but untrained task differed significantly. The average percentage of correct responses for the trained task during pretest was 25.9, while the average trained task posttest score was 31.2 ($t = 1.58, p > .05$). Similarly, the average pretest and posttest scores on the untrained but similar task (28.6 and 32.1, respectively) did not differ significantly.

Discussion

In this study mothers tended to rely most upon verbal modes of communication while attempting to teach their retarded children a specific task. Consistent with the findings reported by Marshall, Hegrenes, and Goldstein (1973), preresponse verbal directions which were generally shorter and repetitive and did not contain specific labels for the stimuli occurred most frequently. Although it is possible that mothers of retarded children are aware of the limited receptive linguistic competencies of their children and thus use simple commands, other data collected during this study suggest that the type of verbal directions used may be more directly related to task variables. Mothers who taught the noncounting tasks, which consisted of familiar stimuli, tended to use proportionately more stimulus-specific labels and descriptions than did mothers who taught counting tasks. Hence, the linguistic styles of mothers may be partly determined by immediate situational factors.

Contrary to the findings summarized by Hess et al., (1971), stimulus-specific verbal directions and instructions were not related to the performance of the children. As Rosenberger, Stoddard, and Sidman (1972) have suggested, the limited receptive language of young retarded children no doubt is restrictive of the effectiveness of elaborate forms of verbal communication. In receptive language the child is required to "match" a word with the actual object or action to which the word refers. A mother who says, "Put the wagon over there with the other wagon," is requiring her child to make a cross-modality conditional discrimination, since the stimulus attributes of the word *wagon* are quite different from those of the picture *wagon*; and, yet, the child must recognize equivalence in order to respond correctly. A number of theorists (e.g., Bruner, 1964; Piaget & Inhelder, 1969; Klausmeier, Note 4) have posited that language is predicated upon precursory nonverbal cognitive structures which are formed as the result of active interaction with responsive aspects of the environment. The child learns first to discriminate one object from another and then to classify objects according to shared characteristics. Thus, the eventual linguistic competencies of children may well depend upon their ability to form less complex within-modality conditional discriminations during the preverbal stages of development.

The pattern of intercorrelations which were observed among measures of maternal behavior suggest at least one salient dimension of teaching style. As Hess et al. (1971) and others have found, the activities of mothers which follow their retarded children's responses and are evaluations of correctness were positively related to one another and did predict performance during training. The failure to observe negative physical feedback (e.g., spanking or slapping) may be a result of a general reluctance by mothers to punish their children while being recorded on videotape. Also, the occasions for what some mothers may have considered to be an extreme form of control were probably limited by the nature of the task.

In summary, the results of this investigation indicated that postresponse feedback is an extremely good predictor of performance during training. However, they do not suggest, as operant theorists have argued, that these aspects of the teaching styles of mothers act to determine the performance of their children. It is equally probable that the activities of mothers occur as the result of the behavior exhibited by their children. Thus, mothers tend to provide positive feedback whenever their children give correct responses. In this sense, then, it is the behavior of the children which controls the potentially reinforcing aspects of teaching style. Correct responding, in turn, could well be shaped by other factors including the nonverbal preresponse activities of mothers which in this study occurred infrequently. The validity of such an interpretation can only be assessed by employing an experimental manipulation approach (Bell, 1968) to the study of parent–child interaction.

Reference Notes

1. Brophy, J. E., Hess, R. D., & Shipman, V. C. *Effects of social class and level of aspiration on performance in a structured mother-child interaction.* Paper presented at the biennial meeting of the Society for Research in Child Development, Minneapolis, March 1965.
2. Olim, E. G., Hess, R. D., & Shipman, V. C. *Relationships between mothers' language styles and cognitive styles of urban preschool children.* Paper presented at the biennial meeting of the Society for Research in Child Development, Minneapolis, March 1965.
3. Robinson, C. C., & Filler, J. W., Jr. *A parent teaching style assessment scale.* Paper presented at the annual meeting of the American Association on Mental Deficiency, Minneapolis, May 1972.
4. Klausmeier, H. J. *Cognitive operations in concept learning.* Division 15 Presidential Address presented at the annual meeting of the American Psychological Association, Washington, DC, September 1971.

References

Bell, R. Q. A reinterpretation of the direction of effects in studies of socialization. *Psychological Review*, 1968, 75, 81-95.

Brophy, J. E. Mothers as teachers of their own preschool children: The influence of sociometric status and task structure on teaching specificity. *Child Development*, 1970, 41, 79-94.

Bruner, J. S. The course of cognitive growth. *American Psychologist*, 1964, 19, 1-15.

Hess, R. D., & Shipman, V. C. Early experience and the socialization of cognitive modes in children. *Child Development*, 1965, 36, 869-886.

Hess, R. D., Shipman, V. C., Brophy, J. E., & Bear, R. M. Mother-child interaction. In I. J. Gordon (Ed.), *Readings in research in developmental psychology*. Glenview, IL: Scott, Foresman, 1971.

Leiter, R. G. *Examiner's Manual for the Leiter International Performance Scale*. Chicago: Stoelting, 1969.

Marshall, N. R., Hegrenes, J. R., & Goldstein, S. Verbal interactions: Mothers and their retarded children vs. mothers and their nonretarded children. *American Journal of Mental Deficiency*, 1973, 77, 415-420.

Olim, E. G. Maternal language styles and children's cognitive behavior. *Journal of Special Education*, 1970, 4, 53-68.

Piaget, J., & Inhelder, B. *The psychology of the child*. New York: Basic Books, 1969.

Rosenberger, P. B., Stoddard, L. T., & Sidman, M. Sample-matching techniques in the study of children's language. In R. L. Schiefelbush (Ed.), *Language of the mentally retarded*. Baltimore: University Park Press, 1972.

Ward, J. H., Jr., & Jennings, E. *Introduction to linear models*. Englewood Cliffs, NJ: Prentice–Hall, 1973.

Modifying Maternal Teaching Style: Effects of Task Arrangement on the Match–to–Sample Performance of Retarded Preschool-Age Children

JOHN W. FILLER, JR.
George Peabody College for Teachers

Twenty-one mothers and their retarded preschool-age children were observed during six teaching sessions. Following the first three sessions, each mother–child dyad was assigned to one of the three groups. Groups were matched on measures of mother and child behavior and on measures of various mother and child background factors. Prior to the last three teaching sessions, mothers received instructions to modify certain aspects of their teaching style. The results indicated that children of mothers who had been instructed to present the materials of the task systematically obtained significantly higher performance scores during training than did children of mothers who either received no instruction or had been told to increase positive feedback for correct responses. Further, 6 of 7 children whose mothers had altered the manner in which they presented the task materials showed improvement on a test administered after training. These results suggest that nonverbal activities which precede responding are critical aspects of teaching style and deserve more attention than they have received in the past.

During recent years there has been an increased tendency to emphasize the role of parents as critical instructional agents in the education of their own retarded children (e.g., Bricker & Bricker, Note 1; Gray & Klaus, Note 2). The current emphasis on parent involvement and training has been influenced by growing concern for the shortage of trained professionals and by demonstrations of relationships among a variety of parental factors and measures of the cognitive development of children (Schaefer, 1970). Other investigators have isolated specific relationships among defined aspects of parental behavior and measures of children's performance during structured teaching situations. For example, Hess, Shipman, and their colleagues (Brophy, 1970; Hess, Shipman, Brophy, & Bear, 1971) suggest that both preresponse measures of teaching style (verbal and nonverbal forms of communication which primarily precede children's responses) and postresponse reactive aspects of teaching style (reward, praise, and promise of reward) are related to children's performance on sorting tasks.

More recently, Filler and Bricker (1976) observed 21 mother–retarded child dyads while the mothers attempted to teach a match–to–sample task. They found that measures of positive postresponse feedback (positive verbal and physical feedback) were highly related to correct performance. However, preresponse verbal directions and instructions, although occurring frequently, were unrelated to child performance as were most of the more infrequently occurring nonverbal preresponse forms of behavior. Although in such correlational studies the importance of a careful specification of both parent and child behavior is emphasized, there is no demonstration of functional or deterministic relationships be-

This study was conducted as part of a dissertation submitted by the author to the Department of Psychology of George Peabody College for Teachers in partial fulfillment of the requirements for the PhD degree. The dissertation was supervised by William A. Bricker and supported by National Institute of Child Health and Human Development Grants No. HD07073 and HD00973. Preparation of the manuscript and analyses of data were supported by the Illinois Institute for Developmental Disabilities, where the author is now affiliated.

The author would like to express his deepest appreciation to Dr. Diane Bricker and to the staff, parents, and children of the Infant, Toddler, and Preschool Research and Intervention Project of the John F. Kennedy Center, George Peabody College for Teachers, for their enthusiastic cooperation.

"Modifying Maternal Teaching Style: Effects of Task Arrangement on The Match-To-Sample Performance of Retarded Preschool-age Children", John W. Fuller, *American Journal of Mental Deficiency,* Vol. 80, No. 6, May 1976, © 1976 American Association On Mental Deficiency.

tween pre- and postresponse parental behavior and the performance of children on learning tasks.

In contrast to the studies cited above, in a number of behavior modification studies, researchers have demonstrated that when parents are taught to apply principles derived from the experimental analysis of behavior, predictable changes occur in the rate or form of their children's behavior (e.g., Hawkins, Peterson, Schweid, & Bijou, 1966; Wahler, 1969). Unfortunately, as Gardner (1969) has noted, in behavior-modification studies, investigators have tended to focus primarily on outcome variables and have not included careful specification of parental variables. Further, most of these studies have involved manipulations of parents' postresponse behavior and have lacked tests of the possible independent contribution of isolated changes in preresponse behavior. Thus, while it is possible to conclude that measures of the behavior of parents predict, in a statistical sense, children's performance and that changes in parents' behavior can result in changes in children's behavior, adequate studies of the contribution of different aspects of parental teaching style to performance gains during learning situations are notably absent from the literature.

In this study pre- and postresponse activities of different matched groups of mothers of retarded children were altered, and the subsequent performance of their children on a learning task was examined.

TABLE 1

CHARACTERISTICS OF THE CHILDREN (N = 21) BY SUBGROUPS

Group	Percentage correct on pretest		MA[a]		CA[a]		IQ[b]		Sex		Etiology	
	Mean	Range	Mean	Range	Mean	Range	Mean	Range	Male	Female	DS[c]	Other
Control	26.8	19–38	23.1	16–32	39.9	20–61	62.2	39–80	3	4	4	3
Feedback	25.8	25–31	24.7	18–42	42.1	32–60	58.3	41–74	5	2	2	5
Manipulation of materials	25.0	19–31	26.1	20–35	47.4	32–64	57.3	48–69	5	2	4	3

[a] In months.
[b] Cattell Infant Intelligence Scale or Stanford-Binet Intelligence Scale, Form L-M.
[c] Down's syndrome.

Method

Subjects

The 21 subjects were the same as those included in the Filler and Bricker (1976) study. Descriptive information about the children, by group to which they were assigned, is presented in Table 1. Ten of the children were diagnosed as having Down's syndrome, and 2 had arrested hydrocephalus. The etiological conditions associated with the retardation of the remaining 9 were not known. Information about the mothers, by group to which they were assigned, is presented in Table 2.

Teaching Task

Each mother taught her child one of six four-choice iconic match-to-sample tasks. The stimuli employed in each task have been described by Filler and Bricker (1976). For each matching task, a picture slot board and four picture blocks were used in a fashion highly similar to that of the Leiter International Performance Scale (Leiter, 1969). The particular task which a given mother taught was one on which her child, during a pretest, had demonstrated only chance performance. Pretest score group means are presented in Table 1.

Recording Equipment

Each teaching session for every mother-child dyad took place in a room located in the Kennedy Center Experimental School at

TABLE 2
Characteristics of the Mothers (N = 21) by Subgroups

Group	Years of education		Family income[a]		Age	
	Mean	Range	Mean	Range	Mean	Range
Control	12.07	10–14	8.36	4.0–15.0	31.0	22.0–37.0
Feedback	13.14	9–16	7.00	3.2–12.0	30.8	19.0–49.0
Manipulation of materials	12.71	11–18	7.92	3.5–13.0	33.6	22.0–44.0

[a] In thousands of dollars.

George Peabody College for Teachers, a place familiar to all of the children and their mothers. Two Sony AVC 3200 cameras were positioned in the experimental room. One, fitted with a Canon 25-100 mm fl.8 zoom lens, was mounted in the ceiling directly above the table at which the mother and child worked. The other camera was fitted with a Cosmicar 8.5 mm fl.5 lens and mounted on a Quick-Set Samson tripod. This second camera provided a wide-angle view of the mother and child. Signals from the two cameras were fed simultaneously into a Sony SEG-1 special-effects generator where they were synchronized such that the image from the wide-angle camera and that from the close-up camera appeared together on a Motorola program monitor. The bottom fourth of the screen contained a view of the materials on the table, and the upper three-fourths of the screen contained the wide-angle view of the mother and child. These synchronized images were then taped on a Sony AV3650 Video Recorder where they were preserved on ½ inch Sony videotape. Sound was supplied through two Sony cardioid microphones, one suspended from the ceiling and the other mounted on the table. A Wollensak T-1500 Magnetic Tape Recorder was used to supply a series of tone signals which were superimposed on the videotape. These signals, which were used during the tape analysis, were not heard by the mother or child. All equipment, except the two cameras and microphones, was located in an adjacent room.

Rating Procedure

Each tape of every mother–child training session was rated in a fashion identical to that employed by Filler and Bricker (1976). Thirteen categories of behavior were recorded: 8 maternal preresponse categories, 2 child response categories, and 3 maternal postresponse or feedback categories. The 8 preresponse categories were:

1. *Information/Verbal directions or instructions.* Verbalizations which contained information the child could use to increase his chances of responding correctly, e.g., "Put the wagon over there with the other wagon" or "This is a wagon and over there is another wagon, just the same."
2. *No information/Verbal directions or instructions.* Verbalizations which contained no information about the task, e.g., "Do it" or "Put it where it goes."
3. *Cue placements of the stimulus materials.* Any placement of a picture which increased the probability of the child making the correct match, e.g., placing a picture of a wagon directly in front of the other picture of a wagon and then asking the child to match them.
4. *Opportunity placements of the stimulus materials.* Any presentation of a picture which did not provide a cue concerning the correct match.
5. *Limited choice presentations.* Any presentation of a to–be–matched picture when choices available for a match were less than four.
6. *Points.* Mother pointed to the materials to emphasize critical aspects of the stimuli.
7. *Guidance.* Mother established physical contact with the child and assisted him in making a task-relevant response.
8. *Demonstration.* Mother demonstrated or modeled a correct response before asking the child to respond.

The two categories of children's responses were correct matches and incorrect matches. Three categories of maternal postresponse feedback were:

1. *Verbal feedback.* Verbal feedback was scored as either positive verbal feedback (i.e., potentially reinforcing statements like "Good boy!" or "That's great!") or negative verbal feedback (i.e., potentially punishing statements like "No!" or "You're wrong!").
2. *Physical feedback.* Physical feedback was scored as either positive (potentially reinforcing physical contact like hugging or kissing) or negative (potentially punishing physical feedback like hitting or restraining).
3. *Rewards.* The mother gave her child a toy, edible, etc. as a consequence of a response.

A research assistant who was unfamiliar with the purpose and design of the study rated each videotaped session. These ratings were used exclusively in all subsequent analyses of the interaction sessions. A second rater independently rated 50 percent of the total number of sessions. Pearson product-moment correlations computed between observations of raters for the frequency of each category of mothers' and children's behavior ranged from .87 to 1.00. The mean correlation across categories was .98 (Fisher's *Z*).

Procedure

Prior to the assignment of dyads to groups, each child had received a pretest to determine the task the mother would teach, each mother had worked with her child for three 6-minute sessions conducted on successive days, and each child had received a posttest on the task the mother had taught. The ungrouped data collected during these phases have been reported previously (Filler & Bricker, 1976). In the present study these initial training and test sessions constituted a baseline phase.

Immediately after the completion of the posttest administered by Filler and Bricker (1976), hereafter referred to as Posttest 1, each mother was assigned to one of three groups. Seven were assigned to the postresponse feedback condition, 7 to the preresponse manipulation of materials condition, and 7 to a control condition. Multiple *t* test comparisons of the descriptive variables listed in Tables 1 and 2 indicated no statistically reliable differences among the groups.

Each mother continued training her child, using the same task she had employed during the three preceding baseline sessions. Whereas during baseline all mothers had been instructed to do whatever they liked to teach their children, mothers now received differential instruction according to group assignment. Each was asked to report for the study 15 minutes earlier for Sessions 4, 5, and 6 (intervention) than they had for each of the three baseline sessions. During this time, they individually viewed a videotape-recording of themselves working with their children and received instructions from the experimenter.

For those mothers assigned to the feedback group, the experimenter focused all of his comments upon instances of the mother providing positive feedback for the correct responses of her child. While viewing the videotape of the last baseline session, the experimenter praised the mother for providing positive verbal feedback, positive physical feedback, and edibles or toys immediately following an appropriate response by the child. In addition, he directly suggested that she increase the incidence of such behavior. Since none of the mothers used rewards during baseline, each was asked, prior to beginning Session 4, to select an edible or toy which she would present to the child after each correct response. Following the completion of the videotape and after reminding the mother to provide response-contingent positive verbal feedback, positive physical feedback, and rewards, the experimenter escorted the mother to the room where the training sessions took place. She was then joined by her child and Training Session 4 began. On the following day, the same procedure was followed, except that mother and experimenter viewed the videotape of Session 4. On the next day, the mother and the experimenter viewed the videotape of Session 5 before beginning Session 6; however, prior to beginning Session 6, the mother was reminded that this would be the last training session.

Mothers assigned to the manipulation of materials condition also viewed tapes of themselves working with their child prior to each of the three intervention training sessions. However, during each of the viewing periods, the experimenter focused all of his comments upon the degree to which the mother systematically maximized the probability of a correct match. Specifically, he emphasized limiting placement choices available to the child by covering some of the placement positions. He also stressed the importance of presenting each picture block in such a manner as to provide cues to the child concerning the correct match. Each mother was told to select a block to be presented, cover all of the alternative placement positions, and place the block directly in front of the correct picture slot. If the child then placed the block correctly, it would be presented again, but this time placed farther away from the correct slot, still with only one choice available. Over several presentations the placement was moved toward a position roughly equidistant from each slot. Once the child correctly placed the block, starting from the standard position, the mother was told to uncover a second choice for block placement and to present the first block again, testing to see whether a correct match would be made. If placed correctly, the first block was removed and the second block presented with two choices available. The child was trained to place correctly the second block in the same manner as he was trained to place the first. The third position on the board was uncovered after the child had correctly placed the first two blocks from the standard position. The same procedure was to be followed for training the child in correct placement of the third block. Finally, the fourth block would be presented after the first, second, and third had been placed correctly. At this point none of the positions would be covered. Each mother was instructed to return to an easier step (i.e., increase cue placement and decrease number of choices available) when an incorrect match occurred. No instructions were given concerning the order of presentation of blocks in reference to position on the slotboard which, as during baseline, varied from session to session. After the videotape had been played, the experimenter reviewed his comments concerning the importance of providing cues and limiting choices in the specified manner. He then took the mother to the experimental room where she and her child began Session 4. On the following day, immediately prior to Session 5, the mother viewed the videotape of Session 4 and was praised for the systematic use of cue placement and limiting choices. On the next day the same procedure was followed; however, just prior to beginning Session 6, the experimenter reminded the mother that this would be the last training session.

The 7 mothers assigned to the control condition individually viewed the videotape of their third training session immediately prior to beginning Session 4, Session 4 immediately prior to Session 5, and Session 5 immediately prior to Session 6 in a manner exactly the same as that used with mothers in the feedback and manipulation of materials conditions. However, the experimenter did not comment on specific aspects of the mother's teaching style. He stated at the end of each videotape that the mother was "doing fine" in her attempts to teach her child and praised her for her efforts.

Following completion of the sixth teaching session, each child received a repetition of Posttest 1 (Posttest 2). Each of the four picture blocks of the task the mother had taught was presented to the child, and he was asked to "Put it where it goes" four times for a total of 16 trials.

Results

Several measures of maternal behavior were deleted from analysis because their average frequency of occurrence per session was extremely low (< 1.0). These were: guidance, demonstration, negative physical feedback, and reward (which never occurred during baseline). Further, for the purpose of efficiency, four measures were expressed as percentages. They were: percentage of verbal directions or instructions which contained stimulus-specific information; percentage of picture block presentations which provided cues; percentage of block presentations when choices available for a response were less than four; and percentage of children's responses scored correct during training. The remaining preresponse category (points) was expressed as frequency measures. The session-by-session measures of postresponse feedback were represented as ratios to avoid the possibility of confounding which might result in the failure to detect a true difference between treatment groups. The ratios were: ratio of the total frequency of positive verbal feedback to the total number of correct responses; ratio of the total frequency of negative verbal feedback to the number of incorrect responses; and ratio of the total frequency of positive physical feedback to the total number of correct responses. Representing postresponse measures as ratios minimized the probability that an increase in the correct responding of children, if accompanied by an increase in positive feedback, would result in a failure to detect postresponse feedback differences among the groups during intervention. Postresponse feedback activities of mothers were also expressed as percentage of correct responses which were immediately followed by positive verbal feedback, percentage followed by positive physical feedback, and percentage followed by reward. However, since the results of these analyses were entirely consistent with those of the ratio analyses, they were not presented.

The first set of analyses performed consisted of two multivariate analyses of variance. The first analysis included the eight measures of mothers' behavior and children's percentage of correct responses averaged across the three baseline training sessions for each of the three groups. The results indicated a nonsignificant multivariate effect for group. The second multivariate analysis was of group differences for the same measures, each averaged across the three intervention sessions. Unlike the results of the previous baseline multivariate analysis, a significant multivariate effect for group was obtained ($F = 9.76$, 16/22 df, $p < .01$). Following the suggestion of Field and Armenakis (1974), I performed individual two-way univariate analyses for each measure included in the multivariate tests.

Analyses of Children's Performance

The first, and primary, univariate Group × Session analysis of variance had, as the dependent variable, children's percentage correct scores during the six training sessions. The group mean for each mother–child teaching session is presented in Figure 1. The analysis of these data revealed a significant effect for group ($F = 3.73$, 2/18 df, $p < .05$), session ($F = 5.09$, 5/90 df, $p < .01$), and the Group × Session interaction ($F = 4.29$, 10/90 df, $p < .01$). Separate one-way analyses of variance, one performed for each level of the between-subjects Group factor, indicated a significant session effect

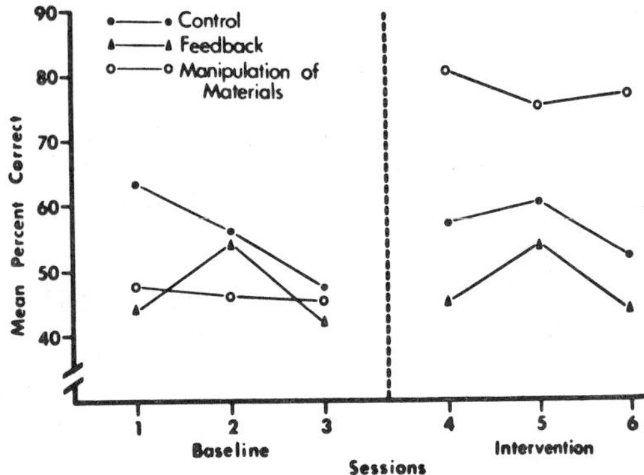

FIGURE 1. Mean percentage correct responses for children assigned to the control, feedback, and manipulation of materials groups across sessions.

only for the manipulation of materials group (F = 10.89, 5/30 df, $p < .01$). Subsequent Newman–Keuls analysis of session differences indicated that children of mothers assigned to the manipulation of materials group obtained significantly higher percentage correct scores during intervention than during baseline ($p < .05$).

A second two-way analysis of variance was used to examine percentage correct scores during the test phases of the study. The results revealed a significant effect for test (F = 9.30, 2/36 df, $p < .01$). Both the group effect and the Group × Test interaction were not significant. Collapsed across groups, the mean scores for Pretest, Posttest 1, and Posttest 2 were 25.90, 30.38, and 40.29, respectively. Newman–Keuls comparisons indicated that the Posttest 1 scores were significantly greater than Pretest scores ($p < .05$) and that Posttest 2 scores were greater than either Pretest or Posttest 1 scores ($p < .05$).

One-tailed sign tests (Siegel, 1956) were used to determine if the number of children within each group who improved across tests was significantly greater than would be expected by chance alone. Each of the three analyses of Pretest to Posttest 1 changes failed to indicate significance. The number of children who improved in the control, feedback, and manipulation of materials groups were 2, 3, and 3, respectively. Similarly, the frequency of positive changes for the control and feedback groups from Posttest 1 to Posttest 2 were nonsignificant. However, the analysis of changes in the manipulation of materials group indicated that a significant number of children (6) did show gains from Posttest 1 to Posttest 2 (p = .02). Thus, the manipulation of materials group was the only group in which a significant number of children showed positive changes in performance on tests.

Analyses of Mothers' Behavior

In order to determine whether or not group differences in children's performance were related to changes in mothers' behavior, the 8 measures of mother's behavior included in the multivariate analysis were dependent variables in separate univariate two-way analyses of variance. Of primary interest were the analyses of the two preresponse measures, percentage cue presentations and percentage limited choice presentations, and the two ratio measures of positive postresponse feedback. Since mothers had been instructed differentially to modify these activities during the intervention phase, significant Group × Session interactions were expected.

The top half of Figure 2 illustrates the mean percentage cue presentation scores for the three groups of mothers during the six teaching sessions. Analyses of these data yielded a significant main effect for session (F = 16.10, 5/90 df, $p < .01$) and a significant Group × Session interaction (F = 12.73, 10/90 df, $p < .01$). Separate one-way analyses revealed a significant session effect for the manipulation of materials group (F = 38.91, 5/30 df, $p < .01$); however, the scores for the feedback and control groups did not differ significantly across the six sessions. Newman–Keuls analysis revealed that the mothers in the manipulation of materials group exhibited significantly higher percentage cue scores during each intervention session than during each baseline session ($p < .05$).

The mean percentages of limited choice presentations for each group across the six teaching sessions are presented in the lower half of Figure 2. Since two-way analysis of group and session differences during the three baseline sessions revealed a significant group effect (F = 5.68, 2/18 df, $p < .05$), with mothers subsequently assigned to the manipulation of materials group receiving lower scores (mean = 29.90) than mothers later assigned to either the feedback (mean = 58.61) or control (mean = 62.71) groups, analyses of covariance were performed. The results indicated that mothers in the manipulation of materials group provided proportionately more limited choice presentations than did mothers in the feedback or control groups during Session 4 (F = 11.60, 2/17 df, $p < .01$) and during Session 5 (F = 11.50, 2/17 df, $p < .01$). However, the difference among groups during Session 6 failed to reach significance (F = 2.75, 2/17 df, p = .09). All of the mothers in the manipulation of materials group increased both cue placements and limited choice presentations in a manner consistent with the instructions

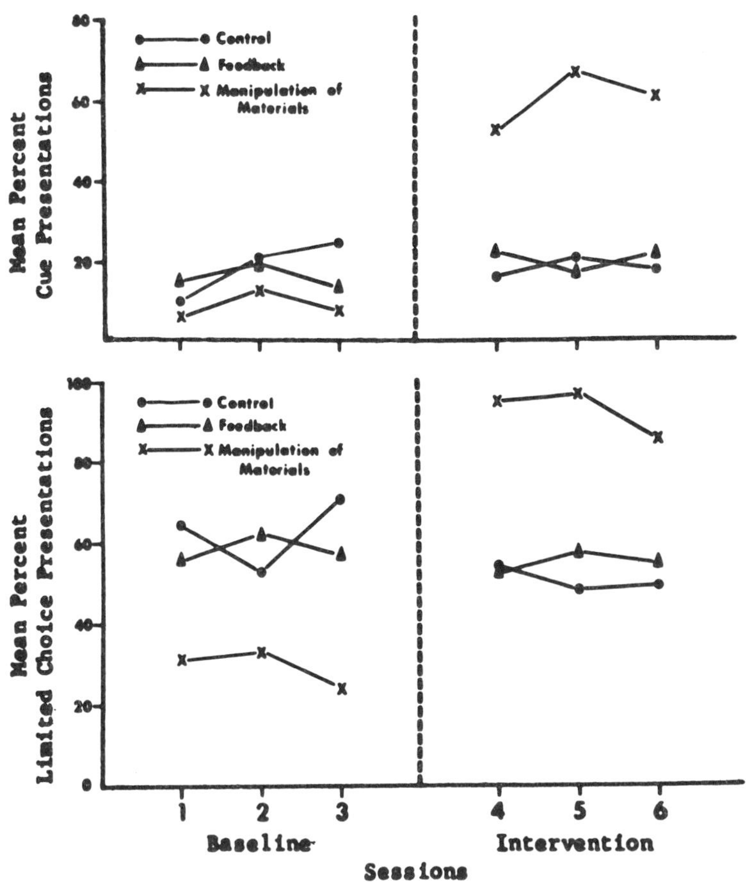

FIGURE 2. Mean percentage cue presentations and mean percentage limited choice presentations for the control, feedback, and manipulation of materials groups across sessions.

they were given during intervention.

The lower half of Figure 3 shows the average ratios of positive verbal feedback to correct responses for each of the three groups during baseline and intervention. The analysis of the ratio scores of positive verbal feedback to correct responses showed a significant main effect of session ($F = 2.73$, 5/90 *df*, $p < .05$) and, as expected, a significant Group × Session interaction ($F = 4.11$, 10/90 *df*, $p < .01$). Subsequent one-way analysis revealed a significant session effect for the feedback group ($F = 16.40$, 5/30 *df*, $p < .01$) but not for the control or manipulation of materials groups. Newman–Keuls comparison of the feedback group's session means indicated that scores for each intervention session were significantly greater than scores for each baseline session ($p < .05$).

Mean ratios of positive physical feedback to correct responses for each group during each session are illustrated in the upper portion of Figure 3. The two-way analysis of the ratio of positive physical feedback to correct responses indicated significant main effects for group and session. As expected, a significant Group × Session interaction was also indicated ($F = 13.77$, 10/90 *df*, $p < .01$). Subsequent tests for simple effects indicated that the obtained interaction resulted from the fact that mothers assigned to the feedback condition obtained significantly higher scores during intervention than during baseline ($p < .05$) and that their mean scores for Sessions 5 and 6 were significantly greater than their mean score for Session 4 ($p < .05$).

Since mothers assigned to the control and manipulation of materials groups failed to provide rewards during any of the training sessions and mothers assigned to the feedback group did so only during intervention, assumptions of normality of distribution and homogeneity of variance necessary for *F* test comparisons could not be met. Thus, formal analyses of these data were not conducted. The feedback group mean ratios of reward to correct responses were .71, .86, and .91 during Sessions 4, 5, and 6, respectively.

The univariate analysis of preresponse percentage information-containing verbal instructions and directions and the uni-

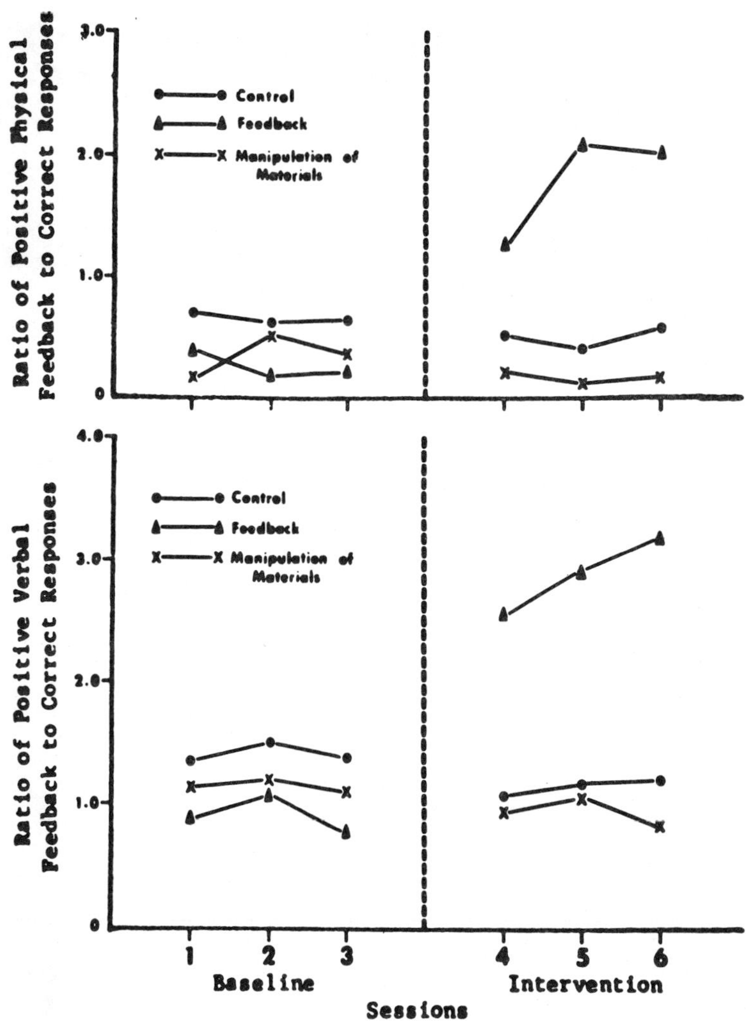

FIGURE 3. Mean ratio of positive verbal feedback to correct responses and mean ratio of positive physical feedback to correct responses for the control, feedback, and manipulation of materials groups across sessions.

variate analysis of the postresponse ratio of negative verbal feedback to incorrect responses failed to reveal significant group and session main effects or Group × Session interaction effects. The analysis of material preresponse pointing to specific aspects of the stimuli yielded a significant main effect for group ($F = 6.50$, 2/18 *df*, $p < .01$) and a significant main effect for session ($F = 5.95$, 5/90 *df*, $p < .01$). A Newman–Keuls comparison indicated that mothers assigned to the control condition pointed more often than did mothers assigned to the manipulation of materials condition. Also, mothers in each group pointed more often during Sessions 1 and 3 than during Sessions 4 and 5.

Discussion

The results of this study clearly suggest the importance of nonverbal preresponse activities of mothers. Children of mothers assigned to the manipulation of materials condition showed dramatic improvement in performance after their mothers altered the manner in which they presented the stimuli. Further, 6 of the 7 children assigned to the manipulation of materials group showed gains on a test administered after intervention while only 3 of 7 improved in the feedback and control groups. It would be erroneous to conclude, however, that such effects can be achieved in the complete absence of positive feedback since, in this study, the postresponse activities during intervention were very nearly the same as those during baseline. Thus, during intervention, mothers in the manipulation of materials condition were also providing positive feedback for correct responses in a manner consistent with their natural tendencies to do so. Had mothers not maintained baseline levels of positive feedback, it is doubtful that their children would have responded as they did during intervention. Nevertheless, the data do suggest the validity of Brophy's (1970) contention that activities which precede responding deserve more attention than they have received from operant and social-learning theorists.

Although mothers assigned to the feedback group showed significant increases across sessions in both percentage and ratio measures of response-contingent positive verbal feedback, positive physical feedback, and rewards, the performance of their children did not change. In operant terms, the praise provided by mothers did not constitute reinforcement, since an increase in these activities failed to be associated with an increase in the probability of correct responding. As Ray and Sidman (1970) have noted under similar conditions, the establishment of a particular form of stimulus control (correct matching) does not seem to be affected by the manipulation of events which occur subsequent to correct responding.

Given the fact that the performance of children assigned to the feedback group did not improve during intervention, the reason for the observed positive relationship between performance of children and positive feedback during baseline, reported by Filler and Bricker (1976), is not entirely clear. A possible explanation is that preresponse forms of behavior control children's performance which, in turn, influences the frequency of positive feedback provided by mothers. Thus, increasing the amount and variety of positive feedback during intervention had no effect upon correct responding because the controlling relationship was in the opposite direction. A test of this hypothesis would require the manipulation of performance levels of different groups of children with pre- and postintervention measures of the postresponse activities of parents.

The growing tendency to include parents as integral parts of the amelioration process demands research that concentrates upon the delineation of functional aspects of teaching style. In the past, interaction researchers have been concerned with descriptions of what mothers do while working with their children and have concentrated upon the enumeration of aspects of behavior of mothers that predict the acquisition of various forms of their children's behavior. Although rarely stated, the implicit assumption has been that those aspects of mothers' behavior which predict performance also cause performance. Bell (1968), noting this tendency, has argued for the adoption of an "experimental-manipulation" approach to the study of mother–child interaction. The present investigation demonstrated that the experimental method is feasible and that the results gained may well provide constructive insights into the functional nature of relationships between the behavior of mothers and the performance of their children.

Illinois Institute for Developmental Disabilities
1640 W. Roosevelt Rd.
Chicago, IL 60608

Reference Notes

1. Bricker, D. D., & Bricker, W. A. *Toddler research and intervention project report: Year II* (IMRID Behavioral Science Monograph, No. 21). George Peabody College for Teachers, 1972.
2. Gray, S. W., & Klaus, R. A. *The early training project: A seventh year report.* John F. Kennedy Center for Research on Education and Human Development, George Peabody College for Teachers, 1969.

References

Bell, R. Q. A reinterpretation of the direction of effects in studies of socialization. *Psychological Review*, 1968, 75, 81-95.

Brophy, J. E. Mothers as teachers of their own preschool children: The influence of socioeconomic status and task structure on teaching specificity. *Child Development*, 1970, 41, 79-94.

Field, H. S., & Armenakis, A. A. On use of multiple tests of significance in psychological research. *Psychological Reports*, 1974, 35, 427-431.

Filler, J. W., Jr., & Bricker, W. A. Teaching styles of mothers and the match–to–sample performance of their retarded preschool-age children. *American Journal of Mental Deficiency*, 1976, 80, 504-511.

Gardner, J. M. Behavior modification research in mental retardation: Search for an adequate paradigm. *American Journal of Mental Deficiency*, 1969, 73, 844-851.

Hawkins, R. P., Peterson, R. F., Schweid, E., & Bijou, S. W. Behavior therapy in the home: Amelioration of problem parent–child relations with the parent in a therapeutic role. *Journal of Experimental Child Psychology*, 1966, 4, 99-107.

Hess, R. D., Shipman, V. C., Brophy, J. W., & Bear, R. M. Mother–child interaction. In I. J. Gordon (Ed.), *Readings in research in developmental psychology*. Glenview, IL: Scott, Foresman, 1971.

Leiter, R. G. *Examiner's Manual for the Leiter International Performance Scale*. Chicago: Stoelting, 1969.

Ray, B. A., & Sidman, M. Reinforcement schedules and stimulus control. In W. N. Schoenfeld (Ed.), *The theory of reinforcement schedules*. New York: Appleton–Century–Crofts, 1970.

Schaefer, E. S. Need for early and continuing education. In V. H. Denenberg (Ed.), *Education of the infant and young child*. New York: Academic Press, 1970.

Siegel, S. *Nonparametric statistics for the behavioral sciences*. New York: McGraw–Hill, 1956.

Wahler, R. G. Oppositional children: A quest for parental reinforcement control. *Journal of Applied Behavior Analysis*, 1969, 2, 159-170.

IT'S NEVER TOO EARLY: DEVELOPING LANGUAGE SKILLS IN THE YOUNG CHILD

Dorothy M. Unger

All teachers, especially those who work with younger exceptional children, are vitally interested in the language development of their students. It is important that the child make consistent progress and that language development become a positive and successful experience for the child and his teachers.

Since language development begins with imitation of sounds the child hears spoken in the home, the teacher of the exceptional child can elicit the help of parents in the development of their child's language competencies.

When initiating a cooperative language teaching experience with parents, teachers can alert parents to the following basics:

- When language patterns are given in a large number of sound units, and at a rate faster than the child can carry and integrate, confusion ofter results.
- The addition of an extra sound to a language pattern is enough to throw the entire language pattern into confusion.
- Since language is learned by sound imitation, a child diagnosed as having a short auditory memory will need greater assistance.
- Although the younger child with a speech delay can learn to understand many of the most common words spoken at home, the child is often unable to reproduce words containing three or more different sounds until he is between 3 and 6 years of age.

DEVELOPING THE TECHNIQUE

As a language and speech therapist working with very young exceptional children who needed help in their speech development, the author developed a technique which parents of young children can use in the home. The method involves reading with a child, instead of reading to him. If a child is able to imitate sounds, as some children can at the age of 18 to 24 months, and he is willing to sit and look at pictures in a book, the child is ready for such a program.

The first requirement is a specific and consistent quiet place and time each day for this uninterrupted "together reading." Having appropriate reading matter is also essential. The easy to read beginner books such as Hop on Pop (Seuss, 1963) are excellent material for this activity.

APPLYING THE TECHNIQUE

The following is a description of the technique, using Hop on Pop as an example. The parent should turn to the first page of the book and say "up", showing the child that the dog is up in the air. After repeating this, the parent should extend a hand toward the child, indicating that it is the child's turn. Usually the child will understand what is expected of him. If he does not, however, the parent can explain simply, "We are reading together, First I will say the word; then you will say the word."

The length of the phrase should then be extended to "Up pup" and then to "Pup is up." At this stage the parent can judge whether or not the child has an auditory memory for two or three words. If the child's auditory memory is short (for example the child says "Puh ih uh"), then the input should be shortened. The ending letters should be stressed as the input is repeated slowly, "Pup is up."

On the next page of the book there is a puppy inside a cup. The parent should first say "cup" for the child to repeat. The phrase should then be extended to "pup in cup." If this phrase is too long for the child to repeat, it should be broken into "pup" and "in cup," emphasizing "in" in the second part. Inflection on the "in" can be changed for variety and fun.

This procedure should be followed on the next page for the phrase "cup on pup." If the child is 4 years of age or older and can see that each of these groups of black letters represents a "word", the reading process has begun.

At first a child may have to be coaxed to repeat the words. With a young child the parent may have to say, "Now you" or "You say --------." With an older child, the parent

"It's Never Too Early: Developing Language Skills in the Young Child", Dorothy M. Unger, *Teaching Exceptional Children*, Vol. 8, No. 3, Spring 1976, © 1976 by The Council For Exceptional Children.

may simply instruct the child "I say the words first; then *you* have *your*turn." If a child omits a word, he should be encouraged to "say it *all.*"

Units should be kept short. An input of two or three words is a good start. They should be related to one story or idea. For example, if one is reading the story *Put Me in the Zoo* (Loopshire, 1960), when the imaginary animal says, "I will go into the zoo," the units to be repeated by the child might be "I," "will go," "into," "the zoo." In this manner, the child who has a short immediate memory is not overtaxed. The child with a longer auditory memory will be able to repeat a presentation of "I will go" and "into the zoo" with success.

For a short time it may be necessary to have the child repeat one word at a time or even allow him to say the last word of the unit. The idea is to have fun together while reading. As the child becomes able to repeat longer units with ease, the syllable input, should be lengthened.

EMPHASIZING THE SOUNDS

After the parent has established this reading together time and used the same story at least two to three times so that the child is familiar with the words, the parent could then say, "Now let's have different fun." At this stage he should try to develop more auditory awareness for sounds by calling the child's attention to the sameness of some sounds, to rhymes, and to rhythm.

In the phrase "Up pup," to continue with the *Hop on Pop* examples, the parent can clap his hands or tap his foot as he emphasizes the word *pup.* Then the phrase could be changed to "cup, pup," with emphasis on *pup*, and then to "pup in cup,"with emphasis on *cup* . In this manner the parent can clap on rhyming words to emphasize rhythm, and rhyme. With the next lines, "All, tall. We all are tall," the words *all* and *tall* can be emphasized. Then on "All, small. We all are small," the words *all* and *small* can be emphasized.

Children enjoy joining in on the clapping and mutual pronunciation of the words. Often a parent will find it effective to hesitate before the paired rhymed word. As the child develops more facility in listening and rhyming, he will happily produce the word. Although *Hop on Pop* has been used as the example here, there are numerous other beginning books with end rhyming words that may be used.

STRUCTURING THE AUDITORY ENVIRONMENT

Another problem in speech and language development occurs with auditory figure-ground confusion. The child is unable to pick out a sound from a general background of other sounds. As a result, the meaning is confused. He hears a jumble; all the sounds run together. There may also be a high element of distractibility; that is, the child's attention is drawn to the slightest auditory stimulus in the background, making him unable to concentrate on a given task. Thus, a child trying to comprehend what is being read to him while a plane drones overhead or a refrigerator hums will be unable to select the sounds he needs from the total auditory input, even though neither the plane nor the refrigerator actually drowns out the spoken words.

In reading with children, the author developed another technique that is useful in developing or extending auditory memory and in focusing the child's attention on the desired response. The parent should first listen carefully to how the child repeats the input. If the final or end sounds or words are omitted, as previously described when the child omitted the p on *up*,the parent can repeat the phrase changing the vocal inflection on the omitted word.

For example, if the parent says, "play all day," and the child omits the *all*, the phrase should be repeated with inflection changed to stress the omitted word. If a nonplosive final consonant such as *l, m, or n* is omitted, the parent should repeat the word and prolong the final sound. Thus the child who say *"baw"* for "ball" should hear the parent say "bal-l-l."

The technique of tapping one's foot or clapping hands on a similar or rhymed word is another effective aid in structuring the auditory environment.

KEEPING THE READING TIME SHORT AND PLEASANT

A child who has the multiple problems of short auditory memory, high distractibility to other environmental sounds, and perhaps auditory figure-ground confusion often has a short attention span. He finds it difficult to sit and focus his attention. If this is the case, the parent may find it necessary to make the reading together sessions short. If 5 minutes is all that can be sustained with interest and pleasure, the session should stop after that. A parent may have to be content with lengthening the sessions by intervals of only 1 minute more at a time.

Even this is a good beginning. The ability to attend and to repeat the word, phrase, or sentence will develop as the parent and child continue to read together.

FACILITATING PROGRESS

Parents of children with communication problems are often anxious and concerned about their child's progress. Teachers can inform parents about their child's academic development and suggest techniques parents can use to facilitate consistent progress as the child develops language skills at home and at school.

LEARNING DISABILITIES

Camp Challenge: A Preschool Program for Visually Handicapped Children and Their Parents

By Jean Grogan M.Ed. and Sheldon Maron Ph.D.

While Camp Challenge is designed primarily for children with visual disabilities, it is a model that can be adapted to provide an effective program for all children with disabilities and their families.

Camp Challenge is a program for visually disabled (and multiply-disabled) preschool children and their parents. It began in 1973 as a cooperative venture between the Bureau of Blind Services (part of the Florida State Department of Education) and the Visual Disabilities Track (part of the Special Education Program) at Florida State University. The camp itself is owned and operated by the Easter Seal Society of Florida.

The camp's purpose is threefold: 1) to provide direct services to visually disabled preschoolers and their parents; 2) to serve as a resource for parents and professionals who care for such children and who seek preschool services for them; and 3) to provide practical experience in a unique setting for Florida State University students majoring in visual disabilities (and related areas).

The program is conducted twice yearly — in October and in April. Each session runs for five days and is funded by the Bureau of Blind Services (BBS). The camp is located in a picturesque setting in central Florida, close to the city of Orlando.

From twenty-seven to thirty families attend each session. Families are referred by BBS caseworkers who recommend that they submit applications to the state BBS office or to us at Florida State University. In the past two years we have been unable to accept all the applications for Camp Challenge, the need for such a service has been so great. In January 1976, a BBS study indicated that there are more than 250 visually handicapped preschoolers in Florida, many of whom receive few or no services.

To accommodate as many families as possible, we give first priority to those who have not previously participated in Camp Challenge. Occasionally an "alumnus" is accepted, especially if he or she has shown signs of development regression over the past year. Moreover, some families should return, particularly families from rural areas where there are no preschool or infant stimulation programs and those with more severely disabled children.

At least one parent, guardian or foster parent must accompany each child. Each session begins on a Saturday and is concluded on the following Thursday; this weekend start has enabled a number of fathers to attend. We try to encourage both parents to participate whenever possible because the growth and development of children with disabilities requires the support and participation of both parents, especially in the early years. All too often fathers are not involved to the degree that is necessary, leaving an awesome burden for the mother to bear alone.

In the past, 35 per cent of all our families have had both parents in attendance at camp — a good percentage considering that most fathers and some mothers miss a week of work, and salary, in order to participate in the program.

The Parents' Program

The camp program is comprised of two distinct, simultaneous subprograms, one for the parents and one for the children. The parents' program includes a series of demonstrations, simulations of visual limitations and discussions by professionals from a wide variety of disciplines and settings (see chart). Parents are divided into small groups to maximize participation and individual attention. In addition, a nightly program for parents (see chart) includes speakers, movies, seminars, project demonstrations, and the like, designed to enhance

Parents' Daily Program

Monday

9:00 a.m.	The Handicapped Child in the Family—Dealing with Emotional Problems
11:00	Promoting Motor Development in Preschool Blind Children
12:00	Lunch (parents eat under blindfold)
1:00 p.m.	Rest hour
2:00	Common Eye Disorders in Young Children
3:00	Orientation and Mobility Simulation — Basic Sighted Guide Techniques
8:00	Feedback session from daily program. Crafts program: Parents make educational toys. Teachers demonstrate toys.

Tuesday

9:00 a.m.	Developing Readiness Skills — Emphasis on Parent-made Materials
11:00	Teaching Feeding Skills
12:00	Lunch
1:00 p.m.	Rest hour
2:00	Parents Observations of Teachers and Students Working with Children
3:30	Demonstration of Educational Materials Commercially Available
8:00	Feedback session from daily program. Demonstration on Teaching Dressing Skills.

Child's Daily Program

Time	Group 1	Group 2
9:00 - 10:00	Physical Education	Sensory Stimulation
10:00 - 11:00	Sensory Stimulation	Swimming
11:00 - 12:00	Swimming	Nature
12:00 - 1:00	Lunch	Lunch
1:00 - 2:00	Rest hour	Rest hour
2:00 - 3:00	Nature	Crafts
3:00 - 4:00	Crafts	Physical Education

parents' understanding of their children's situation.

The programs are designed to give parents practical information that can help them to help their child. For instance, after the presentation on readiness skills (social and academic skills that help prepare the child for school), the parents are given an opportunity to construct materials to use later with their own children. These toys are made from common materials found at home such as egg cartons, fabric scraps, rice, etc. Each parent has a chance to try his "finished product" with his child during the course of the week. These skills and methods will continue to be useful after they have returned home.

Some parents participate in panel discussions in which they have an opportunity to offer their experiences and ideas concerning the special care their children require. These panels stimulate discussions among all parents present.

Parents also spend one morning during the session in nearby Orlando where they observe a local public school program (with well-equipped resource rooms) for visually disabled children of elementary school age. Parents get a reassuring firsthand glimpse of programs many of their children will soon be entering. While there, parents have ample opportunity to talk with teachers and get further suggestions regarding the readiness skills their children need to develop before entering school.

As the week progresses, friendships are made and parents usually find themselves exchanging addresses, toys, children's clothes, etc. Shortly after the close of camp, a list of addresses of camp participants is sent to each family.

On the last day of each session, each family is asked to complete an evaluation of the camp program. These evaluations are carefully tabulated to enable us to make modifications and improvements in the program.

The philosophy at Camp Challenge emphasizes the similarities of our children to all children . . .

The Children's Program

The children's program is conducted concurrently with the parents' program. Approximately thirty children are divided as evenly as possible into five groups. The groups are staffed by twelve teacher-consultants (certified workers with the visually handicapped) and eighteen Florida State University students so that the child-staff ratio is just about one to one. This ratio is necessary because of the increasing number of young children and severely multiply-disabled children who attend. In addition, the Easter Seal Society provides a full-time swimming instructor, camp director and cooks.

On the first day of camp the staff administers a battery of tests to each child to assess skills in motor development, communication and daily living skills (feeding, dressing, grooming, etc.). For example, each child is tested to ascertain his ability to indicate the need to use the bathroom, to roll independently from stomach to back, and to use facial and bodily gestures to indicate wants and needs. This information, together with direct observations, parent conversations and background information from application forms, determines the individualized instructional program for the next four and one-half days. A teacher-consultant may already have worked with some of the children, and this familiarity helps provide more comprehensive planning.

The children's program (see chart) involves activities based on the child's needs. Teachers in each group, together with students and in consultation with us, formulate the program for each session. For some children the program may include learning to focus attention and to make basic responses of acknowledgement. For others it may involve gross motor activities (crawling, walking, running, etc.), toileting and mastering skills of daily living (feeding and dressing). For still others, developing fine motor skills (manual dexterity) and utilizing residual vision (as well as hearing, touch and smell) may be taught.

Parents spend one afternoon observing the teacher-consultants and the students working with their children. Before the close of camp, each family meets with the staff members who have worked with their child. At this time, specific objectives and recommendations are made to parents. The staff suggests activities, materials and procedures to help the child meet these objectives. A comprehensive written report is sent to the appropriate BBS caseworker so that the objectives established at camp can be worked on and realized at home. Parents have access to the report through their caseworker.

Objectives

We realize that objectives must be limited in a five-day program. On the other hand, we never cease to be amazed at the progress that can be made even in this short period of time. With an intensive stimulation program, children have made significant gains in growth and development. The prognosis for these children becoming as independent as they can be improves significantly if intervention programs begin long before school age.

While the children's program represents a short-term source of help, the parents' program represents a continuing resource worth far more than the time spent at Camp Challenge. Parents are not only referred to specific personnel and agencies to contact back home, but, more important, they learn that they can play a crucial role in their child's growth and development.

A great deal can be done if begun early enough to eliminate the negative emotional connotations of blindness and the stereotype of dependency that blindness conveys to the public — including parents of children who are visually disabled. The camp program stresses the idea that while a visual handicap does imply certain restrictions and/or special provisions, a visually handicapped child is a *child* first, with needs similar to those of *all* children. He or she goes through the same developmental sequences and stages as all children. Vision problems are usually not only conspicuous, they often reinforce parents' perceptions that their child is somehow "different." The philosophy at Camp Challenge emphasizes the similarities of our children to all children, disabled or not: we build on these common aspects of growth and development. If we do this, we build on strengths not weaknesses, and that is the cornerstone of a sound educational program.

FUTURE TRENDS

Research has definitely documented the necessity for early childhood education programs for the handicapped. Psychologist and language specialists among others have shown that by the time a child fails in school, it may be too late to recapture the losses that may have transpired.

Some states, such as Kansas and Iowa, have responded to this fact and are providing services to children from birth. Connecticut and other states have enacted laws that make handicapped children eligible for an education at the age of 3. However, in 1976 the National Advisory Committee on the Handicapped reported that 29 states have not enacted legislation mandating the education of pre-school handicapped children. Since then some states have passed positive laws regarding the education of this population, but many others still remain outside the coverage of the provision in P.L. 94-142 that opens the door to Federal support for the pre-school child.

The National Advisory Committee on the Handicapped made the following recommendation in its 1976 Annual Report:

> That the Governors and Legislatures of the several states join forces in making sure that educational services are authorized and provided for every handicapped child in their states, beginning at the child's birth, and that the Commissioner of Education lend his active support to the achievement of this goal.

Progress is being made, but the future must also bring with it further concern for the commitment to early education programs for the handicapped. The future must also deal with the problems of how to capitalize on research evidence being provided by early childhood projects. Some crucial issues are:

1. How valid and useful are our screening instruments in identifying high-risk children with severe and mild handicaps?
2. How does assessment information translate into remedial suggestions in the most effective manner?
3. Do the benefits of early identification outweigh the possible negative effects?
4. At what age is it most beneficial to begin services? 1 month old? 1 year old? 2 years old? 3 years old?
5. What competencies should be expected of an individual who teaches these children?
6. Do we provide services to the gifted pre-schoolers?

Classroom Planning for Young Special Children

JOYCE STEWART EVANS

Joyce Evans is Resource Specialist, Early Childhood Program, Southwest Educational Development Laboratory, Austin, Texas.

■ **Organizer, Architect, Decorator—all are roles of the classroom teacher who carefully plans the educational setting in which her students actively participate. Rooms for young children with special problems require careful planning.**

ROLES DEFINED

An Organizer determines the individualized needs of the students and how to meet these needs through room planning. Careful planning of room arrangement can provide children with a sense of stability, security, and order. In addition, careful planning can save the teacher time needlessly spent moving furniture for various activities, hunting for lost equipment, and picking up at the end of the day.

An Architect takes the space available and maneuvers the space to match the needs of the organizational plan. Although all classrooms should be planned to make best use of available space, careful planning is especially important for rooms used by preschool and early elementary age special children. Programs for these children feature large group, small group, and individual activities. Thus the potential for crowding, chaos, and possible dangers exists in an unplanned room. Such problems can be minimized by dividing the classroom area into learning centers planned for various types of activities.

A Decorator utilizes various mediums to enhance the planned surroundings of a room. This includes the use not only of commercially-produced and teacher-made materials, but also of children's work. Careful decorating thus becomes an expression not only of the teacher's personality, but that of the children as well.

ROOM ARRANGEMENT

In organizing a classroom, certain basic principles of room arrangement are applicable for all rooms, although no single plan could possibly meet the specific needs in all situations. Variables such as children's ages, special handicapping problems and special equipment, the number of children and adults, planned curriculum program, and available resources must be considered. However, all programs should include provisions for individual, small group, and total group activities.

Chart 1 provides a general list of areas which might be included within a room. Obviously, not all areas can be included in the average classroom. Only the individual teacher can determine which areas are most important in meeting the needs of her class. Become an organizer by evaluating which areas are most important to you and your students. Number the areas according to importance for your classroom. After

"Classroom Planning For Young Special Children", Joyce Stewart Evans, *Selected Readings in Early Education of Handicapped Children*, © by The Council for Exceptional Children..

deciding which areas are a necessity, determine which areas can be combined. For example, the storytelling area for reading to a small group can also be an area for individual activity as children select their own books to picture-read. The art area can be used by individual children as well as for small groups working together. Dual or multiple use of room areas depends upon how you schedule the day's activities.

FUNCTION OF ROOM AREAS

Next, determine which of these areas are noisy, quiet, and semi-quiet areas. For example, the construction and motor areas will be noisy while the storytelling area will be semi-quiet. In contrast, areas for planned lesson instruction or a time-out area should be as free from noise and distractions as possible.

Become an architect by maneuvering the available space to meet your specific needs. Space for large group activities should have no partitions or dividers which require moving and should be free for use by the total group as needed during the day. This space may also serve as the snack area, naptime area, or as the traffic lane for movement to smaller areas for individual or small group activities. This area will usually be the center area of a room.

Space for small group lessons by the teacher and assistant teacher should be located in the quietest parts of the room in order to decrease distractions as much as possible during instructional periods. Usually these areas are most successfully located in corners of the room which provide two sound absorbant sides. Visual distractions are also reduced by seating the children with their backs toward the rest of the room. In addition, this allows the teacher to watch other children in the room while working with the small group. More than one such area may be needed if the assistant teacher as well as the teacher will be conducting planned lessons.

Space for small group or individual activity of a noisy nature, such as the construction or housekeeping areas, should be located as far as possible from quiet areas. Once the best places for quiet activities have been determined, areas for noisier activities can be planned. To provide a buffer zone, place areas for relatively quiet activities such as book reading, creative arts, or science between noisy and quiet areas. Figure 1 shows one example of room area arrangement.

Chart 1
Room Areas

Large Group Area: Motor activities, music, snacks, rest period

Small Group Areas: Group size = ________

Housekeeping or Make-Believe Area: household items, dress-up clothes, role-playing clothes
Storytelling Area: pictures, books, catalogs, magazines, flannel board
Manipulative Area: puzzles, stacking toys, pegboards, inch cube blocks
Construction Area: blocks, building items
Art Area: paints, paper, brushes, clay
Science Area: pets, plants, other collections
Lesson Area: areas for specific instruction by teacher and/or assistant
Motor Area: climbing stairs, punching clown, softballs
Special Areas: specific to problem, such as auditory training unit
Other ________

Individual Area

Time Out Area (quiet area with only a chair)
Picture-Reading Area
Manipulative Area
Construction Area
Art Area
Other ________
Special Equipment

DISTINGUISHING AREAS FROM ONE ANOTHER

Each area should be clearly defined and set off from the others. This can be accomplished through separation by distance; the use of bookcases, cabinets, or similar items as dividers; or the use of area rugs. When arranged appropriately, the effect is noticeable as one enters the room—the room looks like a large space divided into several smaller areas, not simply one large room filled with a lot of equipment.

Plan your room arrangement on paper before beginning to move furniture. Measure your room and reproduce an outline on graph paper to save later rearranging. Cut out shapes scaled to the furniture from a second sheet of graph paper. Place the furniture arrangement on paper with accurate measurements, and you will avoid finding yourself with leftover furniture at the end of moving.

OPTIMAL LEARNING THROUGH DECORATION

Once room areas have been determined and the major task of furniture arrangement is completed, attention should be directed toward decorating each area for optimal learning. Too much equipment exposed at one time is distracting and reduces the learning which can take place through use of specific items. Select equipment displayed on shelves to reinforce specific learning related either to unit content under study or skills being taught. For example, during a unit on body awareness, puzzles of body parts should be displayed, not puzzles of animals. The storage space which is imperative in areas for small group activity may be provided by bookcases which also act as area dividers. Decorative use of the back of the bookcase can also be incorporated by covering it with colored paper and using the space for displaying the art work of the children. An alternative is covering the bookcase back with contrasting fabrics or contact paper to provide a tactile wall for learning.

WALL, FLOOR, AND SHELF DECOR SERVE PURPOSE

All wall displays should have a purpose—reinforcing learning, stimulating new learning, or serving as a reward area for displaying the children's work. Children's pictures may be enhanced by the method of display. Use large colored sheets of construction paper to provide a mat for displaying pictures. Rotate the pictures in order to display the work of all the children rather than attempting to display all the pictures at the same time. A critical point to remember in decorating is that this is a room for children. All wall displays should be at the child's eye level. To check for correct placement, kneel down and pretend you are the height of your students. Can you see the pictures easily without having to tilt your head back?

Floor decor as well as wall decor can become very attractive with a little planning. In a tile floored room, small scatter rugs not only add color but also help define learning areas. Carpet installation leftovers, obtained from carpet sales companies, can be pieced together for small areas. If rugs are used, be sure they do not slip. Apply a double surface adhesive tape to fix the rug to the floor along all sides.

Add a decorative note as well as organization to the shelves which hold small pieces of equip-

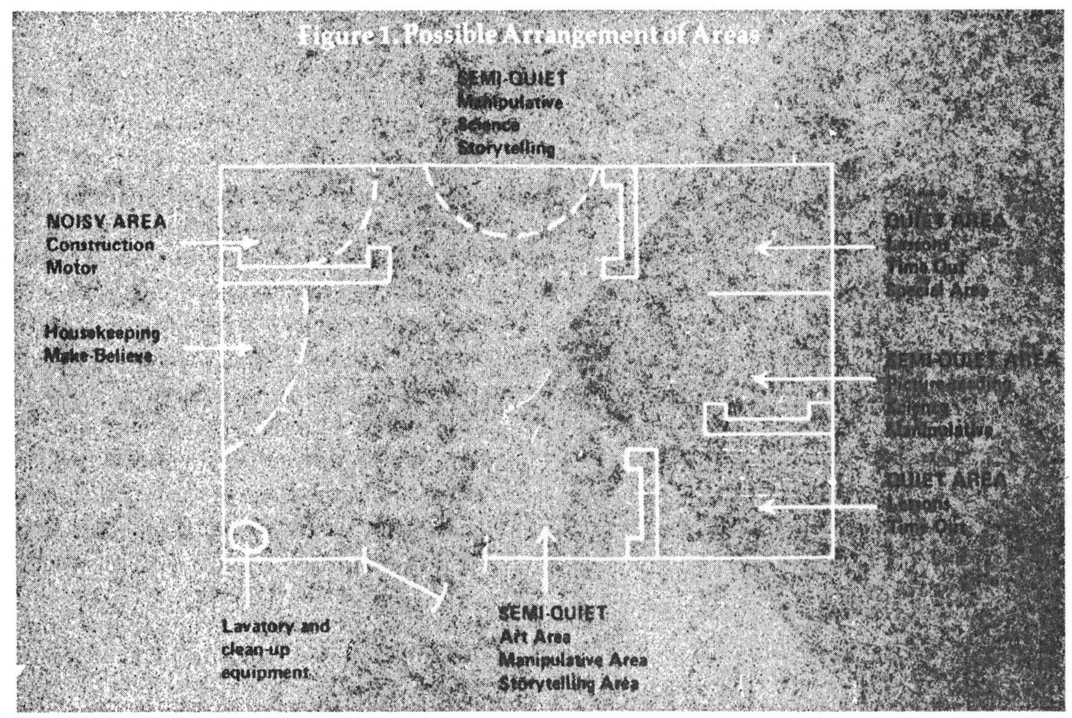

Figure 1. Possible Arrangement of Areas

ment such as beads, inch cube blocks, and pegs. Commercial containers for such items are often difficult for the small hands to manage. Small boxes, plastic containers, egg cartons, and other containers painted in bright colors or covered with contact paper can be used to hold these items. In addition, color concepts can be reinforced by color coding or color matching items. Place all materials so children can easily see the contents of each box. Providing a specific place for each piece of material plus verbal encouragement by the teacher will help the children learn to replace items in their proper place.

CLASSROOM ARRANGEMENT OF PRIMARY IMPORTANCE

During the school year, you and your students will spend more waking hours within the four walls of the classroom than in any other single space. The extra time spent as an Organizer, planning for the needs of your students; an Architect, planning effective use of space; and a Decorator, enhancing the visual appeal of the room, is time well spent when measured by the dividends of more effective teaching and learning.

Developing Individualized Education Programs for Young Handicapped Children

ALICE H. HAYDEN
EUGENE EDGAR

Early education for handicapped children is a top priority of Public Law 94-142, the Bureau of Education for the Handicapped, as well as many professionals in the field of special education. The obvious rationale for early intervention is that young children are more amenable to skill acquisition than are older children and that secondary handicapping conditions can possibly be prevented. Many very young children who should be receiving special services are unserved. Although there have been some who have questioned the effects of early intervention, logic dictates that regardless of the reason for intervention, precise, appropriate programing is absolutely necessary if any intervention is to be effective. Individualized education programs (IEP's) are a safeguard that is available to insure appropriate planning.

THE RATIONALE

The IEP's are described in the rules and regulations, *Federal Register, 41* (252), December 30, 1976 in S121A 220-S121A 226, and *42* (163), August 23, 1977, pp. 42507ff. The only interpretation that can be made with regard to this Congressional mandate is that the IEP is an accountability check for the teacher, administrator, parent, and school system to translate the federal goal of an "appropriate education for every handicapped child" into reality. The IEP is not a binding contract between the teacher and the child in the sense that one or the other is liable if the goals of the IEP are not achieved. Rather, it is a discrete planning process designed to systematize educational planning into an individualized, child oriented approach.

"Developing Individualized Education Programs For Young Handicapped Children", Alice H. Hayden, Eugene Edgar, *Teaching Exceptional Children,* Spring 1978, © 1978, The Council For Exceptional Children.

Most educators will agree that there are five major steps that must be included in the educational process for handicapped children. First, there is an *assessment/diagnostic process* in which it is determined what the child can and cannot do. From this information a determination is made as to what the child needs to begin with—what he or she must *learn next*. Activities are then *planned* to facilitate learning. The plan is then *implemented* and at some point *child performance is measured* in order to evaluate the effectiveness of the entire plan. This process—assessment, goal setting, planning for instruction, implementation, and evaluation—is common to almost all educational strategies for handicapped students. Any good educational program will have these components.

In reality, almost everything required for the IEP is currently being done by competent teachers. The law clearly states that the *minimum* membership of the planning committee is to be the child's referring or present teacher, a representative of the local school district (or preschool program serving the child), and the parent(s). Additional members may be included *(Federal Register, 41,* (252), December 30, 1976, p. 56986). However, Section 121a432, (p. 56991) states that the committee contain individuals "knowledgeable about the child, the assessment results . . . . "

To our way of thinking, the committee is the most appropriate group to determine a child's individual program. Each member of the committee certainly can collect information and generate possible ideas for the IEP before the formal meeting. The professionals (teachers and local education agency personnel) need to recognize that the parents have a basic right to be involved in their child's education. There may be instances when parents (like any other member) could impede the process. However, we believe that these will be the exceptions rather than the rule.

Another major concern about the use of a committee to develop the IEP relates to the scheduling and number of committee meetings. The law allows flexibility to the extent that individuals can be assigned various tasks and the committee need meet only to agree on the final program. Certainly each individual case must be handled in a way that facilitates adequate program planning for the child. The intent of the law is clear—a group of responsible, competent individuals will develop each child's IEP. The method by which this is accomplished is left to the discretion of the group.

PROCEDURES: HOW TO DEVELOP AN IEP

Each IEP must contain the following elements:

1. A summary of present levels of the child's performance.
2. Yearly goals.
3. Short term objectives for each yearly goal.
4. A list of the specific educational and support services needed to meet each objective.
5. Evaluation criteria for each objective.
6. Procedures for re-evaluating the IEP.

There are four major procedures that need to be carried out in order to develop an appropriate IEP: collecting relevant assessment information on the child, deciding on the main priorities for educational intervention (establishing yearly goals), determining how to achieve these goals, and evaluating the IEP. The responsibility for these activities belongs to the committee. However, the committee does not necessarily have to perform each function or meet as a group in each phase, but must agree on each component of the final program.

5. FUTURE

The committee is responsible for insuring that there is an overall service delivery program for each child, that the program is implemented exactly, that the results of the program are reviewed, and that the program is revised, at least yearly. Some considerations regarding parents are that:

1. Meetings must be scheduled at a convenient time for the parents.
2. If the parents' native language is other than English an interpreter must be provided.
3. The parents need to be informed of their rights and responsibilities and should be trained in the IEP process.

The first task of the committee is to collect data on the child. Data must be included that relate to the child's current level of performance and the possible effects of the child's handicapping condition on learning.

Data To Be Collected and Analyzed

Medical Assessment Data

There can be no substitute for a thorough medical examination. Even though there might be very little that can be done to *correct* the child's medical or health problems, these conditions very often influence instructional planning. Therefore, not only must these problems be noted but an interpretation must be made as to how they affect the child's instructional programing.

- Such matters as seizures, medication, heart defects, allergies, susceptibility to illness, strength and stamina, and special feeding instructions are types of assessment information that must be considered in the formation of the IEP.
- Heart defects may require a curtailment of certain types of physical activity or specific amounts of rest periods.
- The possibility of surgical techniques to alleviate physical problems (club foot, cleft palate, leaking heart valve, etc.) must be explored and considered.
- In the rare cases of degenerative central nervous system diseases the IEP must focus on the best strategies for maintaining current functioning and retarding the loss of current skills.
- The types of medications being used must be noted, as well as possible side effects. Procedures for conducting controlled studies of varied dosages should also be established.
- Specific physical limitations may alter educational priorities (a paralyzed arm, for example, might dictate that instruction be geared to the good arm and that physical therapy be given to the immobile arm).
- Allergies may limit the types of food that can be used as possible reinforcers.
- The need for rest will certainly be a factor in determining the daily schedule of activities (a child with a serious heart problem might need to have complete rest three or four times a day).

The basic purpose of this medical information is to permit development of a *comprehensive* IEP. Thus, this information must be used to provide for ongoing medical treatment (medications, diet control, seizure control) as well as to determine considerations for educational programing. All of this information needs to be gathered *and* summarized in the IEP.

Physical Assessment Data

Many preschool aged handicapped children have physical involvement. Programing considerations will concern the procedures that can be used. Positioning, for example, is of prime importance for severely/profoundly handicapped individuals, not only as it may relate to a therapeutic program but also how various positions may facilitate or hamper other educational programing. Techniques to relax children who are spastic and strengthen those who are athetoid, procedures for lifting and moving the children, and the possible use of prosthetic devices are all critical pieces of information that must be collected during the assessment phase.

For any child who is experiencing physical problems, the initial assessment information should attend to three major points. First, a competent occupational therapist or physical therapist needs to determine the specific therapeutic needs of the student. These needs, of course, will be responded to by the IEP as special services. Second, the information gained from this evaluation should point out any of the child's specific physical limitations that will affect educational programing. Third, especially for the severely involved child, specific positioning and handling techniques need to be specified. The occupational therapist or physical therapist should be able to determine how best to position the child so that the child will be *physically* able to make the desired responses. This position should be noted on the IEP as the *desired educational position.*

In the great majority of instances, occupational therapists or physical therapists will be used as consultants to the teacher in the classroom. The initial assessment information, therefore, should include specific information on how the teacher and therapist will interact throughout the school year. Information should be included on the types of behaviors that might occur which would demand immediate therapeutic attention.

As with the medical assessment information, these physical assessment data need to be recorded on the IEP both for special program considerations and also to see how they interact with all educational programing.

Educational Assessment Data

Although assessment for instructional programing is a complex issue, several pertinent areas need to be discussed. First, the process of assessment involves teachers looking directly and frequently at specific child behaviors. Second, the materials the teachers use contain procedures for measuring objective behaviors that are sequenced developmentally in various content areas, but always including gross motor, fine motor (or cognitive), communication (language), social, and self help behaviors. Third, the formats in which the materials are presented should be program specific; that is, they are derived from the specific goals of the educational

Determining Priorities

Analysis of Data

When all the assessment data are collected the committee must meet and determine the child's current level of functioning and special needs. The analysis of the assessment data in order to establish service priorities is the major task of the committee and they

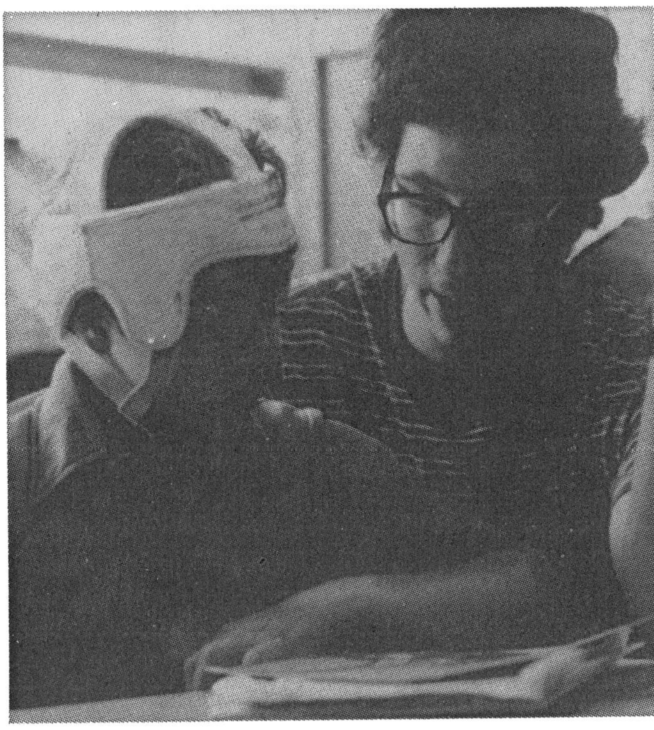

must establish a process for making these decisions. In most cases the professionals on the committee must carry the brunt of the decision making process. Parental input is critical, especially as to desired goals, but the professionals, who should understand the assessment data and program capabilities, will have the basic responsibility for determining priorities.

Probably the most important activity of the committee is to analyze the assessment data and establish priority areas of instruction. This activity determines the appropriateness or inappropriateness of the IEP, because the most technically correct IEP, if focused on inappropriate instructional goals, will result in low quality instruction.

Current Functioning Level

Before any meaningful program can be developed, an accurate statement of the child's current functioning level in each content area must be made. This is interpreted as the highest level of the skills the student has in each area. The priority area for instruction should be at the next level. When programing is planned at a lower level, valuable instructional time will be lost. If programing occurs at too high a level there will be little, if any, success, as well as a high degree of frustration on the part of both student and teacher. A caution should be noted at this point: regardless of the appropriateness of the initial assessment data, mistakes will be made. With the careful use of ongoing assessment procedures teachers are able to detect quickly any pinpoints that are too high or too low for a given child. Thus, daily instructional data should probably take precedence over initial assessment data in determining level of instruction. If the daily data indicate a lower level of functioning than did the initial assessment, a careful explanation of the initial assessment data is called for. In this case the teacher will have to consult with the individuals who collected the initial assessment information and try to determine the cause of the discrepancy.

Physical Limitations

There are very obvious physical limitations that will necessitate alterations in priorities. For example, completely deaf children should not be expected to acquire basic auditory skills. Obvious cases of physical limitations will certainly alter the instructional priorities. However, specific functions (i.e., motor manipulation, receptive language) still must remain as instructional priorities; only the specific skill descriptions will change. A very special caution is needed here because many times these obvious physical limitations are poorly documented. Many cerebral palsied children and partially sighted children have been poorly programed because teachers *assumed* they could never use their fingers or see. Any case of physical limitations must be precisely documented before priorities are changed.

Functionality of Skills

The ultimate criterion for programing must be: "Will this skill provide the individual with a functional behavior that will directly enhance his ability to live independently?" This priority should direct all goal setting activities. Unfortunately, many educational objectives are established simply because these objectives are "aways used." *Each skill that is taught should either be a functional behavior in and of itself or should be a building block skill* (a skill that is part of a functional behavior).

Re-evaluation of IEP's

As priorities are determined, objectives must be developed for each skill area. Each objective should contain a specific procedure for determining when the child evidences the desired skill. With this procedure, re-evaluation of the IEP focuses on three questions: (1) Are the goals appropriate for the child? (2) Are the listed services being delivered to the child? and (3) Is the child evidencing skill gains? In reality all these questions are related to child performance data. Hence, the committee's task is to monitor the child's progress and to make sure that the child is receiving the services that are listed in the IEP. If the child is evidencing satisfactory gains the IEP is probably appropriate. If the child is not experiencing success the committee must determine if the goals need to be altered or if different educational procedures are called for. In any instance, the committee has the responsibility to act as a team to insure that each child is receiving the most appropriate education.

Measuring Preschools' Readiness to Mainstream Handicapped Children

A. GEOFFREY ABELSON

A. Geoffrey Abelson, M.Ed., is doctoral candidate in Early Childhood Education, University of Michigan, Ann Arbor, Michigan, and Research Assistant, Institute for the Study of Mental Retardation and Related Disabilities, University of Michigan. *The research described was supported by the Office of Education, U.S. Department of Health, Education and Welfare, Research Grant OEG-0-74-0463, to M.S. Moersch of the Institute for the Study of Mental Retardation and Related Disabilities, University of Michigan. The author acknowledges the contributions of Carol Alexander to this study.*

With the current trend in special education toward mainstreaming, rather than segregating, handicapped children, techniques are needed for evaluating preschool programs and facilities to prepare such youngsters for normal educational settings.

Early identification of children with handicaps and developmental delays concurrent with immediate intervening programming and treatment is one prevailing trend among professionals concerned with the care and education of children. Another trend, related mainly to special education, is mainstreaming or normalization, meaning an effort to integrate, rather than segregate, exceptional youngsters with so-called normals in educational settings.

Early identification and intervention are indicated by Bloom [1:197–199] in discussing human development as being most pliable and susceptible to environmental forces during critical periods of rapid growth. The first 5 years of life, and especially the first 3, are a prime time to redirect environmental influences that may positively effect growth in the areas of speech and language, perceptual-motor skills, socialization and self-concept.

A policy of mainstreaming or normalization of handicapped and developmentally delayed children has received a plethora of support, as well as words of caution. Wolfensberger wrote that traditional special education and rehabilitation too often remediated in an artificial, segregated and nonnormative setting [6:46]. Thus, transfer of training into realistic, normative settings is unsuccessful. Forness reported little evidence that special class placement results in any gains not promoted in a regular classroom [2:117–126]. Social learning theorists have shown the powerful influence of imitation and modeling on the learning of all children [5:274–292]. Clearly, socialization and speech and language development of children are

"Measuring Preschools' Readiness to Mainstream Handicapped Children," A. Geoffrey Abelson, *Child Welfare*, Vol. LV No. 3, March 1976. ©1976 The Child Welfare League of America, Inc.

influenced by children's exposure to peer-group situations. Public Law 92424, as passed by Congress in 1972, requires Head Start programs to enroll at least 10% handicapped children. Reger warns, however, that to place all handicapped children in classes with nonhandicapped children would put many handicapped children back where they were before the advent of special education [4:513–515].

Problem

The Early Intervention Project of the Institute for the Study of Mental Retardation and Related Disabilities, University of Michigan, has shown concern for the movement toward mainstreaming because of a need to direct parents of handicapped children to "normal" preschool settings offering satisfactory educational and social experiences. To ascertain whether programs and physical facilities exist in Washtenaw County, Michigan, that can be recommended to parents, 45 preschools were observed and surveyed. About 90 preschools exist in Washtenaw County. The ones included in this study are of the following categories: parent cooperative, traditional proprietary, church-controlled, Montessori (proprietary), drop-in center, and college laboratory.

Method

About 2 hours were spent in observation of each of the preschools. A form was constructed to record such information as physical plant design, adult-child ratio, availability of learning materials, toys and cots, and the management style of the teachers. At the end of the observation period, the head teacher or director was interviewed to determine staff responsibility for individual children, previous enrollment of handicapped children, willingness to accept referrals of handicapped children, and the nature of the handicap the school would accommodate. Finally, a questionnaire concerning staff qualifications, parental involvement and educational philosophy was given to each interviewee, to return by mail.

Results

Of the 45 preschools in the study, none indicated that it was unwilling to accept handicapped children. However, questions on accepting children with a particular handicap produced the data shown in Table 1.

Table 1 shows that the most frequently accepted handicaps are speech delay and mental retardation. The least desirable handicaps include confinement to wheelchair, upper extremity problems and blindness.

In response to the question, "Would you be willing to accept a child who is not yet toilet trained?" 22 schools said "yes" and 23, "no." Most of the "yes" responses were conditional on either the possibility for training or training being in process. Forty-one schools responded to the question whether a handicapped child had ever been enrolled, 25 answering "yes." Only five schools of the 45 reported that individual staff members are responsible for specific children. The adult-to-child ratio ranged from 1:4 to 1:30, with a mean of 1:8.

5. FUTURE

The physical plants of most of the preschools observed revealed few settings without architectural barriers. Thirty-five of the 45 settings had stairways, only 13 had handrails on both sides of the stairways, and none had ramps. In addition, nine settings were split level in design. Other physical constraints that limit the integration of handicapped children included the following: 27 schools provided ample parking space adjacent to the building while 18 had no parking space, no drop-off space, or a parking space some distance away; only 13 preschools offered child-size toilets and none of the facilities provided handrails adjacent to the toilets.

TABLE 1
Acceptance of a Particular Handicap

Handicap	Accepting		Nonaccepting	
Blind	14	(31%)	31	(69%)
Partially sighted (with travel vision)	34	(76%)	11	(24%)
Deaf	21	(47%)	24	(53%)
Hard of hearing	38	(84%)	7	(16%)
Speech delay	43	(96%)	2	(4%)
Motor impairment				
a) Nonambulatory but able to crawl and sit in a chair	15	(33%)	30	(67%)
b) Confined to wheelchair	13	(29%)	32	(71%)
c) Ambulating but in braces (would have problems with stairs and rough terrain)	19	(42%)	26	(58%)
d) Upper extremity problems that would interfere with feeding and dressing	13	(29%)	32	(71%)
Mentally retarded (independent ambulation, able to feed, might have language delay, and cognitive skills below age level)	41	(92%)	4	(9%)
Cardiac and respiratory condition (such as asthma where the child's activity level might have to be monitored)	17	(38%)	28	(62%)

No quantitative conclusions can be reached regarding either the management styles of teachers or the availability of various learning materials and accessories. However, there is agreement with Goodlad's nationwide study that most of the schools are offering about the same type of program, with a more limited range of experiences than is expressed by their goals and philosophies [3].

Summary

The vast majority of preschool directors and teachers included in this study revealed a positive attitude toward integrating handicapped and developmentally delayed children into their programs. Clearly, this is indicative of changing beliefs and values regarding the handicapped. The adage, "Those who are different should remain with their own kind," seems to be changing. Furthermore, it is encouraging that the personnel of the preschools felt enough self-confidence and adequacy to expect benefits to handicapped children from their programs.

The information compiled from this study offers parents and caretakers some sense of direction toward providing normal educational experiences for their handicapped children. But they are urged to visit and thoroughly investigate any preschool before enrolling their child.

It is strongly recommended that surveys of this nature be conducted in all communities every few years, with provisions for updating. Appropriate placement of individual handicapped children is dependent on the type of information compiled here. Because of the financial and personnel requirements of such an endeavor, it is reasonable to expect either local school districts or intermediate school districts to conduct such surveys under the mandate of state law.

Certification for Teachers of Preschool Handicapped Children

ALFRED HIRSHOREN
WARREN UMANSKY

ALFRED HIRSHOREN *is Associate Professor and* WARREN UMANSKY *is Assistant Professor, College of Education, University of Georgia, Athens.*

Under Public Law 94-142, the Education for All Handicapped Children Act of 1975, state education agencies will, on September 1, 1978, be responsible for seeing that a free public education is provided for all children with handicaps who are between 3 and 18 years of age.

Early education for children with handicaps offers a number of benefits that warrant serious consideration by school systems. Early intervention with children who have some handicaps may alleviate many of the manifestations of the handicaps that could inhibit development and learning. Furthermore, provision of services in the early years could substantially reduce the costs of later education.

In order to assess the planned movement of states toward meeting the legislative mandate, a survey of preschool handicapped children teacher certification guidelines was undertaken. Certification of teachers in the area of special education exists in all states and the District of Columbia (Abeson & Fleury, 1972). Teachers who graduate from an approved program of special education usually qualify for kindergarten through 12th grade certification in their specialty area. Education of children below the kindergarten level has with few exceptions remained outside the area of responsibility of the state education agencies. As Karnes (1975) cogently points out, teachers who are trained to work with normal young children or with older handicapped children are unprepared to assume the multiple responsibilities of the teacher of preschool handicapped children. Such an individual "is often a diagnostician, curriculum developer, manager and team leader, parent worker, trainer of volunteers and paraprofessionals, and public relations expert" (p. 81), as well as a teacher of a unique population of children. From this job description, it is apparent that the teacher does not fit into traditional certification categories for early childhood education or special education kindergarten through 12th grade that are used in most states. It appears essential, then, that state education agencies recognize a separate category of certification for teachers of preschool handicapped children since implementation of Public Law 94-142 will shift the responsibility for the preschool handicapped area to the public schools. The purpose of this study is to assess the current status of teacher certification practices in the area of preschool handicapped children throughout the country.

Methods

Offices of teacher certification in the 50 states and the District of Columbia were contacted by mail questionnaire. Thirty-six responses resulted from this mailing. Followup letters were sent to the remaining states. Only one state failed to respond to the second mail request. This state was contacted by telephone to obtain the required information.

Results and Discussion

Certification for teachers of preschool handicapped children is offered in 12 states. An additional five states are currently in the process of developing certification guidelines for the area of preschool handicapped. Results of the survey are shown in Table 1.

It is apparent that few states currently have or are concerned about developing separate certification standards for teachers of preschool handicapped children although several states do require at least some course work in special education for all prospective teachers. This leaves some question as to the future status of staffing mandated programs for these children. The orientation of training for special educators is usually directed toward the school age child who has already passed through crucial developmental periods. Therefore, consideration is given not so much to emerging basic skills as to the application and refinement of basic skills for higher levels of performance.

The early childhood educator is knowledgeable in normal patterns of development and

"Certification For Teachers of Preschool Handicapped Children", Alfred Hirshoren and Warren Umansky, *Exceptional Children*, Vol. 44, No. 3, November 1977, © 1977, The Council For Excceptional Children.

TABLE 1

Teacher Certification and Known Training Programs in Early Childhood Special Education in the United States

State	Teacher Certification			Known Training Program	
	Yes	*No*	*In Development*	*Yes*	*No*
Alabama	X			X	
Alaska		X			X
Arizona		X		X	
Arkansas		X			X
California		X		X	
Colorado		X			X
Connecticut		X			X
Delaware		X			X
Florida		X		X	
Georgia		X		X	
Hawaii		X		X	
Idaho		X		X	
Illinois	X			X	
Indiana		X		X	
Iowa	X			X	
Kansas			X	X	
Kentucky	X			X	
Louisiana		X			X
Maine			X		X
Maryland	X				X
Massachusetts	X			X	
Michigan		X		X	
Minnesota	X			X	
Mississippi	X				X
Missouri			X		X
Montana		X			X
Nebraska		X		X	
Nevada		X		X	
New Hampshire		X			X
New Jersey		X		X	
New Mexico		X			X
New York		X		X	
North Carolina		X		X	
North Dakota	X			X	
Ohio		X		X	
Oklahoma		X		X	
Oregon		X			X
Pennsylvania		X		X	
Rhode Island		X		X	
South Carolina		X		X	
South Dakota			X	X	
Tennessee		X		X	
Texas		X		X	
Utah		X			X
Vermont	X			X	
Virginia	X			X	
Washington		X		X	
West Virginia		X			X
Wisconsin	X			X	
Wyoming			X	X	
District of Columbia		X		X	

may be skillful in working with children who show minor deviations in development that still fall within the normal range. Nevertheless, the needs that will be generated by Public Law 94-142 to provide staff to serve young children with moderate to severe handicaps demand recognition by the states of a separate training area in early childhood special education. The need for specialized personnel in this area has already been recognized by many colleges and universities that operate programs to train early childhood special educators (Umansky & Hirshoren, 1977). In fact, the survey indicated that although 25 states plus the District of Columbia have no certification standards for these personnel, they have institutions of higher education that provide training in the area. The discrepancy between the training and certification processes reflects at least some lack of communication between the state education agencies and training institutions, which may leave the state education agencies a step behind in personnel procurement. It is anticipated that the gap between training and certification will close as programs for young children with handicaps become more prevalent in response to the law.

References

Abeson, A., & Fleury, J. B. *State certification requirements for education of the handicapped.* Arlington VA: The Council for Exceptional Children, 1972.

Karnes, Merle B. Education of pre-school age handicapped children. In W. P. McLure, R. A. Burnhan, & R. A. Henderson (Eds.), *Special education: Needs, costs, methods of financing. Report of a study.* Urbana IL: Bureau of Educational Research, College of Education, University of Illinois, 1975.

Umansky, W., & Hirshoren, A. *Teacher training programs in early childhood special education.* Manuscript in preparation, 1977.

Head Start for the Handicapped: Congressional Mandate Audit

GAIL L. ENSHER
BURTON BLATT
JAMES F. WINSCHEL

Abstract: The 1972 Amendments to the Economic Opportunity Act mandated that not less than 10% of the Head Start enrollment nationwide be made available to handicapped children. This article reports research evaluating the effect of the mandate during the first year of its implementation. The findings indicate reasonable progress in meeting the needs of the handicapped; however, labeling appears to have increased and serious problems remain in accommodating youngsters with severe disabilities. Recommendations for the enhancement of Head Start efforts on behalf of the handicapped are including a suggestion for reducing society's inclination to segregate or exclude children with major differences in development.

GAIL L. ENSHER *is Associate Professor of Special Education,* BURTON BLATT *is Professor of Special Education and Dean of the School of Education, and* JAMES F. WINSCHEL *is Professor of Special Education, Division of Special Education and Rehabilitation, Syracuse University, Syracuse, New York.* *The research reported herein was performed under a contract with Policy Research Incorporated, East Lansing, Michigan, pursuant to Contract No. HEW-OS-73-222 from the Office of Child Development, US Department of Health, Education, and Welfare. The opinions expressed do not necessarily reflect the position or policy of the Office of Child Development and no official endorsement should be inferred.*

In an age of national criticism it would be easy to lose sight of significant gains registered by public education over the past decade. Two of the advances recorded—the trend toward preschool programs and the right to education for all children—have found meaningful convergence in the 1972 Amendments to the Economic Opportunity Act. This mandate required that not less than 10% of the Head Start enrollment opportunities nationwide be made available to handicapped children (Public Law 92-424, 1972).

Since the inception of Head Start, the Office of Economic Opportunity (OEO) and the Office of Child Development (OCD) have sought to serve a heterogeneous population of children, principally drawn from the socioeconomic "have nots" of American society. Deliberate efforts have been made to meet the developmental needs of disadvantaged children irrespective of intelligence, physical condition, emotional stability, or language development. In the face of such conviction, it is puzzling that Head Start has, to a large degree, neglected the seriously disabled child.

The concern of Congress was evident in the following excerpt from a 1972 Senate committee report of S.2007 (LaVor, 1972):

> The history of Headstart clearly shows that severely handicapped children have been systematically excluded from programs and, in fact, children with only moderate handicaps have generally been refused access to such services. These refusals have normally been based on the feeling that the national program is not primarily oriented toward treating handicapping conditions, and expertise is not available at the local level for developing effective programs. (p. 250)

Enlarging the Scope

The Economic Opportunity Act Amendments of 1972, which finally mandated services to

 © 1977 CEC

the demonstrably handicapped, were hailed as a critical statement of federal concern for children with special needs. Professionals viewed the legislation as a harbinger of the future, while parents saw in the mandate a new concern for the welfare of their children. The task that confronted Head Start was to enlarge the pool of those eligible for its services, with particular reference to children with significant impairments.

Coinciding with passage of the 1972 Amendments, the nation witnessed a reiteration of the concepts of freedom of choice, options, due process under the law, and consumer protection. In education this expression of human rights and potential was evident in the concept of human development as plastic, capable of modification, and influenced by motivation, practice, and training (Blatt & Garfunkel, 1969). This concept of human educability, central to the development of compensatory education, was integral to the Head Start movement and inherent in the 1972 Amendments to the Economic Opportunity Act. Thus, from an affirmation that people can change, that the young can change most, and that the handicapped are in most need of opportunities to change, it was logical that Head Start be entrusted with responsibility for children with special needs.

Unexplored Challenge

The extent to which handicapped children could be meaningfully served by Head Start and other preschool programs remained a largely unexplored challenge. With reference to the disadvantaged, Blatt and Garfunkel (1969) gave evidence of the problems of preschool intervention:

> Inferences from our data revealed that disadvantaged children are influenced more by the home setting than by the external manipulation of their school environment. In light of what we believe to have been the face validity of an enriched preschool program, the inability of this program to produce measurable differences between experimental and nonexperimental children causes us to suggest that it is not enough to provide preschool children with an enriched educational opportunity. Families need a great deal of help toward becoming stronger and better integrated units to provide more powerful stimulants and models for intellectual attainment. (pp. 119-120)

Among many studies that have more directly examined the general effectiveness of Head Start efforts, the Westinghouse study (Frost, 1973) compared the cognitive and affective development of first, second, and third graders who had participated in Head Start with a matched sample of children from the same grades who had not had such an experience. The report concluded that:

> Although this study indicates that full-year Head Start appears to be a more effective compensatory education program than summer Head Start, its benefits cannot be described as satisfactory. Therefore we strongly recommend that large-scale efforts and substantial resources continue to be devoted to the search for finding more effective programs, procedures, and techniques for remediating the effects of poverty on disadvantaged children. (p. 404)

Extensive interviews with individuals from Head Start and other community action, educational, and health related services were the focus of the Kirschner study (1970). This investigation sought to determine the impact of Head Start programs on community change. Although the Kirschner investigation suffered the limitations of all retrospective studies, it produced evidence that Head Start and other community action programs can be effective instruments in bringing about institutional change in both education and health.

Services to handicapped children in Head Start were examined by Cahn (1972) who found that many children identified as handicapped for program purposes did not meet the criteria of significant impairment stipulated in the Economic Opportunity Act Amendments. Disproportionate enrollments of children with mild problems of vision, hearing, and speech were noted, while services to mentally retarded and more severely impaired youngsters were relatively rare.

National Evaluation

The studies just cited have served as an impetus for a national evaluation of Head Start services to the disabled. This article summarizes the findings of that national investigation and addresses itself to major policy recommendations for the improvement of Head Start services to handicapped children. In total, the observations confirm both the potential of the mandate and its limited impact to this time.

Method

Program Selection

Preliminary to the main investigation, site visits were made to 16 regularly funded Head Start programs and 14 experimental preschool programs funded by OCD and the Bureau of Education for the Handicapped (BEH). The regularly funded programs were selected from a total of 1,353 Head Start delegate and grantee agencies, using a quasi-stratified sampling technique. The 14 experimental projects served as one of two comparison groups and represented the total population of such programs specially designated for study by OCD. This pilot study used participant observation, which is a procedure "widely used in sociological and anthropological studies of complex social situations or organizations" (DeGrandpre, 1973, p. 46). The study led to the development of standard procedures for major site visits to 36 Head Start programs and to 10 independent preschool enrichment programs, the latter serving as a second comparison group.

Observers

The 11 field investigators (participant observers) were university affiliated special educators, advanced graduate students, and individuals from an independent consulting agency. Each field investigator received a minimum of 25 hours training in observation techniques and use of a specifically designed observation schedule. Skill in use of the schedule was certified by both the project's codirector and an independent consultant trainer.

Instruments

Preliminary observations of Head Start programs led to the development of an interview schedule covering three main areas of investigation: (a) program administration, (b) classroom management and instruction, and (c) case study information on individual children. The schedule permitted the recording of both quantitative and qualitative data as provided by the methodology of participant observation.

Procedures

Field investigators visited each setting for a minimum of two days. Program level information was obtained through interviews with Head Start directors and coordinators of programs for the handicapped. This part of the schedule was directed toward definitions, recruitment, staff training, resources, and evaluation. Two 3 hour observations were conducted in each class serving handicapped children and information was recorded on instructional techniques, teacher child interactions, and peer relationships. Specific attention was directed toward possible differences in the delivery of service and instruction to typical and handicapped children. Finally, case study information on 74 children randomly selected from the handicapped population was obtained through interviews with teachers and other agency personnel.

Findings and Discussion

The Handicapped Population

Handicapped clients constituted 13.29% of the total Head Start population (see Table 1), a figure 3% greater than the legislative requirement and 4% above the prevalence estimate for school age children. The tendency to overidentify children as handicapped dictates a certain caution in the interpretation of these statistics. It became apparent in the study that prior to the mandate disabled children had been routinely enrolled in Head Start without recourse to labels and their inclusion in program activities was not markedly new in concept or practice.

Table 1 indicates that the visually impaired, hearing impaired, and physically and other health impaired children are enrolled in Head Start in excess of their expected prevalence. Several explanations of this phenomenon are available. First, these groups of children are more easily identified and more precisely diagnosed during the preschool years than are children with other handicapping conditions. Thus, in programs serving preschool youngsters, children with visual, hearing, and physical impairments constitute a larger percentage of the total enrollment than would similar children in the school age population from which the prevalence estimates were generated. A second explanation is that the emotionally disturbed and the mentally retarded are enrolled at levels equal to or below the prevalence estimates since the more mildly disabled in these two groups are not normally identified during the preschool years.

The findings in the area of speech impairment (4.72% as compared with a school age prevalence of 3.5%) are not easily explainable. The developmental nature of speech and language would dictate that the presence of speech impairments in preschool youngsters be interpreted at a level not greater than the school age prevalence. However, in this study, children identified as speech impaired constituted a disproportionate percentage of the total Head Start population, significantly exceeding the prevalence estimate for school age youngsters. Whether this resulted from ignorance, the pressures of the mandate, or both was not fully determined.

Of the handicapped children enrolled in the Head Start programs, 21% were classified as severely impaired; they comprised 2.8% of the total enrollment. The legislation makes it difficult to render any clear judgment of this accomplishment. The relevant OCD policy statement (HEW, 1973b) reads as follows:

> While children with milder handicapping conditions (e.g., children with visual problems correctable with eyeglasses) will continue to be identified and receive appropriate Head Start services, they fall outside the scope of this issuance. The intent is rather to insure that Head Start serves more fully children who have severe vision and hearing impairment, who are severely physically

TABLE 1

Handicapped Enrolled in 36 Head Start Programs, 1973–74

Disability group	*Level*	*Prevalence estimates in percentage* [a]	*Number enrolled*	*Percentage of total handicapped served*	*Percentage of total Head Start enrollment*
Visually	Severe		26	2.03	0.27
impaired	Nonsevere	0.1	83	6.49	0.86
	Total		109	8.52	1.13
Hearing	Severe		23	1.80	0.24
impaired	Nonsevere	0.6	99	7.73	1.03
	Total		122	9.53	1.27
Speech	Severe		84	6.56	0.87
impaired	Nonsevere	3.5	371	28.99	3.85
	Total		455	35.55	4.72
Emotionally	Severe		34	2.65	0.35
disturbed	Nonsevere	2.0	161	12.58	1.67
	Total		195	15.23	2.02
Mentally	Severe		26	2.03	0.27
retarded	Nonsevere	2.3	71	5.55	0.74
	Total		97	7.58	1.01
Physically	Severe		77	6.01	0.80
and other	Nonsevere	0.5	225	17.58	2.34
health impaired	Total		302	23.59	3.14
Combined	Severe		270	21.10	2.80
disability	Nonsevere	9.0	1,010	78.90	10.49
groups	Total		1,280	100.00	13.29

Note. Total enrollment in 36 programs = 9,635.

[a] Prevalence estimates are based on school age population as cited in Dunn (1973, p. 14).

and mentally handicapped, and who otherwise meet the legislative definition of handicapped children in terms of their need for special services. (p. 3)

To those who interpret the policy as exclusively relevant to the severely handicapped (in a continuum of mild, moderate, and severe), it is apparent that only one-fourth of the 10% goal has been attained. On the other hand, it is possible that the 10% mandate was directed toward the inclusion of handicapped children at all levels of impairment and the use of the word *severe* in the guidelines was not classificatory in its intent, but merely a convenient adjective used to differentiate the minor problems of childhood from truly handicapping conditions. Under this interpretation, the percentage of severely involved children enrolled in Head Start (21% of the handicapped population) is probably congruent with prevalence estimates for this level of severity.

Largely unresolved in the analysis of the data were problems related to the mislabeling of children as a recourse in meeting the legislative mandate. Programs were identifying as handicapped those children who required minimal assistance or special services and who manifested no obviously disabling condition beyond minor problems of speech, health, or behavior.

Although handicapping conditions were to be verified by a qualified professional, this mandate was loosely construed and identification as handicapped often appeared to be a subjective judgment applied as much for the imperatives of the program as the welfare of the child. The conflict between the need to meet the mandate and professional-moral aversion to overlabeling was repeatedly evident in the concerns of program personnel. The new legislation, with its 10% quota, has probably promoted overlabeling and has brought Head Start personnel under seemingly unresolvable pressures.

While the tendency to overlabel may be viewed as evasive of the legislative intent, the practice is partially explainable in terms of genuine recruitment problems confronting approximately 50% of the programs in this study. In spite of efforts by most programs to use the assistance of other community agencies in locating handicapped children, the procedures followed were largely standard to Head Start recruitment and insufficient to the identification and enrollment of an elusive population. An uninformed populace, misguided parental resistance, and the self serving competition of community agencies protecting imaginary domains were significant obstacles to recruitment. Exceptions were found in those Head Start programs characterized by aggressive leadership and active parental involvement. In those programs, severely handicapped children were enrolled in significant numbers concomitant with or exceeding prevalence estimates.

Assessment and Instruction

The mandate effected an increase in diagnosis and assessment by qualified professionals within the community for the purpose of certifying suspected disabilities and securing special services. While this action was not always instrumental in modifying classroom practice, it did promote among teachers a new interest in assessment and the continuous monitoring of the progress of all children. Particularly in programs serving the largest number of severely involved youngsters, teachers were becoming increasingly conversant with the use of formal and informal evaluative techniques. Unlike assessments made by consultants from other agencies, appraisals carried out by Head Start personnel were more frequently translated into meaningful practice.

Possibly as a result of better assessment, teachers serving a higher proportion of the severely impaired employed more individualized techniques. Speech and language development were stressed and children were more frequently encouraged to respond verbally. In these classes, more imaginative methods of instruction were observed and children more often participated in independent learning activities. The exigencies of dealing with severely involved preschoolers required teachers to rely more heavily on child initiated learning and, in so doing, promoted in all children those independent skills necessary to school success.

Integration and Exclusion

The most persistent problems accompanying the integration effort invariably centered on the most severely impaired. Clinical observations suggested that seriously handicapped children were often the victims of an emotional distancing, or psychological separateness, even when physical proximity with other children was maintained. Teachers in one-third of the programs indicated that nonhandicapped children and staff both failed to accept the severely impaired child, although only three programs acknowledged the exclusion of children once admitted. Even typically confident teachers questioned their ability to serve the severely handicapped, and such doubts contributed to the instances of physical or attitudinal separation. Head Start directors and teaching staffs often agreed on their inability to serve the blind, deaf, severely retarded, and children with gross motor development. Although the extent to which these groups were excluded is worthy of further investigation, the phenomenon is possibly related to inadequate support and lack of special training, which characterized most Head Start staffs.

Head Start personnel also reported evidence of exclusionary practices in the actions of other community agencies. Agencies with a history of work with seriously impaired clients reportedly viewed Head Start as a potential service rival or as a novice incompetent to offer appropriate training. They were reluctant, therefore, to recommend these programs to parents and others. This climate of distrust was moderated over time as contacts with these agencies were increased and the mutual expertise of personnel was more widely recognized.

Persistent exclusionary practices were evident in the actions of public school personnel. The attempt to build continuity between Head Start and public schools was fraught with difficulties. Schools usually admit mildly and moderately handicapped children, but in manner and attitude do not always welcome them. By contrast, severely impaired youngsters are rarely admitted and are even less often welcomed. Of 74 subjects selected for case study from among the 1,280 handicapped children enrolled in 36 Head Start programs, one-third were to remain in Head Start for a second year, primarily as a result of the public schools' real or imagined inability to offer appropriate training.

Parent Involvement

Parents of children in this study testified to their influence in program planning and policy and to their involvement in day to day Head Start activities to an extent equal to or greater than that of parents of nonhandicapped children. In addition, parents of the handicapped increased their knowledge in the areas of child care and community resources and otherwise benefited from a variety of instructional endeavors carried on by Head Start personnel and consultants. Parents of severely impaired children also noted that the program provided relief, care, and service which might not otherwise have been available prior to formal school enrollment or the attainment of school age.

Training and Technical Assistance

Most programs would have benefited from additional training and technical assistance. Personnel training was superficial and sporadic and often unrelated to the perceived needs of programs. Staffs frequently noted overtraining in matters largely peripheral to instruction, while the practicalities of program implementation went unattended. While personnel did have the benefit of a variety of preservice and inservice workshops and courses, the total training effort appeared marginally effective in terms of cost, time, or the improvement of instruction.

Cost

Existing accounting practices in Head Start do not permit adequate documentation of the true costs of accommodating handicapped youngsters. Undoubtedly, these vary with the nature and severity of the disability and with the service to be rendered. In general, little additional expense is involved in Head Start services to the mildly handicapped. Such modest expenditures are most often accounted for by minor shifts in personnel assignments and by an increased reliance on consultant services. Cost projections for optimal service to moderately and seriously impaired children suggest a differential of two or three times the average expenditure, although such estimates are based on insufficient data and are largely conjectural.

Experimental Programs

Prior to the major investigation of Head Start programs, OCD and BEH had funded 14 experimental projects charged with responsibility to "develop and test alternative approaches to more effective delivery of services to preschool handicapped children and their families" (HEW, 1973a). These programs, representing a diversity in size, location, and the social and ethnic backgrounds of their clients, constituted one of two comparison groups employed in this study. The main finding was that increased funding accounted for modest improvements in service delivery, although only a few programs provided genuinely innovative instruction.

More children with moderate and severe disabilities were enrolled in the experimental programs and a greater reliance on special education for program development was evident. Increased contacts with community agencies, a greater emphasis on individual assessment, and improved personnel training characterized these settings as compared with the regular Head Start programs.

The overall evaluation of the experimental settings indicated modest gains in the face of familiar and continuing problems. Recruitment difficulties, staff training relative to the severely impaired, and resistance by entrenched community agencies plagued the experimental projects little less than they did regular Head Start programs. The problems of definition had not yet been resolved and some experimental projects were found to be offering services to the severely handicapped in separate settings—a clear evasion of the legislative intent.

One finds in the experimental effort sufficient cause for optimism and ample reason for concern. Money alone has seldom solved serious human problems, and in ways yet undefined, preschool efforts for the handicapped may call for a more imaginative effort. The experimental programs did not fail in their mission; they just never quite lived up to expectations.

Select Programs

Ten independent early childhood projects and six Head Start programs comprised a second comparison group. Each select program met to the highest degree obtainable two basic criteria: First, at least 5% of their enrollment consisted of moderately and severely handicapped children; and second, each was actively engaged in integration efforts through program operated demonstration classes or other regular class settings in the community.

The field observations of the select programs revealed a general superiority of service to handicapped children. The quality of these programs is manifest in the following findings as compared with either regular Head Start or the experimental programs:

1. More favorable staff to client ratios accompanied by greater attention to the problems of individual learners.
2. Personnel more highly trained in preschool education and supported by inservice training and technical assistance as needed.
3. Family oriented services as opposed to either child centered programs or treatment of child and parent as separate entities.
4. Intense involvement with public schools and other community agencies. (Followup

of children who left the program was common and tended to assure the continuity of services from one setting to the next.)

5. Program directors who asserted their leadership in planning, training, curriculum instruction, funding, and community relationships.

Many of the select programs began with services to the handicapped and gradually accommodated typical children, an approach alien to most integration efforts. Success with all children—whether handicapped or not—was rooted in ample resources, skilled personnel, and dynamic leadership. The problems of serving handicapped children in integrated preschool settings were largely surmounted in the select programs because the resources existed to accomplish the objective.

Conclusion

In its first year of implementation, the legislation mandating Head Start services to handicapped children has been modestly effective. These accomplishments, more directional than revolutionary, are indicative of both success and failure. Improvements are evident in the level of parent involvement, community contacts, awareness of individual needs, and services to the more seriously impaired. On the other hand, many seriously handicapped children are still not enrolled in programs, the labeling of children with minor problems has increased, and Head Start staffs have sometimes grown openly resentful or highly anxious about the assumption of new responsibilities for which they feel ill equipped in terms of time, energy, and training. The experimental programs were plagued by identical problems and were only slightly more successful in meeting the needs of their handicapped clients. Only a few of the select programs demonstrated the present capacity and inclination to deal effectively with the handicapped population in ways which accrued to the advantage of all children. To the extent that special educators can learn from their accomplishments, it would appear that resources, skill, dedication, and leadership still make the difference. How to assure these qualities in all Head Start programs is a resolvable problem; it is one within special education's present capacity to achieve. The following recommendations and statements of policy may prove useful in giving further direction to current efforts.

Identifying and Educating Gifted/Talented Nonhandicapped and Handicapped Preschoolers

MERLE B. KARNES
JANE D. BERTSCHI

At age 3, Billy's speech was totally unintelligible. Consequently, he had great difficulty communicating with other children and his usual means of interaction was to strike or grab them. However, Billy also clearly demonstrated superior psychomotor ability; he displayed unusual strength and markedly advanced motor skill development. His severe speech and language delay and related behavior problems coupled with outstanding motor skill development qualified Billy for placement in the RAPYHT program for talented handicapped preschool children.

RAPYHT Open Classroom teachers set goals for Billy that would foster his motoric talent as well as improve his speech and social behavior. The teachers provided Billy with many and varied opportunities for movement and motor activities and suggested that other children ask Billy for help with tasks that called for particular strength or skill. The teachers also set strategies for dealing with his social behavior and, in addition, Billy received speech therapy from a specialist.

As Billy helped other children and began to realize how much he could do, his self image grew. Interaction with others helped him to develop social skills which, in turn, provided more natural opportunities to speak. All these played a part in giving Billy more confidence in speaking and in social interactions, as well as in providing opportunities to practice and further develop motor skills. By the end of his second year in the project, Billy was speaking in sentences appropriate to his age level, his behavior had dramatically improved, and he continued to make gains in psychomotoric development.

Teacher planned lessons actively involve children in the SOI classroom.

"Identifying and Educating Gifted/Talented Non Handicapped and Handicapped Preschoolers", Merle B. Kanes, Jane D. Bertschi, *Teaching Exceptional Children,* Vol. 10, No. 4, Summer 1978, © 1978 by The Council For Exceptional Children.

Gifted preschoolers (ages 3 to 5) have often been overlooked in educational planning. Even more neglected have been handicapped children in that age group who are also gifted. In 1975, however, the Bureau of Education for the Handicapped (BEH) funded two First Chance Projects to develop and demonstrate models for identifying young gifted and talented children and programing for them. One project is located in the public schools of Chapel Hill, North Carolina; the other, in the Institute for Child Behavior and Development at the University of Illinois, Champaign-Urbana Campus. The latter program referred to as RAPYHT* (the Retrieval and Acceleration of Promising Young Handicapped and Talented) is part of the Joint Early Education Program for the Handicapped (JEEPH), an early childhood program for the handicapped based on a joint agreement among 15 rural Champaign County school districts, the Champaign County Educational Service Region Office, and the University of Illinois. Only the RAPYHT program, however, will be discussed in detail in this article.

THE RAPYHT PROGRAM

It was essential at the outset that the RAPYHT staff have a clear understanding of who was to constitute the gifted and talented handicapped population. Determining the characteristics of the handicapped presented the lesser problem since programs for young handicapped children had been in existence at the University of Illinois for several years and since Illinois state guidelines had already been formulated. For the purpose of the project, however, the handicapped child was defined as one whose full development was impaired through physical, social-emotional, and/or learning deficits. The term *gifted* is usually applied to the child with extraordinary academic, verbal, and/or intellectual abilities. The term *talented* usually refers to children who are socially, artistically, or physically gifted. In RAPYHT, however, the term *talented* covers six areas of function: intellectual, academic (reading, math, science), creative, social (leadership), artistic (art, music), and psychomotoric.

Obviously, the first step in establishing an educational program for the gifted handicapped preschooler was to identify the target population. Then, educators faced a second challenge: how best to nurture those talents so that the gifted child—whether handicapped or not—might achieve his or her potential. This article, then, begins with a discussion of how the gifted and talented handicapped child may be identified (similar procedures can be followed in identifying the gifted and talented nonhandicapped) and concludes by outlining two approaches for educating these young children.

IDENTIFICATION OF THE GIFTED/TALENTED HANDICAPPED

Identification of gifted and talented handicapped children is a complex process that begins when children are screened and evaluated for placement in a preschool special education program and continues throughout the intervention period. So extended a procedure is necessary because the talents of the handicapped child are often obscured by conditions relating to his or her handicaps and may not be recognized during initial diagnosis. Later, however, hidden talents may emerge after the child has spent several weeks or months in an intervention program. Thus, the RAPYHT approach to identification consists of two parts: procedures implemented as part of a screening and diagnostic process used to identify children who are eligible for a preschool special education program, and procedures employed with children already enrolled in an intervention program.

LOCATION, SCREENING, AND ASSESSMENT PRIOR TO PLACEMENT IN THE PROGRAM

Location of children to be screened in the JEEPH communities relies on a variety of techniques including lists generated by local school principals, media announcements, flyers sent home with children in school, and a telephone census. Location activities in a given school district vary according to the size of the district, the mobility of its population, and the policy of its administration.

Children located in the 15 school districts are then screened using the Comprehensive Identification Process or CIP (Zehrbach, 1975) to detect behavior that suggests developmental delays in one or more of eight areas—cognitive, speech and language, fine motor, gross motor, vision, hearing, medical history, and socio-affective. The primary objective of this screening is to identify potentially handicapped children; however, information obtained from parent reports or observation of children during screening activities that suggests potential talent is noted. For example, the CIP Parent Interview Form includes questions about special talents that may be displayed by the child, advanced vocabulary and expressive language, the child's special interests, and social skills, all of which may produce information suggestive of talent. Children selected during the screening process are then referred for detailed study by a diagnostic team consisting of a psychologist, a speech clinician, and a social worker.

Diagnostic procedures include a battery of standardized instruments. Members of the interdisciplinary team are alert to characteristics that may indicate talent in one or more of six areas (intellectual, academic, creative, leadership, visual and performing arts, and psychomotor). Information gathered by the diagnostic team is presented at a staff meeting where placement eligibility is determined. Consensus as to whether each handicapped child is is potentially and functionally talented is also determined at this time. Such children, with parental consent, are placed directly in a RAPYHT demonstration classroom.

OBSERVATION OF CHILDREN AFTER ADMISSION TO THE PROGRAM

Not all gifted or talented children are identified at the diagnostic stage. Some emerge only after they have been in a program that remediated their handicaps to the extent that their behavior began to suggest talent. RAPYHT staff, with the assistance of faculty at the University of Illinois and advisory board members, devised talent checklists to evaluate the six previously listed areas of talent on the basis of teacher ratings. Of characteristics found to be associated with each area of talent, 7 to 10 were selected and stated in terms of behaviors that could be observed in the 3 to 5 year old child. To conduct a classroom screening using the talent checklists, the teacher studies the items for each area of talent, observes the children in the classroom, and then rates each child's performance in relation to the items on the checklist. The Intellectual Talent Checklist in Figure 1 is an example of the types of items used and the rating procedures.

Specific criteria for selection of children for followup talent assessment are based on the checklist scores of a normative group of 194 preschool handicapped children. Cutoff scores were established at 1½ standard deviations above the mean score of the normative group on each talent checklist. A followup of the children identified by the talent checklist involves three major steps:

1. *Teacher interview.* The purpose of the interview is to obtain general background information on the child and to validate the teacher's checklist responses by collecting specific anecdotal/observational data related to the child's potential talents. A Teacher Interview Report form has been de-

veloped to record this information as well as to structure the interview. At this stage, children may be screened out for a variety of reasons (e.g., lack of teacher information supporting talent, child's age rather than talent accounting for high score).

2. *Individual child assessment.* This step involves a comprehensive assessment of the child's abilities using a variety of instruments and data sources, including parent interviews, examination of historical records, standardized tests, and structured observations of the child in a variety of settings. Specific procedures vary according to the area of talent under investigation.

3. *Consultation and trial programing.* Because a child's handicap(s) may obscure expression of talent and because assessment methods may not fully reveal abilities, talent programing and prolonged observation are often necessary before definite diagnosis is possible. Teachers, therefore, consult with dissemination specialists regarding talent development activities to use in their classrooms in order to provide opportunities for selected children to express potential talents. Figure 2 presents a flow chart that summarizes the followup of talented handicapped preschoolers identified by the checklists.

TWO APPROACHES FOR EUCATING GIFTED/ TALENTED PRESCHOOLERS

The SOI and the Open Classroom

It is generally agreed that there is no single best approach for educating any group of children, and this tenet holds for the gifted as well. A major consideration may well be that the approach selected be compatible with the philosophy of the teacher. Of course, certain program components are essential if a program is to be judged exemplary (Karnes & Lee, in press). Nevertheless, a model program may be built around radically different approaches for educating young gifted and talented children—particularly handicapped. RAPYHT incorporated an open or informal approach as well as a structured, teacher directed approach based on an instructional model, Guilford's Structure of the Intellect (SOI).

Certain commonalities cut across the boundaries of each approach. In each, center based classes meet for 2½ hours in the morning. Each class is directed by a certified teacher in early childhood handicapped who has special training in the particular approach used in that classroom. Each head teacher is assigned a teacher aide with 30 hours of professional training. In addition, teacher aides receive on the job training in the specific approach they are helping to implement. Family involvement is an integral part of each approach.

Both approaches incorporate classroom assessment procedures for determining developmental levels in critical areas. Both adhere to Public Law 94-142 in writing individualized education programs (IEP's) for each child in areas of deficit. In addition, IEP's are written in areas of strength. Periodic charting of the children's progress is required in both approaches. Special attention is given in each approach to challenging and motivating each child through individualized instruction and to avoiding holding any child back to the level of children with lesser abilities and talents.

Each approach relies on ancillary staff as part of the team that provides service to the child and his or her family. Team members vary according to the needs of a given child and, in addition to the head teacher and the teacher aide, may include a speech and language specialist, a psychologist, a social worker, and an occupational or physical therapist. Team members in each approach are committed to meeting the special needs of each gifted and talented handicapped or nonhandicapped child. Considerable effort is given to matching the child's stage of development with

FIGURE 1

INTELLECTUAL TALENT CHECKLIST

A. Strongly agree
B. Agree
C. Neutral
D. Disagree
E. Strongly disagree

Date: ______________ Classroom: ______________________

Observer: ____

	Names and Ages of Children														
1. Is highly alert and observant.															
2. Demonstrates exceptional retention of material presented.															
3. Is very curious about a great variety of things.															
4. Is often absorbed in activity.															
5. Learns easily and readily.															
6. Conveys ideas exceptionally well.															
7. Demonstrates advanced ability to apply knowledge to practical situations.															
8. Knows about many things of which other children his or her age are unaware.															
9. Demonstrates advanced understanding of abstract relationships (e.g., cause and effect).															
10. Demonstrates exceptional ability to solve problems.															
Totals															

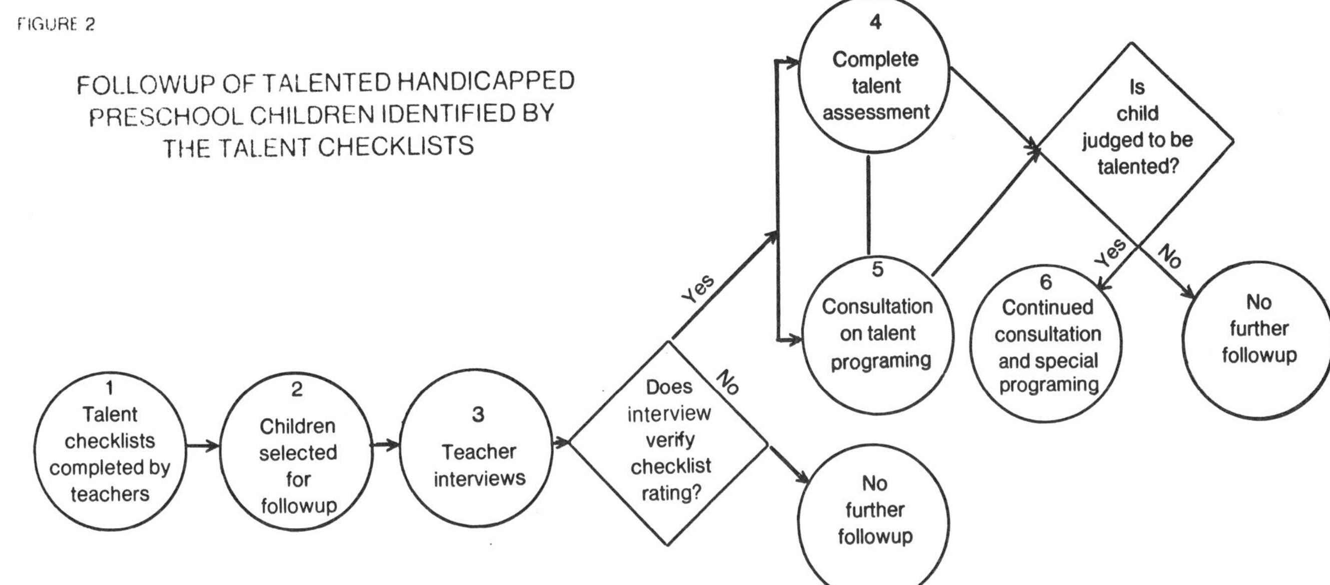

activities that provide opportunities to accelerate development as well as to pursue an area of talent in breadth.

CONTRASTING THE TWO APPROACHES

The differences between the two approaches are best understood by examining the performance of each in determining the following: theoretical base, curriculum, instructional methods and materials, child assessment, teacher role, teacher-child interactions, use of time, and use of space.

THEORETICAL BASE

The Structure of Intellect approach assumes that children learn best when teachers provide sequenced activities based on individualized instructional objectives. The SOI model helps teachers stimulate a variety of intellectual abilities, including convergent, divergent, and evaluative thinking. The SOI model aids in programing for talent development as well as in the remediation of handicaps.

The Open Classroom assumes that children, with teacher help, are capable of determining the direction, scope, means, and pace of their education. The teacher helps children to acquire basic skills, the learning tools that will enable them to explore, observe, describe, and organize experience. It provides an environment that encourages and nurtures talent in children and also meets their special needs.

A game teaches the relationship between letters and beginning sounds in an SOI classroom.

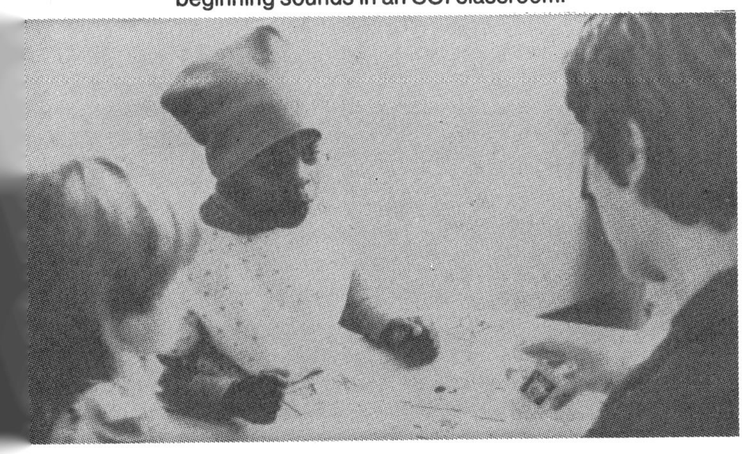

Teachers are more likely to work with individual children in the Open Classroom.

CURRICULUM

SOI teachers rely on prepared curriculum and materials to plan lessons. They also use a game format to present math, language, and prereading lessons. Artistic and music activities are included in the daily plan. Children learn songs, use musical instruments, and participate in yoga, dance, and creative movement exercises. Teachers also plan lessons using talk sheets, puppets, and role plays that help children explore their feelings and learn appropriate social behavior.

In the Open Classroom children initiate their own learning activities. Instead of planning structured lessons, teachers attempt to extend or channel the child's activities in ways that integrate the learning of specific skills. Thus, teachers base instruction on their knowledge of each child and use the child's interests as a springboard to facilitate skill development. For example, if Billy is playing with his favorite animal, a gray rubber hippopotamus, his teacher may ask what the hippopotamus eats. Billy, some of the other children, and the teacher may decide to find out by looking up the answer in an animal book. The group may spend a half hour learning about the eating habits of hippopotamuses and other wild animals.

INSTRUCTIONAL METHODS AND MATERIALS

SOI lesson plans are matched to individual needs. Sometimes children with similar needs are grouped together for an activity, and sometimes teachers place materials and instructions for an activity in a separate envelope for each child. The children call these tasks "workjobs" and perform them independently, usually sitting together in small groups with a teacher nearby to provide help when needed.

During directed play time, children in the SOI classroom have access to a variety of materials. This is a time for child initiated projects, play, and individual tutoring. Teachers encourage social interaction between children interested in using the same materials and take advantage of every opportunity to teach children directly.

A variety of materials are available at all times in the Open Classroom. They are placed so that children can reach them easily. Teachers listen carefully in order to engage children in dialogue and activities that lead to an exploration of subjects in which they have expressed interest. Content areas such as math, reading readiness, and fine motor coordination are integrated into a child's activity whenever possible. Teachers and children also discuss problems that come up and make decisions together.

CHILD ASSESSMENT

Both the SOI and the Open Classroom approaches use the same sequenced set of skills in six developmental areas as a guideline for child assessment and as an aid in determining individual priorities. In the SOI classroom, skills are observed in gamelike activities that provide an opportunity for the child to demonstrate specific skills. In the Open Classroom procedure, teachers observe and record each child's performance of specific skills during spontaneous classroom activity. For skills unlikely to be demonstrated spontaneously, the teacher gives each child a simple task in which the desired skill can be observed. Such tasks are generally incorporated into the child's normal activities.

TEACHER ROLE

SOI teachers plan precisely the daily experiences for all children in the classroom. They meet together daily to discuss their plans, to record child progress, and to set new objectives. Although teachers provide materials and direct children in using them, they take care to involve them actively in the learning situation and encourage them to act as freely as possible within the context of planned activities.

In the Open Classroom, teachers help children to understand their environment and their feelings. Teachers give encouragement, feedback, guidance, information, and clarification to children throughout the day. Teachers create a purposeful atmosphere by expecting and helping children to use time productively and to value work and learning. Teachers in the Open Classroom meet for at least one hour each day to discuss their observations and to devise new strategies for extending learning experiences.

TEACHER-CHILD INTERACTIONS

Most interactions between teacher and children in the SOI classroom are initiated by the teacher. Teachers make a conscious effort to ask questions that require divergent, convergent, and evaluative thinking when working with groups of children as well as when working with individuals.

In the Open Classroom interactions are spontaneous and informal and usually initiated by the child. Teachers are more likely to work with individuals than with a group.

USE OF TIME

A specific daily schedule is followed in the SOI classroom. During the first period of the day, children are allowed to choose their own activities. Fifteen minute lessons for small groups of children are alternated with periods of less structured activity and with activities, such as music, when the whole group is together. Snacks are served in a family atmosphere, and self help, social, and expressive language skills are encouraged. Children spend about 20 minutes each day on the playground.

The daily schedule in the Open Classroom consists of flexible blocks of time. Many learning activities take place simultaneously. A child may work alone, with a friend, or in a group. Snacks are available on a small table throughout the day. When children are hungry, they may help themselves to the portions illustrated on a menu card. Group meeting is the only time of the day when all children and teachers meet together. During each day's meeting teachers record topics or activities in which individual children wish to participate. The children involved in planning usually share responsibility for leadership during the meeting. Each child cleans up his or her own work space and everyone helps put the room in order at the end of the day. In the Open Classroom, as in the SOI classroom, children spend about 20 minutes each day on the playground.

USE OF SPACE

The use of space varies in the SOI classroom. During directed play, children and teachers are scattered in various parts of the room. During structured lessons, there may be two or three small clusters, each including one teacher and three to five children. During music and snack, teachers and children are together in one part of the room.

The use of space in the Open Classroom changes to meet the interests and needs of the children. Children move freely about the room throughout the day. The classroom is divided into areas with consideration for the type of work likely to occur, the supplies needed, and the proximity to other areas. The art area, for example, has a large table with bins underneath it that contain ingredients and tools for making playdough. On the wall is an illustrated recipe for making playdough, and next to that table is a toaster oven where playdough creations can be baked. Other art supplies—paper, crayons, tape, glue, paint, scissors, boxes, and "junk" are at the child's level in the same work area. A corner for reading is set off from noisy activity areas and contains a carpet, pillows, and a wide variety of children's books, attractively displayed.

SUMMARY

The gifted and talented handicapped child belongs to the most underserved segment of the preschool population. This article has focused on two major concerns in providing new opportunities for these children: identification and educational programing.

Obviously, identification of the gifted and talented handicapped preschooler presents a real challenge. It is difficult to identify gifted children among the nonhandicapped, but the problem of identification becomes even more difficult when compounded by handicapping conditions. In this article, the identification procedure was broken down into three steps: location, screening, and assessment prior to placement in the program. Even more importantly, however, the identification process was extended into the intervention period. Through prolonged observation and trial programing more accurate diagnosis is possible.

No single approach to educating gifted handicapped children is advocated in this article. Instead, two approaches are reviewed—the Open Classroom and the SOI model. Certain commonalities exist between the two approaches: staffing patterns, assessment to determine the developmental level of each child, adherence to Public Law 94-142 in writing IEP's, involvement of parents in planning and programing for their child, charting of child progress, and reliance on ancillary personnel. Both programs meet the standards for an examplary program for young handicapped children delineated by Karnes and Lee (in press). Differences between the two approaches center around the following: theoretical base, curriculum, instructional methods and materials, child assessment, teacher role, teacher-child interaction, use of time, and use of space. Because the philosophical differences are sharp, it may be more important to match the teachers with the approach than to attempt to match child and program. The important consideration in programing for young gifted and talented children is to help them overcome or compensate for areas of weakness and develop areas of potential or functional talent.

The SOI classroom is teacher directed. The Open Classroom is teacher-child directed. Both approaches stimulate and nurture the talents of handicapped children as well as meet their special needs. Both are viable ways of providing programs for gifted and talented handicapped preschool children.

REFERENCES

Karnes, M. B., & Lee, R. *What research and experience say to the teacher of exceptional children: Early childhood.* Reston VA: The Council for Exceptional Children, in press.

Zehrbach, R. R. *CIP—Comprehensive Identification Process* (screening test for 2½- to 5½-year-old handicapped children). Bensenville IL: Scholastic Testing Service, 1975.

Planning for Early Childhood Programs for Exceptional Children

James J. Gallagher, Ph.D.
University of North Carolina
Chapel Hill

There has been a startling growth in special education programs during the past decade. Over a 6-year period (1966–1972) there has been a 300% increase in funds made available for special education at both state and federal levels (Gallagher, Forsythe, Ringelheim, & Weintraub, 1975). One of the most universally accepted propositions in special education has been that the earlier one can apply appropriate treatment resources to the child and family, the more effective special education will be (Karnes, 1973).

One of the most serious questions that we should ask ourselves is whether we can avoid the problems of quality control faced in the past by rapidly expanding programs such as Head Start (Rivlin, 1971). Useful tools that can help us avoid such pitfalls are the emerging techniques of program planning and evaluation. This article will point out some ways in which these techniques can be used.

EMERGENCE OF PROGRAM PLANNING

One major change on the American educational scene over the past decade is the rapid rise of program planning and evaluation as an expected component in federal, state, and local educational activities (House, 1973). This change has taken place so quickly that we forget the very different attitude, widespread only a few years ago, that "planning" was a foreign invention and vaguely unpatriotic.

America is the only nation that has considered "ad hocism" as a desirable way to meet our problems. The fact that we survived two World Wars with little advance preparation contributed to our feeling that anything was possible any time America put her heart and soul into it. We believed in our invulnerability against the ravages of time or unpleasant surprises, but now our limitations are more evident. The growing popularity of program planning is associated with the realization of our limited abilities and resources. The experiences of Vietnam and the energy crisis make it clear to us that there need not always be a happy ending to our undertakings, and that our national resources are not unlimited.

This acceptance leads to the notion that we must systematically conserve and apply our limited resources to the educational problems most important to us. In addition to the need to allocate its limited resources in a maximally efficient way, education is also faced with the general public's growing doubts as to its ability to perform effectively.

From the public's standpoint, educators did not succeed sufficiently in improving the scholastic performances of economically disadvantaged children. With the experience of a decade of federal spending came the gloomy realization that education was capable of spending any amount of money provided, with no clearly discernible improvement (House, 1973). The growing need to order priorities and maximize limited resources has led to a new determination to review what educators are doing and to improve or eliminate unworthy efforts.

A number of planning models are now available, each with its own strengths and weaknesses (Gallagher, Surles, & Hayes, 1973; Provus, 1969; Stake, 1967; Stufflebeam, 1968). In order not to become enmeshed in the details of any one system and forget the purpose of planning models, I will identify four or five major components that should be part of *any* planning system. Figure 1 presents a typical schematic of a planning model. The basic question is, what does planning make us, as special educators, do that we might not otherwise do?

Defining the scope of the problem

One advantage of any planning system is that it forces the decision-maker to collect some useful data on the size and true nature of the problem. For example, now many preschool handicapped children are there in our community, our state, our country? What handicaps do they have? What are their major needs? It is essential that these questions be answered as accurately as possible so that sensible planning progresses from these baselines. If we have 1,000 children to serve, very different strategies will be needed than if we have 100,000 children to serve.

"Planning For Early Childhood Programs For Exceptional Children", James J. Gallagher, ph.D., *Journal of Special Education*, Vol. 10, No. 2, Summer 1976, © Butterwood Farms, Inc.

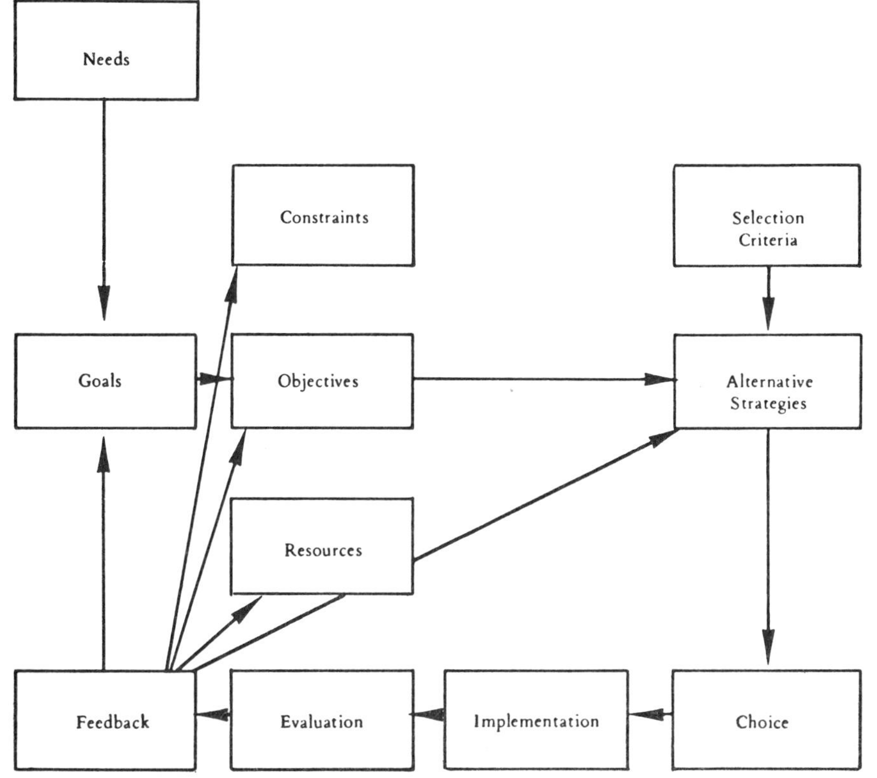

Figure 1. Program planning and evaluation model.

1970).

I have calculated the impossibility of widespread application of three models currently in use in limited special education programs. These strategies are special classes for the emotionally disturbed, resource teachers for gifted children, and resource teachers for children with special learning disabilities (Gallagher, 1973, 1974). If these models are projected on the state or federal level, along with the support services needed to train the necessary professionals, they are beyond any reasonable attainment.

For example, to provide services to gifted students in the resource teacher model, 50 universities must each turn out 15 master teachers (MS+) per year for 10 years. Not one university is producing anything like that number now. The planning model helps to identify those strategies that are incapable of rational completion by analyzing the needed support services for each. Certain models are useful if our goal is to serve only 10% of the target group. Other strategies may be needed if we wish to serve 50% of that group.

Identifying alternative strategies

Another unique part of the planning effort is the identification of alternative service strategies. There are likely to be a number of different service models (e.g.), special class, resource teacher, itinerant specialist, etc.) that are potentially available (Reynolds, 1962). A planning model would estimate the costs of these strategies on a multi-year basis, forcing one to consider alternative strategies and to weigh them against each other. Further, it is entirely possible that different situations require different strategies. For example, one strategy (special classes) may suffice for the urban areas of a state, while a very different one (itinerant teachers) may be needed for the rural areas.

In special education we have employed certain treatment strategies developed before the advent of systematic planning. For example, many states have adopted strategies of organizing special classes for emotionally disturbed children, and we would not want them to cease helping these children while other strategies are considered. On the other hand, in the area of preschool special education we have not had a single well accepted delivery system; thus, it is particularly important for professionals planning in this area to consider all viable alternatives.

Criteria for strategy choice

One other important by-product of the planning system is that we must specify the criteria by which we choose the most favorable of the alternative strategies. For example, we might list economy, proven achievement, availability of professionals, as some of the criteria by which we would choose between strategies. We might like to provide a psychiatrist for every person in the United States to help deal with emotional problems. However, this is not feasible because there are just not enough psychiatrists to go around. Thus, when we weigh each strategy and its alternatives in terms of feasibility we find that a program which is feasible on a limited community basis may not be a likely strategy for the state level (Hobbs,

Needed resources

The "ad hoc approach," or crisis planning, that we in special education often use causes us to put aside the important support needs that are the necessary backup to quality service. Our immediate tendencies are to spend what little resources we have dealing with service needs in the best way possible. This is a human approach, but like many human approaches to large problems, it unfortunately is both inefficient and inappropriate. We need appropriate teacher training, curriculum development, research, and technical assistance programs to provide quality programs for preschool handicapped children.

If we establish a large number of new programs in preschool education, then we must have reasonably trained personnel to operate those programs. It then follows that we must have a plan, or strategy, for the preparation of these personnel, either by changing existing university training programs or expanding inservice or on-site training. We must calculate needed training resources and then allocate the necessary support funds to bring these training programs into being.

Another need that special educators often put aside is the need for a comprehensive plan of continuous research and development activities. We often try to comfort ourselves with the misconception that in some laboratory somewhere dedicated scientists or educators are putting together sets of curriculum materials or program activities which will benefit and upgrade special education. Some significant, if rare, efforts by Cawley (1972), Goldstein (1969), and Meyer (1970) point up the infrequent systematic efforts in this area. If in fact, we are going to improve our ideas and procedures and make the next generation of special educators more proficient, we have to plan for those support services that will make better teachers a likely reality.

Technical assistance

Another area of support services needed is an organized system of technical assistance, or outreach, to systematically deliver new educational ideas and procedures to special educators already in the field (Gallagher, 1973; Lillie, 1975). We need continued emphasis on the establishment and execution of these technical assistance programs to systematically upgrade personnel and maintain a quality effort. Since technical assistance is often delivered over a large geographic area, state planning may be the answer.

At the Frank Porter Graham Child Development Center at the University of North Carolina, Chapel Hill, we currently operate three major technical assistance programs: the Technical Assistance Development System (TADS); the Developmental Disabilities/Technical Assistance System (DD/TAS); and the Mideast Learning Resource System (MELRS). The purpose of these systems is to provide the latest knowledge and skills in such issues as program planning, curriculum, evaluation, and communication to three very different groups of clients: a set of national demonstration centers for preschool handicapped children; the 50-state Developmental Disabilities Councils; and the state Departments of Education in an eight-state Mid-Atlantic region.

While the nature of the technical assistance varies according to the client, several principles apply to all and should apply to any program:

1. The assistance is based on the perceived needs of the client.
2. A contract is established between the client and the technical assistance program that clearly states the kind of help to be delivered, when, and by whom. Such a contract provides documented accountability.
3. A "talent bank" of special consultants—lawyers, psychologists, pediatricians, and educators—is on call to aid the client's special needs (Gallagher, 1973).

Evaluation and accountability

The final aspect of any planning model involves an evaluation of whether we have approached our desired standard of performance. This is a most difficult task, from a psychological standpoint, for anyone (House, 1973) because the news that we get from educational evaluations is almost always "bad news." The best that can happen is discovering that we have done what we promised we were going to do. Anything short of this becomes a problem to us and to our credibility. However willing we might be to put off the onerous task of self-evaluation, the public is increasingly unwilling to let us do so. Therefore, a systematized attempt to collect a wide variety of data to display our accountability to our funding sources and to the public is an inevitable part of any current planning effort.

The five support system components, if properly executed, can provide the basis for continued quality service to those in need of special education. Their absence will likely lead to another decade of hit-or-miss, trial-and-error efforts guaranteed to disillusion our clients and ourselves. In recent congressional testimony, I have suggested that the appropriation of funds for those support systems be directly tied to the level of service funds committed. That is, instead of separate appropriations for training, research, technical assistance, etc., a percentage figure (about 15%) of the service funds should be allocated for these support services to prevent economy-minded state or federal legislatures from cutting individual services which can be more easily reduced without screams of consumer anger.

POLITICAL REALITIES AND PLANNING

Additional money does not guarantee that the funds will be allocated to the necessary preschool programs for the handicapped. Despite impressive statements of the priority of programs for preschool handicapped children (Caldwell, 1973), we must face the fact that unless state decision-makers grab hold of the reins with a planning model, preschool education for handicapped children will not develop as rapidly as needed.

Political realities and pressures within the special education establishment to expand existing programs often determine the allocation of resources. An example is the application of ESEA Title VI-B which allocated funds on a general formula grant to the states. When this provision was originally put into the federal handicapped legislation, a number of suggested directions and priorities were listed. These priorities came not just from the staff members in the federal establishment, but also from a consensus of special education experts from state departments and the professional field. One top priority was preschool education.

Although many states began or expanded their preschool efforts with these funds, they did not invest as much as one might have anticipated. Federal staff members were convinced that the variety of special educators interested in school-age retarded, the emotionally disturbed, or sensory handicapped children had put pressure on state leaders to invest more resources in *their* areas. As a result of this pressure, state department personnel or other decision-makers allocated much of the Title VI-B resources to expanding existing programs rather than beginning new efforts in preschool education.

The lesson is clear. If preschool education is one of our priorities, then we must systematically plan to insert it into the total special education program where it can obtain the allocation of the necessary resources. A long-range plan with a clear and visible priority for preschool programs is one of the best weapons the state decision-maker has against these spasmodic political pressures from professionals and local communities.

PROBLEMS WITH PLANNING

It is not wise to leave a discussion of planning without mentioning some of the substantial weaknesses in the current planning models, even as they change and improve. One weakness at state and federal government levels has been a separation of the planning process from budget control. Unless these areas are coordinated, planning becomes unrealistic and loses the attention of the practical program managers. The multitude of tiny decisions in monthly reallocation of budget monies really influences policy more than long-range planning.

A second major weakness is that too often planners forget their role as aides to decision-makers and start acting as the decision-makers themselves. Instead of providing a template upon which the decision-makers can make more rational decisions, the planners insert their own personal priorities into the plans, alienating themselves from the political leaders and losing their effectiveness.

Another major weakness is our inability to effectively evaluate our total programs. Consequently, we sometimes underestimate the impact of programs by not thoroughly describing the results. A program to improve the lot of educable retarded children is not adequately evaluated by the results of a reading achievement test. The complex self-image and subtle attitudinal changes, the reshuffling of family values and interests, and the attitudes of others in the community all need evaluation before a complete program assessment is possible.

Finally, there is the continued difficulty of significantly changing the original plan once it is set. Theoretically there should be adequate opportunity to change the original plan. In actual practice a powerful inertia tends to establish the 1st-year version of a 5-year plan as "the plan."

Still, with all of these weaknesses requiring improvement in current models, program planning and evaluation is one of the more useful tools available to educational decision-makers. We need to acquaint ourselves with this tool to aid us in programming for preschool handicapped children.

References

Caldwell, B. The importance of beginning early. In M. Karnes (Ed.), *Not all little wagons are red.* Reston, Va.: Council for Exceptional Children, 1973.

Cawley, J. Teaching arithmetic to mentally handicapped children. In E. Meyen, G. Vergasen, & R. Whelan (Eds.), *Strategies for teaching exceptional children.* Denver: Love Publishing Company, 1972.

Gallagher, J. J. The psychology of planned change. In M. Karnes (Ed.), *Not all little wagons are red.* Reston, Va.: Council for Exceptional Children, 1973.

Gallagher, J. J. Technical assistance—a new device for quality educational services for the gifted. *TAG Newsletter*, 1974, 5–8.

Gallagher, J. J., Forsythe, P., Ringelheim, D., & Weintraub, F. Funding patterns and labeling. In N. Hobbs (Ed.), *Issues in the classification of children* (Vol. 2). San Francsico: Jossey-Bass, 1975.

Gallagher, J. J., Surls, R., & Hayes, A. *Program planning and evaluation.* Chapel Hill: University of North Carolina. Frank Porter Graham Child Development Center, 1973.

Goldstein, H. *Social learning curriculum.* New York: Yeshiva University, 1969.

Hobbs, N. Project Re-Ed: New ways of helping emotionally disturbed children. In *Crisis in child mental health: Challenge for the 1970's* (Joint Commission on Mental Health of Children). New York: Harper & Row, 1970.

House, E. (Ed.). *School evaluation.* Berkeley, Calif.: McCutheon, 1973.

Karnes, M. (Ed.). *Not all little wagons are red.* Reston, Va.: Council for Exceptional Children, 1973.

Lillie, D. *Early childhood education.* Chicago: Science Research Associates, 1975.

Meyer, W. *Me now. Life sciences: A special education program.* Boulder: Biological Sciences Curriculum Study, University of Colorado, 1970.

Provus, M. Evaluation of ongoing programs in the public system. In R. Tyler (Ed.), *Education evaluation: New roles, new means* (68th Yearbook of the National Society for the Study of Education, Part 2). Chicago: University of Chicago Press, 1969.

Rivlin, A. *Systematic thinking for social action.* Washington, D.C.: Brookings Institute, 1971.

Stufflebeam, D. Toward a science of educational evaluation. *Educational Technology*, 1968, *8*, 5–12.

Aa Bb Cc
sun

INDEX

STAFF

Publilsher	John Quirk
Editor	Dona Chiappe
Editorial Ass't.	Carol Carr
Permissions Editor	Audrey Weber
Director of Production	Richard Pawlikowski
Director of Design	Donald Burns
Customer Service	Cindy Finocchio
Sales Service	Diane Hubbard
Administration	Linda Calano
Index	Mary Russell
Cover Design	Donald Burns
Cover Photo	Richard Pawlikowski

Appendix: Agencies and Services for Exceptional Children

Alexander Graham Bell Association for the Deaf, Inc.
Volta Bureau for the Deaf
3417 Volta Place, NW
Washington, D.C. 20007

American Academy of Pediatrics
1801 Hinman Avenue
Evanston, Illinois 60204

American Association for Gifted Children
15 Gramercy Park
New York, N.Y. 10003

American Association on Mental Deficiency
5201 Connecticut Avenue, NW
Washington, D.C. 20015

American Association of Psychiatric Clinics for Children
250 West 57th Street
New York, N.Y.

American Bar Association
Commission on the Mentally Disabled
1800 M Street, NW
Washington, D.C. 20036

American Foundation for the Blind
15 W. 16th Street
New York, N.Y. 10011

American Medical Association
535 N. Dearborn Street
Chicago, Illinois 60610

American Speech and Hearing Association
9030 Old Georgetown Road
Washington, D.C. 20014

Association for the Aid of Crippled Children
345 E. 46th Street
New York, N.Y. 10017

Association for Children with Learning Disabilities
2200 Brownsville Road
Pittsburgh, Pennsylvania 15210

Association for Education of the Visually Handicapped
1604 Spruce Street
Philadelphia, Pennsylvania 19103

Association for the Help of Retarded Children
200 Park Avenue, South
New York, N.Y.

Association for the Visually Handicapped
1839 Frankfort Avenue
Louisville, Kentucky 40206

Center on Human Policy
Division of Special Education and Rehabilitation
Syracuse University
Syracuse, New York 13210

Child Fund
275 Windsor Street
Hartford, Connecticut 06120

Children's Defense Fund
1520 New Hampshire Avenue NW
Washington, D.C. 20036

Closer Look
National Information Center for the Handicapped
1201 Sixteenth Street NW
Washington, D.C. 20036

Clifford W. Beers Guidance Clinic
432 Temple Street
New Haven, Connecticut 06510

Child Study Center
Yale University
333 Cedar Street
New Haven, Connecticut 06520

Child Welfare League of America, Inc.
44 East 23rd Street
New York, N.Y. 10010

Children's Bureau
United States Department of Health, Education and Welfare
Washington, D.C.

Council for Exceptional Children
1411 Jefferson Davis Highway
Arlington, Virginia 22202

Epilepsy Foundation of America
1828 "L" Street NW
Washington, D.C. 20036

Gifted Child Society, Inc.
59 Glen Gray Road
Oakland, New Jersey 07436

Institute for the Study of Mental Retardation and Related Disabilities
130 South First
University of Michigan
Ann Arbor, Michigan 48108

International Association for the Scientific Study of Mental Deficiency
Ellen Horn, AAMD
5201 Connecticut Avenue NW
Washington, D.C. 20015

International League of Societies for the Mentally Handicapped
Rue Forestiere 12
Brussels, Belgium

Joseph P. Kennedy, Jr. Foundation
1701 K Street NW
Washington, D.C. 20006

League for Emotioally Disturbed Children
171 Madison Avenue
New York, N.Y.

Muscular Dystrophy Associations of America
1790 Broadway
New York, N.Y. 10019

National Aid to the Visually Handicapped
3201 Balboa Street
San Francisco, California 94121

National Association of Coordinators of State Programs for the Mentally Retarded
2001 Jefferson Davis Highway
Arlington, Virginai 22202

National Association of Hearing and Speech Agencies
919 18th Street NW
Washington, D.C. 20006

National Association for Creative Children and Adults
8080 Springvalley Drive
Cincinnati, Ohio 45236
(Mrs. Ann F. Isaacs, Executive Director)

National Association for Retarded Children
420 Lexington Avenue
New York, N.Y.

National Association for Retarded Citizens
2709 Avenue E East
Arlington, Texas 76010

National Children's Rehabilitation Center
P.O. Box 1260
Leesburg, Virginia

National Association for the Visually Handicapped
3201 Balboa Street
San Francisco, California 94121

National Association of the Deaf
814 Thayer Avenue
Silver Spring, Maryland 20910

National Cystic Fibrosis Foundation
3379 Peachtree Road NE
Atlanta, Georgia 30326

National Easter Seal Society for Crippled Children and Adults
2023 W. Ogden Avenue
Chicago, Illinois 60612

National Federation of the Blind
218 Randolph Hotel
Des Moines, Iowa 50309

National Paraplegia Foundation
333 N. Michigan Avenue
Chicago, Illinois 60601

National Society for Autistic Children
621 Central Avenue
Albany, N.Y. 12206

National Society for Prevention of Blindness, Inc.
79 Madison Avenue
New York, N.Y. 10016

Orton Society, Inc.
8415 Bellona Lane
Baltimore, Maryland 21204

President's Committee on Mental Retardation
Regional Office Building #3
7th and D Streets SW
Room 2614
Washington, D.C. 20201

United Cerebral Palsy Associations
66 E 34th Street
New York, N.Y. 10016

COMMENTS PLEASE:

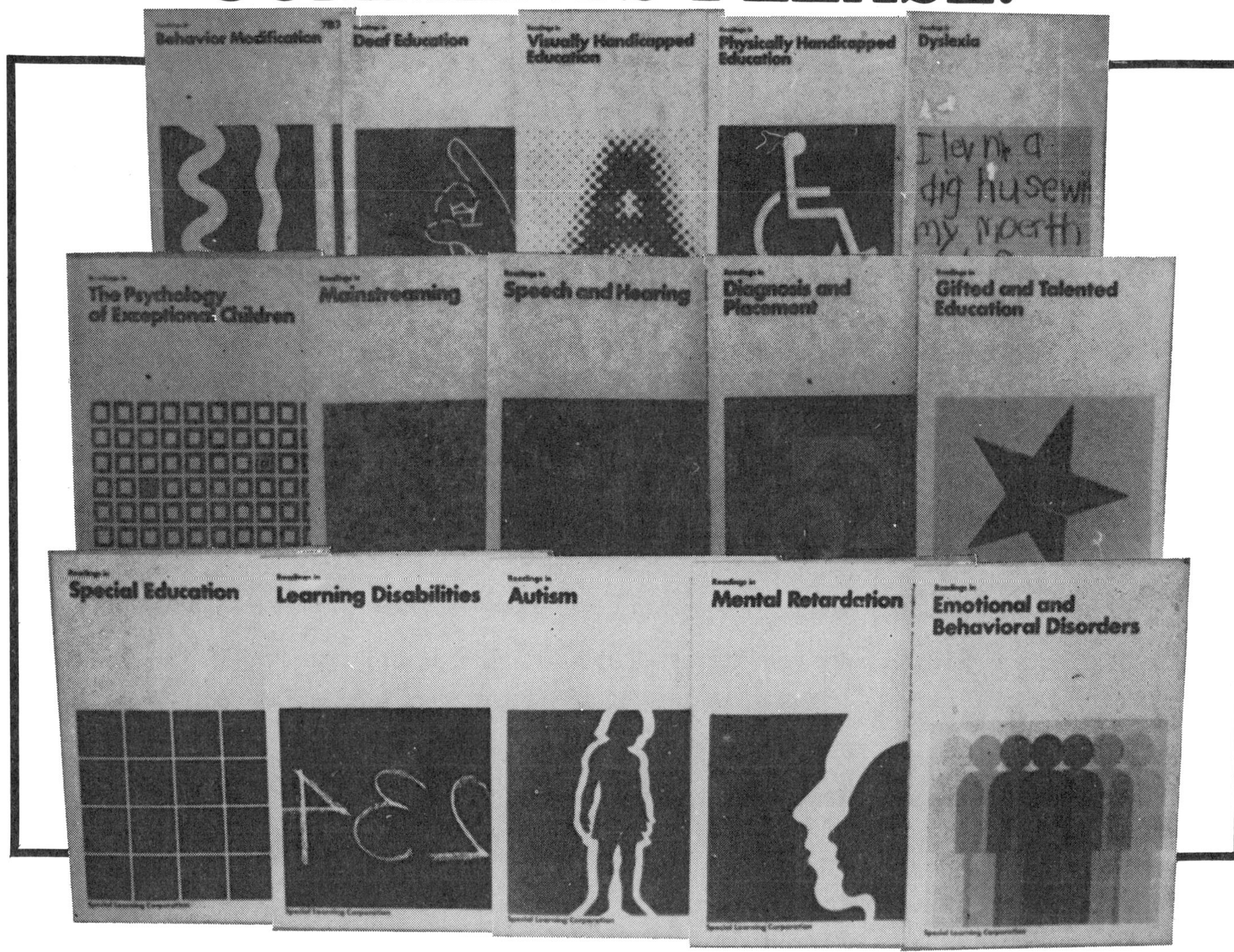

SPECIAL LEARNING CORPORATION

42 Boston Post Rd.

Guilford, Conn. 06437

SPECIAL LEARNING CORPORATION

COMMENTS PLEASE:

Does this book fit your course of study?

Why? (Why not?)

Is this book useable for other courses of study? Please list.

What other areas would you like us to publish in using this format?

What type of exceptional child are you interested in learning more about?

Would you use this as a basic text?

How many students are enrolled in these course areas?

_____ Special Education _____ Mental Retardation _____ Psychology _____ Emotional Disorders

_____ Exceptional Children _____ Learning Disabilities Other _____

Do you want to be sent a copy of our elementary student materials catalog?

Do you want a copy of our college catalog?

Would you like a copy of our next edition? ☐ yes ☐ no

Are you a ☐ student or an ☐ instructor?

Your name _____ school _____

Term used _____ Date _____

address _____

city _____ state _____ zip _____

telephone number _____

P/S

CUT HERE ● SEAL AND MAIL

BELMONT COLLEGE LIBRARY

DATE DUE

RETURNED DEC 14 1983

DEC 14 1983

RETURNED NOV 19 1985

NOV - 6 1985

GAYLORD PRINTED IN U.S.A.